The Daring Decade

The Exciting, Influential, and Bodaciously Fun American Movies of the 1970s

VOLUME TWO: 1975–1979

Chris Strodder

Pulp Hero Press
The Most Dangerous Books on Earth
www.PulpHeroPress.com

© 2020 Chris Strodder

No part of this publication may be reproduced, distributed, or transmitted in any form or by any means, including photocopying, recording, or other electronic or mechanical methods, without the prior written permission of the publisher, except for brief quotations embodied in critical reviews and certain other non-commercial uses permitted by copyright law.

Although every precaution has been taken to verify the accuracy of the information contained herein, no responsibility is assumed for any errors or omissions, and no liability is assumed for damages that may result from the use of this information.

The views expressed in this book are those of the author and do not necessarily reflect the views of Pulp Hero Press.

Pulp Hero Press publishes its books in a variety of print and electronic formats. Some content that appears in one format may not appear in another.

Editor: Bob McLain
Layout: Artisanal Text
ISBN 978-1-68390-279-9
Printed in the United States of America

Pulp Hero Press | www.PulpHeroPress.com
Address queries to bob@pulpheropress.com

Contents

Foreword by Candy Clark xi
Introduction xv
Notes on the Text xix

The Strongest Man in the World 3
Shampoo 4
The Stepford Wives 6
At Long Last Love 8
The Great Waldo Pepper 9
Tommy 11
Escape to Witch Mountain 12
Death Race 2000 14
Aloha, Bobby and Rose 16
French Connection II 17
The Eiger Sanction 19
Love and Death 20
Nashville 22
Night Moves 24
Jaws 26
Bite the Bullet 29
Cooley High 30
The Apple Dumpling Gang 32
Smile 34
Mandingo 35
The Rocky Horror Picture Show 37
Dog Day Afternoon 40
Three Days of the Condor 43
Hester Street 44
The Adventures of the Wilderness Family 46
One Flew Over the Cuckoo's Nest 47
The Man Who Would Be King 50

Barry Lyndon 52
The Hindenburg 53
Lucky Lady 56

1976

Taxi Driver 61
Gable and Lombard 63
Breakhart Pass 65
Robin and Marian 66
All the President's Men 68
The Bad News Bears 71
Silent Movie 72
The Big Bus 74
Logan's Run 75
Murder by Death 77
Buffalo Bill and the Indians, or Sitting Bull's History Lesson 78
The Omen 80
The Outlaw Josey Wales 82
Treasure of Matecumbe 83
The Shootist 85
Burnt Offerings 87
At the Earth's Core 88
The Front 90
Marathon Man 92
Car Wash 94
The Song Remains the Same 96
Carrie 98
Network 100
The Last Tycoon 103
Rocky 104
Silver Streak 107
Bound for Glory 108
Freaky Friday 110
King Kong 112
A Star Is Born 114

1977

Fun with Dick and Jane 119
Slap Shot 120
Airport '77 123
The Many Adventures of Winnie the Pooh 125
Eraserhead 126
Black Sunday 128
3 Women 130
Annie Hall 131
Smokey and the Bandit 134
Star Wars 135
The Deep 139
The Hills Have Eyes 140
The Rescuers 142
New York, New York 144
Sorcerer 146
MacArthur 148
The Spy Who Loved Me 149
The Last Remake of Beau Geste 151
Orca 152
Empire of the Ants 153
The Kentucky Fried Movie 155
Julia 156
Oh, God! 158
Pete's Dragon 159
The Turning Point 161
Close Encounters of the Third Kind 162
The Goodbye Girl 165
Saturday Night Fever 167
Candleshoe 168
High Anxiety 169

1978

Coma 175
The Betsy 176
Coming Home 178

An Unmarried Woman   181
The Fury   182
Gray Lady Down   184
Pretty Baby   185
Rabbit Test   187
The Last Waltz   188
The Buddy Holly Story   189
Big Wednesday   191
Capricorn One   192
Grease   194
Jaws 2   197
Heaven Can Wait   198
Sgt. Pepper's Lonely Hearts Club Band   200
Foul Play   201
Animal House   203
The Driver   206
Eyes of Laura Mars   207
Interiors   209
Days of Heaven   210
The Boys from Brazil   212
Midnight Express   213
Halloween   215
The Deer Hunter   217
Superman   220
California Suite   222
Every Which Way But Loose   224
Invasion of the Body Snatchers   226

The Warriors   231
Norma Rae   232
The China Syndrome   233
Hair   236
Old Boyfriends   237
Manhattan   239
A Little Romance   241
Saint Jack   243
Hanover Street   244

Alien 246
Escape from Alcatraz 249
The Muppet Movie 251
Moonraker 252
Breaking Away 254
The Amityville Horror 255
Rock 'n' Roll High School 258
Apocalypse Now 260
Starting Over 262
10 264
The Black Stallion 266
Meteor 267
The Great Santini 269
The Rose 270
Star Trek: The Motion Picture 271
1941 273
The Jerk 275
All That Jazz 276
Kramer vs. Kramer 279
The Black Hole 282
Being There 283

Afterword by Michael O'Keefe 285
Appendix 289
Bibliography 299
Index 301
About the Author 319

FOREWORD

Born in Oklahoma and raised in Texas, Candy Clark moved to New York in the late 1960s and was working as a fashion model when a casting director suggested she audition for *Fat City* (1972), an upcoming movie being directed by Hollywood legend John Huston. Not only did she land a role in this critically acclaimed drama, but the next year the same casting director brought her into George Lucas's blockbuster comedy *American Graffiti*. Her delightful performance as Debbie, the fun-loving Connie Stevens/Sandra Dee lookalike with a pile of platinum blonde hair and an enthusiasm for hot cars, brought her an Oscar nomination as Best Supporting Actress. Over the next four decades dozens of movies and TV shows followed, among them prominent movies directed by such luminaries as John Badham, Jonathan Demme, David Fincher, David Lynch, Nicolas Roeg, and Steven Soderbergh. Her '70s highlights include leading roles in *The Man Who Fell to Earth* (1976) with David Bowie, *The Big Sleep* (1978) with Robert Mitchum, and *More American Graffiti* (1979) with Scott Glenn. Today she lives and continues to work in Los Angeles, and as we discovered in our delightful conversation she's still full of lively spirit and is a person who knows how to tell an entertaining story. Our thanks to Candy Clark for joining in on our book.

People sometimes think of the 1970s as a frivolous or insignificant decade, but I loved those years. The 1960s had introduced "people power" and "flower power," civil rights, feminism, and the youth movement, and all that energy fed right into the '70s. Everyone back then seemed more individualistic, and people felt freer to do their own thing. There was more protest about changing the system and ending the war, more rebellion against the establishment, and everything seemed more urgent and vivid. There was no social media in the '70s, so people were more hands-on and involved than they are now.

I loved the camaraderie I felt back then. On any given Saturday night in Los Angeles, there would be four or five parties to go to, so we'd all party-hop and you'd see everyone you know. I loved the discos, where you could just dance and dance to this continual beat under colorful lights. The fashions were wild and creative. Women would wear hot pants with colored pantyhose and platform shoes with thick cork soles for this real rock-and-roll look. Men who were producer-types would leave their shirts unbuttoned to the navel, and some of them would wear chains with coke spoons around their necks. For awhile it seemed like everyone was playing backgammon everywhere, you'd see people carrying around backgammon boards and playing in bars and restaurants.

Naturally the creative energy surging through the decade got channeled into movies. Hollywood seemed to be taking chances, so you got all these new young directors making their first movies, people like Steven Spielberg and George Lucas. Film became a director's medium, so directors were allowed to express themselves and do what they wanted. The result was that the '70s welcomed some truly artistic movies that still hold up, classics like *American Graffiti, Two-Lane Blacktop, Harold and Maude, Soylent Green, The Last Detail, Paper Moon, One Flew Over the Cuckoo's Nest,* and *Being There*. Balanced against these daring, artistic movies were highly commercial hits like *The Poseidon Adventure* and *Earthquake*. When you see those old special-effects movies of the '70s you have to remember that they were cutting-edge movies at the time, and everything was done by hand without the digital effects we have today. These were movies you were meant to enjoy, not study, and they appealed to adults, not like many of today's superhero blockbusters that are aimed at teenagers.

One of my most vivid movie experiences of the 1970s was seeing *The Exorcist* on opening day in Westwood. The movie was sold out, so we waited in line for two chilly hours. The line was so long that there were vendors selling hot dogs to the people who were waiting. The theater had set up an open window up on the building with a curtain blowing outwards to create this eerie effect. As we were waiting to go in, all the people from the previous showing were exiting, all of them with wobbly knees and shocked looks on their faces. Once the movie started, I had this experience I'd never felt before. At the first sight of the little girl after she's transformed into a monster, I had this weird, creepy feeling that started at my feet and ended at the top of my head. All the hair on my body stood straight up on end like I was electrified. At the scariest moment someone outside the theater rattled the exit door, and everybody inside simply flipped out. We were all losing our minds, there was chaos everywhere, and the ushers gave up trying to control the audience or stop people from smoking. It was fabulous! For months afterwards my friends and I all quoted lines from *The Exorcist* to each other.

The first movie I was in was *Fat City*, which I think is an underrated treasure. At the time I was young and oblivious to how significant it was to be working with the legendary director John Huston. Leonard Gardner's script was so good that, in my opinion, it was writing on the level of Steinbeck. It told the story of people who are not usually featured in movies, all the down-and-outers who don't make it. We shot it in Stockton, California, and we all stayed in the Holiday Inn right next door to the Civic Center where they had roller derby and boxing, so the small-town feel in the movie is

With Jeff Bridges in Fat City.

genuine. Susan Tyrrell, who got nominated for an Oscar, was jaw-droppingly good in that movie. Unfortunately, the advertising campaign didn't tell you what the story was about. The title didn't register with people—was Fat City a weight-loss camp?—and the poster didn't suggest boxing, which is a major part of the movie. If you haven't seen it, give *Fat City* a chance, it's one of John Huston's best.

Next came *American Graffiti*. George Lucas was one of the quietest, most introverted people on planet Earth, and he was the last person you'd think would become a billionaire. He was exhausted working on *American Graffiti* because he was literally

FOREWORD

American Graffiti.

working around the clock, shooting the movie all through the night and editing it during the day. We worked with an extremely low budget, so as an actor you knew you had only one or two chances to get your lines right before George moved on to the next scene. The experience of making movies was very different back then. We used real big cameras loaded with actual film, not like today's small digital cameras. There were lots of lights and everything took longer so the movie felt more like a big group project with everybody working together as a team. These days the director would be sitting at a video monitor away from the actors doing the scene. The difference between making movies then and now is like the difference between a coach who gets right on the field to talk to his players and a coach who is up in the stands yelling down to them.

The professional highlight of my entire life came when I got nominated for an Academy Award for *American Graffiti*. I went to the ceremony with my boyfriend at the time, Jeff Bridges. These days there's a lot of conformity at awards shows, all the women wear these million-dollar dresses and jewels, but back then we just bought our own clothes, dressed ourselves, and did our own makeup and hair. I wore a long white dress that I had bought myself, and I added a turquoise boa. I'm pretty sure Jeff was wearing a rented tux. And we didn't arrive in a limo, we simply drove ourselves to the Shrine Auditorium. I was sitting in the second row, and as they announced my category I looked down the row to watch Sylvia Sidney, who was nominated for *Summer Wishes, Winter Dreams*. I was sure she was going to win, and I wanted to watch her face when her name was called out. Then, as they announced the Best Supporting Actress nominees, when they got to my name, for some reason the camera focused on somebody else, not me! When they announced the winner, I was waiting to hear Sylvia Sidney, but instead it was Tatum O'Neal! WHAT?! Sylvia Sidney, who had been working in movies since the 1920s, didn't win? I'm sorry, but it seemed too soon for nine-year-old Tatum O'Neal to

With David Bowie in The Man Who Fell to Earth.

Candy in 2020. Photo courtesy Candy Clark.

be winning an Oscar. Plus, she was the co-star of the movie! She should have been up for Best Actress, not Best Supporting.

Later in the decade Hollywood got carried away with sex in movies. It was almost mandatory for actresses to do nude scenes. I was never comfortable doing nudity, but I did, in *The Big Sleep*, for example. My best memories of that movie were getting to work with all these famous people, like Robert Mitchum, James Stewart, and Joan Collins. I also got to be in London for two months when the punk movement was at its peak. I really got into the punk scene, and I had a lot of fun going to nightclubs and pogoing out on the dance floor. It was all so exciting, and making movies was so artistic and satisfying, it really felt like the era would go on forever. Nothing does, of course, but the memories last. It's been so much fun to reminisce and celebrate this great era of movies with Chris Strodder's book, *The Daring Decade*!

—Candy Clark

The Force Is Strong with This One

Anyone who has attended one of my live presentations based on my book *The Daring Decade* has heard me use the words "greatest of all time" in relation to various movies of the 1970s. I had repeatedly encountered this phrase back when I was a newly minted teenager in the early '70s and I was reading about the dazzling new movies I was seeing in my local theaters. As I studied all the contemporary newspaper and magazine reviews, I kept running into the phrase "greatest of all time": *The French Connection* (1971) had the greatest car chase of all time, *The Godfather* (1972) was the greatest gangster movie of all time, *The Exorcist* (1973) was the greatest horror movie of all time, etc. Critics, fans, friends—everybody, it seemed, was lauding these movies as the greatest of all time in various categories. Not only were they some of the greatest of all time, they were among the most popular of all time, too. In the early '70s more and more blockbusters—*Airport* (1970), *Love Story* (1970), *American Graffiti* (1973), *The Sting* (1973), *Blazing Saddles* (1974), and others—were crossing the magic $100 million threshold at the box office. *The Godfather* even set the new *all-time* box-office record. Hollywood was making us all offers we couldn't refuse.

How lucky I was in those years to be a fledgling moviegoer experiencing these classic movies first-hand at a significant moment in history. As I later learned, in the late 1960s powerful forces— including the destructive impacts of colossal box-office bombs, changes in long-time leadership at the major studios, the surprising success of non-traditional counter-culture movies like *Easy Rider* (1969), Hollywood's abandonment of the archaic Production Code (which limited what directors could say and show in their movies), and the surge of new societal freedoms and energies—had combined to end one era and start another. And there I was in the early 1970s, an enthusiastic eyewitness to a revolution that I would one day call the Daring Decade.

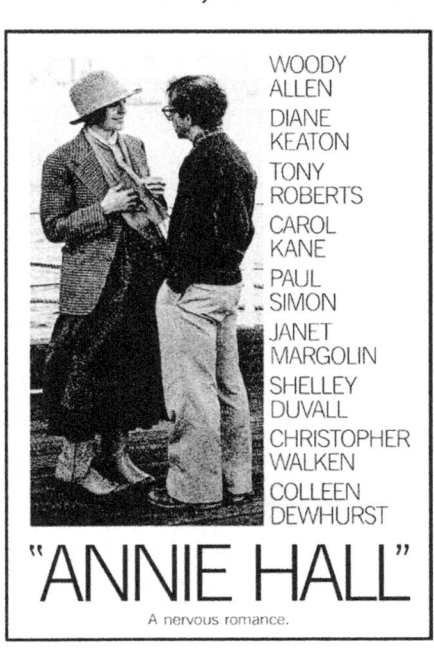

Moving from high school to college in the mid-'70s, I watched in joyous amazement as the revolution flourished. By 1975 the cinematic insurgency that had been sparking for a couple of years had become a towering inferno (literally—1974's number-one box-office smash was *The Towering Inferno*). The spirited, inventive directors who had made strong impressions between 1970 and 1974 with their early movies—Woody Allen, Robert Altman, Brian De Palma, George Lucas, Martin Scorsese, and Steven Spielberg, to name just a half-dozen—were, by 1977, making some of the most successful, artful, and influential movies of all time, among them popular award-winning milestones like Allen's *Annie Hall* (1977), Altman's *Nashville* (1975), De Palma's *Carrie* (1976), Lucas's *Star Wars* (1977), Scorsese's *Taxi Driver* (1976) and Spielberg's *Jaws* (1975). By the end of the '70s, young actors and actresses who had begun their rise to fame early in the decade—Jeff Bridges, Jill Clayburgh, Robert De Niro, Richard Dreyfuss, Sally Field, Jodie Foster, Diane Keaton, Marsha Mason, Al Pacino, Sissy Spacek, Sylvester Stallone, and John Travolta, to name a dozen—had cleared the

launching pad and soared to stardom. New movie-making tools and technology, such as the innovative low-light lenses that captured candlelit scenes in 1975's *Barry Lyndon*, the pioneering Steadicam that provided smooth handheld-camera movements for 1976's *Marathon Man*, and the groundbreaking computer-controlled motion photography that enhanced 1977's *Star Wars*, were taking cinematography and special effects into hyperspace. Ticket sales in the second half of the '70s zoomed to record levels: in 1975 *Jaws* relentlessly chomped its way past Hollywood's legendary blockbusters to become the all-time box-office champ, and soon *Star Wars* flew right past *Jaws* and into a galaxy all its own. Even theater construction was accelerating (1978's eighteen-screen multiplex, at the time the world's largest, in Toronto). The rebels had stormed Hollywood's citadel, and they, and their audiences, had won.

Spielberg and Lucas were the ones who really cracked the code. The two mid-'70s masterpieces they made less than two years apart affected audiences in unprecedented ways. Fans who can't remember their wedding anniversaries can still recall every detail of their

experiences seeing *Jaws* in a theater for the first time. Similarly, in past decades audiences had swooned for *Gone with the Wind* (1939) and *The Sound of Music* (1965), but nobody collected a complete set of Tara action figures or slept in von Trapp-themed pajamas; fans of *Star Wars* did both via the abundant toys and apparel promoting that magnum opus, which became more of a transcendent religious experience than perfect popcorn entertainment. *Jaws* and *Star Wars* dramatically changed Hollywood by leading the charge toward energetic crowd-pleasing spectacles, by dramatically magnifying a studio's advertising possibilities, by multiplying the number of opening-week theaters for new movies, by inaugurating summer as "blockbuster season," and by creating entire catalogs of merchandising opportunities. Critics extolled them, the Academy respected them—they earned a combined fourteen Oscar nominations (both were up for Best Picture) and won nine Oscars—and "greatest of all time" lists still include them anytime someone tallies up the greatest

INTRODUCTION xvii

movie soundtracks, the greatest movie villains, the greatest movie explosions, or simply the greatest movies. Just as Hollywood had restarted the moment sound arrived in 1927, you could arguably divide movie history into two pre-and post-*Jaws*/*Star Wars* epochs.

All these marvelous '70s movies, I felt, were talkin' to me (hopefully you recalled *Taxi Driver*'s Travis Bickle talkin' to a mirror as you read that). They seem to have been talkin' to everyone else, too, since these movies have had powerful, lasting influences on filmmakers and audiences for fifty years now. One way you can tell how influential the great movies released from 1975 to 1979 have been is by seeing how many of them generated decades of sequels—*Rocky* (1976), *Star Wars* and *Alien* (1979), for instance, which started stories that continued well into the twenty-first century. Another way is by seeing how many 1975-'79 movie quotes made it into the common vernacular, everything from "follow the money" and "may the Force be with you" to "la-de-da" and "I love the smell of napalm in the morning." Still another way is to count the number of mid- to late-'70s movies that are still considered the best in their particular genres. To illustrate with just four of many possible examples, presented here in chronological order: 2016, CNN nominated *All the President's Men* (1976) as "the gold standard of journalism movies"; 2017, *Rolling Stone* named *The Rocky Horror Picture Show* (1975) as the "best movie musical"; 2018, the Virgin Media conglomerate picked *Superman* (1978) as the "greatest superhero movie"; and 2019, *National Review* declared *Apocalypse Now* (1979) as the "greatest war movie ever made." These and other powerhouses weren't merely ahead of the curve; they *became* the curve that subsequent movies hoped to reach.

In the introduction to the first volume of *The Daring Decade* I noted that the prestigious American Film Institute had produced lists in 1998 and 2007 identifying the hundred greatest movies of all time, and both lists had included more movies from the 1970s than from any other decade. To add to that accolade, both AFI lists had more movies from 1975-'79 than from 1970-'74. Clearly, the decade's movies had started strong, and they finished even stronger. What's more, these late-'70s movies didn't merely entertain, they inspired. *The Rocky Horror Picture Show* gave unique confidence to its intensely loyal fan community; *All the President's Men* led to increased enrollment in journalism classes; *Rocky* sent its devotees sprinting up the seventy-two steps of the Philadelphia Museum

of Art; *Star Wars* got people to dress up as Lukes and Leias for Halloween; *Saturday Night Fever* (1977) propagated discos and disco fashions; *Animal House* (1978) put togas on America's collegians, *Grease* (1978) put a number-one soundtrack album on everybody's turntables, and *10* (1979) put cornrows in women's hair. People saw these movies and not only loved them, they lived them.

I've been avidly watching, studying, and researching these movies for five decades now. So here at the end of these opening remarks, I feel like I'm Lacombe, François Truffaut's character, in the last scene of the majestic sci-fi epic *Close Encounters of the Third Kind* (1977). Lacombe sends Roy Neary, Richard Dreyfuss' character, off to his starry adventure with a short, heartfelt affirmation: "I envy you." I offer that same encouragement to anyone who is encountering these glorious, memorable, wonderfully affecting movies for the first time, or for the first time in ages. Either way, I envy you.

—Chris Strodder

Notes on the Text

The methodology for choosing this volume's 1975-1979 movies was the same one used for the previous volume's 1970-1974 movies. See that book's Introduction for a detailed explanation, but basically I chose Oscar winners, blockbusters, cult classics, artistic or technological breakthroughs, a sprinkling of freaky "drive-in delights," and some personal favorites. All are feature-length American movies that were released in theaters (so no short films, no subtitled foreign films, no TV movies). As you'll see, it's an eclectic, flavorful buffet that serves up the fantastic, the fun, and the flops, everything from timeless masterpieces that have endless repeatability to catastrophes that generate the kind of commentary usually reserved for zeppelin explosions. Right on.

As in volume one, the movies are presented chronologically with a theater-style format. They open with a listing of main credits and a seventy-character "Preview." Then comes "Now Showing"—an opinionated four-hundred-word critical essay—followed by an "Added Attraction" that further develops something from or related to the movie. Within each separate year, I've identified five movies that are especially **FAR-OUT**, a '70s accolade that's spoken aloud in movies as diverse as *Car Wash* (1976), *Smokey and the Bandit* (1977), *Foul Play* (1978), *Up in Smoke* (1978), *North Dallas Forty* (1979), and *Apocalypse Now* (1979). The **FAR-OUT** movies I've picked aren't necessarily the best movies (though some of them clearly are), but they all do something distinctive that makes them stand out, so they're explored via a longer format that adds a "Fine Line" (an important quote), a "Close-Up" (a specific scene), and a *nine*-hundred-word essay. Finally, throughout the book everything is based on my own original research (not on recycled Internet trivia), and I've copied the quotes exactly as they're spoken in the movies (you'd be amazed how often movie quotes are transcribed incorrectly in print and on the Internet).

For purposes of information, commentary, and history, this book makes reference to various copyrighted titles, trademarks, and registered marks (including Academy Award and such titles as *Casablanca* and *MAD* magazine) that are the property of their respective owners and are used here solely for informational purposes under the Fair Use Doctrine. Neither the author nor the publisher makes any commercial claim to their use. All images were acquired via the Movie Stills Database (moviestillsdb.com) for editorial use only.

James Joyce called errors "the portals of discovery." I think of them the same way. Should you doubt a fact or notice a possible "portal of discovery," please do two things: first, forgive my mistake (and it is my mistake, nobody else's); and second, let me know what you found by politely writing to me via www.encycoolpedia.com. I'll reply with interest and gratitude.

—C.S.

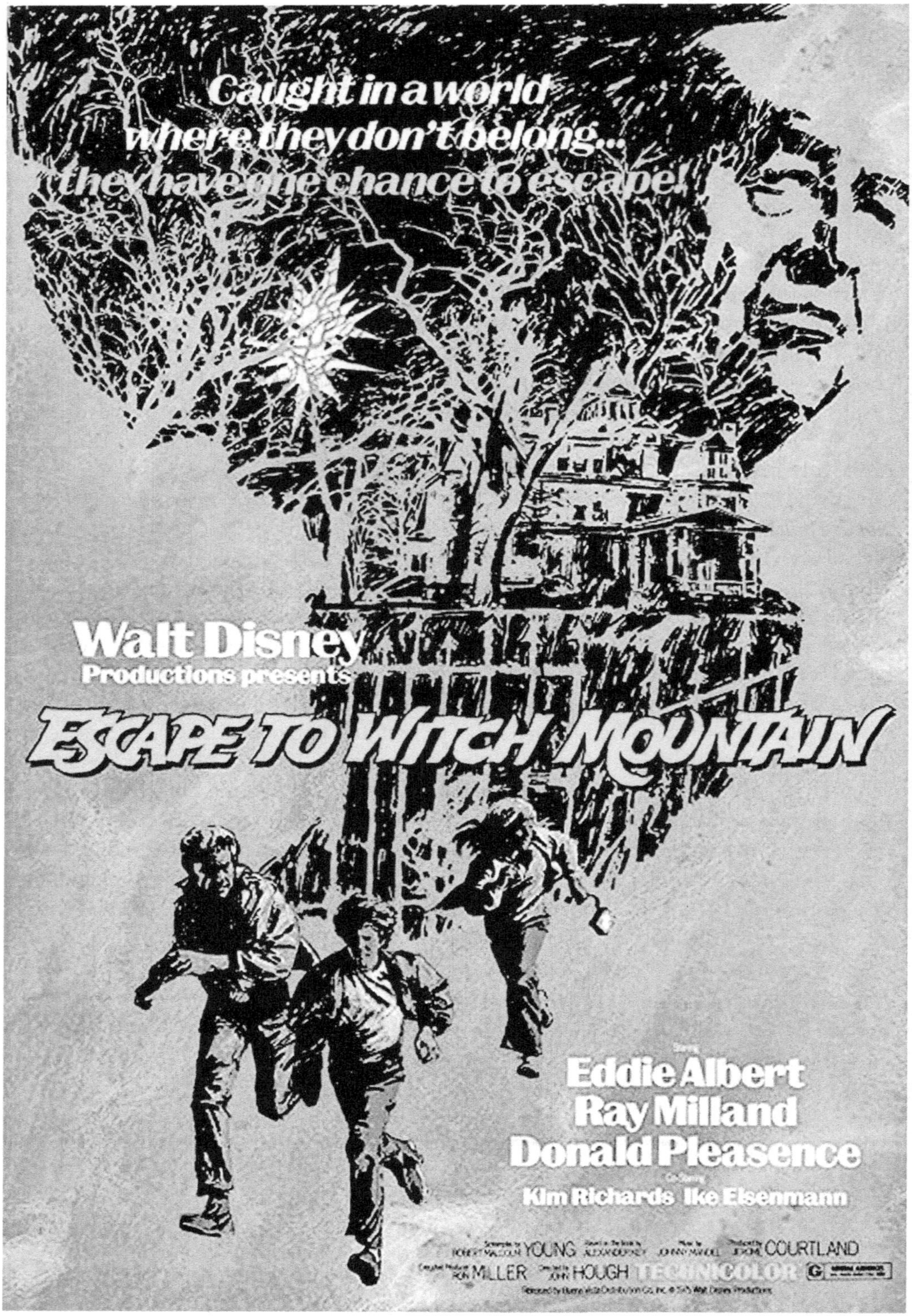
Caught in a world
where they don't belong...
they have one chance to escape!
Walt Disney
Productions presents
ESCAPE TO WITCH MOUNTAIN
Eddie Albert
Ray Milland
Donald Pleasence
Kim Richards Ike Eisenmann
YOUNG
COURTLAND
MILLER
HOUGH
TECHNICOLOR
G

1975

In Film

- Oscar for Best Picture: *One Flew Over the Cuckoo's Nest*.
- Most Oscar wins (five): *One Flew Over the Cuckoo's Nest*.
- Most Oscar nominations (nine): *One Flew Over the Cuckoo's Nest*.
- *One Flew Over the Cuckoo's Nest* becomes the first movie since *It Happened One Night* (1934) to sweep the Oscars in the five top categories: Best Picture, Actor, Actress, Director, and Screenplay.
- Top-grossing movie*: *Jaws*.
- Top-grossing comedy: *The Return of the Pink Panther*.
- Top-grossing horror or sci-fi: *Escape to Witch Mountain*.

- *Jaws* supplants *The Godfather* (1972) as the highest-grossing movie of all time.
- *The Adventures of the Wilderness Family*, *Escape to Witch Mountain*, and *Jaws* launch new movie franchises.
- George Lucas founds Industrial Light and Magic, the company that will create the innovative special effects he'll need for *Star Wars* (1977).
- *Sneak Previews*, featuring reviews by movie critics Gene Siskel and Roger Ebert, debuts on TV.
- Average price for an adult movie ticket: $2.05.
- Five memorable actors: Warren Beatty, George Burns, Gene Hackman, Jack Nicholson, Al Pacino.
- Five memorable actresses: Louise Fletcher, Lee Grant, Carol Kane, Ann-Margret, Brenda Vaccaro.
- Movie debuts: Laurence Fishburne, Carrie Fisher, Richard Gere, Christopher Lloyd, Lily Tomlin, John Travolta, director Joan Micklin Silver.
- Deaths include Larry Fine and Moe Howard of the Three Stooges, Susan Hayward, Fredric March, composer Bernard Herrmann, screenwriters Rod Serling and Bill Walsh, directors George Stevens and William Wellman.

* Throughout the book, box-office rankings are for domestic releases, shown at Box Office Madness: https://boxofficemadness.wordpress.com.

In America

- President Gerald Ford makes his State of the Union Address and declares that "the state of the union is not good."
- Sara Jane Moore and Manson Family-member Lynette "Squeaky" Fromme make separate attempts to assassinate President Ford.
- Helicopters dramatically evacuate the last Americans from Saigon.
- Watergate conspirators John Mitchell, H. R. Haldeman, and John Ehrlichman are found guilty and given prison sentences.
- Heiress and armed-robbery fugitive Patty Hearst is arrested.
- Jimmy Hoffa, the controversial ex-president of the Teamsters Union, goes missing.
- Bill Gates and Paul Allen found Microsoft Corp.
- Now open: Disney World's Space Mountain, New Orleans' Superdome.
- "Thrilla in Manila": Muhammad Ali beats Joe Frazier.
- *Chicago*, *A Chorus Line*, and *The Wiz* open on Broadway.
- Average price for a gallon of gas: Fifty-seven cents.
- New technology: Cromemco Cyclops (first digital camera), Pong (home version).
- New transportation: AMC Pacer, Cadillac Seville, Volkswagen Rabbit.
- New products: Bubble Yum, Country Time lemon drink, Famous Amos cookies, Miller Lite beer, the Pet Rock, Pop Rocks.
- Sports champions: Pittsburgh Steelers at Super Bowl IX, Philadelphia Flyers in hockey, Golden State Warriors in basketball, Cincinnati Reds in baseball.
- Bestselling books include Charles Berlitz's *The Bermuda Triangle*, James Clavell's *Shōgun*, E.L. Doctorow's *Ragtime*, Judith Rossner's *Looking for Mr. Goodbar*.
- Music: Ron Wood joins the Rolling Stones; new albums include Bob Dylan's *Blood on the Tracks*, Led Zeppelin's *Physical Graffiti*, Bruce Springsteen's *Born to Run*; new songs include the Bee Gees' "Jive Talkin'," Captain & Tennille's "Love Will Keep Us Together," Queen's "Bohemian Rhapsody."
- TV debuts: *Good Morning America*, *Saturday Night Live*, *Wheel of Fortune*.
- Deaths include Thomas Hart Benton, Casey Stengel, Thornton Wilder.

The Strongest Man in the World

Released: February 1975
Director: Vincent McEveety
Stars: Kurt Russell, Joe Flynn, Cesar Romero
Academy Awards: None

PREVIEW: An experiment makes a student super-strong prior to a big weight-lifting contest.

NOW SHOWING: Dexter Riley's Last Hurrah

Disney had already made a popular sports comedy in the 1970s called *The World's Greatest Athlete* (1973), starring Jan-Michael Vincent as a Tarzan-like college track star with a tutor named Jane. Two years later the studio decided to get its most popular young male star into athletics. Unfortunately, *The Strongest Man in the World* (1975), the last of Kurt Russell's five Disney comedies for the decade, is one of his weakest.

Strongest Man concludes the "Dexter Riley" trilogy that started with *The Computer Wore Tennis Shoes* (1969) and peaked with *Now You See Him, Now You Don't* (1972). As in those two movies, Russell (now twenty-four years old and with his longest hair yet) plays Dexter, a charismatic, trouble-prone student at fictional Medfield College. After an amusing animation during the opening credits (Disney usually did these animations well), Medfield's long-suffering dean (Joe Flynn) is presented with the college's serious financial problems. Meanwhile, a science-lab accident creates a fizzing liquid that Dexter unintentionally swallows. Immediately he gets super-strong, easily pushing over a steel lamp post and lifting students above his head one-handed. Seeing a money-making opportunity, the dean allies the school with the Crumply Crunch cereal company and arranges a weight-lifting contest against Medfield's rivals in hopes of winning big prize money. Naturally, spies from another cereal company, including the villain from the earlier Dexter Riley movies (Cesar Romero), try to steal the formula. After some cloak-and-dagger shenanigans and a wild car ride when Dexter pours the energizing formula into an old jalopy, the strength contest comes to a Disneyfied conclusion.

The best parts of this unexceptional movie all involve the formula's strength-enhancing properties, especially when the dean himself does a four-minute demonstration. *Strongest Man* boasts a supporting cast of veteran performers, like Eve Arden, Phil Silvers, and the always-irritable Joe Flynn (sadly, it's his last on-screen appearance before his premature death). Viewers may note that the weight-lifting sight gag featuring impossibly elongated arms is a direct steal from Jerry Lewis's *The Nutty Professor* (1963).

The movie's main weakness is Dexter—or rather, his absence. Dexter's the most appealing character, but he's gone for long sections, including forty straight minutes in the middle. An odd bit when an acupuncturist hammers two thick needles into a student's forehead may make parents squirm uncomfortably; you almost expect an on-screen warning, "Kids, don't try this at home."

ADDED ATTRACTION: SuperDisney

Disney's live-action '70s comedies gave all kinds of extraordinary powers to ordinary characters. These weren't scary stories where the characters turned into monsters or bizarre creatures after receiving their special abilities. Everyone basically still looked the same as they did before, so the fun was watching them and everyone around them deal with these unexpected enhancements. Even at the time some of Disney's efforts seemed pretty dopey, and none of these movies has improved with age, but they can still generate nostalgic smiles. Here are a half-dozen prime (and even primate) examples in chronological order.

- *The Barefoot Executive* (1971): A monkey somehow has the ability to pick hit TV shows.
- *The Million Dollar Duck* (1971): A normal duck is accidentally irradiated and suddenly lays solid-gold eggs.
- *Now You See Him, Now You Don't* (1972): College-student Dexter Riley creates an invisibility spray.
- *The Strongest Man in the World* (1975): Dexter Riley develops a super-strength formula.
- *Freaky Friday* (1976): A mother and daughter literally switch bodies.
- *The Cat from Outer Space* (1978): What looks like a regular housecat is actually an alien that uses telepathy, levitates objects, and open doors.

Shampoo

Released: February 1975
Director: Hal Ashby
Stars: Warren Beatty, Julie Christie, Goldie Hawn
Academy Awards: One win (Best Supporting Actress—Lee Grant), plus three more nominations (Best Supporting Actor—Jack Warden; Best Writing; Best Art Direction)

PREVIEW: A charming hairdresser juggles lovers as he starts to get serious about his future.

NOW SHOWING: Hairport 1975

Like many '70s hairstyles, *Shampoo* (1975) has layers. During a thirty-six-hour period in 1968, George (Warren Beatty), an irresistible, free-lovin' hairdresser, sleeps with four women. This Casanova rides his motorcycle (a Triumph, naturally) to his encounters with a blow dryer tucked in his belt and beguiling words on his tongue. Much of the movie is a smart, witty sex farce, and George even pretends to be gay momentarily to distract a jealous rival. But entertaining bedroom adventures aren't what *Shampoo* is about. Haircare flair becomes despair.

Hypocrisy and selfishness undermine every relationship. For example, George's youngest partner (Carrie Fisher, in her movie debut) propositions him just to get

Julie Christie and Warren Beatty.

back at her mother; beautiful Jackie (Julie Christie) abandons her ideal match to relocate with a rich old man (she's literally hair today, gone tomorrow); the rich old man boasts that he's "trying to make this a better place to live in," but he's got dark business dealings and hired thugs. George, meanwhile, helplessly ruins his life. He adores and effortlessly seduces women, makes sincere declarations (he tells two women he could see himself retiring with only her), but is faithful to nobody. In the moving final scene, he's alone, facing a somber future.

Running steadily alongside this romantic carousel is the 1968 presidential election being held that very day. Nixon's and Agnew's images are often in the background, with TV announcements constantly updating the returns. The hip hedonists are so focused on their own pleasures and problems, however, that they ignore the coming storm (nobody votes or discusses politics). The myopic libertines lose. Money and power win. Tellingly, *Shampoo* opens and closes with the Beach Boys' exquisite "Wouldn't It Be Nice"; initially, the words are hopeful, but 110 minutes later, after nearly every couple has come undone and Nixon wins, the song sounds wistful.

Shampoo unites a 1970s all-star team. Besides the stellar cast, there's screenwriter Robert Towne, fresh off *Chinatown* (1974) and earning his third consecutive writing nomination (daringly, he has Julie Christie deliver the most profane line). Director Hal Ashby, having succeeded with *The Last Detail* (1973), here uses visuals to subtly convey meanings (note how most interiors are dim, except for the white, bright salon filled with women, George's idea of heaven). Paul Simon contributes snippets of melancholy music that discreetly punctuates George's decline. And the time-capsule fashions are perfect. It's an essential '70s movie. *Shampoo*, and repeat.

ADDED ATTRACTION: Lost Fortune

In *Shampoo*, Jill (Goldie Hawn) obliquely refers to Warren Beatty's *Bonnie and Clyde* (1967): "The only way you're ever gonna get money out of a bank is to rob one." While it wasn't the game-changing landmark that *Bonnie and Clyde* was, *Shampoo* was another hit for Beatty, so everyone expected similar success when *The Fortune* (1975), directed by Oscar-winner Mike Nichols and co-starring Beatty and Jack Nicholson, premiered three months later. Surprisingly, *The Fortune* flopped. Therein lies the mystery, because this modest screwball comedy has its charms and some fun performances. In the 1920s, Beatty, playing an anxious philanderer, and Nicholson, as a wild-haired dimwit, collaborate to swindle a naïve heiress (Stockard Channing, making her big-screen debut and delightfully stealing the movie from the two big stars). Everything meanders toward an amusing second half when the inept guys attempt to execute half-baked murder plans. Stylish but uneven, *The Fortune* could've been better, but it could've been much worse, too.

The Stepford Wives

Released: February 1975
Director: Bryan Forbes
Stars: Katharine Ross, Paula Prentiss, Peter Masterson
Academy Awards: None

PREVIEW: A newcomer to a small town gradually uncovers a secret about the women living there.

NOW SHOWING: "Robots in Disneyland"

By now the term "Stepford wife" is so familiar that modern audiences won't find many surprises in *The Stepford Wives* (1975). In the '70s, though, this moderately suspenseful movie generated attention and controversy. Based on the 1972 bestseller by Ira Levin, author of *Rosemary's Baby*, the movie starts with a scene of a mannequin being carried down a Manhattan street, a sign of artificial bodies to come. A family then leaves the city for leafy, suburban Stepford, where young, pretty Joanna (Katharine Ross) befriends another newcomer, the ebullient Bobbie (Paula Prentiss). Wearing hip casual fashions, they both start noticing odd behavior among the staid local women: a fender bender, for instance, generates zero emotion from the injured wife. To liberate the town's passive women, Joanna and Bobbie initiate a "consciousness-raising group" (how '70s!), but the other wives only want to discuss cleaning products. Uninitiated viewers should catch on quickly to the movie's gimmick, especially when one of the inexpressive wives calmly repeats the same non sequitur over and over again midway through the movie.

Joanna and Bobby investigate the town's dark secret, leading to their first guess about polluted water (another timely topic). When Bobbie herself comes back from a weekend getaway as a completely changed person—old-fashioned clothes, submissive attitude, a sudden obsession with housework—Joanna realizes she's next and her husband will soon make her "like one of those robots in Disneyland." Near the end the movie intensifies with seventeen minutes set on one stormy night. Domestic violence and a startling knife thrust lead to a dark mansion where director Bryan Forbes marshals every cliché possible (a man relentlessly pursuing a fleeing woman, shadowed halls, lightning flashes, creepy music, etc.). The only question left is, will Joanna succumb or survive?

Critics who said the movie somehow denigrates the feminist movement miss the point; the controlling men who strip their wives of personalities and careers are villains.

Katharine Ross (center) and the other Stepford wives.

It's more accurate to note that this horror movie isn't very scary. Perhaps the best way to enjoy *The Stepford Wives* is as a black comedy, because the submissive wives continually speak with amusing TV-commercial vocabularies ("you need a fresh-perked cup of coffee!"), and the climactic big-breasted android is so plasticized and overdone it's almost funny. Ross is compelling as the curious, rebellious wife, but in truth *The Stepford Wives* feels more like a TV movie, which is what the three sequels actually were.

ADDED ATTRACTION: Born Again

While *The Stepford Wives* was still in theaters, another subdued horror movie opened, this one produced by … Bing Crosby Productions? Yes, *der Bingle*'s company made *The Reincarnation of Peter Proud* (1975), plus the creepy *Willard* (1971) and many other movies and TV shows. Like *The Stepford Wives*, *The Reincarnation of Peter Proud* was based on a book (this one by Max Ehrlich); and like *Stepford*, *Reincarnation* is about identity issues and is more eerie than horrific. Michael Sarrazin plays Peter Proud, a troubled man who investigates his recurring dreams and decides he "must have lived before," circling him back toward the same place and the same tragic situation he's been seeing in his sleep. Margot Kidder has a daring soft-core sex scene alone in a bathtub and wears unconvincing old-lady makeup much of the time (at one point she's supposed to be the mother of beautiful Jennifer O'Neill, who in real life is eight months older than Kidder). More unsettling is Proud's incestuous romance with the daughter of the man he used to be in a former life. The movie is occasionally interesting, but it's too uneven to be truly chilling. Coming out a couple of months after *Peter Proud* was another horror movie, *The Devil's Rain* (1975). Though it does have some genuine scares and monstrous effects, including a bubbling, melting face in the first seven minutes, this confusing, poorly received movie is more notable for its cast, which includes Ida Lupino, William Shatner, and John Travolta in his first movie role.

At Long Last Love

Released: March 1975
Director: Peter Bogdanovich
Stars: Burt Reynolds, Cybill Shepherd, Madeline Kahn
Academy Awards: None

PREVIEW: Two sophisticated 1930s couples sing, dance, and try to make their lovers jealous.

NOW SHOWING: "Well Did You Evah!"

Many directors working in various genres have tried to recapture the joyful spirit of classic movie musicals. Both Mel Brooks and Steven Spielberg incorporated 1930's-style musical scenes into their movies (1974's *Young Frankenstein* and 1984's *Indiana Jones and the Temple of Doom*, respectively). Peter Bogdanovich, who had already scored with his Depression-era *Paper Moon* (1973), daringly patterned an entire movie after the great Fred Astaire/Ginger Rogers musicals. All-white sets, glamorous costumes, vintage cars, sixteen sprightly Cole Porter songs including "Well Did You Evah!" and "It's De-Lovely," and a silly plot about romantic jealousy fill *At Long Last Love* (1975) with enough fizz to fill a magnum of champagne.

Unfortunately, the performances make the movie go flat. In the 1970s Bogdanovich had a blind spot for his paramour, Cybill Shepherd. Previously the title character of his disappointing *Daisy Miller* (1974), here she tries hard as one of the leads. As a singer she's passable, but as a dancer, like in the "Most Gentleman Don't Like Love" showcase, she's whatever is the opposite of "light on her feet." Meanwhile, Burt Reynolds, gamely playing a musical millionaire, occasionally resorts to the non-singer's trick of talk-singing, and he dances like someone trying to keep time. During some of the numbers the singers are standing behind furniture, or sitting, or swimming, all to conceal the absence of true terpsichorean talent. Of the leads, only Madeline Kahn emerges unscathed.

The movie is so effervescent it floats along with no real dialogue: characters quip back and forth and then sing their feelings. To Bogdanovich's credit, he shows everyone performing live, not lip-synching, to recapture the spontaneity and authenticity of those old musicals; this ambitious effort might've succeeded with a star like Barbra Streisand. Bogdanovich's 1930s costumes and sets look great, though, so it's a stylish movie to watch. If only those sets could sing.

While it's a daring, misguided experiment, *At Long Last Love* is not as de-lousy as its harsh reviews suggest. Its famous names all moved on to something better—Bogdanovich to *Saint Jack* (1979), Shepherd to *Taxi Driver* (1976), and Kahn to *High Anxiety* (1977). Reynolds immediately rebounded with the successful *W.W. and the Dixie Dancekings* (1975), another music-filled movie (this time, however, he doesn't sing). This Southern-fried car-chase romp, with Reynolds as a charming robber and Jerry Reed as a country singer, is an amiable warm-up for Reynolds' mega-hit, *Smokey and the Bandit* (1977).

ADDED ATTRACTION: Singing Actors, Part One

Besides Burt Reynolds, these actors were not afraid to croon a tune in 1975-1977 movies. For actors who sang in 1978-1979 movies, see the entry for *1941* (1979).

- Marlon Brando, *The Missouri Breaks* (1976): Brando sings a minute of a sweet train song while playing a mandolin.
- Mel Brooks, *High Anxiety* (1977): Swinging like he's Frank Sinatra, Brooks serenades a bar with the theme song.
- Sean Connery, *The Man Who Would Be King* (1975): Connery briefly sings "The Son of God Goes Forth to War" solo midway through the movie; Michael Caine joins him for a sad reprise at the end.
- Robert De Niro, *New York, New York* (1977): De Niro attempts ten wobbly seconds of "Blue Moon" before the real singer takes over.
- Bob Newhart, *The Rescuers* (1977): He's one of the lead singers on "Rescue Aid Society."
- Jack Nicholson, *Tommy* (1975): As Tommy's doctor, he tentatively talk-sings one song and slow dances with Tommy's mom.

The Great Waldo Pepper

Released: March 1975
Director: George Roy Hill
Stars: Robert Redford, Bo Svenson, Susan Sarandon
Academy Awards: None

PREVIEW: With barnstorming coming to an end in the 1920s, a biplane pilot becomes a stuntman.

NOW SHOWING: End of an Era

After *Butch Cassidy and the Sundance Kid* (1969) and *The Sting* (1973), *The Great Waldo Pepper* (1975) is the final teaming of director George Roy Hill and Robert Redford. *Pepper* doesn't reach the lofty heights of those earlier Oscar-winning blockbusters—not many movies do, obviously—but it soars extremely high.

Like *The Sting*, *Pepper* opens with the old black-and-white Universal Pictures logo and is set between the two world wars. And like *The Sting*, *Pepper* is filled with terrific period details, here evoking a time when early flying was transitioning to modern aviation. Redford plays Waldo Pepper, a handsome, charismatic flyer who flashes a movie-star smile anytime he needs something. After barnstorming around the Midwest to take customers for short five-dollar flights in his yellow biplane, Pepper ends up performing risky wing-walking stunts in a flying circus that offers blood-thirsty spectators the possibility of "sudden death" (the movie makes a strong point about the public's need for increasingly intense thrills). Though the feats are dangerous, the movie's first half is generally light and includes amusing sights like Pepper bashing into a barn and dressing in drag.

Everything changes when a reckless stunt causes the adorable "It Girl of the Skies" (Susan Sarandon) to plunge to her death. Perhaps the audience should've been prepared for unexpected fatalities, since the movie's first minute shows vintage photos of dashing flyers who died young. But the It Girl isn't an experienced daredevil; she's a petrified victim who shockingly falls from Pepper's grasp. An even more horrifying death follows twelve minutes later when someone burns inside a wrecked plane and Pepper is seriously injured. After these grim tragedies, the pilots' foolhardy pursuits seem more pointless than courageous, and the movie's joy flies away.

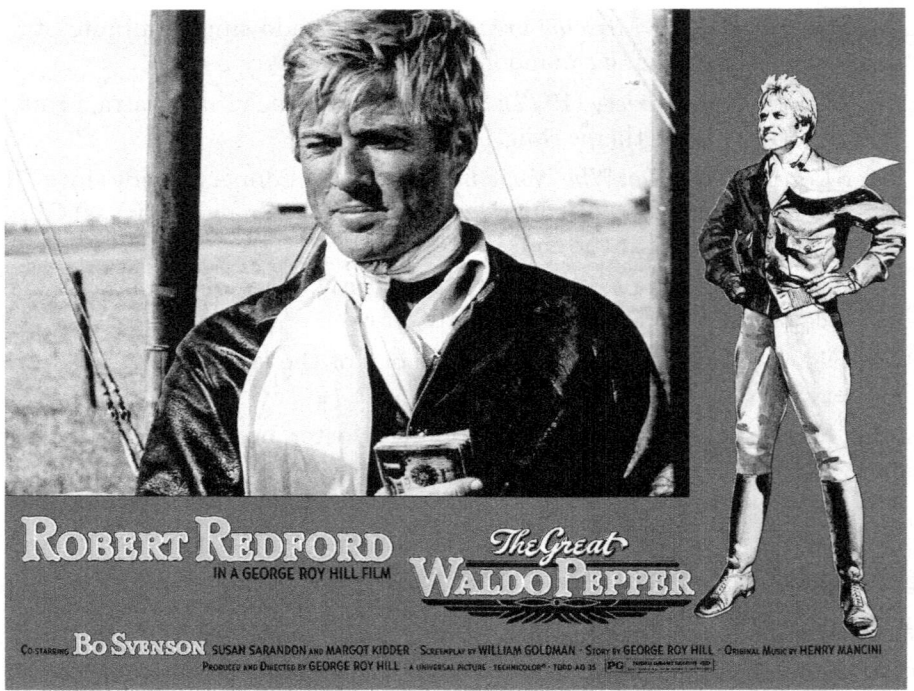

Pepper heads west to become a stuntman in Hollywood, where the action is grounded for twenty-three minutes. But in a last dogfight being staged for movie cameras, he goes airborne against a real German ace. These two anachronistic knights joust with the poignant resignation that their time is finally over. This spectacular eleven-minute duel, like all the aerial footage, keeps the movie aloft.

The Great Waldo Pepper is always stylish and often very entertaining, and it has stirring dialogue about "courage, honor, and chivalry." While much of the movie celebrates the joy of flying, the alarming deaths bring this high-spirited tale crashing down with dark warnings about the high price of obsession.

ADDED ATTRACTION: Biplane Movies

The Great Waldo Pepper wasn't the only '70s movie that featured biplanes. Here are fourteen additional American movies that took vintage aircraft aloft.

- *Ace Eli and Rodger of the Skies* (1973): The title characters are 1920s barnstormers.
- *Boxcar Bertha* (1972): A biplane crashes early in the movie.
- *Capricorn One* (1978): Near the end, there's a dramatic helicopter-vs.-biplane pursuit.
- *The Cat from Outer Space* (1978): The alien feline turns biplane pilot in a final chase.
- *Charley Varrick* (1973): A car-vs.-biplane duel ends the movie.
- *Darling Lili* (1970): Rock Hudson commands the Flying Eagles squadron in this World War One musical.
- *Days of Heaven* (1978): A flying circus makes a brief appearance.
- *Lucky Lady* (1975): Several scenes include biplanes.
- *Murphy's War* (1971): His war includes a biplane-vs.-submarine battle.

1975

- *Nothing by Chance* (1975): A documentary celebrating modern barnstormers.
- *The People That Time Forgot* (1977): A biplane flies to a lost continent.
- *Silver Streak* (1976): Thrown off the modern train, the hero catches up via an old biplane.
- *Tora! Tora! Tora!* (1970): Before the Pearl Harbor attack, a flying lesson in a biplane provides comic relief.
- *Von Richthofen and Brown* (1971): Biplanes (and a triplane) fill this story of the German ace.

Tommy

Released: March 1975
Director: Ken Russell
Stars: Roger Daltrey, Ann-Margret, Oliver Reed
Academy Awards: Two nominations (Best Actress—Ann-Margret; Best Music)

PREVIEW: A deaf, dumb and blind young man becomes a pinball champion and inspires followers.

NOW SHOWING: Pinball Wizard

For music fans, *Tommy* (1975) might've been the year's coolest movie. Not only is *Tommy* great visual fun, but it showcases famous rock stars and Hollywood stars who all sing in an operatic movie that replaces dialogue with wall-to-wall songs. Another popular 1975 musical, *The Rocky Horror Picture Show*, was also outrageously entertaining, but its performers were mostly unknowns (the audiences participating in the theaters were the real stars). *Tommy*, on the other hand, has Eric Clapton cranking out a fast blues song to Marilyn Monroe's statue, Jack Nicholson as a doctor talk-singing his diagnosis, Roger Daltrey joyously belting an anthem while running undersea, and Ann-Margret cavorting in a room flooded with liquid chocolate. Now THAT'S entertainment!

The movie is based on the Who's landmark double album that was released to instant acclaim in 1969. The muddled (okay, preposterous) story has a traumatized deaf, dumb, and blind boy becoming a pinball champion, regaining his senses, and inspiring a cult of followers who eventually turn against their "new messiah." On the album, the four

Roger Daltrey.

male band members sing all the parts, including those for women and kids. The movie clarifies the narrative a bit by casting men, women, and children in their correct roles, and also by adding new songs to connect scenes. The undeniable highlights include Elton John's show-stopping "Pinball Wizard" at the rowdy pinball tourney (the mighty Who back him and finish by destroying their instruments); Tina Turner amped up as the nightmarish "Acid Queen"; Roger Daltrey, mute kid, finally liberated to become Roger Daltrey, rock star, two-thirds of the way through the movie with the exhilarating "I'm Free"; and the uplifting "Listening to You" sunrise finale.

Unfortunately, not all the stars qualify as singers. Nicholson gingerly tiptoes through his one number, and a new verb is required to properly categorize Oliver Reed's vocals. Ann-Margret is fully committed, however, bringing genuine talent and glamour to the role of Tommy's mother in an Oscar-nominated performance. Matching the wildly varied musical numbers are director Ken Russell's eccentric visuals. Every scene is loaded with dazzling, sometimes cartoonish, frequently hilarious elements. The five-minute saga of young acolyte "Sally Simpson," culminating with her zany marriage to a glittery Frankenstein, is an imaginative merging of story and style into a flamboyant mini-movie. *Tommy* isn't for everyone, but it doesn't try to be. To millions of faithful fans, it's one of the decade's weird, wonderful experiences.

ADDED ATTRACTION: Who's Next

Arguably the world's greatest rock group in the 1970s (sorry, Rolling Stones and Led Zeppelin fans), the Who finished the decade with two more movies. *The Kids Are Alright* (1979) is a terrific documentary that recaps the group's career with rare footage, dynamic concert performances that end in total destruction, live studio work ("Barbara Ann" is an impromptu hoot), and interviews. Drummer Keith Moon (who died seven months before the movie came out) was a madcap reality show waiting to happen. Fans will be in Who heaven. Later that year, *Quadrophenia* (1979) was director Franc Roddam's dramatic version of the Who's ambitious 1973 concept album about a troubled teen (Phil Daniels) in working-class London who gradually loses his girl, job, family, friends, and illusions. On the album, the "quad" of the title represents the four songs that illustrate different sides of the hero's personality, and each member of the Who is identified with one of the songs. The movie doesn't make any of those connections, and the cast members don't sing any songs, though music from the Who and hits from early-'60s groups play in the background throughout the movie. *Quadrophenia* effectively captures the era and the Mod subculture, and it also gives Sting his first movie role.

Escape to Witch Mountain

Released: March 1975
Director: John Hough
Stars: Kim Richards, Ike Eisenmann, Eddie Albert
Academy Awards: None

PREVIEW: Authorities pursue two psychic kids who struggle to recall their mysterious past.

NOW SHOWING: Sci-Fi Siblings

2001: A Space Odyssey (1968) was a wondrous science-fiction milestone that toured the universe via pioneering special effects. It was an expensive movie to make, however, and its ambiguities polarized audiences, so in the early 1970s studios ditched the rocket ships and brought sci-fi settings and themes closer to home. *Silent Running* (1972) notwithstanding, movies like *The Omega Man* (1971), *THX 1138* (1971), *Soylent Green* (1973), *Sleeper* (1973), *Westworld* (1973), and the four *Planet of the Apes* sequels cleverly used modern city streets, unusual homes, underground structures, desert landscapes, and other existing environments to represent dystopian futures right here on Earth for stories barbed with relevant social criticism. For these few years, smaller sci-fi was potentially better sci-fi.

A new Earth-bound sci-fi movie for kids rolled out in early 1975. *Escape to Witch Mountain* is an appealing Disney thriller that generated solid reviews and audiences large enough to elevate this one movie into a franchise. Two orphans with paranormal powers are coveted by a greedy millionaire (Ray Milland) to assist his investments. The kids escape in an RV with a self-described "crusty old man" (Eddie Albert), but soon the millionaire, police, and reward hunters are close behind for a long pursuit through scenic Northern California. Balancing the comical scenes and friendly animals is a darker side in which the girl (Kim Richards) gradually recalls a tragedy. Foreshadowing *E.T.* (1982), the kids turn out to be from "a whole other solar system" and hope to reunite with other extraterrestrials (an old-school flying saucer finally arrives to take them "home"). It's a suspenseful, entertaining movie that doesn't devolve into silliness like many other Disney live-action movies did back then. Today's kids should still be fully engaged, though modern parents won't be as enamored of the dated special effects as '70s audiences were.

The sequel, *Return from Witch Mountain* (1978), keeps the psychic siblings (now teenagers), drops Milland and Albert, adds Bette Davis and Christopher Lee as villains, and moves the story to Los Angeles. The two kids are separated most of the time until an implausible plutonium-plant climax. Despite this movie's weak slapstick and routine action, some of it involving Disney's family-friendly version of a street gang, somehow the series continued for decades. Meanwhile, in 1975 two more sci-fi movies were imminent; they too stayed on the ground, since the high-flying revolution launched by *Star Wars* (1977) was still two years away ...

ADDED ATTRACTION: More '75 Sci-Fi

Three months after *Escape to Witch Mountain*, *Rollerball* (1975) raced into theaters for the summer. Norman Jewison, already an Oscar winner, directed this well-crafted, surprisingly thoughtful action movie about a barbaric roller-derby-with-motorcycles sport in a future when "corporate society takes care of everything"; that far-off year, the movie declares, is 2018. "To demonstrate the futility of individual effort," all-powerful corporations have created the violent, fast-paced rollerball game, which is indeed action-packed, though the movie unfortunately goes an hour between games. James Caan is the star player whose open defiance poses a threat that must be eliminated. The year's quirkiest sci-fi movie was *A Boy and His Dog* (1975), a November release that's understandably become a cult favorite. After a five-day nuclear war destroys civilization in the remote future (2024), Don Johnson, baby-faced and a decade before *Miami Vice* superstardom, plays a sex-obsessed, gun-toting survivor named Vic. He wanders through the Southwestern desert looking for food and girls, his only companion a witty dog that talks to him telepathically and detects nearby humans. The thugs Vic encounters have makeshift costumes and vehicles that anticipate *The Road Warrior* (1981). The movie's last third slows down when Vic, lured by a pretty girl, abandons the dog (voiced by Tim McIntire) to venture into a weird underground community where everyone is slathered in mime makeup and death is apparently impending. A mix of tension and humor, this imaginative, offbeat movie ends with a twisted, pitch-black joke that's unforgettable.

Death Race 2000

Released: April 1975
Director: Paul Bartel
Stars: David Carradine, Sylvester Stallone, Simone Griffeth
Academy Awards: None

PREVIEW: Costumed drivers in a wild cross-country race win points for hitting pedestrians.

NOW SHOWING: Road Kill

An unexpected hit, *Death Race 2000* (1975) is a wild, outrageous splatterfest for people who enjoy Quentin Tarantino's *Grindhouse* movies. But keep the kids away, because *Death Race 2000* earns its R rating.

Producer Roger Corman, famous for his quick, cheap movies, applies a simple formula here: fast cars + blood + sexy girls = "the greatest sporting event since the days of Spartacus." That event, a parody of all violent sports, is the Transcontinental Road Race using small super-fast cars. There's a touch of science-fiction (a futuristic cityscape, a reference to "the world crash of '79"), but mostly there's gory action that's accelerated by the under-cranked camera.

Simone Griffeth and David Carradine.

The race spans the country, with sex breaks in St. Louis and Albuquerque (the locations all look like Southern California, however). The five souped-up cars are customized with fangs, spears, machine guns, etc. to match the campy themes of their costumed drivers, which include a female Nazi (Roberta Collins) who brags about "the master race," the masked Frankenstein (David Carradine) who has an actual hand grenade for a hand, and a flamboyant gangster (Sylvester Stallone, a year before *Rocky*) who wants to win "in the name of hate."

After fifteen minutes a car impales a highway worker and everyone cheers, because racers earn points for killing pedestrians and spectators. Soon the racers are intentionally driving through picnics ("Go for the baby and the mother," the driver is advised), they're crushing doctors during Euthanasia Day at the geriatric hospital, and they're running over loyal fans who willingly sacrifice themselves for their heroes. Things are complicated by a revolutionary group intent on disrupting the race, but many of those saboteurs fall to the cars.

Not all viewers will laugh at the crazy carnage that makes this movie almost as silly as a Road Runner cartoon (it even implements Wile E. Coyote's "fake tunnel" trick). But violence is what the movie is satirizing: "Our American way of life," the race announcer declares, "sure it's violent! But that's the way we love it! Violent, violent, violent!" Other targets are the French and "their evil power" that has caused all of America's problems, and an all-powerful president who self-righteously calls his audience "my children." And yes that's Fred Grandy from TV's *The Love Boat* in one of the cars. The surprisingly happy ending arrives in a fast eighty minutes. For some viewers, that's too soon, for others, not soon enough. Either way, fasten those seatbelts.

ADDED ATTRACTION: Corman's *Capone*

In theaters concurrently with *Death Race 2000* was another blood-spattered Roger Corman movie. Directed by Steve Carver, who had made *Big Bad Mama* (1974) for Corman, *Capone* (1975) is a low-budget crime drama that attempts to capitalize on the monumental success of *The Godfather* (1972) by showing the rise and fall of America's most famous real-life mobster. Al Capone's exploits are heavily fictionalized (in the movie he gets his facial scars from flying through a window, but actually he received them in a knife fight), history gets rearranged (in real life the enforcer Frank Nitti died before Capone, not after), and at times the machine-gun fire seems almost continuous. Still, the movie will appeal to anyone who likes uncomplicated over-the-top action. As Scarface, Ben Gazzara chews up scenery like he's ending a hunger strike, and he's got so much wadding stuffed into his cheeks he seems to be parodying the old-man jowls Marlon Brando added when he played Don Corleone. While Gazzara doesn't have big Al's physical heft, he does have the man's volcanic malevolence that suddenly erupts in violence or profanity. John Cassavetes briefly plays a fellow hood, beautiful Susan Blakely has daringly sexy scenes as Al's girl, and Sylvester Stallone appears as Nitti just a year before *Rocky* (1976) makes him a superstar.

Aloha, Bobby and Rose

Released: April 1975
Director: Floyd Mutrux
Stars: Paul Le Mat, Dianne Hull, Tim McIntire
Academy Awards: None

PREVIEW: Two lovers inadvertently cause a death and hit the road to escape what they've done.

NOW SHOWING: Hello Goodbye

Aloha, Bobby and Rose (1975) sets itself up as a likeable romance, but it crashes in the second half. Paul Le Mat, reprising his hot-rodding role from *American Graffiti* (1973), plays an unambitious L.A. mechanic and bad pool hustler. When he meets Rose (Dianne Hull), an attractive single mom, she initially doesn't like him, but she quickly warms to his boyish charms and wolfman hair.

The movie then shows their next two days together. During an enjoyable first date, Bobby stupidly pulls a childish prank at a liquor store that accidentally leaves the clerk dead. Racing away, Bobby wrecks Rose's car and bloodies them both. They drive south in his Camaro, briefly (and pointlessly) reach Mexico, turn around and come back in one of the most unscenic road trips ever. Ominous sirens and repeated police sightings suggest there won't be a happy ending. Rose, desperately missing her child and feeling guilty, turns herself in; Bobby refuses because he doesn't think the truth will be credible. He pays for that cynicism when he is shot dead by the police. Aloha, Bobby.

"I never dreamed it would happen like this," says a tearful Rose near the end. The audience could say that too because the movie had started so affably with light scenes that endeared us to these humble characters. But what might have been a sweet story with a little playful rebellion turns to tragedy once Bobby and Rose dig themselves into a deep, depressing hole with a series of dumb decisions. Though the movie disappointingly veers from the early expectations it creates, audiences still wanted to come along for the ride, and *Aloha, Bobby and Rose* became a surprise box-office hit

What director Floyd Mutrux really gets right is the setting. Great music from the decade (especially by Elton John), cool car scenes, and real L.A. locations like Pink's Hot Dogs authentically evoke the time and place. We especially like Bobby and Rose's fun two-minute cruise down the Sunset Strip; along the way the camera spotlights ten big ads for new albums by Ringo Starr, the Rolling Stones, the Electric Light Orchestra, and other nostalgic faves, plus concerts at the Greek Theater by Al Green and at the Universal Amphitheatre by Bette Midler. One billboard announces Neil Young's *Time Fades Away* album. Maybe time does, but those nostalgic feelings sure don't.

ADDED ATTRACTION:
American Hot Wax Is Here to Stay

Floyd Mutrux's next movie was much more joyful. Ostensibly *American Hot Wax* (1978) is about the pioneering DJ Alan Freed, one of the founding fathers of rock and roll. Persuasively brought to life by Tim McIntire, who is also in *Aloha, Bobby and Rose*, Freed spins records on the radio, auditions new groups, presents the first big rock concerts, defiantly challenges the authorities who think the music is "smut," and eventually gets tangled in his infamous payola scandal. His meandering story, however, becomes secondary to the raucous music swirling around him. It's no coincidence that the movie borrows the first word of its title from *American Graffiti* (1973): like that beloved classic, *American Hot Wax* offers wall-to-wall music, and that's really where the movie succeeds. Anytime Freed isn't playing records on the air, live performances of vintage rock songs are spontaneously breaking out on sidewalks, in office hallways, and in homes. The last twenty-five minutes celebrate the era with a live concert that closes with two titans, Chuck Berry and Jerry Lee Lewis, working the crowd into a frenzy. When Freed defiantly announces, "You're never gonna stop rock and roll," you can believe it, especially when the last shot is of a lone kid bangin' away on garbage-can lids. Adding to the movie's fun are budding TV stars Fran Drescher, Jay Leno, and Laraine Newman, who all play significant supporting characters.

French Connection II

Released: May 1975
Director: John Frankenheimer
Stars: Gene Hackman, Fernando Rey, Bernard Fresson
Academy Awards: None

PREVIEW: A tough New York detective goes to France to finish his hunt for an escaped drug lord.

NOW SHOWING: Popeye's Back

Viewers with sequelphobia—a fear of bad movie sequels—need not worry about *French Connection II* (1975). It's a worthy follow-up to *The French Connection* (1971), and together they'd make a satisfying double-feature.

Not only is "*The*" absent from the title, part two makes some interesting changes to part one's thrilling formula. *French Connection II* moves the setting from New York to Marseilles and replaces part one's famous car-vs.-train chase with a suspenseful foot chase. With Roy Scheider off making *Jaws* (1975), part two doesn't have Cloudy, the reasonable partner who balanced the unorthodox detective Popeye Doyle (Gene Hackman); instead, it has a by-the-book French inspector who barely tolerates Doyle. Importantly, the taut, relentless investigation of part one re-starts in part two but is interrupted for thirty-six minutes when Doyle becomes ... indisposed.

Doyle arrives in Marseilles as the proverbial fish out of water, a metaphor symbolized by his exit from a taxi that's decorated with a fish and early scenes of marketplace fish being gutted. Amusing sequences show his French disconnection as he struggles to order food, meet women, and watch French TV. Doyle has come for part one's drug lord, Charnier (Fernando Rey), who mysteriously escaped at the end of that movie. Still hot-tempered and unconventional, but now out of his element, Doyle ruins the first bust he witnesses when he tackles a fleeing suspect who is actually an undercover ally.

A third of the way through the movie, Charnier's henchmen kidnap Doyle and repeatedly inject him with heroin, turning him into a helpless, dazed junkie. Three weeks later he's forced to go cold turkey, a harrowing sequence that reduces this ferocious pit bull of a detective to a screaming, weeping mess. When he's finally clean, he casually incinerates the hotel where he was held captive. Back on Charnier's trail,

Doyle's last exhausting pursuit through the streets ends abruptly on a Marseilles dock. Viewers hoping to see Popeye get revenge on his smug tormentor will enjoy the outcome.

Like part one, part two contrasts the lifestyles of elegant criminals and frazzled cops. And like its predecessor, *French Connection II* shows the gritty, ugly side of its city. Director John Frankenheimer also employs the same kind of handheld shots that William Friedkin used in part one to intensify the immediacy. Frankenheimer has followed-up Friedkin's masterpiece with a powerhouse of his own, though his isn't a true story. Darn it.

ADDED ATTRACTION: French Reconnection

French Connection II adds more information to the case that was at the center of *The French Connection*. In that first movie, Doyle and Cloudy tracked an incoming shipment of heroin and eventually pulled off what was at the time the biggest drug bust in American history, but the French mastermind slipped out of their grasp. In the second movie, the French police acknowledge Doyle as "an authentic American hero" for this "big arrest" in part one, but they also remind him that the sixty kilos of captured heroin were later stolen "right out of police headquarters." We also learn that Popeye has been on the force for fourteen years and has killed five men, two of them policemen. But it's Charnier himself who briefly explains how he escaped at the end of the first movie, even though he was seemingly trapped in a building with Popeye and other policemen in close pursuit. "It was very simple, and very droll," he brags in *French Connection II*, "eighty-three policemen wanted to talk to me, and fifty-two of them talked to my money instead. I love a city where you always know where you stand."

Gene Hackman.

The Eiger Sanction

Released: May 1975
Director: Clint Eastwood
Stars: Clint Eastwood, George Kennedy, Vonetta McGee
Academy Awards: None

PREVIEW: A retired assassin returns for a job that sends him climbing up a perilous mountain.

NOW SHOWING: Eastwood, Clint Eastwood

Name Universal's exciting action movie for mid-1975, based on a popular novel, produced by the Zanuck/Brown team, filmed on outdoor locations by a soon-to-be-famous director early in his directing career, with music by John Williams. *Jaws*? Sure, but also *The Eiger Sanction* (1975), a good-but-not-great Clint Eastwood movie that preceded *Jaws* by a month and made a tidy profit before the big shark swallowed it up.

Eastwood isn't just the star of *The Eiger Sanction*, he was also the director. As in another early movie where he directed himself, Eastwood plays against his stereotypical tough-guy heroes; he'd been a jazz DJ in *Play Misty for Me* (1971), and now he's a bespectacled art professor, Dr. Jonathan Hemlock, using words like "involuted." Hemlock is a former government assassin recruited back to work via a contrived espionage plot that's one of the movie's many James Bond-style elements. Like the Bond movies, this one has a weird leader of a spy-organization (an albino who can't stand light), scenic locations, thrilling exploits, and exotic women. And like Bond, Hemlock is "extravagant but effective" on the job. That job is to join an international

Clint Eastwood.

mountain-climbing team and "sanction" (assassinate) a killer, but the complicated story soon becomes nonsensical. For instance, Hemlock knows that his unnamed target limps, but that character accompanies Hemlock for two-thirds of the movie and even makes a hazardous climb before his conspicuous limp suddenly appears in the final nine minutes.

More troubling are the movie's Cro-Magnon social behaviors. Hemlock thinks he's being witty when he says, "I thought I'd given up rape, but I've changed my mind" to seduce a "black chick" (his words) who induces some lame Aunt Jemima/Uncle Ben jokes. A gay character minces, a dog is named with an ugly gay slur, and a friend teases Hemlock that he's "a pansy." To his tough Indian trainer Hemlock says, "Just scalp me! I wish Custer would've won." Men pat sexy women on the butt. Hemlock punches a woman. They don't make 'em like this anymore. Thankfully.

Get past the outdated attitudes and focus on the sky-high altitudes, because the terrific action sequences and spectacular photography—in Arizona's Monument Valley and on Switzerland's 13,000-foot Eiger—overcome lapses in logic and taste. Eastwood does the climbs himself, and that's really him suspended over the void in the exciting climax. Stunt-wise, the movie scales impressive heights, but in unfortunate ways *Sanction* slips and falls.

ADDED ATTRACTION: A Different Mountain to Climb

If *The Eiger Sanction* offers a mountain of macho thrills, its opposite is *The Other Side of the Mountain* (1975), a sensitive tear-jerker that was a major Christmas hit. Telling the true story of champion skier Jill Kinmont (Marilyn Hassett), this bio-pic shows beautiful mountains and exciting skiing action for the first thirty-eight minutes, but then Kinmont, speeding downhill to qualify for the 1956 Olympics, careens off a cliff and breaks her neck, leaving her paralyzed below the shoulders. The rest of the movie shows her redoubtable "iron-willed spirit" as she slowly rebuilds her life from a wheelchair. As if she needs more challenges, her best friend gets polio, her boyfriend dumps her, and her supportive new fiancé (Beau Bridges) gets killed in a plane crash. Kinmont's optimism endures, however, and this touching movie inspires. The slower, less-successful sequel, *The Other Side of the Mountain Part 2* (1978), opens with a replay of her part-one crash and continues her true story in 1976 with many flashbacks to past events. Though she's reluctant to start a new romance, a sweet trucker (Timothy Bottoms) helps her try to love again and they get engaged. Eerily, he too almost gets killed in a crash, but this time the fiancé makes it back for a teary reunion and a golden outdoor wedding.

Love and Death

Released: June 1975
Director: Woody Allen
Stars: Woody Allen, Diane Keaton, Olga Georges-Picot
Academy Awards: None

PREVIEW: In the 1800s, a cowardly Russian pacifist and his wife try to assassinate Napoleon.

NOW SHOWING: Love and Death and Lunacy

With *Love and Death* (1975), Woody Allen showed that he had fully developed as a movie-making triple-threat. He'd been writing/directing/starring in movies since *Take the Money and Run* (1969), progressing through the 1970s from the rough-but-riotous *Bananas* (1971) to the more polished *Sleeper* (1973). Smart and stylish, *Love and Death* advances Allen to the brink of his masterpiece, *Annie Hall* (1977).

Love and Death represents a departure for Allen. While he's still got his black horn-rimmed Moscot eyeglasses, he wears them in nineteenth-century Russia with a soldier's uniform, not in a twentieth-century America city with the familiar urban casuals seen in *Play It Again, Sam* (1972). It's the first movie Allen narrates himself, here playing Boris, a cowardly pacifist who marries his distant cousin (Diane Keaton) and plots to assassinate Napoleon. Additionally, *Love and Death* is his first movie to make extensive use of classical music (especially Prokofiev), something he'll do in many later movies. Atypically for Allen, there's bloody violence, and, surprisingly, Boris scores with Europe's sexiest courtesan (Olga Georges-Picot), who even compliments him as her "greatest lover" (Allen's characters usually bemoan their bad luck with women). It's his first movie with a three-word title that has "and" in the middle (he'll do this five more times, starting with 1989's *Crimes and Misdemeanors*), and, in a minor point, for the first time somebody saves string, a hobby that resurfaces in *Zelig* (1983).

Despite these dissimilarities, *Love and Death* shares traits with Allen's previous movies. As in *Bananas*, there's "a strange and vivid dream" sequence, this one showing a field with caskets and waiters. In *Sleeper*, Keaton's character is a poet who recites a nonsensical poem; in *Love and Death*, Boris decides to become "a great poet" and composes aloud (his first line is actually from T.S. Eliot's "The Love Song of J. Alfred Prufrock"). More importantly, it's yet another hilarious teaming with Diane Keaton and moves her closer to her Oscar-winning triumph as Annie Hall.

Besides the wonderful sight gags that are equal to the Marx Brothers' best (or anyone's best in the '70s), what really elevates this movie above Allen's previous works is its intelligence. Allen spins sublime comedy out of philosophical discussions, and in one conversation he incorporates ten titles from Dostoyevsky's canon (*The Gambler*, *The Idiot*, "Bobok," etc.). Compared to Mel Brooks's hysterical-but-lowbrow *Blazing Saddles* (1974), the brilliant *Love and Death* is like *Blazing Dissertations*.

ADDED ATTRACTION: Allen's Homages

As he did in *Bananas* (1971), Woody Allen points to earlier movies throughout *Love and Death*. One of them is his own *Take the Money and Run* (1969), which includes a punchline—"What's today? Monday, Tuesday, Wednesday … ten years"—that's recycled almost verbatim in *Love and Death*. More references follow.

- *Battleship Potemkin* (1925)
  Three lion statues are shown in this order: a lion asleep, awake, and then alert; *Love and Death* reverses the order so it looks like a lion is collapsing in exhaustion. Also, both movies include a battlefield scene that shows someone being shot directly in the eye.
- *Monsieur Beaucaire* (1946)
  Bob Hope's comedy and *Love and Death* both have a character named Don Francisco. Also, both movies show the hero leaning forward and inadvertently poking a woman behind him with a sword.

- *Casanova's Big Night* (1954)
  Bob Hope's comedy and *Love and Death* both include the lines, "There's been a mistake. I know. I made it."
- *The Seventh Seal* (1957)
  Ingmar Bergman's drama and *Love and Death* both open with a shot of a cloudy sky. Also, Death leads six characters in a solemn *danse macabre* at the end of *The Seventh Seal*. Woody's movie ends with Boris dancing off with the Grim Reaper.
- *Persona* (1966)
  Bergman occasionally positions two women so that one head is half-hidden behind the other as both face forward, or sometimes the foreground actress is in profile. Allen similarly positions overlapping faces as two women discuss wheat.

Nashville

(One of 1975's five **FAR-OUT** movies)

Released: June 1975

Director: Robert Altman

Stars: Keith Carradine, Ronee Blakely, Lily Tomlin

Academy Awards: One win (Best Song), plus four more nominations (Best Picture; two for Best Supporting Actress—Ronee Blakley, Lily Tomlin; Best Director)

PREVIEW: Musicians gather in Nashville as organizers plan a big outdoor political concert.

FINE LINE: "Well if makin' love were margarine, then she is the high-priced spread." (From "My Baby's Cookin' in Another Man's Pan," performed by Jonnie Barnett.)

CLOSE-UP: One of *Nashville*'s charms is its perfectly imperfect music. Many of the singing actors and actresses aren't real musicians, so they perform with varying degrees of skill. This range of abilities makes the movie more authentic, since many of these characters are amateurs hoping for a stardom they'll obviously never attain. Two hours into the movie, singer Cristina Raines actually coughs slightly in the middle of "Since You've Gone."

NOW SHOWING: Visiting Nashville

A year after they made the underrated *Thieves Like Us* (1974), director Robert Altman, screenwriter Joan Tewkesbury, stars Keith Carradine and Shelley Duvall and others all reteamed for *Nashville* (1975). It quickly became a critical darling, major reviewers named *Nashville* the year's best movie, and at the Oscars it was up for Best Picture. Audiences weren't quite as enthusiastic, but they still pushed *Nashville* into the top thirty of the year's box-office successes.

All this *Nashville* news is impressive, but it may baffle some viewers who are frustrated by this defiantly plotless *160-minute* movie. Anyone looking for a clear storyline has come to the wrong movie, because Altman always preferred atmosphere to plot. Here, to capture different sides of country music's colorful epicenter at the start of the post-Watergate era, he shows two-dozen characters roaming around the city and occasionally interacting with each other over a five-day period. Their activities are generally organized around an outdoor political concert that several characters are arranging with hopes of recruiting other characters as performers. We see some of that concert, plus many other musical performances, because *Nashville* is, at heart, a musical. Singing—in studios, on stages, and in clubs—constitutes over half the movie. Many of the actors and actresses play professional musicians, others are wanna-be singers or fans, and with the slightest encouragement a party guest or a waitress will croon a quick a cappella number.

To film this wide-ranging panorama, Altman created settings and circumstances in real locations (actual houses, churches, a junkyard, a racetrack, a hospital, the Grand Ole Opry, nightclubs, etc.), he populated the backgrounds with local citizenry, and he gave his actors and actresses permission to improvise dialogue. Altman then documented the results. This daring experimental style includes sophisticated sonic techniques that place microphones everywhere, enabling Altman to record layers of sound so the audience perceives various voices, music and effects without always knowing what's most important. Altman had done something similar in excellent predecessors like *M*A*S*H* (1970) and *McCabe & Mrs. Miller* (1971). With *Nashville* he achieves the pinnacle of this subtle art.

After credits that run like old-time music ads, the first scene isn't actually musical. A van drives around broadcasting speeches from an unseen political candidate; the van's later appearances will strengthen the connection between politicians and entertainers. Next we're in a music studio listening to a strident patriot (Henry Gibson), then we move to an enthusiastic gospel singer (Lily Tomlin), and in the following twenty minutes we meet nearly all the main characters in different locations. Tenuously connecting the vignettes is a ludicrous English journalist (Geraldine Chaplin) who talks with almost everybody. She takes herself much too seriously, while they don't take her at all.

By this point modern audiences might be exasperated: all these characters are weaving in and out of this cinematic tapestry, but to what end? Jeff Goldblum, for instance, rides around on a three-wheeled chopper and silently performs amateur magic tricks to strangers. Why? Maybe he replicates some real person in the actual city, but his appearances are more puzzling than entertaining. Shelley Duvall is an impossibly thin groupie in crazy outfits and ever-changing wigs. Noted. Lily Tomlin's character relates a bizarre anecdote about a bulging eyeball. Surprising, but irrelevant. Keith Carradine's rock-star character is a jerk. Rock stars, jerks? That's not news. Pop-cultural touchstones—Marlon Brando, Barbra Streisand, JFK, *Easy Rider*, *The Wizard of Oz*—get mentioned. It's all vaguely interesting, some episodes more than others, but the parts never jell into a coherent whole.

At times Altman does induce some provocative incongruities. Girls twirling batons are immediately succeeded by girls twirling rifles; when a popular singer faints at the airport, a political supporter photobombs the news report with a campaign poster; a man talks about his wife's surgery while his disinterested niece scans the radio for rock music; a blasé woman continues walking as a car accident happens right behind her. The best scenes really are captivating: Elliott Gould and Julie Christie briefly appear as themselves, and the Nashvillians struggle to identify them; Ronee Blakely plays a fragile star who has a nervous breakdown onstage; Keith Carradine sings his Oscar-winning ballad "I'm Easy" in a nightclub where four rapt lovers each think he's serenading only her; naïve Gwen Welles plays a lovely waitress who "cannot sing a lick" but tries hard and is sadly compelled to undress for jeering men. Memorable scenes, however, don't fill this long movie, they punctuate it.

The final concert concludes with an assassination attempt by a loner with no agenda other than a desire for attention. After momentary chaos, the movie segues into a hopeful song from the one performer we haven't heard yet, the spitfire played by Barbara Harris. Credits roll, and then the screen goes black for two minutes while the same song is given a gospel treatment. So the music endures. Most issues in the movie, however, are left unresolved.

Some viewers regard this shooting and aftermath as a powerful metaphor for Altman's message about ambition, politics, and the celebrity-obsessed American psyche; others viewers may feel it's simply been tacked on to add some drama to a mostly undramatic movie that never clarifies what it's really doing (is it observing? celebrating? or satirizing?). While everyone should see *Nashville*, and everyone will find things to admire in this significant '70s movie, not everyone will swoon.

ADDED ATTRACTION: Singing Actresses

Gwen Welles and Lily Tomlin aren't the only non-singing actresses who fearlessly crooned tunes in 1975-1979 movies.

- Candice Bergen, *Starting Over* (1979): Her cringe-worthy "Better Than Ever" is intentionally hilarious.
- Eileen Brennan, *At Long Last Love* (1975): She joins in on four songs.
- Goldie Hawn, *The Duchess and the Dirtwater Fox* (1976): She sings bawdy music-hall numbers with an English accent.
- Jill Ireland, *From Noon Till Three* (1976): Ireland performs the Golden Globe-nominated "Hello and Goodbye."
- Diane Keaton, *Annie Hall* (1977): Keaton sings two numbers as a budding night-club singer.
- Sondra Locke, *Every Which Way But Loose* (1978): Her songs include a duet with Phil Everly.
- Mary Kay Place, *New York, New York* (1977): She's the new band singer who knocks out "Blue Moon."
- Susan Sarandon, *The Rocky Horror Picture Show* (1975): Her songs include "Touch-a Touch-a Touch Me."
- P.J. Soles, *Rock 'n' Roll High School* (1979): When she sings the title song, the whole gym class starts dancing.

Night Moves

Released: June 1975
Director: Arthur Penn
Stars: Gene Hackman, Jennifer Warren, Edward Binns
Academy Awards: None

PREVIEW: A private eye struggles to solve a missing-person case that seems to lead to murder.

NOW SHOWING: New Noir

After the success of *Chinatown* (1974), a wave of noir thrillers quickly surged into theaters (see "Added Attraction"). One of these, *Night Moves* (1975), doesn't rise to the heights of Roman Polanski's masterpiece, but it's as good as *Klute* (1971), *The Long Goodbye* (1973), and other highly regarded crime-solving movies from the '70s.

Night Moves is so complicated that even the movie's private eye ends up completely baffled. As per the title, many scenes take place at night, when things are barely seen and dark motivations become shadowy actions. Gene Hackman is excellent as Harry, a modern-day ex-football player who's now a jaded gumshoe working, like Jake was at the start of *Chinatown*, on low-level divorce cases in L.A. What seems like a straightforward request—to track down a missing teenage girl, which was also one of Jake's *Chinatown* assignments—tangles him in a web of intrigue involving stolen archaeological artifacts and a New Mexico movie location. Harry retrieves the free-spirited girl (Melanie Griffith, in her movie debut) but she later dies mysteriously, sending him to Florida where a sunken wreck, a sexy femme fatale, and an attacking airplane make him plead, "What the hell is going on?" In the final shot, he's circling endlessly on the ocean in a powerboat called *Point of View*.

That last image perfectly expresses this movie's unanswered questions. Viewers could rightly wonder about the girl's death—was it an accident, or murder? And if murder, by whom? In the exciting climax, the pilot of a crashed plane is glimpsed through a window as he sinks below the waves—he mouths something, but what? Clues, names, explanations, accusations? Hackman's last lines, "You bastard, bastard, bastard"—is that the dead pilot? Himself? Multiple characters? Harry admits "I didn't solve anything," because the twisting plot is just like the chess match shown in the movie: it has an unexpected outcome that we acknowledge but can't really understand. In a way, Hackman's character is a livelier version of the solemn, focused loner he played in *The Conversation* (1974); neither man can trust anyone as he gets dragged into an impenetrable maze.

Director Arthur Penn had already made one of the best crime movies of the '60s, *Bonnie and Clyde* (1967). With *Night Moves* he makes one of the best of the late 1970s and shows that, after *Chinatown*, easy answers and tidy resolutions will be hard to come by.

Melanie Griffith.

ADDED ATTRACTION: Next Noir

Two months after *Night Moves* brought noir forward to a modern setting, *Farewell, My Lovely* (1975) returned it to 1941. This respectable adaptation streamlines Raymond Chandler's labyrinthine novel and ends it differently (for instance, the movie's femme fatale gets killed by the private eye, but in the book she escapes and later commits suicide). Iconic actor Robert Mitchum plays iconic shamus Philip Marlowe, now world-weary and "getting old" (he's about twenty years older than the book's Marlowe). Using a snappy vocabulary, Marlowe narrates this L.A. story where all the men wear fedoras and everyone, even the dames, is packin' heat. A search for, what else, a missing girl leads to a jewel heist, a whorehouse, a scruffy widow (Sylvia Miles, in an Oscar-nominated performance), murders, and an off-shore gambling boat. Mid-movie Marlowe is drugged, a weird sequence that has him so "shot full of hop" he goes as "crazy as two waltzing mice." Sylvester Stallone, pre-*Rocky* (1976), briefly plays a gangster. The noir year ended with December's spoofy *The Black Bird* (1975). George Segal plays the son of Sam ... Sam Spade the great detective, that is, the same private eye Humphrey Bogart had famously defined in *The Maltese Falcon* (1941). When junior takes possession of a Maltese Falcon statuette, dark characters (including a Nazi dwarf who has goons wearing Hawaiian shirts) take interest. Uneven and never laugh-out-loud funny, the movie is still amusing, Segal is a pro (as usual), and Lee Patrick and Elisha Cook, Jr. reprise their roles from the original *Maltese Falcon*.

Jaws

(One of 1975's five **FAR-OUT** movies)

Released: June 1975

Director: Steven Spielberg

Stars: Roy Scheider, Richard Dreyfuss, Robert Shaw

Academy Awards: Three wins (Best Editing; Best Music; Best Sound), plus one more nomination (Best Picture)

PREVIEW: Three men take to sea to hunt a killer shark that is terrorizing a popular beach area.

FINE LINE: "You're gonna need a bigger boat." (Chief Brody, upon seeing the shark's gaping jaws up close for the first time.)

CLOSE-UP: Steven Spielberg sure likes meteors. Eighty-six minutes into the movie, with the *Orca* silhouetted against the dark horizon, a shooting star flashes in the upper-left section of the sky. Ten minutes later, as Chief Brody anxiously loads his pistol in the foreground, a much slower meteor streaks across the night sky from the upper-right corner of the screen to the lower-left, leaving a long trail behind it. Twelve seconds pass, and one more moves diagonally from the screen's upper-left corner and disappears into clouds above the *Orca*, which floats quietly in a long-distance shot.

NOW SHOWING:
You're Gonna Need a Bigger Theater

Few movies have been as influential as *Jaws* (1975). Not only did it skyrocket the career of young Steven Spielberg, who would go on to become the highest-grossing movie director of all time, *Jaws* launched the era of the summer blockbuster. Before *Jaws*, movies with big box-office potential debuted in different seasons (*The Godfather* in March 1972, *The Exorcist* in December 1973, for example). After *Jaws*, summer became the prime movie-going season; *The Omen* (June 1976), *Star Wars* (May 1977), *Alien* (May 1979) and many other blockbusters followed in the wake of *Jaws*'s summer success.

What's more, *Jaws* established a new release pattern for big-event movies. Instead of opening in a few theaters, or just in major cities, so that positive reviews and word-of-mouth referrals could give good movies time to "find" their audience one region at a time, *Jaws* opened in over four-hundred theaters in tandem with a nation-wide TV-advertising blitz. The studio's goal was not a steadily rising surge of attention, but rather an overwhelming must-see juggernaut that had to be experienced immediately. And experienced *live*, too, as *Jaws* and *Star Wars* eventually became actual attractions at Universal Studios and Disneyland. These were movies too big for mere theaters.

Movies ever since have tried to emulate *Jaws*'s impact and success, but not all of these pretenders have what *Jaws* does: a plot structure that disrupts expectations, an inventive young director working at the top of his game, and one of Hollywood's most suspenseful musical themes. The plot of *Jaws* follows the classic three-part structure used for centuries in the theater. A situation is introduced, complications follow, and there's a compelling resolution. But if the formula is ancient, the presentation feels new. *Jaws* famously kicks off with a savage killing that instantly taps into fundamental terrors. The movie is lethal from the get-go, like a roller coaster that immediately rockets its riders toward sharp curves and steep plunges.

As a temporary respite from the thrills, the movie includes some bureaucratic disarray. The town's leaders try to counter their sudden tourist-repelling infamy with distractions and a cover-up scheme involving another, smaller shark they've happened to kill. But once the three principals take to the ocean to battle the monster, the movie is stripped down to a pure fight for survival, a fight that the most experienced character surprisingly won't survive and the least likely hero will. The experienced seadog runs out of tricks and gets devoured, the scientist's technology completely fails, and only the police chief's unduplicatable improvisation succeeds. There are no ecological warnings, and no lessons about dealing with sharks that anyone could apply later, other than what *not* to do. Based on what we see, basically the best advice is not to go swimming in the first place.

What makes the fast-moving plot even more effective is that the mechanical shark used for filming was rarely working and so couldn't actually be shown (see "Added Attraction"). Delayed reveals intensify many great horror movies, obviously, including different versions of *The Phantom of the Opera*, *The Fly* (1958), and on to *Predator* (1987) and beyond. In *Jaws*, the first-hour suspense builds in the viewer's mind as the unseen threat gets larger and smarter, and those imagined teeth get longer and sharper.

Though the long, difficult shoot at Martha's Vineyard went way over budget and over schedule, director Spielberg seems to be working confidently all throughout the movie. Chucking out some of the book's unseemly episodes—like the tacky affair between the young scientist, Hooper (Richard Dreyfuss), and the chief's wife—and adding a more audience-pleasing finale than the book's ending that killed Hooper and let the shark expire from exhaustion, Spielberg seems to know just what the audience wants at any given moment. He adds a little comic relief ("He ate the light," a nervous joke when the boat's power goes out) and some riveting historical perspective about the real-life tragedy of the *U.S.S. Indianapolis* before he fully unleashes the shark.

Perhaps Spielberg's most inspired choice was to place his camera at water level, a technique that other directors quickly copied. Scene after scene is shown with the camera right where the victims are splashing, splitting the screen horizontally between sky and ocean. This way it's not just the on-screen victims who are being attacked; it's the audience that's treading water while the unseen shark ambushes them. Spielberg also moves his camera underwater like it *is* the shark, showing the audience what the predator sees as it maneuvers toward its helpless victims.

The ominous music by John Williams dramatically amplifies the suspense. His simple two-note theme (dun-DUN, dun-DUN) starts deep and slow but adrenalizes higher and faster as the shark approaches, exploding into a frenzy at the moment of ferocious attack. Williams's Oscar-winning music is now one of the most recognizable movie themes in history. Rarely has camera technique matched music technique so effectively.

Ultimately, the success of *Jaws* was the result of a perfect blend of story, ideas, and technique. *Jaws* quickly became the all-time champion in ticket sales as audiences flocked to see it again and again. Increasingly lame sequels followed up to *Jaws 4*, and feeble imitators tried to duplicate its success with swarms of killer fish, big bugs, and other featured creatures. All these efforts might have made money, but they didn't make history. *Jaws* did, because it was first, and it's still the best.

ADDED ATTRACTION: Shark Sightings

In the first half of *Jaws*, killer sharks are depicted in photos, on a billboard, in a chalkboard drawing, and on an arcade-game screen; we even peer into the mouth of a dead tiger shark that's been strung up on the dock. But what's barely seen in that first half is the great white that's terrorizing Amity Island. Mechanical problems forced Steven Spielberg to limit the shark's exposure to under *five* minutes (only about four percent of the 124-minute movie). In fact, before the eighty-one minute mark, the shark appears for a total of thirteen seconds. Don't believe us? Here's where the jaws in *Jaws* appear before the first major sighting 65% of the way through the movie.

- 17 minutes into the movie:
  A two-second glimpse of snout and fins as the shark drags the young Kintner boy below.
- 62 minutes:
  Dorsal fin and tail pass by for six seconds as the shark swims into "the pond." For three seconds the shark's gaping jaws pull the teacher from the capsized rowboat. A two-second shot of the dorsal fin as the shark glides under the bridge and out to the sea.
- 81 minutes:
  As Chief Brody chums the water behind the *Orca*, the shark surfaces for one second and flashes its teeth. Moments later, everyone gets their first long look at the full-length shark as it slowly swims by for thirty seconds.

Bite the Bullet

Released: June 1975
Director: Richard Brooks
Stars: Gene Hackman, Candice Bergen, James Coburn
Academy Awards: Two nominations (Best Music; Best Sound)

PREVIEW: In 1906, seven riders on horseback try to win a tough endurance race across the West.

NOW SHOWING: Race to the End of an Era

Bite the Bullet (1975) is an entertaining but troubling adventure movie. It reinvents the traditional western by using familiar elements—horses, cowboys, guns, vast landscapes, etc.—for a seven-hundred-mile endurance race on horseback in 1906 (there actually was such a thing in 1908). Among the seven competitors is a heroic cowboy, Sam (a convincing Gene Hackman). This admirable "champion of dumb animals, ladies in distress, lost kids and lost causes" consistently helps others, especially animals: he rescues an orphaned colt, he protects a jackass from abuse, and throughout he acts and speaks against animal cruelty.

That cruelty might upset sensitive viewers. The race starts after thirty-three minutes, and soon the horses are doing most of the suffering. One is driven over a cliff by a bear, another is literally ridden to death for two excruciating slow-motion minutes, one is injured and destroyed by its rider, and another is gunned down in full gallop and does a somersault. After a week of sprinting through deserts and mountains, the last surviving horses are so exhausted and overheated they can barely stagger to the finish line.

The riders, meanwhile, have their own problems. Bandits attack the beautiful cowgirl (Candice Bergen); the old man (Ben Johnson), hoping to be "a man to remember," poignantly dies of a heart attack mid-race; Sam is mysteriously drugged, suggesting the race may be fixed; and the poor Mexican rider has a terrible toothache that requires an impromptu extraction (afterwards, he bites on a bullet casing to plug the hole, giving the movie its title). Near the end, the race becomes a chase when escaping prisoners steal the riders' horses. After using a motorcycle (symbolizing the new century) to retrieve their mounts, the riders resume the race. Three of them make it to the slow-motion finish.

The best parts of the movie are in the dialogue by screenwriter/director Richard Brooks, the eight-time Oscar nominee famous for *In Cold Blood* (1967). He takes his time and lets his characters develop, giving some resonance to what otherwise could be redundant race scenes. Throughout, the western details feel accurate, and the rugged scenery in Nevada, New Mexico, and Colorado looks spectacular (unfortunately, much of the "vile, treacherous" terrain looks so similar that during the race it's often impossible to know who is ahead). The finale may feel a little anti-climactic, but by then this epic, well-crafted movie will have already won over the audience.

ADDED ATTRACTION: Another Kind of Horse

In *Bite the Bullet*, a Mexican rider is suffering from an agonizing toothache. A lady bartender offers him the "latest thing in miracles, heroin," and she gives it to him in pill form. "One of these painkillers with a chaser of whiskey," she boasts, brings "four hours of joyhouse." The pills do indeed work, but soon he's taking "six pills in one hour instead of one every four hours," and he almost dies of an overdose. All of this may seem unlikely for 1906, but the movie's inclusion of opiates is actually accurate. Opium derivatives really did exist as medicinal treatments at this time, heroin having been synthesized from morphine in 1874 and first sold as a painkiller in 1888 (something this powerful would be especially useful in an era when the main dental tool was the pair of pliers frontier dentists and blacksmiths used for rough extractions). The movie's inclusion of heroin is one of the ways *Bite the Bullet* transitions from traditional old-fashioned westerns set in the nineteenth century to a modern interpretation moved up to the twentieth. *Butch Cassidy and the Sundance Kid* (1969) did this by adding an early bicycle to a few lighthearted scenes; in the Daring Decade, *Bite the Bullet* does it by adding heroin.

Cooley High

Released: June 1975
Director: Michael Schultz
Stars: Glynn Turman, Lawrence Hilton-Jacobs, Cynthia Davis
Academy Awards: None

PREVIEW: Chicago, 1964, and teenage friends have dangerous, fun and romantic experiences.

NOW SHOWING: Chicago Graffiti

After the Oscar-nominated success of *Sounder* (1972) and *Lady Sings the Blues* (1972), Hollywood started making movies about black characters who were more authentic than the make-believe pushers and avengers in the violent blaxploitation genre. Joining a likeable group that includes *Claudine* (1974) and *Uptown Saturday Night* (1974), *Cooley High* (1975) is an endearing comedy that was warmly received by critics and audiences.

Often compared with *American Graffiti* (1973), *Cooley High* shares many qualities with that Oscar-nominated classic: both present fun/dramatic/romantic stories of ordinary teens (many played by unknown actors and actresses) in the early '60s against a background of the era's great songs (here lots of Motown classics), with epilogues summarizing the main characters' futures. Additionally, both movies inspired nostalgic TV sitcoms, with *Graffiti* leading to *Happy Days* and *Cooley* to *What's Happening!!* Unlike *Graffiti*, *Cooley* covers weeks, not just a single night, it includes scenes inside classrooms and homes, and it shows parents, nudity, sex, and weed. *Graffiti* had its characters cruising around in their own cool cars, pranking the dozing cops and getting away with it; *Cooley*'s guys race a stolen Cadillac from *pursuing* cops and later get arrested. In the biggest departure from *Graffiti*, a main *Cooley* character is beaten to death.

Whereas *Graffiti* ambitiously braided stories about four friends, *Cooley* concentrates on two seniors attending Cooley High (a real Chicago school) and living in rough housing projects. The movie follows them through energetic episodes—hijinks at the zoo, gambling in a diner, a brawl at the movies—that lack the gravity of *Graffiti*'s experiences, which built upon serious imminent decisions the characters were confronting. Cooley's seriousness doesn't emerge until the last twenty minutes when a startling death leads to a funeral and one character's subsequent escape to a brighter place.

Though the charismatic stars occasionally mug instead of act, they're still engaging and pull the audience right in to their adventures. The most distinctive teen is played by twenty-eight-year-old Glynn Turman. Smart, funny, and independent, he wears a tie to school, recites poems, and dreams of a Hollywood screenwriting career that will get him out of the inner-city world. Lawrence Hilton-Jacobs convincingly plays a super-smooth jock, and Garrett Morris, soon to be a regular on *Saturday Night Live*, has a small role as a sympathetic teacher. So it's not as great as *American Graffiti*—few movies are; *Cooley High* endures as a thoughtful, entertaining achievement.

ADDED ATTRACTION: Grier's Year

Cooley High was from American International Pictures, known for 1950s and '60s teen-oriented sci-fi, horror, and beach flicks. In the '70s AIP binged on blaxploitation, adding three more movies in 1975 that all showcased the genre's superstar, Pam Grier. In March, *Sheba, Baby* presented Grier as an energetic private eye who busts up Louisville gangsters. Despite her stylish fashions, chrome pistol, and speedboat, she can't overcome the weak dialogue or save this routine movie. July brought the grittier, slightly better *Bucktown*, with Grier co-starring as an anxious bystander, and little else, unfortunately. Ex-football star Fred Williamson dominates as "a different kinda man" who eliminates a town's corrupt cops and battles a crime boss. December delivered *Friday Foster* (sounds like a Disney movie—with Grier as the star, that would be the most kick-ass Disney movie *ever*). Based on a 1970-1974 comic-strip and comic-book character, Friday (Grier) is a spunky photographer tangled in a confusing assassination conspiracy; a lighter tone and a lively cast that includes Eartha Kitt and Godfrey Cambridge make this the most entertaining of these three AIP action movies. The '70s blaxploitation revolution was quickly losing momentum, though, as seen by the Grier career: after starring in a dozen movies from 1971 to 1975, this memorable screen queen was in just one American movie in 1976, one in '77, and none in '78 or '79.

The Apple Dumpling Gang

Released: July 1975
Director: Norman Tokar
Stars: Bill Bixby, Susan Clark, Don Knotts
Academy Awards: None

PREVIEW: Old West townspeople and crooks want to get the huge gold nugget found by three kids.

NOW SHOWING: Frontierland Fun

The Apple Dumpling Gang is one of the decade's better live-action movies from Disney. Before your eyes start to roll like they're in a slot machine, we already know how faint that praise is, and we'll concede that Disney set its live-action bar pretty low in the 1970s (sliding under that low-set bar was Disney's very next live-action comedy, *One of Our Dinosaurs Is Missing*, which came out just a week after *The Apple Dumpling Gang*). But we're willing to give credit where credit is due, and *The Apple Dumpling Gang* deserves some light applause. Set in California's Tulare County in 1879, this genial western brings together some old pros (including Harry Morgan, Don Knotts, Tim Conway, and Slim Pickens) for a story about a confirmed bachelor (Bill Bixby) who accidentally becomes the caretaker of three young orphans (the movie's title comes from the orphans' preferred food). Midway through the movie the kids are exploring a mine when an earthquake reveals a 356-pound gold nugget worth $87,425. From then on, competing gangs try to steal the nugget, various townsfolk want to become wards of the suddenly rich trio, and it takes a big shoot-out, a saloon brawl, a bank-destroying explosion, a quick wedding, and a wild ride down river rapids to sort everything out.

Despite all this exciting action, Knotts and Conway hilariously steal the movie by playing two hapless thieves. They're perfectly matched and pull off their physical-comedy hijinks as if they were already a long-running comedy duo, though this was actually their first big-screen collaboration. Their teaming proved to be so popular that Disney quickly paired them as nitwits in three more '70s comedies: *Gus* (1976), *The Apple Dumpling Gang Rides Again* (1979), and *The Prize Fighter* (1979).

This being Disney, the happy ending that reinforces traditional family values is predictable. But, this also being Disney, those kids are sure cute (especially the little girl, who constantly stops the proceedings because she's "gotta go"), the outdoor scenery is attractive, and that western town built on the studio's Burbank lot looks authentic. Modern viewers might regard this movie as half-baked entertainment, but 1975 audiences quickly warmed to *The Apple Dumpling Gang* and made it such a big box-office hit that the studio cooked up a decent sequel (see "Added Attraction"), a TV movie (1982's *Tales of the Apple Dumpling Gang*), and even a short-lived TV series (1983's *Gun Shy*).

Tim Conway and Don Knotts.

ADDED ATTRACTION:
Second Helpings of Apple Dumplings

A sequel as good as the original? It's rare, but *The Godfather: Part II* (1974) definitely qualifies. But *Jaws 2*, *Exorcist II*, and most of the decade's other 2's and II's? Not so much. Surprisingly, considering how most sequels go, *The Apple Dumpling Gang Rides Again* (1979) is not awful. This time Tim Conway and Don Knotts are the stars, not just intermittent comic relief. Hoping to go straight, the two clumsy thieves try to open a bank account but accidentally get identified as criminals. To escape they shift into various costumes, transforming themselves into soldiers, prisoners, even showgirls and squaws (some viewers may think a little of these two clowns goes a long way, but others will delight in their stumbles and fumbles). The wildest scenes come midway through the movie, when the fort burns down, and at the end, when Indians suddenly ride into the story and attack a train that's being robbed. The great scene-stealer Kenneth Mars, playing a tough marshal who ends up a twitching, drunken wreck, dominates the strong supporting cast that has Tim Matheson, following up his break-out role in *Animal House* (1978), playing the moustached romantic hero. The original stars (Bill Bixby, Susan Clark, and the three kids) are absent, but they're mentioned in the sequel's first line and again at the very end, with little discussion about them. Their collective name, the Apple Dumpling Gang, gets recycled to show that the fun spirit of the first successful movie is still here.

Smile

Released: July 1975
Director: Michael Ritchie
Stars: Bruce Dern, Barbara Feldon, Michael Kidd
Academy Awards: None

PREVIEW: Teenage girls and small-town organizers prepare for a California beauty pageant.

NOW SHOWING: "Winners and Has-Beens"

In the mid-1970s, Michael Ritchie directed three consecutive movies that examined American contests. Between the political campaigns of *The Candidate* (1972) and the Little League championships of *The Bad News Bears* (1976), Ritchie explored beauty pageants in *Smile* (1975). Though it wasn't a big hit, *Smile* is as smart and satisfying as the other two movies, and it's one of the year's comedic highlights.

Smile resembles *Nashville* (1975), where director Robert Altman roamed the city to observe various characters preparing for a concert. Ritchie's Nashville is Santa Rosa, California, site of the state-wide Young American Miss Pageant. For a week contestants practice their routines and prepare for the big night while enthusiastic adults organize the show. Bruce Dern and Barbara Feldon head the ensemble cast that features many teenage girls, some of them actual beauty contestants. Broadway legend Michael Kidd is the bitchy choreographer who thinks the novice dancers are like a famous Rogers—Roy, unfortunately, not Ginger. And as she proved in another 1975 movie, *Night Moves*, eighteen-year-old Melanie Griffith seemed to have a hard time keeping her top on.

Like Altman, Ritchie pokes his camera around to catch small amusing details—the refrigerator packed with TV dinners—and to overhear screenwriter Jerry Belson's delightful lines—the girl who competed for Miss Teen Complexion and "won $200 and had a wart removed," and the introduction of "former winners and has-beens." The "talent" portions of the pageant are especially entertaining, like the girl whose talent is packing a suitcase because "it's the only thing she could do without falling off the stage." Also hilarious is a trio of panting boys who are trying to sneak racy photos of the girls (Ritchie's skill with kids will flourish in the following year's *Bad News Bears*). Throughout, Ritchie's tone is gentle, not cruel, so there's laughter but no ridicule.

Smile slows down when it leaves the pageant and the sincerely striving girls and instead follows the adults, who are even more juvenile but not as funny (Feldon even takes a bullet). It's nice to see Dern as an eager, optimistic character, not in the violent role he sometimes played. *Smile* was out concurrently with another good Dern movie, *Posse* (1975), in which he stars as a charismatic outlaw. Kirk Douglas directed and stars as a politically ambitious Texas marshal. Like *Smile*, which ends with an out-of-the-blue pageant winner, this movie-with-a-message ends with a surprise.

ADDED ATTRACTION:
Silver Screen to Great White Way

The 1975 movie *Smile* became a 1986 Broadway musical when it opened on the Great White Way and ran for forty-eight performances. Seven other 1970s movies, shown below alphabetically, similarly made Hollywood-movie-to-Broadway-musical transitions. We're listing only musicals here, so not included are movie-to-stage-play transitions, as when the 1971 movie *Harold and Maude* became a 1980 Broadway play (Hollywood legend Janet Gaynor played Maude, but the show still closed after only four performances). Incidentally, Michael Kidd, who plays the choreographer in the *Smile* movie, earned a Tony Award nomination for directing the second musical on the list.

Movie (Year)	Broadway Musical (Year)	Performances
Carrie (1976)	*Carrie: The Musical* (1988)	5
The Goodbye Girl (1977)	*The Goodbye Girl* (1993)	188
Monty Python and the Holy Grail (1975)	*Spamalot* (2005)	1,575
Rocky (1976)	*Rocky the Musical* (2014)	188
Saturday Night Fever (1977)	*Saturday Night Fever* (2000)	501
The Sting (1973)	*The Sting* (announced)	
Young Frankenstein (1974)	*Young Frankenstein* (2007)	485

Mandingo

Released: July 1975
Director: Richard Fleischer
Stars: James Mason, Susan George, Perry King
Academy Awards: None

PREVIEW: Before the Civil War, cruel Southern masters buy, sell and sleep with their slaves.

NOW SHOWING: Completely Gone with the Wind

Imagine unsuspecting viewers hoping to see *Mahogany*, the Diana Ross movie about the glamorous fashion world, but accidentally stumbling into *Mandingo*, one of the decade's most sordid and controversial dramas. They might still be trying to recover.

Mandingo takes the new cinematic freedoms of the 1970s to trashy, ugly extremes. Set in the pre-Civil War South, this lurid, simple-minded soap opera concerns entitled white masters and the impoverished black slaves they have sex with. Among the many distasteful elements that fill the movie: incest; a naked slave hung upside-down and beaten; a five-minute bare-knuckle brawl that's so vicious the mauled victor doesn't even know he won; a female buyer evaluating her new slave by rummaging her hand inside the front of his pants. In the gruesome finale, white family members murder a white mother and her new-born mulatto baby, and a master shoots, pitchforks, and shockingly boils alive the baby's black father.

The language alone is enough to offend. Besides the countless uses of the N-word, all black women are "wenches," and black babies are "suckers." Here's one of the serious medical suggestions offered in the movie: "Sleepin' with one of them nekkid Mexican dogs, they say it drains the rheumatiz right out of the man and into the dog." A concerned father-in-law's marital advice to his naïve daughter-in-law: "You are gonna do dirty things just so you git him in your bed and keep him there." It wasn't much of a stretch when a 1978 *Saturday Night Live* parody called *Mandingo II* had Bill Murray wooing a cow and begging, "Take me, Clover, take me."

Other than Muddy Waters, who sings the bluesy "Born in This Time" three times, nobody was putting this grubby movie on a résumé. Director Richard Fleischer had been making good movies for decades—*20,000 Leagues Under the Sea* (1954), *Fantastic Voyage* (1966), *Soylent Green* (1973)—but he throws out all restraint with *Mandingo*. James Mason, playing a reprehensible plantation lord, growls out history's worst Southern accent. Another English star, Susan George, fares better linguistically, but she's always on the edge of her emotions and overacts every scene.

Somehow, audiences wanted what *Mandingo* was selling, since the movie, like the 1957 bestseller it was based on, became a major hit. An excessive sequel, *Drum* (1976), extends the salacious story with some lusty new characters and new stars (including Pam Grier) but the same bad taste.

ADDED ATTRACTION:
Mahogany Agony

Three months after *Mandingo* sleazed into theaters, *Mahogany* opened to dismal reviews, though it too did strong business. A rags-to-riches story about a poor Chicago secretary (rail-thin Diana Ross) who rises through the fashion world to become a jet-setting model and a top designer, *Mahogany* strives to deliver messages about self-empowerment and true love. Unfortunately, this fractured fairy tale is often ludicrous. Campy scenes include a ridiculous tussle between good-guy politician Billy Dee Williams and bitchy photographer Anthony Perkins, plus a weird dance where Ross drips melted candle wax onto her cheeks and chest. The clothes (Ross's own designs, according to the movie's credits) range from glamorous to bizarre (as a designer, Ross is a great

Diana Ross.

singer, as demonstrated by her three renditions of the Oscar-nominated theme song). Overall *Mahogany* is closer to *Valley of the Dolls* (1967) and other screamy, overwrought melodramas than to Ross's previous movie, the powerful *Lady Sings the Blues* (1972). With *Mahogany*, music impresario/director Berry Gordy joined Robert Culp, Larry Hagman, Jack Lemmon, Joan Rivers and Dalton Trumbo on the list of people who made a single '70s movie that was their only directorial effort ever.

The Rocky Horror Picture Show

(One of 1975's five **FAR-OUT** movies)

Released: August 1975
Director: Jim Sharman
Stars: Tim Curry, Susan Sarandon, Barry Bostwick
Academy Awards: None

PREVIEW: A conservative young couple takes refuge in a castle filled with eccentric people.

FINE LINE: "Rocky's behaving just the way that Eddie did. Do you think I made a mistake, splitting his brain between the two of them?" (Dr. Frank-N-Furter, lamenting the misbehavior of his two creations.)

CLOSE-UP: The ballad during the opening credits identifies classic science-fiction movies and stars, such as *Forbidden Planet* (1956) and Fay Wray. The movie then presents a radical, modern variation on Mary Shelley's *Frankenstein* story, and it offers various homages to the classic movies of the 1930s, including these three: at fifty-one minutes, Riff-Raff torments Rocky with fire in a scene reminiscent of *Frankenstein* (1931); at sixty-nine minutes, the "floor show" curtain lifts to reveal the towering Radio Pictures antenna from *King Kong* (1933), which Rocky will soon climb a la Kong; at eighty-four minutes, Magenta enters wearing the bride's streaked hair from *Bride of Frankenstein* (1935).

NOW SHOWING: "Be" Movie

Like disco and the Three Stooges, you either get *The Rocky Horror Picture Show* (1975) or you don't, with no hard feelings either way. *Rocky Horror* isn't for everybody, which is fine. No science-fiction rock-and-roll musical starring an outrageous transvestite who advocates unfettered sex was meant to appeal to all demographics. But millions of fans, especially teens and twenty-somethings who are ripe for the picking, have made *Rocky Horror* the world's most successful "midnight movie" and the longest-running movie of all time (incredibly, it's *still* playing in some cities). Some devotees have seen the movie in theaters hundreds of times—the only other '70s movie to command such intense, continuous devotion is *Star Wars* (1977).

Interestingly, the movie, which was based on a successful stage musical, flopped when it debuted in 1975. In desperation the studio re-released *Rocky Horror* for midnight showings, and there it found its audience. Soon people weren't just watching the movie, they were memorizing it, singing along and interacting with it, dressing in costumes, bringing props and brandishing them at appropriate moments during the movie. *Rocky Horror* transitioned from being a movie to a party, a community, and a cultural phenomenon.

What were audiences finding in *Rocky Horror*? Zany entertainment, for one thing. That's not to say it's a great movie, because it's not; it's just good and giddy enough to overcome its huge plot holes, cheesy special effects, and occasionally amateurish presentation. The craziness starts immediately when the familiar 20th Century Fox logo at the beginning is accompanied by a tinny piano version of Alfred Newman's famous "Fox Fanfare." After disembodied lips sing the nostalgic theme song, the movie seems to unfold as a campy parody of 1950s melodramas with a young couple chirpily singing about their innocent love next to a small-town church (that the song's title is "Dammit Janet" may suggest this isn't your parents' typical musical). But then an aristocratic English criminologist (Charles Gray) stops the movie to address the audience with dire warnings (he'll periodically interrupt the proceedings to add mock-serious observations). For now, the light story darkens as the couple's car breaks down on a stormy night and they walk to an old castle, where a creepy hunchback in a bloody shirt escorts them into the cobwebbed interior. What feels like a horror movie suddenly becomes a noisy bash as the rollickin' "Time Warp" number revs up and fifteen "unconventional conventionists" in tuxedos, sunglasses, and hats vigorously dance out the song's suggestive moves. Even the criminologist illustrates the steps (what a hoot, the distinguished Gray had been James Bond's nemesis in 1971's *Diamonds Are Forever*).

Now twenty-four minutes in, the star finally arrives, and from here on it's his movie. The heavily made-up Dr. Frank-N-Furter (Tim Curry) makes a spectacular entrance, whipping off his cape to reveal tattoos, lingerie, fishnet stockings, and long glittery gloves. Transitioning to the doctor's lab, for awhile the movie goes full *Frankenstein* (1931). Sort of. The male monster is "an exceptional beauty" in glittery gold underwear who's intended to be the doctor's ideal boy toy. More songs, and more surprises—once the doctor slays a '50s-style biker (Meatloaf) with an axe, anything is possible. The second half is a kitchen-sink of jumbled options: several characters turn out to be related and/or aliens, a musical "floor show" leaps from a stage to an indoor swimming pool, three main characters are killed, and the entire castle flies to the planet Transsexual. Along the way there's man-on-woman, man-on-man, man-on-monster, and woman-on-monster action, plus an elderly scientist in a wheelchair wearing nylons. Got that?

We'd be overthinking the movie if we raised all the questions we have about the plot. For instance, why are the castle's inhabitants working in the church in the opening wedding scene? Are we to think they all have quotidian day jobs? And isn't the doctor being hypocritical when he encourages everyone to indulge in "forbidden fruit" but then yells at his creature and slaps Janet (Susan Sarandon) once they become close?

Little Nell, Patricia Quinn, Tim Curry, and Richard O'Brien.

This is a movie that makes you surrender critical perspectives so you can simply enjoy the silly, amusing ride. Maybe the design details—the Mickey Mouse ears, the *Titanic* life preserver—will make you smile. Or the appeal will be the youthful Sarandon, still early in her career and blushing with shy innocence. The songs are catchy, often clever. There's a creative let's-put-on-a-show exuberance to the entire enterprise, and the spirited performers fully engage the audience by looking into the camera to make faces, deliver conspiratorial comments, or playfully fling water.

For fans, it's all that, and more. *Rocky Horror* was a brave departure from tightly controlled musical masterpieces like *Cabaret* (1972) and bloated traditional musicals like *Mame* (1974); its closest cousin was the energetic *Phantom of the Paradise* (1974), but *Rocky Horror* goes much farther. Borrowing fashion styles from early-'70s glam rock and lifestyles from the accelerating gay-liberation movement, *Rocky Horror* was probably the first major-studio movie to openly encourage pansexual freedom. In addition, the movie works like a Trojan Horse, so it's entertaining on the surface but holds more inside. "Give yourself over to absolute pleasure" and "don't dream it, be it" are key lines in the big musical finale that inspires experimentation and self-redefinition, an envelope-pushing mantra eager disciples can celebrate as they chant along and take the hedonistic message to heart. This B-movie is really a "Be" movie: for all its goofy fun, *Rocky Horror* has serious intentions.

ADDED ATTRACTION: Midnight Movies

The Rocky Horror Picture Show is the most famous midnight movie of the 1970s, but it's not the only one. Here are ten more oldies and newies that frequently played in theaters to late-night crowds.

- *El Topo* (1970): Alejandro Jodorowsky's bizarre and violent western.
- *Eraserhead* (1977): Nightmarish black-and-white images from David Lynch.
- *Freaks* (1932): Tod Browning's horror movie about unusual carnival performers.
- *The Grateful Dead* (1977): A concert film that shows the legendary rock band performing in San Francisco in 1974.
- *The Harder They Come* (1972): A crime drama starring reggae singer Jimmy Cliff.
- *The Last Waltz* (1978): The Band's star-studded farewell concert, directed by Martin Scorsese.
- *Pink Flamingos* (1972): John Waters' infamous monument to bad taste.
- *Plan 9 from Outer Space* (1959): Hilariously amateurish and inept science-fiction from low-budget specialist Ed Wood.
- *Reefer Madness* (1936): Originally intended as a serious dramatization of the disturbing effects of the marijuana "menace."
- *The Song Remains the Same* (1976): Led Zeppelin's powerful 1973 Madison Square Garden concerts, interspersed with short fantasy sequences featuring the band's members.

Dog Day Afternoon

(One of 1975's five **FAR-OUT** movies)

Released: September 1975

Director: Sidney Lumet

Stars: Al Pacino, John Cazale, Charles Durning

Academy Awards: One win (Best Writing), plus four more nominations (Best Picture; Best Actor—Al Pacino; Best Supporting Actor—John Cazale; Best Director; Best Editing)

PREVIEW: Mistakes and tragedy result when two inept amateurs attempt to rob a Brooklyn bank.

FINE LINE: "I'm robbing a bank because they got money here." (Sonny, explaining why he's committing this crime.)

CLOSE-UP: The movie opens with three minutes of Brooklyn street life on a hot summer's day. The music backing these scenes is Elton John's "Amoreena," a countryish pop song about "my lady," a "cornfield," and a "cattle town." "Amoreena" seems like an unusual choice for a modern urban crime drama, but perhaps this pleasant song is letting the audience know that things might get a little quirky, a la another popular heist movie, *The Hot Rock* (1972). And, since the song is playing on a radio inside the car where the bank robbers wait, "Amoreena" might also be showing that the gang is made up, not of hardcore killers, but of ordinary guys who listen to Elton John, at the time the world's biggest pop star.

NOW SHOWING: "It's Just a Freak Show"

Propelled by textbook acting, *Dog Day Afternoon* (1975) is an essential '70s drama. Unfortunately it came out in the same season as *One Flew Over the Cuckoo's Nest* (1975), another riveting powerhouse that claimed all the top Oscars. But decades later, *Dog Day Afternoon* still impresses, and it showcases important stars who may have been in bigger movies but who never gave better performances.

Based on a true story (as the audience is told in opening text), the movie takes place during one sweltering summer evening in 1972. It's a New York movie, but this isn't the upscale Manhattan of *Annie Hall* (1977); this is working-class Brooklyn, a gritty setting closer to *The French Connection* (1971). Three men enter a neighborhood bank just as it's closing so they can rob it. Unfortunately, two minutes into the holdup, everything starts to go wrong. The youngest robber immediately abandons the other two, who quickly discover that there's only $1100 in the vault. The brains of the operation, Sonny (Al Pacino), optimistically declares that he and his sullen, scary partner, Sal (John Cazale), will "get this thing done in half an hour," but Sonny inadvertently draws attention to the bank and within minutes the street is filled with gawking onlookers and over two-hundred policemen, plus sharpshooters on the roofs and helicopters in the air. Not only are these two crooks inept, they're unlucky: when they take hostages, two of them soon need medical attention.

For the first sixty-five minutes, *Dog Day Afternoon* plays like a sly comedy. Sonny must orchestrate bathroom breaks for the hostages, he tosses money to win over the cheering crowds, the head teller scolds his bad language, and Sonny lets one of the hostages hold his rifle so he can teach her a drill. Hoping they might escape on a jet, Sonny asks Sal, "Is there any special country you want to go to?" Sal answers, "Wyoming."

The movie also makes an observation about our celebrity culture. After a hostage briefly talks to a reporter outside, she comes back excitedly, "Girls! I was interviewed!"

Al Pacino.

Another hostage giddily waves into the TV cameras. Sonny is almost proud when he tells Sal, "They got everybody out there, the whole media," and he's bemused as he watches himself on TV. A pizza-delivery guy gets on camera and yells that he's now "a star!" Everybody, the movies seems to be saying, loves media attention.

Then the reason for the robbery becomes clear. Sonny's "wife" arrives, but it's not the woman he's legally married to who is also the mother of his two children. It's Leon (Chris Sarandon). Sonny has robbed this bank to get the money to pay for a sex-change operation for his gay lover. Instantly, of course, this turns the media circus into what Sonny calls "a freak show." While the robbers wait for their requested transportation to arrive, the movie changes from a scatter-brained bank robbery to emotional stories as the police interrogate Leon, Sonny's wife relates her experiences, Sonny's mother comes to talk to him, and Sonny dictates his will (starting with, "To my darling wife, Leon, whom I love more than any man has loved another man in all eternity"). Some viewers criticize this section of the movie, and indeed it does temporarily slow things down, but the momentum accelerates once the action moves from the bank to the bus headed for the airport, where retribution awaits (despite all the guns brandished in the movie, there are only two shots fired and just one death). In the last three minutes, Sonny, who has been a chatterbox all movie long, speaks only one line—"Don't shoot me"—even as the camera is on him almost the entire time.

Each of the principals working on this movie was operating at the top of his game. Best Actor-nominee Pacino was on a streak of four consecutive Oscar nominations (1972's and 1974's *Godfather* epics, and 1973's *Serpico*). Here he shows all sides of this complex character, taking him from clumsy nervousness to buoyant confidence to flummoxed exasperation, sometimes all within a few minutes. In Pacino's hands, what might be absurd actually becomes poignant. Cazale, terrific as a dangerous dimwit who perfectly contrasts Sonny, was on a movie streak of his own (memorable appearances in four straight Best Picture nominees—the 1972/1974 *Godfather* movies, 1974's *The Conversation*, and *Dog Day Afternoon*). Complementing these two intense characters are their background hostages, who all seem so completely natural and believable we feel like we're watching real people (though admittedly Carol Kane, who just a month later would establish herself as a fascinating actress with *Hester Street*, is severely underused as a little-seen bank employee).

Director Lumet was also enjoying a run of acclaimed hits that included *Serpico* (1973) and *Murder on the Orient Express* (1974). As he did in *Orient Express*, Lumet limits *Dog Day Afternoon* to just a few locations and focuses mainly on one, the bank (its interior and doorway). Lumet is also able to generate both tension and sympathy without using a melodramatic emotion-steering music score. He presents the robbers as vulnerable, even considerate men, not as the vicious hard-nosed criminals who often populate heist movies, so we end up rooting for these two hapless losers. There would be tighter, more suspenseful and more action-packed dramas in the 1970s, but there wouldn't be many that were any better than *Dog Day Afternoon*.

ADDED ATTRACTION: Movies from Magazines

Dog Day Afternoon was based on "The Boys in the Bank," P.F. Kluge and Thomas Moore's article that ran in *Life* magazine in 1972. The following '70s movies were also based on articles or short stories that were first published in magazines in 1950 or later.

1970s Movie (Year)	Original Magazine Article/Story Author (Magazine, Year)
Big Wednesday (1978)	"No Pants Mance" Dennis Aaberg (*Surfer*, 1974)
A Boy and His Dog (1975)	"A Boy and His Dog" Harlan Ellison (*New Worlds*, 1969)
Casey's Shadow (1978)	"Ruidoso" John McPhee (*The New Yorker*, 1974)
Death Race 2000 (1975)	"Death Race 2000" Ib Melchior (*Escapade*, 1956)
The Last American Hero (1973)	"The Last American Hero Is Junior Johnson. Yes!" Tom Wolfe (*Esquire*, 1965)
A Man Called Horse (1970)	"A Man Called Horse" Dorothy M. Johnson (*Collier's*, 1950)
Pete's Dragon (1977)	"Pete's Dragon and the U.S.A. (Forever After)" Seton I. Miller/S.S. Field (unpublished, 1957)
Rollerball (1975)	"Roller Ball Murder" William Harrison (*Esquire*, 1973)
The Beast Must Die (1974)	"There Shall Be No Darkness" James Blish (*Thrilling Wonder Stories*, 1950)
Saturday Night Fever (1977)	"Tribal Rites of the New Saturday Night" Nik Cohn (*New York*, 1976)

Three Days of the Condor

Released: September 1975
Director: Sydney Pollack
Stars: Robert Redford, Faye Dunaway, Cliff Robertson
Academy Awards: One nomination (Best Editing)

PREVIEW: A CIA researcher becomes a CIA target when he uncovers a plan to take over oil fields.

NOW SHOWING: The Suspicion Business

Both stars of *The Sting* (1973) got their own thrillers two years later. In *The Drowning Pool* (1975), Paul Newman reprises his private-investigator role from *Harper* (1966). Here his investigation into blackmail leads to a sadistic oil magnate, deaths, and an exciting watery climax that has Newman wearing his boxers in a rapidly flooding room. Complicated and deliberate, the movie is more of a decent diversion than essential entertainment, and audiences never warmed to it.

In contrast, Robert Redford's *Three Days of the Condor* (1975) is a taut, well-crafted hit that's based on James Grady's 1974 novel *Six Days of the Condor*. Like *The Parallax View* (1974) and other Watergate-era thrillers, a major conspiracy fuels this intriguing movie. Redford plays Turner, a CIA researcher code named Condor. When his Manhattan colleagues are shockingly murdered, Turner escapes, shoots an assassin, and kidnaps a random stranger (Faye Dunaway) at gunpoint. Hiding in her Brooklyn apartment, he threatens her, makes her lie to her boyfriend, and ties her up; later that night, they tenderly make love. The next morning she calls him "sweet" and offers enthusiastic help. Her abrupt switch from anxious, innocent victim to adoring, skillful accomplice may echo Patty Hearst's 1974 abduction, but it's still the movie's most implausible feature.

Robert Redford.

On Day Two Turner survives another assassination attempt and realizes he can't trust his CIA contacts, who are all in "the suspicion business." The last twenty minutes are talky and procedural as the CIA tracks Turner while he struggles to uncover "another CIA inside the CIA" with secret designs on Middle East oil fields. Like *The Parallax View*'s sinister conspiracy, this one isn't easily beatable, and the movie ends on Day Three with ongoing unease, not a tidy solution.

Audiences in 1975 easily connected with *Condor*. Not only were the government-conspiracy and gas-crisis themes relevant, but this first-rate movie is populated with excellent big-name stars. Initially it's a little difficult to accept the athletic Redford as a playful, bookish nerd in glasses, but ultimately he makes this scared, smart character convincing. Dunaway isn't in the movie much, and she's closer to the vulnerable casualty of *Chinatown* (1974) than the commanding leader of *Network* (1976). In the background are Oscar winners Cliff Robertson and John Houseman, plus Max von Sydow as an elegant, emotionless assassin. Engrossing and classy, *Three Days of the Condor* is one of the decade's best and timeliest thrillers.

ADDED ATTRACTION: Redford Goes *Electric*

Sydney Pollack directed *Three Days of the Condor* and three other popular 1970s movies with Redford. B.C. (Before *Condor*): *Jeremiah Johnson* (1972) and *The Way We Were* (1973); A.C.: *The Electric Horseman* (1979). If *Condor* is slightly reminiscent of *North by Northwest* (1959) with its complicated plot that drags an unwary man into a battle against a dangerous government agency, *The Electric Horseman* recalls *It Happened One Night* (1934) with its appealing adventure about a reporter who follows (and falls for) an attractive fugitive. An ex-rodeo star (Robert Redford) has embarrassingly sold out to become the garishly electrified cowboy who makes public appearances to promote a breakfast cereal. Knowing he has lost "the best part of himself," he tries to do something honorable by stealing a legendary horse so he can release it into the wild. An intrepid reporter (Jane Fonda) comes along for a story and the two characters share an unexpected romance. Redford and Fonda are well matched, the Utah scenery is stunning, and the cast includes Willie Nelson. Fonda hurts her leg fifty-three minutes in and asks, "What are you gonna do, shoot me?," a clever nod to her earlier movie with Sydney Pollack, *They Shoot Horses, Don't They?* (1969).

Hester Street

Released: October 1975
Director: Joan Micklin Silver
Stars: Carol Kane, Steven Keats, Mel Howard
Academy Awards: One nomination (Best Actress—Carol Kane)

PREVIEW: In 1896, a young Jewish wife comes to New York and tries to adapt to American culture.

NOW SHOWING: Coming to America

Hester Street (1975) is a warm, sweet period piece that has relevance to the feminist issues surging in the 1970s. The deceptively simple story takes place on New York's Lower East Side in 1896, when horse carts clatter on busy neighborhood streets and gas lamps light ramshackle rooms. For the movie's first twenty minutes, struggling immigrants get along by exchanging favors and helping each other find better living situations. Then Gitl (Carol Kane) quietly arrives. She's a young Jewish wife with a child, coming from Russia to meet up with her handsome husband (Steven Keats). He's already been in America for awhile, setting up cheap lodgings and landing a tedious job. To Gitl's surprise, he has eagerly assimilated into his adopted country and has even changed his name from Yankel to Jake. Feeling like he now belongs, he's increasingly frustrated that Gitl holds onto her traditional ways and remains a "greenhorn." When Gitl realizes that Jake has a vivacious girlfriend, she takes some neighborly advice— "Fix yourself, look like a woman that lives in America!"—and tries to update herself with a corset, fashionable clothes, and a new hairstyle. After her efforts generate only tears and shouting, Gitl finally asserts herself—"I don't want him back. Enough"—and slyly starts to turn the tables on him.

The elfin Kane is a marvel. Early on she's a timid, wide-eyed innocent, naïvely thinking that a love potion can somehow save her troubled marriage. By the end, when she has outmaneuvered her cheating husband, engineered a proposal from the ideal man, and even planted the seeds of a new business, Gitl has blossomed into a modern American woman who can skillfully navigate the big city and successfully apply her enterprising ideas. Kane, who had small roles in *Carnal Knowledge* (1971), *The Last Detail* (1973), and *Dog Day Afternoon* (1975), conveys this remarkable growth without any overt histrionics, just with subtle facial expressions and the quiet strength of her steely determination.

Writer/director Joan Micklin Silver confidently makes daring choices. It's a black-and-white movie, for one thing, a rarity in the 1970s but a perfect way to evoke the familiar look of old photographs. Additionally, to further the Old World authenticity established by the quaint décor and costumes, some characters speak Yiddish, with English subtitles translating. It all works splendidly. *Hester Street* isn't profound drama, but it is a lovely, wise, and often amusing little charmer.

ADDED ATTRACTION: May and *Mikey and Nicky*

Joan Micklin Silver's *Hester Street* is something rare for the 1970s: an American feature film directed by a woman. That short list includes Silver's *Between the Lines* (1977), Barbara Loden's *Wanda* (1970), Joan Darling's *First Love* (1977), Joan Rivers' *Rabbit Test* (1978), and Elaine May's *A New Leaf* (1971) and *The Heartbreak Kid* (1972), among a few others (a more complete list of movies directed by women is with the entry for 1979's *Old Boyfriends*). Elaine May's only other '70s movie was a departure for her because it's so grim. Set in one long night, *Mikey and Nicky* (1976) has Mikey (Peter Falk) helping his childhood friend Nicky (John Cassavetes) after Nicky steals money from the mob. With a hit man tracking them, the friends roam the streets to argue, reminisce, and meander through vague plans. Nicky is such an unappealing character—he slaps a woman, willfully destroys Mikey's prize watch, and constantly changes his mind—that we started rooting for the hit man. May's art-house technique includes seemingly improvised dialogue and a handheld camera that conveys the jittery immediacy of the men's situation. Despite intense performances from the two stars and a violent ending, *Mikey and Nicky* is more tedious than satisfying.

The Adventures of the Wilderness Family

Released: November 1975
Director: Stewart Raffill
Stars: Robert Logan, Susan Damante Shaw, Hollye Holmes
Academy Awards: None

PREVIEW: An L.A. family builds a cabin in the Rockies and faces an endless series of problems.

NOW SHOWING: American Family Robinson

What *Jeremiah Johnson* (1972) does for a nineteenth-century man tired of civilization, *The Adventures of the Wilderness Family* (1975) does for a mid-1970s family living in smoggy Los Angeles. During a ninety-second conversation that includes the words "you're crazy," the disgruntled Robinson parents decide to sell everything, pack up their two young kids, and go live off the land. In literally the next scene they're flying deep into the pristine Rockies, where they're dropped off at a tiny cabin.

The first impressions are deflating: a raccoon lives inside the dilapidated cabin, a big bear arrives in the first minute, and rain pours in the second. Quickly the family gets busy. Together they chop down trees and build a large new cabin that even has a see-saw outside, they hunt, fish and pick berries for their food, and they make pets of two orphaned bear cubs. Dad (Robert Logan) never seems to waver in his optimism or abilities, though it's never made clear how this big-city construction worker knows so much about wilderness survival. Mom (Susan Damante Shaw) and the two kids improvise, explore, and pitch in like real troopers. Amazingly everyone stays pretty much committed to the lifestyle, even though some new adversity, including a dangerous rock slide and dad's bloody fight with an angry cougar, seems to pop up daily. At the end, disasters pile atop each other when both a destructive windstorm and a destructive grizzly bear assault the cabin just when dad is away on a treacherous canoe trip and the eleven-year-old girl is seriously sick in bed.

Some of the adventures are rather far-fetched, like when that girl outruns a pack of wolves and a pursuing grizzly, and the family dog battles ferocious opponents without really getting injured. That downpour on the first day? That's the last of the inclement weather until the windy climax. And somehow almost every wild animal they confront is so friendly that this could be a Disney movie.

The triumph is the cinematography. The majestic mountains, tranquil meadows, and vibrant colors are real and extraordinarily beautiful, making almost every outdoor scene suitable for framing. The movie ends before the harsh high-altitude winter sets in, so everything stays green and inviting. Add in the wholesome family values without even a hint of harsh language, and you've got an appealing story that will be an exciting adventure for kids and a picturesque fantasy for parents.

ADDED ATTRACTION: More Wilderness Adventures

The Adventures of the Wilderness Family was successful enough to warrant two sequels and several similarly themed movies in the 1970s, all with Robert Logan. None, surprisingly, are by Disney, though they all boast the wholesome family values, the spectacular scenery, and the polished production values generally associated with Disney's outdoor movies.

- *Across the Great Divide* (1976): In 1876, a frontier rogue (Logan) helps two orphans make a perilous journey through the Rocky Mountains to reach family members in Oregon.
- *The Sea Gypsies* (1978): A family trying to sail around the world gets shipwrecked on an uninhabited Alaskan island and struggles to survive.
- *The Further Adventures of the Wilderness Family*, aka *Wilderness Family Part 2* (1978): A harsh winter brings new problems to the original wilderness family.
- *Mountain Family Robinson*, aka *Adventures of the Wilderness Family 3* (1979): Spring brings a legal threat to the original wilderness family.

One Flew Over the Cuckoo's Nest

(One of 1975's five **FAR-OUT** movies)

Released: November 1975

Director: Milos Forman

Stars: Jack Nicholson, Louise Fletcher, Will Sampson

Academy Awards: Five wins (Best Picture; Best Actor—Jack Nicholson; Best Actress—Louise Fletcher; Best Director; Best Writing), plus four more nominations (Best Supporting Actor—Brad Dourif; Best Editing; Best Cinematography; Best Music)

PREVIEW: Led by a rebellious newcomer, mental patients defy their hospital's strict rules.

FINE LINE: "I must be crazy to be in a loony bin like this." (McMurphy, talking to Billy Bibbit.)

CLOSE-UP: In the dramatic final sequence, the Chief embraces the lobotomized McMurphy and whispers, "I'm not going without you, Mac. I wouldn't leave you here this way. You're coming with me." Just before he smothers McMurphy with a pillow, he mutters the movie's simple but significant last words: "Let's go." Infused with McMurphy's soaring spirit, the Chief finally escapes from the institution by smashing the window and jumping through to freedom.

NOW SHOWING: "The Feeb's Brigade"

On March 29, 1976, *One Flew Over the Cuckoo's Nest* (1975) accomplished something that had only been done once before. At that night's Academy Awards, *Cuckoo's Nest* won Oscars in the top five categories, a feat only *It Happened One Night* (1934) had achieved (1991's *The Silence of the Lambs* would later join this select group). That 1976 Oscar sweep was appropriate recognition for what is still one of Hollywood's most powerful and inspiring dramas.

This movie has aged well because its basic conflict—individuals rebelling against tyrants—is timeless. The cuckoo's nest of the title is a mental institution, where Nurse Ratched (Louise Fletcher) comes to work in the opening scenes wearing a black hat, coat, and cape. While white-clad patients and orderlies go through their routines, Randall McMurphy (Jack Nicholson) arrives as the only person in rough, casual clothes (he's also wearing handcuffs). Unlike all the quiet, well-ordered people around him, McMurphy injects immediate energy into the building by laughing out loud and kissing a guard. He's gotten out of prison work detail by pretending to be a mental patient, and he thinks he's got it made.

Jack Nicholson and Danny DeVito.

    McMurphy shrugs off the report that says he's "belligerent" and "lazy" with "five arrests for assault" on his record. For awhile he's a savvy, streetwise outsider, bemusedly watching a group-therapy session where patients yell at each other. Given his strong personality as a natural-born instigator, he quickly becomes their leader and starts orchestrating bets, organizing basketball games, and championing revisions to their schedule. Midway through the movie he escapes, audaciously commandeers a bus, and takes the patients on a riotous fishing trip. This long comic sequence is the only time we leave the institution's grounds.

    By now the other patients have revealed themselves to be like children. They're easily distracted, they quickly push and shout at each other, and they bend the rules of games to suit their immediate situations. After the fishing trip, however, it's apparent that McMurphy is having a profound effect on them. By giving them reasons to cheer, by standing up to the domineering Ratched, and by joyfully uniting them as "the feeb's brigade," McMurphy becomes their Wizard of Oz, restoring to them powers they think they have lost. Billy Bibbit (Brad Dourif), for instance, momentarily overcomes his stutter when Ratched confronts him. Cheswick (Sydney Lassick) declares himself "no little kid" and demand his cigarettes. The silent, towering Chief (Will Sampson) starts talking again, eventually feels "big as a damn mountain," and unleashes his brute strength to liberate himself. In the last group scenes, the guys calmly play cards like adults would, which they hadn't been able to do before. McMurphy pays a tragic price for his unruly antics, but by the time he dies, his work is done.

    Nicholson catalyzes the movie and fully asserts himself as a charismatic, unpredictable, screen-filling superstar. He'd already put together a remarkable run of movies from *Easy Rider* (1969) and *Five Easy Pieces* (1970) to *The Last Detail* (1973) and *Chinatown* (1974), all of them bringing him Oscar nominations, but McMurphy is the career-defining role that put him on the Mount Rushmore of 1970s actors. McMurphy is a volatile mix of outrageous behavior (like the hilarious scene when he feigns brain damage) and subtler, quieter emotions. During his wild, disastrous farewell party late in the movie, he sits silently in close-up for a full minute as a range of thoughts sprint through his mind. Fascinating.

Louise Fletcher, whose previous movie work was limited to small roles, balances McMurphy's exuberance and animalistic sex-drive by playing Nurse Ratched with steely control and frigidity. He's hot-blooded and aggressive; she's icy and passive-aggressive. Though her heartless, spirit-crushing methods border on sadism, she's not a simple, cackling witch or horned demon (despite the hairstyle that's swirled into horns). While we root for her comeuppance, Ratched isn't truly evil because she's convinced she's doing what's best for the patients. The inflexible Ratched is as committed to enforcing the institution's rules as the free-wheeling McMurphy is to breaking them. They're titanic adversaries, and in this movie Fletcher is Nicholson's equal. Imagine if the other actors and actresses who were considered for these roles had been hired; according to the special-feature interviews on the movie's 2002 DVD, Marlon Brando, Gene Hackman, or Burt Reynolds would've been challenging Anne Bancroft, Colleen Dewhurst, Angela Lansbury, or Geraldine Page. Reynolds vs. Lansbury, what a different movie that would be.

If the relatively unknown Fletcher was a surprise, so too was Czechoslovakian director Milos Forman. He'd made only one previous English-language feature film, a modest, well-received comedy called *Taking Off* (1971). Forman confidently intensifies the *Cuckoo's Nest* drama by filming at the actual prison-like Oregon State Hospital and by including real patients in the scenes. He keeps the camera close to his characters for maximum impact, and he skillfully stages most of the action indoors so that the Chief's final breakaway into the countryside has more resonance. Additionally, Forman makes significant and risky changes to Ken Kesey's bestselling novel. In the book, the Chief narrates the story; McMurphy is big and physically intimidating; Cheswick drowns; and many patients finally leave the ward.

On film, everything works, spectacularly. *One Flew Over the Cuckoo's Nest* blends robust entertainment with a stirring anti-authoritarian message into a box-office smash and one of the decade's pivotal cinematic experiences. Many viewers don't just watch this movie—they love it.

ADDED ATTRACTION: *MAD* Magazine's Parodies of 1975-1976 Movies

Cuckoo's Nest got its own movie parody, "One Cuckoo Flew Over the Rest," in *MAD* magazine (the parody ran in July 1976). Below are seventeen other 1975-1976 movies that were similarly honored, followed by the titles of the parodies. *MAD*'s parodies of 1977-1979 movies are with the entry for *The China Syndrome* (1979).

- 1975 movies
  Dog Day Afternoon: "Dum Dum Afternoon"
  Barry Lyndon: "Borey Lyndon"
  Funny Lady: "Fun Lady"
  Jaws: "Jaw'd"
  Rollerball: "Rollerbrawl"
  Shampoo: "Shampooed"

- 1976 movies
  All the President's Men: "Gall of the President's Men"
  The Bad News Bears: "The Bad Mouth Bears"
  King Kong: "King Korn"
  Marathon Man: "Marathon Mess"
  The Missouri Breaks: "The Misery Breaks"
  Network: "Nutwork"
  Obsession: "Sobsession"
  The Omen: The Ominous"
  Rocky: "Rockhead"
  The Shootist: "The Shootiest"
  A Star Is Born: "A Star's a Bomb"

The Man Who Would Be King

Released: December 1975
Director: John Huston
Stars: Sean Connery, Michael Caine, Christopher Plummer
Academy Awards: Four nominations (Best Editing; Best Writing; Best Art Direction; Best Costume Design)

PREVIEW: Two Englishmen head into a small country in hopes of taking it over and getting rich.

NOW SHOWING:
Long Live the Man Who Would Be King

For rousing adventure, don't underestimate *The Man Who Would Be King* (1975). Fans of *Raiders of the Lost Ark* (1981) might prefer that energetic escapade (*Raiders* was a Best Picture nominee, but *TMWWBK* wasn't). *TMWWBK* isn't as action-packed as *Raiders*; it slows somewhat in the second half; its lingo may be challenging; and it's not politically correct (the year is 1885, when the colonial British casually mistreat India's "heathens" and "savages"). However, place *TMWWBK* in the context of the mid-1970s, when many up-to-the-minute movies were gritty, urban, and profane, and this gloriously old-fashioned movie jumps out as immense entertainment.

Faithfully adapted from Rudyard Kipling's 1888 novella, *TMWWBK* fits alongside director John Huston's earlier adventure classic, *The Treasure of the Sierra Madre* (1948), where Americans in Mexico search for gold but end up losing everything. *TMWWBK* begins with the framing device of a half-dead Peachy (Michael Caine) staggering up to Kipling (Christopher Plummer) to tell an incredible tale that started three years earlier. Peachy and Danny (Sean Connery, boldly going without his James Bond toupee) are two British "scoundrels" in India who decide they're "not little men" and will become "kings of Kafiristan," an isolated kingdom they're certain they can easily plunder. A perilous journey over snowy mountains gets them to "the promised land." After they successfully lead the villagers in battles, Danny really is crowned king and takes possession of limitless treasures. Unfortunately, he starts believing he's fulfilling some divine "destiny": he calls the others "mortals," takes a queen (played by Caine's actual wife), and wants Peachy to to bow to him. Such hubris must be punished, obviously, and Danny takes a terrible fall (literally). Peachy miraculously survives to bring Kipling a gruesome souvenir.

Huston's storytelling is masterful, the adventure magnificent, the locations spectacular, but it's the two perfectly matched rogues who make this movie transcendent. Huston says in the DVD's special features that he'd wanted to make *TMWWBK* for two decades with Clark Gable and Humphrey Bogart; "Connery and Caine," he adds, "are ideal." He's right, and it's hard now to imagine anybody but these two in the roles. We'd willingly extend the 129-minute length just to enjoy more of Peachy and Danny's pleasurable camaraderie (the reward of loyal friendship is one of the movie's morals, along with the dangers of ambition and gold lust). See *The Man Who Would Be King*; think "they don't make 'em like this anymore."

Michael Caine and Sean Connery.

ADDED ATTRACTION:
Connery and Huston, Together Again

Sean Connery and John Huston teamed up in another 1975 adventure movie, though this time Huston isn't directing, he's acting, playing a role as a statesman in 1904. In John Milius' ambitious *The Wind and the Lion*, Connery stars as a horseback-riding Moroccan outlaw who audaciously abducts an American woman (Candice Bergen) and her children, takes them deep into the desert, and uses them as political bargaining chips. Back in America, the "vigorous and active" President Teddy Roosevelt (Brian Keith) is looking for "some issue to hang his campaign on," so he abandons the diplomatic negotiations of the movie's first half for the military intervention of the second. Connery's Scottish brogue is briefly a distraction, but he otherwise expresses the spirit and strength of the "formidable brigand" who pulls off thrilling exploits. Loosely based on actual 1904 events, this rousing movie has rugged scenery, vivid action sequences, and an Oscar-nominated score by Jerry Goldsmith.

Barry Lyndon

Released: December 1975
Director: Stanley Kubrick
Stars: Ryan O'Neal, Marisa Berenson, Patrick Magee
Academy Awards: Four wins (Best Cinematography; Best Art Direction; Best Costume Design; Best Music), plus three more nominations (Best Picture; Best Director; Best Writing)

PREVIEW: An idle, unprincipled Irishman in the 1800s achieves wealth but then squanders it.

NOW SHOWING: The Rake's Progress

By the early 1970s, Stanley Kubrick had directed three consecutive cinematic landmarks: *Dr. Strangelove* (1964), *2001: A Space Odyssey* (1968), and *A Clockwork Orange* (1971). So what followed his up-to-the-minute black comedy, his science-fiction milestone, and his savage drama? A stately eighteenth-century epic, naturally.

Not only was *Barry Lyndon* (1975) a bold departure for Kubrick, but it was a radical movie in an era when Hollywood was telling contemporary stories (consider that year's other Best Picture Oscar nominees besides *Barry Lyndon*—*Jaws, Dog Day Afternoon, One Flew Over the Cuckoo's Nest*, and *Nashville*). Making *Barry Lyndon* even more unique was its extreme length (184 minutes) and its deliberate, slow-motion pace. Tellingly, *MAD* magazine (September 1976) spoofed it as *Borey Lyndon*.

Patient audiences, however, are rewarded with visual splendor. For his long, languid story, Kubrick introduced cutting-edge filming techniques to create one of the most gorgeous movies ever made. Pairing special new lenses with John Alcott's Oscar-winning cinematography, Kubrick captured intimate candlelit scenes and spectacular panoramic landscapes inspired by actual paintings. Sumptuous settings, meticulous historical details, ravishing costumes, and lavish wigs, all backed by the century's greatest composers (Bach, Vivaldi, Handel, etc.), make this more of an artwork than a mere movie.

The flaw is Ryan O'Neal. He plays the handsome scoundrel Redmond Barry, "born clever enough at gaining a fortune, but incapable of keeping one." In Part I we meet this "boy," "schoolboy," "meddling brat," "lad," and "poor child"; the miscast O'Neal, famous for *Love Story* (1970), is thirty-four years old. He shows the same wooden expression for the first forty minutes, finally half-smiling when he wins a fistfight.

After ninety-two minutes he meets the Countess of Lyndon (Marisa Berenson), "a woman of vast wealth and great beauty" who rarely talks. Their sad married life fills the more melodramatic Part II, "an account of the misfortunes and disasters which befell Barry Lyndon." Unfaithful and profligate, Redmond is doomed to "finish his life poor, lonely, and childless," especially after his beloved son dies tragically and his stepson shoots him in the

Ryan O'Neal and Marisa Berenson.

last of the movie's four duels. In our final look at Redmond, he's pathetically limping away on one leg to become an unsuccessful gambler who will never see Lady Lyndon again.

Barry Lyndon is a movie by and for sophisticated grown-ups who love the classics and a good museum. Anyone willing to invest the time will relish the magnificence of this elegant masterpiece.

ADDED ATTRACTION: All in the Family

Stanley Kubrick's daughter, Vivian, has an uncredited role as a spectator in *Barry Lyndon*. Here are other directors who put their own children in their 1975-1979 movies, usually as background kids, though not always—Victoria Russell, for instance, stars in a long musical number in her father's movie.

- Michael Anderson
  Michael Anderson, Jr., *Logan's Run* (1976)
- Peter Bogdanovich
  Alexandra and Antonia Bogdanovich, *At Long Last Love* (1975)
- Clint Eastwood
  Kyle Eastwood, *The Outlaw Josey Wales* (1976)
- Bob Fosse
  Nicole Fosse, *All That Jazz* (1979)
- David Lynch
  Jennifer Lynch, *Eraserhead* (1977)
- Daniel Petrie
  Mary Petrie, *The Betsy* (1978)
- Sidney Poitier
  Sherri Poitier, *A Piece of the Action* (1977)
- Joan Rivers
  Melissa Rivers, *Rabbit Test* (1978)
- Ken Russell
  Victoria Russell, *Tommy* (1975)
- Mark Rydell
  Christopher Rydell, *Harry and Walter Go to New York* (1976)
- Michael Schultz
  Derek Schultz, *Car Wash* (1976)

The Hindenburg

Released: December 1975
Director: Robert Wise
Stars: George C. Scott, Anne Bancroft, William Atherton
Academy Awards: One win (Special Achievement Award for Sound Effects and Visual Effects), plus three more nominations (Best Cinematography; Best Art Direction; Best Sound)

PREVIEW: A Nazi officer tries to identify the saboteur who could destroy the famous airship.

NOW SHOWING: "Oh, the Humanity"

Whereas other major disaster movies—*The Poseidon Adventure* (1972), *The Towering Inferno* (1974), etc.—were fictional, *The Hindenburg* (1975) is based on a real catastrophe. And like many movies with historical foundations, it supplements the facts with invented melodrama so that audiences can experience the disaster through the travails of fictional characters. In *The Hindenburg*, the "real catastrophe" part of that formula soars; it's the melodrama that deflates this long, slow movie.

Director Robert Wise, a four-time Oscar winner, uses a twenty-five-foot model and top-notch special effects to get the look right, making the enormous "queen of the skies" the movie's true star. Exteriors of the *Hindenburg* gliding majestically across the sky or parked imposingly on the ground, and interiors of its intricate support structure, are all impressive and led to multiple Oscar nominations.

Nobody really knows why the "world symbol of Nazi power" exploded in New Jersey in 1937, so *The Hindenburg* presents one plausible theory involving an anti-Nazi crewmember and a time bomb. The movie is essentially a mystery story, with George C. Scott aboard as an intense Nazi colonel conducting an investigation so he can prevent possible sabotage. Though the colonel realizes who the villain is long before the explosion, he still can't stop it.

As per the disaster-movie template established earlier in the decade, *The Hindenburg* includes past Oscar winners, the requisite romantic flirtation, a musical number, and preliminary perils (dangerous mid-flight repairs, wind gusts at the landing site). Satisfyingly, there's a protracted sequence showing the disaster. Wise makes an interesting choice at the end by switching this color movie to black and white, thus enabling him to seamlessly blend vintage newsreel footage with shots of his characters frantically escaping from the collapsing inferno (hold on—isn't it false advertising to show the fiery blast in blazing color on the movie's poster?).

Ultimately the real-life sixty-second explosion and crash are drawn out to nine riveting minutes. It's taken almost two hours to get to this point, though, and that's the problem. The time-filling run-up to these last scenes is often boring, and most of the characters are either underdeveloped, unsympathetic, or outright annoying.

Many critics shot down the movie upon release, but enthusiastic audiences made it a solid hit. Modern viewers might note the movie's mention of the R.M.S. *Titanic*, reminding them of James Cameron's 1997 blockbuster that does real-life disaster much better and with much more emotion.

ADDED ATTRACTION: Legends in Peril

A screen legend from Hollywood's pre-1960 Golden Age is a key ingredient in the disaster-movie recipe. The *Hindenburg*'s legend is Burgess Meredith, playing a passenger who survives the disaster. Listed chronologically are more 1975-1979 disaster movies with their Hollywood legends and their movie fates.

- *Two-Minute Warning* (1976)
  Charlton Heston plays the police captain who helps slay the murderous sniper.
- *Airport '77* (1977)
  Joseph Cotton, a passenger, survives the crash.
  Olivia de Havilland, a passenger, also survives.
  James Stewart, not aboard the 747, is never in jeopardy.
- *Gray Lady Down* (1978)
  Charlton Heston, the sub's captain, doesn't go down with the ship.
- *Avalanche* (1978)
  Rock Hudson survives and takes responsibility for the disaster.
- *The Swarm* (1978)
  Henry Fonda's character dies from the bees' venom.
  Olivia de Havilland's character dies in a train derailment.
- *The China Syndrome* (1979)
  Jack Lemmon's character is shot inside the nuclear plant.
- *The Concorde ... Airport '79* (1979)
  Mercedes McCambridge, a Russian gymnastics coach, survives the crash.
  Robert Wagner, the corrupt villain, shoots himself when his crimes are exposed.
- *City on Fire* (1979)
  Henry Fonda, the fire chief back at headquarters, is never in danger.
  Ava Gardner, the TV anchorwoman back at the studio, is never in danger.
  Shelley Winters, a nurse, dies in the conflagration.
- *Meteor* (1979)
  Henry Fonda, playing the president, survives.
  Natalie Wood, a Russian interpreter, survives.

Lucky Lady

Released: December 1975
Director: Stanley Donen
Stars: Gene Hackman, Liza Minnelli, Burt Reynolds
Academy Awards: None

PREVIEW: In 1930, a rum-running trio with a yacht eludes the coast guard and rival smugglers.

NOW SHOWING: Three's a Crowd

The 1970s were filled with movies about earlier decades. *The Great Gatsby* (1974) showed the 1920s, *The Sting* (1973) the '30s, *Summer of '42* (1971) the '40s, *The Last Picture Show* (1971) the '50s, and *American Graffiti* (1973) the '60s, to name just five of many examples. *Lucky Lady* (1975), set in 1930, continued that nostalgic trend. The big difference is that all the aforementioned movies were box-office successes; *Lucky Lady* was a big-budget disappointment that temporarily halted several movie careers.

Lucky Lady's principals entered with impressive résumés. Stanley Donen had directed major stars in the much-loved crime caper *Charade* (1963), screenwriters Willard Huyck and Gloria Katz had co-written *American Graffiti*, Gene Hackman (who gets top billing) and Liza Minnelli (blonde and tattooed) were both recent Oscar winners, and Burt Reynolds was one of America's busiest movie stars (four movies just in 1975!). As Einstein said when he incorrectly wrote down $E=mc^3$, what could go wrong with this formula?

Miscalculation, that's what. Supposedly a comedy, *Lucky Lady* doesn't have one memorable line or inventive sight gag. It does have a tasteless "joke" delivered by Minnelli, Reynolds forces his signature cackle at different times like he's witnessing incontrovertible hilarity, and the '30s lingo sounds vaguely amusing. But there's also a disturbing cockfight, the gentle character played by Robby Benson is violently murdered, and the ending comes after a long, noisy battle.

The story is about three smugglers running liquor via a yacht named *Lucky Lady*. Minnelli sleeps with both men: "I like you both," she rationalizes, "I don't see anything wrong or unfaithful about that." They're all briefly in bed together, but the movie doesn't explore this daring development. Where the movie excels is in its visual presentation (the coastal locations are lovely, the main hotel glamorous), plus Minnelli performs a number live. But *Lucky Lady* doesn't float like a sassy screwball comedy should. Minnelli and Reynolds quickly moved on to other projects, but the screenwriters wouldn't do another movie for four years, Donen for three years, and Hackman for two. Though critics sank it, *Lucky Lady* resurfaced in *MAD* magazine in a June 1977 feature called "We'd Like to See the Day When …," which included this entry: "… theaters that raise prices when they show biggies like *The Godfather* cut prices when they show a bomb." The movie shown on a marquee to represent "a bomb"? *Lucky Lady*. Ouch.

ADDED ATTRACTION: The Hustler

Burt Reynolds didn't go down with the ship. In fact, he had a better, more acclaimed movie come out the very same day that *Lucky Lady* opened (that day, as it happens, was Christmas Day in 1975). In *Hustle*, Reynolds re-teams with Robert Aldrich, director of their football-themed hit, *The Longest Yard* (1974). Reynolds plays a cynical L.A. detective who teams with his partner (Paul Winfield) to start investigating a death that may be either a suicide or a murder. The mystery soon unravels into a tangled, sordid story. *Hustle* is tough and dark, so dark, in fact, that Reynolds' character doesn't survive, an unusual turn of events for one of his movies and the kind of conclusion that makes this one more like classic film noir than *Fuzz* (1972) and *Shamus* (1973), the lightweight cop comedies Reynolds had made earlier in the decade. Catherine Deneuve plays a stunning hooker who is involved with both the case and the detective. An excellent supporting cast of reliable pros (Eddie Albert, Ernest Borgnine, Eileen Brennan, and Ben Johnson) help make *Hustle* an unusual and interesting thriller.

Prepare yourself for a perfectly outrageous motion picture
NETWORK
Television will never be the same
METRO-GOLDWYN-MAYER presents
FAYE DUNAWAY WILLIAM HOLDEN PETER FINCH ROBERT DUVALL in
NETWORK
By PADDY CHAYEFSKY Directed by SIDNEY LUMET Produced by HOWARD GOTTFRIED
R RESTRICTED
METROCOLOR
PANAVISION®
MGM
United Artists

1976

In Film

- Oscar for Best Picture: *Rocky*.
- Most Oscar wins (four): *All the President's Men* and *Network*.
- Most Oscar nominations (ten): *Network* and *Rocky*.
- *Network* is one of the few films ever to receive Oscar nominations in all four acting categories; Peter Finch, one of the stars in *Network*, wins for Best Actor, making him the first posthumous winner of an Oscar for acting.
- For the first time a woman is nominated as Best Director: Lina Wertmüller (*Seven Beauties*).
- Top-grossing movie: *Rocky*.
- Top-grossing comedy: *Silver Streak*.
- Top-grossing horror or sci-fi: *The Omen*.
- A flop as a mainstream release, *The Rocky Horror Picture Show* (1975) is re-released into theaters in 1976 as a midnight movie and eventually becomes the longest-running midnight movie ever.
- *The Bad News Bears*, *The Omen*, and *Rocky* launch new movie franchises.
- The Steadicam, a new camera-stabilizing mount, is used in a movie for the first time (*Marathon Man*).
- *Family Plot*, the last movie directed by Alfred Hitchcock, is released.
- Average price for an adult movie ticket: $2.15.
- Five memorable actors: David Carradine, Robert De Niro, Dustin Hoffman, Jason Robards, Sylvester Stallone.
- Five memorable actresses: Faye Dunaway, Jodie Foster, Talia Shire, Sissy Spacek, Beatrice Straight.
- Movie debuts: Albert Brooks, Amy Irving, Jessica Lange, Mariel Hemingway, Ernie Hudson, Theresa Russell, Brooke Shields, Debra Winger, director Alan Parker.
- Deaths include Godfrey Cambridge, Lee J. Cobb, Sal Mineo, Paul Robeson, Rosalind Russell, cinematographer James Wong Howe, director Busby Berkeley, screenwriter Dalton Trumbo.

In America

- Democrat Jimmy Carter defeats Republican incumbent Gerald Ford in the presidential election.
- Commemorative events are held all across America to celebrate the bicentennial.
- Heiress and armed-robbery fugitive Patty Hearst is sentenced to prison.
- At the Winter Olympics in Innsbruck, Austria, America sends the largest delegation (106 athletes) and wins ten medals (the third-highest total among competing nations), including a gold medal for figure-skater Dorothy Hamill.
- At the Summer Olympics in Montreal, Canada, America wins ninety-four medals (the third-highest total among competing nations), including a gold medal for decathlete Bruce Jenner and five golds for the boxing team led by Sugar Ray Leonard and Leon Spinks.
- The U.S. Treasury issues the new $2 bill adorned with Thomas Jefferson's portrait.
- NASA's Viking 1 and 2 landers reach Mars and start sending photos back to Earth.
- Average price for a gallon of gas: Sixty-one cents.
- New companies: Apple Computer Company; Conrail (Consolidated Rails Corp.); Gymboree, Price Club, Ticketmaster, TJ Maxx.
- New technology: Apple I desktop computer ($666.66), the 5.25" floppy disk, Fairchild's "Channel Fun" (the first cartridge-based home video game console).
- New transportation: Chevy Chevette, Ford Fiesta, Honda Accord, the supersonic airliner *Concorde*.
- New products: California Cooler, Roach Motel, the oozy toy Slime.
- Sports champions: Pittsburgh Steelers at Super Bowl X, Montreal Canadiens in hockey, Boston Celtics in basketball, Cincinnati Reds in baseball.
- Bestselling books include Alex Haley's *Roots*, Anne Rice's *Interview with the Vampire*, Robert Ringer's *Winning Through Intimidation*, Gail Sheehy's *Passages*.
- Music: The Band gives its farewell concert; new albums include Boston's *Boston*, the Eagles' *Their Greatest Hits (1971-1975)*, Peter Frampton's *Frampton Comes Alive*, Boz Scaggs' *Silk Degrees*, Paul Simon's *Still Crazy After All These Years*, Stevie Wonder's *Songs in the Key of Life*; new songs include ABBA's "Dancing Queen," the Bee Gees' "You Should Be Dancing," C.W. McCall's "Convoy," Starland Vocal Band's "Afternoon Delight," Rod Stewart's "Tonight's the Night," Wings' "Silly Love Songs."
- TV debuts: *Alice, Battle of the Network Stars, Charlie's Angels, Donny & Marie, Family Feud, The Gong Show, Laverne & Shirley, The Muppet Show, What's Happening!!*
- Deaths include Alexander Calder, Mickey Cohen, Paul Gallico, J. Paul Getty, Howlin' Wolf, Howard Hughes, Ted Mack, Man Ray.

Taxi Driver

(One of 1976's five **FAR-OUT** movies)

Released: February 1976

Director: Martin Scorsese

Stars: Robert De Niro, Jodie Foster, Cybill Shepherd

Academy Awards: Four nominations (Best Picture; Best Actor—Robert De Niro; Best Supporting Actress—Jodie Foster; Best Music)

PREVIEW: A cab driver's severe loneliness pushes him to violently attack New York's "scum."

FINE LINE: "Now I see it clearly. My whole life is pointed in one direction. I see that now. There never has been any choice for me." (Travis Bickle, fully armed ninety-three minutes into the movie and about to attempt a political assassination.)

CLOSE-UP: Thirty-seven minutes into the movie, Travis Bickle follows up his dreadful date with Betsy by calling her from a pay phone. He meekly apologizes and asks to see her again, but she refuses. Near the end of this agonizing call, the camera pans past Bickle and stares down an empty hallway for twenty seconds, as if Bickle's pain is too intense for us to witness. In *Scorsese by Ebert*, director Martin Scorsese "calls this shot the most important one in the film."

NOW SHOWING: "Here Is a Man Who Would Not Take It Anymore"

Anyone interested in '70s cinema must confront *Taxi Driver* (1976). Brutal, uncompromising, at times hard to watch, this disturbing movie is Martin Scorsese's first masterpiece, a towering accomplishment that stands alongside *The Godfather* (1972) and a handful of other classics as the decade's best dramas.

Taxi Driver vividly tracks the outer life and inner thoughts of Travis Bickle (Robert De Niro), a lonely cabbie who roams Manhattan from spring through summer and feels increasingly alienated amidst the ugly street life. From the very start we realize that Bickle's descent into madness won't be a long drop, because he's already damaged. The opening titles set the scene—night, a steaming New York street, but it's really Hell, with orange vapors rising as names appear in the reddish colors of flames while eerie music thunders ominously. Bickle enters and speaks his first line—"I can't sleep nights"—as he's applying to be a taxi driver; he then walks outside and drinks liquor from a bottle in a paper bag. Back in his shabby room, he writes in his journal that the city's lowlifes are "sick, venal," and "someday a real rain will come and wash all this scum off the streets." The movie is just six minutes old.

Everything is shown from Bickle's warped perspective, so he's in, or witnesses, almost every scene. A few biographical details emerge (he's twenty-six, an ex-Marine, uneducated), but Bickle's back story is kept vague. Instead of knowing who he was, we observe him as he is. He drives his cab (surprisingly, for only twenty percent of the movie), reads journal entries aloud, and has odd preferences (Schnapps on breakfast cereal, among other counter-productive behaviors). Significantly, Bickle can't relate to anyone. A cashier and a Secret Service man he engages both get suspicious and call for back-up; taking breaks with other cabbies, he barely pays attention. Nobody knows him, so he's called by three different nicknames—Killer (by the cabbies), Cowboy (by a pimp), and *El Titere*, "the puppet" (by a store owner).

Bickle's best attempt at a romantic relationship starts when the idyllic Betsy (Cybill Shepherd) arrives in slow-motion, "wearing a white dress ... like an angel." Bickle spiffs himself up and asks her out by basically describing himself: "I think you're a lonely person. ... You're not a happy person. And I think you need something." Their date collapses when he takes her to "a dirty movie"—she's disgusted, he's confused, and he later berates her. His plummet into rage-filled isolation accelerates.

Bathed in red light midway through the movie, Bickle says, "I got some bad ideas in my head." Writing that he's "God's lonely man" and that "suddenly, there is a change," he arms himself and begins training for some unclear mission of "true force." Famously, he faces a mirror and asks, "You talkin' to me?" Pretending to shoot, he tells his reflection, "You're dead."

Sixty-eight minutes into the movie, Bickle kills an armed robber, his first violent act. But he's not traumatized, he's empowered. He sits and watches *American Bandstand*, where teenagers dance to Jackson Browne's melancholy "Late for the Sky" with its line, "I know I'm alone, and close to the end." Bickle's in front of the TV with a gun.

Over the edge he goes, announcing himself as "a man who would not take it anymore, a man who stood up against the scum." Bickle's been cutting his hair shorter during the movie—now he goes full Mohawk and brings his unlicensed weapons to a political rally. He's chased off, so he moves to an easier target, the sleazy pimp who controls Iris, a twelve-year-old prostitute (remarkably played by twelve-year-old Jodie Foster). The gruesome final bloodbath is over in three intense minutes and is truly horrifying. Using guns and a knife, Bickle kills three men, one right beside the hysterical Iris. Walls are sprayed with blood and brains, and Bickle himself is shot in the neck and arm. Out of bullets, he's unable to kill himself.

Taxi Driver is different from other vigilante movies like *Death Wish* (1974) in that Bickle himself isn't the victim of any wrongdoing; he's a frustrated spectator who wants to correct perceived wrongs. Additionally, *Taxi Driver*, while no less gory, is far more stylish than typical vigilante movies. Scorsese fills the movie with cinematic tricks and flourishes—moments of fast-motion when he's amped up, for instance—to show Bickle's tormented mind. Always a virtuoso of camera movement, Scorsese uses an overhead shot to peer down at the final red-lit crime scene, slowly tracking over blood and bodies like he's literally showing us Hell. Accompanying the many startling images is Bernard Herrmann's Oscar-nominated score, its romantic, yearning saxophone solos countering dark, chaotic chords to reveal both sides of Bickle's personality.

The movie's steady descent to psychotic disaster is disrupted at the end when newspapers treat Bickle like a hero. Perhaps this is the movie's ironic comment on our celebrity-worshipping culture, perhaps we're just meant to feel relief that finally something positive is happening to Bickle, but it seems unlikely that this unhinged killer could openly murder people, no matter how evil they are, with complete impunity. He doesn't even lose his job (seriously? the cab company wants customers to ride with volatile Travis Bickle?). The last unnerving glimpse of Bickle's reflection, synced with a quick "snap" sound, suggests that this human time-bomb hasn't been defused, only reset.

ADDED ATTRACTION: Hollywood Hookers

Playing the young streetwalker, Jodie Foster nabbed an Oscar nomination as Best Supporting Actress. Here are seventeen other prominent actresses who played prostitutes in 1970s movies.

- Carol Burnett: *The Front Page* (1974)
- Julie Christie: *McCabe & Mrs. Miller* (1971)
- Catherine Deneuve: *Hustle* (1975)
- Colleen Dewhurst: *The Cowboys* (1972)
- Faye Dunaway: *Little Big Man* (1970)
- Jane Fonda: *Klute* (1971)
- Claudia Jennings: *Truck Stop Women* (1974)
- Madeline Kahn: *Paper Moon* (1973)
- Carol Kane: *The Last Detail* (1973)
- Sophia Loren: *Man of La Mancha* (1972)
- Shirley MacLaine: *Two Mules for Sister Sara* (1970)
- Rita Moreno: *Carnal Knowledge* (1971)
- Susan Sarandon: *Pretty Baby* (1978)
- Brooke Shields: *Pretty Baby* (1978)
- Stella Stevens: *The Ballad of Cable Hogue* (1970)
- Barbra Streisand: *The Owl and the Pussycat* (1970)
- Kitty Winn: *The Panic in Needle Park* (1971)

Jodie Foster.

Gable and Lombard

Released: February 1976
Director: Sidney J. Furie
Stars: James Brolin, Jill Clayburgh, Red Buttons
Academy Awards: None

PREVIEW: Clark Gable and Carole Lombard fall in love and then have to overcome bad publicity.

NOW SHOWING: The Stars Come Out

The mid-'70s nostalgia craze that put *Happy Days* on TV and the Beach Boys in stadiums inspired numerous movies about Hollywood's Golden Age. Notorious among these was *Gable and Lombard* (1976), which received many derisive reviews. Critics scorned the liberties the movie takes with history (for example, the movie's dramatic courtroom appearance during Clark Gable's paternity suit never happened), but don't all bio-pics dating back to *Cleopatra* (1934) and *Annie Oakley* (1935) take liberties? For facts, read biographies; for entertainment, watch movies.

With that in mind, *Gable and Lombard* isn't the total catastrophe you might've expected. Both leads give it a go, though James Brolin, imitating Gable's voice and mannerisms, never conveys the King's power and settles on making him "a lucky slob from Ohio." His Gable couldn't pull off Rhett Butler. Jill Clayburgh is more successful as the lively, foul-mouthed Carole Lombard who in the first ten minutes punches Gable in the mouth. Starting the movie as Shrill Clayburgh, she gradually softens to become more affecting, though a tasteless late scene at a ladies' meeting diminishes everybody.

The way-too-long 131-minute movie opens with Lombard's plane-crash death and then flashes back through their fictionalized romance and the resulting bad publicity (he's already married). Some scenes are completely implausible: intentionally taking breaks from each other for a few days, they unintentionally end up back-to-back in the same sand trap at the same Palm Springs golf course. Strangely, while Gable and Lombard play at being movie stars, they don't *work* at it. We see movie billboards, movie parties, and studio backlots, we hear names like Gary Cooper and Rin Tin Tin, we recognize Hedda Hopper, Louis B. Mayer, and Vivien Leigh as characters in *Gable and Lombard*, and we even spot the cast of *The Wizard of Oz* (1939), but Clark and Carole actually *make* movies for only two minutes, and those are played for laughs. Two minutes, in an era when this pair made dozens of movies, some of them classics.

What the movie seemingly gets right are the vintage clothes and cars, and maybe the couple's us-against-the-world spirit, like when Lombard rallies her "big ape" with a "nobody's ever gonna beat us" speech. The pair's devoted fans will consider *Gable and Lombard* vulgar trash, uncommitted viewers might think it's shallow fun, but nobody will rate this movie highly. Fortunately both stars quickly accelerated to big hits and left this memory far behind.

ADDED ATTRACTION: Duelling Bios

Two more bio-pics were released in early 1976; neither one succeeded. First was *Goodbye, Norma Jean* (1976), a cheap, ugly movie about Marilyn Monroe's rough pre-fame years. Played by the voluptuous-but-amateurish Misty Rowe, who soon posed for *Playboy*, young Monroe endures a steady stream of degrading encounters that check all the rape/creepy-audition/lesbian-scene boxes. The sleaze isn't graphic, but still, a snuff-film snippet? Give us a break. In comparison, *W.C. Fields and Me* (1976) looks like a masterpiece (next to *Goodbye, Norma Jean*, anything would). Rod Steiger perpetually sneers out the side of his mouth as the irascible comedian, and Valerie Perrine plays the title's "me," his adoring mistress who wrote the book this movie is based on. Sprinting through their Hollywood years to his sad death, the movie has impressive period details, Henry Mancini's graceful music, and too much sentimental melodrama. *Lenny* (1974), a better bio-pic with Perrine, elevated Lenny Bruce into a bold crusader straining for artistic expression; in contrast, *W.C. Fields and Me* reduces Fields to an unpleasant, hard-drinking curmudgeon.

Breakheart Pass

Released: March 1976
Director: Tom Gries
Stars: Charles Bronson, Ben Johnson, Richard Crenna
Academy Awards: None

PREVIEW: In the 1870s, someone on board a train through the mountains is killing passengers.

NOW SHOWING: Murder on the Humboldt Express

It's a western with lots of derring-do, it's a murder mystery with deceptive characters and plot twists—it's Alistair MacLean, which means another strong action-packed thriller based on one of MacLean's popular books. While not as awesome as *The Guns of Navarone* (1961) and *Ice Station Zebra* (1968), two earlier movies that followed MacLean's print bestsellers, *Breakheart Pass* (1976) is still a solid entry in MacLean's canon of books and movies.

This time MacLean the author becomes MacLean the screenwriter. As in his 1974 novel, the story is set in the 1870s and mostly takes place on a rescue train that's heading west to California's Fort Humboldt, where there's been a diphtheria outbreak. A doctor, a reverend, Nevada's governor, a marshal and soldiers are all on board to support the effort. They're also bringing a captured fugitive ("a killer, arsonist, a cheat and a coward") they've arrested along the way. What some of them don't know is that there's no epidemic, prisoners at the fort have taken charge, and the medical supplies aboard the train are actually boxes of guns and dynamite.

As the train winds through snowy mountains (spectacular scenes filmed in Idaho), passengers start dying mysteriously. Lingering stares among the survivors suggest that everyone's concealing a secret; as usual in MacLean's ripping yarns, most of them are. The fugitive, John Deakin (Charles Bronson), is really an undercover Secret Service agent who's trying to expose the conspiracy of killers. Action scenes punctuate the investigation. Before the climactic ambush at Breakheart Pass, we're shown a graphic point-blank shot to the head, a fatal fall into a gorge, a fantastic slow-motion train wreck, and Deakin's realistic one-on-one fight atop the moving train. We also see flattering shots of the lovely Jill Ireland (Bronson's real-life wife) and hear the marshal (Ben Johnson) say, "Let's get 'er done." The cavalry literally rides to the rescue, and a quick-draw duel ends the movie.

Blending espionage, action, and the classic western, *Breakheart Pass* works effectively, though imperfectly. Too many plot holes weaken the story. For instance, the killers stash the bodies on the train: why not toss 'em over the side? And why is the wanted criminal, Deakin, left unshackled so he can wander around? Fortunately there's enough that's worthwhile—including small roles for two NFL stars, Joe Kapp and Doug Atkins, and a champion boxer, Archie Moore—to make *Breakheart Pass* an entertaining ride.

ADDED ATTRACTION: Buckin' Bronson

In the 1970s, Charles Bronson was an acting *machine*, starring in twenty-two movies during the decade, including a major hit, *Death Wish* (1974). After *Breakheart Pass* he soon made two very different westerns. *From Noon Till Three* (1976) is a pleasant romantic comedy with Bronson playing an outlaw who spends an idyllic afternoon with a beautiful widow (Jill Ireland). To seduce her he uses the ol' please-cure-my-impotence ploy that Tony Curtis worked on Marilyn Monroe in *Some Like It Hot* (1959). After the outlaw leaves and is allegedly killed, the widow's story is turned into a bestselling book with the movie's title. The outlaw returns to find the town a tourist attraction and the widow thriving in the myth-making business. It's an offbeat movie, a little long but a charming departure for Bronson and a nice showcase for Ireland. A year later *The White Buffalo* (1977) weakly attempted to remake *Jaws* (1975) as a western by turning a rampaging beast loose in the mountains. Unfortunately director J. Lee Thompson, while capable, is no Steven Spielberg, and the movie looks better on the poster than it does on the screen. Bronson plays Wild Bill Hickok, tormented by nightmares and obsessed with killing Moby Buffalo, which unfortunately isn't that impressive when it's finally revealed. The movie meanders with subplots (Kim Novak gets five minutes) before its inevitable (and disappointing) *mano-y-monstruo* showdown.

Robin and Marian

Released: March 1976
Director: Richard Lester
Stars: Sean Connery, Audrey Hepburn, Robert Shaw
Academy Awards: None

PREVIEW: Older now, Robin Hood returns to England to find Marian and fight his nemesis again.

NOW SHOWING: "It's Better This Way"

Until *Robin and Marian* (1976), Disney's animated *Robin Hood* (1973) was the decade's preeminent Robin Hood movie. The two movies couldn't be more unalike. Instead of Disney's lively cartoon Robin (a dashing fox similar to Errol Flynn's iconic 1938 portrayal), *Robin and Marian* presents a scarred, tired Robin (a balding Sean Connery) who is confronting diminishing abilities. After two decades away from England, Robin and his loyal friend, Little John (Nicol Williamson) return to find Marian (Audrey Hepburn) a nun, the merry men scattered, and the malevolent Sheriff of Nottingham (Robert Shaw) "as powerful as ever" (it's true—Shaw looks younger here than in 1975's *Jaws*). Robin renews his relationship with Marian, unites his Sherwood Foresters, and battles his nemesis one last time.

None of that is as easy as it sounds. Midway through, Robin and Little John team up against multiple opponents; formerly this would've been an easy, laughing conquest, but now they both sweat, struggle, and get hit before awkwardly escaping. When Robin and the sheriff finally agree to a winner-take-all duel, their five-minute clash exhausts them both before Robin desperately stumbles to victory (it's Connery's second tough win over Shaw, following 1962's *From Russia with Love*). "I doubt I'll have a day like this again," he reluctantly admits.

The theme of aging isn't the only major departure from other Robin Hood movies. *Robin and Marian* is, at heart, a beautiful love story. He's strong, simple and direct, while she's feisty, wise and eloquent (her last "I love you" soliloquy is pure poetry). They know they belong together, in life and in death. When Marian mercifully takes them both out, Robin realizes "it's better this way," and they share the most romantic, tear-jerking ending since *Love Story* (1970).

Audrey Hepburn and Sean Connery.

Preferring melancholy over mayhem, director Richard Lester reigns in his usual hyperactive, madcap impulses. There are some lightly humorous touches—soldiers clanging helmets together, a catapulted boulder that falls woefully short—but *Robin and Marian* isn't the energetic action/comedy that Lester's *The Three Musketeers* (1973) was. His first image is of ripe apples; his last shows them withered. In between he uses lush music, brownish tones, and screenwriter James Goldman's wonderful lines to touch audiences who have seen plenty of swashbuckling swordfights and now want to be moved. With its impeccable details and slowly unfolding story, this is a lovely, bittersweet Robin Hood movie for adults. And for the ages.

ADDED ATTRACTION: A *Bridge* Too Long

Robin and Marian was Audrey Hepburn's first movie since *Wait Until Dark* (1967); her only other 1970s movie was *Bloodline* (1979), a forgettable thriller that jumbles international stars, glamorous settings and, egad, pornographic snuff films into a sordid mess. Observations about *Bloodline*'s shortcomings are subordinate to questions about what Audrey Hepburn, one of Hollywood's most beloved stars, is doing in a movie like this. Connery, meanwhile, starred in fifteen '70s movies, including one as James Bond (1971's *Diamonds Are Forever*) and another as a planet-saving scientist (1979's *Meteor*). A year after *Robin*, he joined Robert Redford, Laurence Olivier, Michael Caine, and many, many others to help fight the Nazis in *A Bridge Too Far* (1977). This large-scale war World War Two epic is in the tradition of *Tora! Tora! Tora!* (1970) and *Midway* (1976), and while it's not as compelling as the former, it's better than the latter. *A Bridge Too Far* methodically depicts an actual 1944 battle fought in Holland and won by Germany after a series of Allied mistakes. It takes a long time to get going, but once the first gunshot is finally fired fifty-four minutes in, the movie offers almost continuous combat that looks realistic and expensively produced, but with so many stars nobody has a big role. A wearying three-hour marathon, it's an ending too far.

All the President's Men

(One of 1976's five **FAR-OUT** movies)

Released: April 1976

Director: Alan J. Pakula

Stars: Robert Redford, Dustin Hoffman, Jason Robards

Academy Awards: Four wins (Best Supporting Actor—Jason Robards; Best Writing; Best Art Direction; Best Sound), plus four more nominations (Best Picture; Best Supporting Actress—Jane Alexander; Best Director; Best Editing)

PREVIEW: Two unknown reporters pursue a story that leads to the infamous Watergate scandal.

FINE LINE: "When is somebody gonna go on the record in this story? You guys are about to write a story that says the former Attorney General, the highest-ranking law-enforcement officer in this country, is a crook! Just be sure you're right." (Executive editor Ben Bradlee, frustrated that his reporters are relying on unnamed sources.)

CLOSE-UP: Thirty-eight minutes into the movie, Woodward has his first late-night meeting in a parking garage with the mysterious contact informally called Deep Throat. This government insider encourages Woodward to keep plodding: "Forget the myths that the media's created about the White House. The truth is, these are not very bright guys, and things got out of hand." During the meeting we hear the phrase "follow the money" for the first time. This key line is not in book, but it's the perfect shorthand instruction to steer the investigation.

NOW SHOWING: "Follow the Money"

All the President's Men (1976) opens with fifteen seconds of gray fog that suddenly clarifies into an extreme close-up of the date being typed onto white paper. The typewriter strikes deliberately, as if to ensure the information is correct. Characters pound onto the page with explosive bangs, the metaphorical sound of gunfire in a movie where words will be ammunition in a battle for truth. The movie's last image, 137 minutes later? Another close-up of words.

While *All the President's Men* involves Watergate, America's most infamous political scandal, it's really about words, especially those written by the two reporters who pursued the complicated investigation that led from a single, seemingly unimportant crime to Richard Nixon's resignation. Except for the early scenes of the initial break-in, there's little action, something modern audiences might lament. Instead, there are lots of interesting, natural conversations. Talk—in offices, hallways, elevators, restaurants, residences—is how the movie unspools its mystery. That mystery is slow to reveal itself, and the reporters don't realize they're chasing President Nixon until midway through the movie. So, with little action, abundant talk, a slowly developing story, minimal music, and an ending that most viewers will already know, *All the President's Men* is still one of the decade's very best thrillers. How'd they do that?

"They" begins with screenwriter William Goldman, who won the Oscar for this movie after having already won for *Butch Cassidy and the Sundance Kid* (1969). Based on the 1974 bestselling book of the same name, his intelligent script about two dogged journalists is subtle and methodical. Goldman focuses on the quiet details of their steadily building investigation without dumbing down the material with fabricated love interests, side stories, or fistfights. Diligent procedure and process are the movie's hallmarks, so we get lots of driving around, doors shutting in the reporters' faces, library research, pre-digital-era scribbles on physical notepads, and many, many phone calls. Goldman credits the audience with being smart enough to keep up with all the information (modern viewers may be overwhelmed by the many names, places, and acronyms packed into the movie, but 1976 audiences would've known them). He also assumes viewers will get sly jokes like, "Send it out to the *San Francisco Chronicle*, they need it." Goldman writes for adults.

All the foundational legwork he includes pays off when the investigation teeters on the brink of disaster 121 minutes in, because the audience understands how the reporters got to the edge of this cliff and the implications if they tumble over. The late warning they receive, "Lives are in danger," takes on menacing urgency because we recognize the magnitude of what the reporters have accomplished and fully appreciate how formidable their targets are. Yet they soldier on past threats, stern editors, and bad luck. They earn their triumph.

The other "they" is director Alan J. Pakula, who had already made a successful conspiracy movie in *The Parallax View* (1974). Pakula underscores the reliability of what we're seeing by incorporating actual TV footage and newspaper front pages. Additionally, he films in real locations (most memorably with a spectacular shot that slowly retreats to the ceiling of the Library of Congress, reducing the two reporters below to tiny figures looking for needles in haystacks). Everywhere the look seems genuine and perfectly crafted—the newspaper's brightly lit offices are meticulously re-created, while the exhausted, rumpled reporters live in messy apartments and live on fast food. Where Pakula skillfully ratchets up the tension is in the three ominous parking-garage scenes with the unidentified informant called Deep Throat (Hal Holbrook). Using whispers, shadows, and this secretive contact from a spy novel, Pakula and cinematographer Gordon Willis turn what might have been a long, mundane investigation into great film noir.

Dustin Hoffman and Robert Redford.

For much of the movie the two reporters, the soon-to-be-legendary Woodward (Robert Redford) and Bernstein (Dustin Hoffman), don't seem to like each other. Their first meeting twenty-one minutes into the movie is confrontational, later they snipe at each other, and most of the time they address each other by just their last names. Despite their contrasting styles and backgrounds (cautious Woodward was relatively new to the paper, the more impulsive Bernstein was a veteran), they're both assigned to the story, so there are interesting conflicts as they try to make the best of it.

The other principals are the various editors on the *Post*, especially Ben Bradlee (Jason Robards), who leads fascinating table discussions as the voice of journalistic authority (he's the only one who shouts in the movie). The rest of the cast presents some believable, at times mesmerizing witnesses to unusual activities. The two riveting scenes with Jane Alexander as a frightened bookkeeper brought her an Oscar nomination.

A common complaint about the movie is that it rushes through final landmark events. The last we see of the reporters, they're typing away on January 20, 1973, as Nixon is being sworn in for his second term. A minute of newswires then presents the next twenty months of events, concluding with the August 1974 announcement that "Nixon resigns." It's enough, however, that we've seen the primary detective work, and it's why this movie is still used as a teaching tool in journalism classes. Through perseverance, ingenuity, and plodding effort, these two unknown reporters brought down a monumentally corrupt administration and the most powerful man in the free world. *All the President's Men* isn't just tense; it's inspiring.

ADDED ATTRACTION: More Scoops

There had been other American movies that featured print journalists, radio reporters, or TV newscasters before *All the President's Men*, of course: *His Girl Friday* (1940), *Citizen Kane* (1941), and *Deadline—U.S.A.* (1952), just to name three. Here are eleven more from the 1970s, with their stars noted.

- *Between the Lines* (1977): John Heard, Lindsay Crouse
- *Capricorn One* (1978): Elliott Gould, James Brolin
- *The China Syndrome* (1979): Jack Lemmon, Jane Fonda
- *The Front Page* (1974): Jack Lemmon, Walter Matthau
- *Nashville* (1975): Keith Carradine, Geraldine Chaplin
- *Network* (1976): Faye Dunaway, William Holden
- *The Odessa File* (1974): Jon Voight, Maximilian Schell
- *The Parallax View* (1974): Warren Beatty, Hume Cronyn
- *The Pyramid* (1976): Charley Brown, Ira Hawkins
- *Star Spangled Girl* (1971): Sandy Duncan, Tony Roberts
- *Superman* (1978): Christopher Reeve, Margot Kidder

The Bad News Bears

Released: April 1976
Director: Michael Ritchie
Stars: Walter Matthau, Tatum O'Neal, Jackie Earle Haley
Academy Awards: None

PREVIEW: A misfit Little League team recruits two important new players and rises to the top.

NOW SHOWING: All Good News

In April 1976, two terrific movies about great American sports (politics and baseball) opened almost simultaneously to raves from critics and audiences. The second of the two movies, *The Bad News Bears*, isn't as serious and important as *All the President's Men* (the Bears are often consigned, surprisingly, to the juvenile section in libraries), but to many people it's just as entertaining.

What makes *The Bad News Bears* so effective is its audacity. This isn't a stereotypical sports movie. The coach, Buttermaker (Walter Matthau), isn't a wise, avuncular leader; he's a cantankerous, driving-while-drinking slob. The ace pitcher, Amanda (Tatum O'Neal), is a wise-beyond-her-years eleven-year-old girl who dates and has a lucrative job. The superstar, Kelly (Jackie Earle Haley), is a smoking, motorcycle-riding, twelve-year-old "*bandido*" who talks back to adults. The Bears are insolent misfits who fight each other, use ugly racist terms, and swear. Imagine this motley crew in a Disney version of this story: Coach Dean Jones wouldn't be collapsing drunk on the mound; the poster wouldn't have read, "The star player is waiting for her first bra"; the ringer would be a knuckle-ball-throwing chimpanzee; and the plucky underdogs would've won the championship.

Working from Bill Lancaster's smart screenplay, director Michael Ritchie has fashioned a multi-layered comedy that supplements the hilarious on-the-field comedy of errors (literally) with a more thoughtful theme that balances a merciless winning-at-all-costs philosophy against good sportsmanship. After his hapless team is outscored 45-0 in its first three games, Buttermaker recruits Amanda and Kelly. Their influence is instantaneous (Kelly's batting line = four plate appearances, two game-winning homers, a triple, and a walk), and the cellar-dwelling Bears climb to the title game. As the Bears get better Buttermaker gets worse, sliding from an uninvolved bum to an overinvolved jerk who shoves players, throws beer in Amanda's face, and does whatever it takes to win. Eventually he lightens up, decides he shouldn't take the finals so seriously, and replaces his stars with benchwarmers. Happily, the Bears' beer-soaked celebration of their loss is more joyous than the Yankees' unemotional acknowledgement of their win.

Ritchie had already made acclaimed movies like *Smile* (1975), but *The Bad News Bears* is his best. Matthau and O'Neal are perfect together, the main kids have believable personalities, and the game action is realistic, understandable, and suspenseful. While the language is too rough for children, for everyone else this movie hits a home run.

ADDED ATTRACTION: Worse News Bears

Missing the first movie's director, stars, and originality, *The Bad News Bears in Breaking Training* (1977) is a minor-league sequel that's closer to a mediocre TV movie than one of 1976's best comedies. When the Bears are invited to play an exhibition game in the Houston Astrodome, tough-guy Kelly drives everyone in a stolen van across the Southwest and gets his long-lost father (William Devane) to lead the team. Fortunately dad is a coaching genius, the rowdy Bears pull together, and the big game comes down to a familiar last-inning situation. Unfortunately, the boys' antics and bad language aren't cute anymore, and the father/son melodrama is awkward. The Bears really strike out with *The Bad News Bears Go to Japan* (1978). Tony Curtis plays a sleazy promoter who gets the boys to a game in Japan. Ogilvie and Tanner (two of the most familiar players from the first two movies) are absent, and Jackie Earle Haley, still the team's superstar, now looks like an adult, and when he romances a Japanese girl you almost expect him to propose (when this movie about twelve-year-old Little Leaguers was in theaters, Haley was turning seventeen). With long tangents and fifty-three minutes between the two baseball sequences, *The Bad News Bears Go to Japan* is strictly bush league.

Silent Movie

Released: June 1976
Director: Mel Brooks
Stars: Mel Brooks, Dom DeLuise, Marty Feldman
Academy Awards: None

PREVIEW: Three nitwits drop in on some famous stars to ask them to appear in a new silent movie.

NOW SHOWING: Middling Mel

After successfully parodying musicals with *The Producers* (1967), westerns with *Blazing Saddles* (1974), and horror movies with *Young Frankenstein* (1974), Mel Brooks had "a brilliant idea for a new movie" (a line that we actually read on the screen in this new movie).

Dom DeLuise, Marty Feldman, and Mel Brooks.

His idea may not be "brilliant," but it is original and promising: a silent movie called *Silent Movie* about three nitwits in modern-day Hollywood who are trying to make a new silent movie. To get the reluctant studio to greenlight his daring project, director Mel Funn (Brooks) needs some big-name headliners, so he and two sidekicks drive around L.A. in a cool 1954 Morgan convertible to recruit their stars in person one at a time.

The famous actors and actresses who make entertaining cameo appearances (James Caan, Liza Minnelli, Paul Newman, Burt Reynolds, etc.) seem to be having fun playing off their familiar screen characters (Caan's a tough-guy boxer, Reynolds a self-obsessed stud, and so on). In a more developed role, Bernadette Peters plays a vivacious "bundle of lust" who easily steals all her scenes. Some of the sight gags are predictable (a man walks out of an acupuncturist's office covered in needles, big wow), the fast-motion is overdone, and everything may have been better in black and white rather than in color to capture that silent-movie vibe, but there's enough inventiveness to generate occasional chuckles. The cardiac monitor that becomes a Pong game is a nifty '70s joke.

Despite its title and reputation, the movie is not truly silent, since it has a wonderfully expressive score by Brooks regular John Morris, plus there are plenty of sounds during the slapstick, which is effectively underlined with abundant effects and slide whistles. There's even a single spoken word (ironically, from the one person you wouldn't expect to talk). This being a Mel Brooks movie, there are comical musical numbers, just like there were in *The Producers*, *Blazing Saddles*, and *Young Frankenstein*, and he's invited some veteran funnymen (including Charlie Callas, Henny Youngman, and Harry Ritz) to drop in for quick laughs. As he often does in his movies, Brooks springs some inside jokes: seventy-six minutes into *Silent Movie*, the theater showing the sneak preview has three posters for Brooks's own *Young Frankenstein* on display outside. It all adds up to a fast eighty-seven sprint through some hilarious, some merely diverting situations, making *Silent Movie* a solidly entertaining experiment.

ADDED ATTRACTION: Sherlock Wilder

After *Young Frankenstein* (1974), Mel Brooks delivered *Silent Movie* in 1976. In between, the closest thing to a new Brooks movie for 1975 was written and directed by Gene Wilder, who had starred in three of Brooks's previous comedies (*The Producers*, *Blazing Saddles*, and *Young Frankenstein*). Wilder's *The Adventure of Sherlock Holmes' Smarter Brother*, his first directorial effort, aims for the heights of *Young Frankenstein*: it's visually attractive, incorporates musical scenes, and even includes two of *Young Frankenstein*'s stars, Madeline Kahn and Marty Feldman. Unfortunately, Wilder's uneven movie isn't nearly as funny as Brooks's classic. The uninvolving story puts Sherlock's jealous younger brother, Sigerson Holmes (Wilder), on the trail of missing documents. Wilder's got Sherlock, Dr. Watson, and arch-enemy Professor Moriarty in the movie, and he makes knowing references to actual Holmes stories, so he has affection for the subject. But slapstick scenes go on too long, Wilder often shouts in wild-eyed hysteria like he did in *Young Frankenstein*, and that movie's "Puttin' on the Ritz" number towers over any of *Smarter Brother*'s songs (the two "Kangaroo Hop" scenes seem desperate). Veterans Kahn, Feldman, and Dom DeLuise try hard, and Albert Finney contributes a cameo, but the movie is only mildly entertaining, like some lesser Holmes mystery that would be called "The Adventure of the Missed Opportunity."

The Big Bus

Released: June 1976
Director: James Frawley
Stars: Joseph Bologna, Stockard Channing, John Beck
Academy Awards: None

PREVIEW: A huge nuclear-powered bus finds trouble on its inaugural trip across the country.

NOW SHOWING: The Disaster Outlier

According to the movie's poster, *The Big Bus* (1976) is "the first disaster movie where everybody dies (laughing)." Nicely spoofing the decade's disaster epics, the movie's prologue mentions "movies about Big Earthquakes … about Big Boats sinking … about Big Buildings burning … about Big German Balloons bursting," obvious nods to *Earthquake* (1974), *The Poseidon Adventure* (1972), *The Towering Inferno* (1974), and *The Hindenburg* (1975), all of them star-studded big-budget spectacles. Contrasting those mega-movies, *The Big Bus* humorously scales down to a story about a bus, albeit a ridiculously big nuclear-powered thirty-two-wheeled double-decker bus that's over a hundred feet long. For its 180 passengers, no luxury has been spared, so while on board the elegant *Cyclops* they can access a piano lounge, a one-lane bowling alley, a swimming pool, an opulent dining room, and an extravagant bathroom complete with a tub. Eat your heart out, Greyhound.

Consistent with other '70s movies about disastrous grand openings—the fire in *The Towering Inferno* (1974) erupts on the night of the building's gala dedication—the big bus in *The Big Bus* has just been finished and is on its maiden journey across the country. One of the jokes is that, although this leviathan is making a nonstop New York-to-Denver run, all the scenery looks like Southern California's desert and mountains, and we even glimpse road signs for California's Arrow Highway, Covina Boulevard, and the Angeles Crest Highway. Along the way the dangers pile up: saboteurs, a collision with a truck, even an earthquake. It's unclear if the bus ever arrives, since the movie ends with the vehicle split in half while still en route.

Like other disaster movies, the cast includes some Oscar nominees and Oscar winners (José Ferrer, Lynn Redgrave, and Sally Kellerman, with Ruth Gordon as the token Hollywood legend who always seemed to be aboard any plane or ship that went down in the '70s). Larry Hagman and Ned Beatty are among the familiar faces; a priest, sailor, and sexy stewardesses are among the familiar characters; and a troubled relationship between the driver (Joseph Bologna) and the designer (Stockard Channing) is among the familiar subplots. This being a good-natured comedy, everyone survives. The best moments of pure silliness (like the bus drivers named Goldie, Whitey, Blackie, Red, Pinky, Greenie, and Brownie) suggest that *The Big Bus* inspired an even better disaster-movie parody, *Airplane!* (1980).

ADDED ATTRACTION: One-Hundred-Fifteen-Minute Warning

Five months after *The Big Bus*, the disaster genre lurched forward with *Two-Minute Warning* (1976). Technically a catch-the-sniper thriller, *Two-Minute Warning* incorporates so many disaster-movie elements it's closer to *Airport* (1970) than *The Day of the Jackal* (1973). As in *Airport*, a star-studded cast is united (here at the L.A. Coliseum for a Super Bowl-like football game), some key potential targets are briefly introduced, a venerable Hollywood star (Walter Pidgeon) commits small crimes, a mounting threat endangers everyone, and there's a riveting who-will-survive finale. The movie begins with the first-person perspective of an anonymous sniper warming up by killing an innocent cyclist, and then it basically follows four trails: the spectators in the stadium, the TV crew producing the broadcast, the sniper atop the stadium's peristyle, and the police and SWAT team that strategize and maneuver into position. After Merv Griffin's national anthem, the two pro teams (Stanford and USC, actually) kick off thirty-eight minutes into the movie, and a long, slow hour later the sniper finally, *finally* begins firing. With the crowd stampeding to the exits, for the last few minutes there's genuine tension as the bodies pile up and the cops close in. Disappointingly, the sniper is given no motive beyond being called a "clown," "nut," and "transient from out of state," and we never even get a good look at him. *Two-Minute Warning* falls short of the goal line; a year later a better football-themed disaster movie, *Black Sunday*, will score a touchdown.

Logan's Run

Released: June 1976
Director: Michael Anderson
Stars: Michael York, Jenny Agutter, Richard Jordan
Academy Awards: One win (Special Achievement Award for Visual Effects), plus two more nominations (Best Cinematography; Best Art Direction)

PREVIEW: Residents escape from a futuristic city where nobody is allowed to age past thirty.

NOW SHOWING: Don't Trust Anyone Over Thirty

Some popular '70s movies still hold up as marvelous entertainment. *Logan's Run* (1976), regrettably, isn't one of those movies. Back then it seemed like an entertaining cutting-edge science-fiction adventure, but that was before *Star Wars* (1977) changed everything, especially our sci-fi expectations, less than a year later.

The first hour of *Logan's Run* effectively establishes the setting: 2274, in a perfect domed city where everyone wears color-coded outfits and "lives only for pleasure." Though there's a society-imposed age limit of thirty, a life-regenerating process called "renewal" is attainable through "the fiery ritual of Carrousel." When some citizens realize the ritual is merely large-scale bug-zapping—that the participants are being killed, not reborn—they flee. Logan (Michael York) is an elite policeman who exterminates "runners" but eventually becomes one himself, so he too must be pursued.

Instead of a dystopian future a la *The Omega Man* (1971), *Soylent Green* (1973), *A Boy and His Dog* (1975), and others, here the future looks strong and happy. The high-tech city resembles the ultimate shopping mall, with an Arcade area, New You providing instant pain-free body modifications, and a Love Shop offering rooms of writhing lovers. In his *Playboy*-style bachelor pad, Logan beams aboard willing Playmates. All this hedonism distinguishes *Logan's Run* from most other science-fiction movies up to that time, and from *Star Wars*, too. Farrah Fawcett-Majors gets nine minutes in a sexy miniskirt, and beautiful Jenny Agutter gets completely naked. Hideous alien monsters, please audition elsewhere.

Halfway through, *Logan's Run* becomes Logan's walk when he and Jessica (Agutter) escape. The movie really loses momentum during a ridiculous ice-cave encounter with a malevolent robot that resembles an aluminum-foil gas pump. *Logan's Run* then borrows from *Beneath the Planet of the Apes* (1970), replacing that movie's ruined New York with an ivy-covered Washington, D.C. inhabited by a cat-sheltering old man (Peter Ustinov) who quotes T.S. Eliot. Inconsistencies pile up. Logan knows about oceans, but not the sun? Since Earth obviously isn't irradiated or poisonous, why can't everyone leave the dome and prosper outside? Who's running the city, and why would it totally self-destruct the moment Logan blasts the computers inside one single room? Why is almost every city resident white? Don't question the (il-)logic, just enjoy the impressive miniatures, the early holograms, the sleek vehicles and cool jetpacks, the electronic music, and the '70s hairstyles before *Star Wars* blows all this dated fun away.

Jenny Agutter and Michael York.

ADDED ATTRACTION: ♫ Love to Love You Embryo-o-o ♫

Appearing a month before *Logan's Run* was another sci-fi movie about aging. *Embryo* (1976) is a slow, talky movie about an inquisitive doctor (Rock Hudson) who's using "intravenous injections of placental lactogen" to accelerate fetal development inside his home laboratory. After he makes a dog fetus zoom to full-size, he next tries his serum—just like anyone would—on a living human fetus. Growing two years every *day*, the fetus soon transforms into a slinky twenty-four-year-old vixen (Barbara Carrera). Naturally, the doctor has to sleep with her. Blessed with "overwhelming" intelligence, slinky realizes she's maturing rapidly, actually a little *too* rapidly for her taste, so on her own she experiments and kills, hoping to find an anti-aging formula. Rock the doc tries to eliminate her, but even as a wrinkled hag she manages to ... well, we won't deliver the ending here. Unfortunately, before that surprising moment too many scenes have taken place in the dark, much of the movie's information has been conveyed via repetitive recorded dictation, and there hasn't been much action until the climactic chase. Basically, this one's an embry-no. Seeing *Logan's Run* and *Embryo*, you'd conclude people in the Me Decade were obsessed with maintaining a youthful image. Ya think?

Murder by Death

Released: June 1976
Director: Robert Moore
Stars: Peter Falk, David Niven, Peter Sellers
Academy Awards: None

PREVIEW: An eccentric host challenges five famous detectives to solve an ingenious murder.

NOW SHOWING: The Case of the Unfunny Comedy

Because *Murder by Death* (1976) should be funnier than it actually is, we want to love it more than we actually do. Regrettably, after decades of repeat viewings, we still barely laugh during Neil Simon's overrated murder-mystery parody.

Tapping into a mini-run of complicated '70s mysteries like *Chinatown* (1974) and *Murder on the Orient Express* (1974), Simon has devised a nifty plot: all of "the world's greatest living detectives" are invited to a manor for "dinner and murder," with a million dollars awaiting the one who solves the ingenious crime. Rapid-fire gags are delivered by an all-star cast that includes Peter Sellers, David Niven, and Maggie Smith. So there's real potential for a smart comic romp ... which never arrives.

With its single location, sophisticated banter, disguised characters, and mentions of crime as "a game," *Murder by Death* echoes the great *Sleuth* (1972). Simon's detectives affectionately mimic the famous investigators Sam Spade, Charlie Chan, and more (not Sherlock Holmes, though), and all the hoary clichés of old whodunits, like a thunderstorm, a deadly snake and scorpion, a time bomb, even the phrase "the butler did it," make appearances. But for every clever line—the "room filled with empty people," the infuriating foreigner who absolutely refuses to preface nouns with articles—there are flat jokes that are juvenile (the dinner's host, Lionel Twain, lives at Two Two Twain), or obvious (the blind butler doesn't face his listeners), or lowbrow (a gassy old lady, riffs on a character named Wang), or downright offensive (the buck-toothed Oriental detective is subjected to racist teasing and is actually called "Slanty"). Peter Falk is good as a Dashiell Hammett-style private eye who uses hard-boiled lingo ("a patsy being set up to take the fall"), and Alec Guinness has fun as the blind butler, then a corpse, then Twain's daughter, and then … and then … (we won't spoil the multiple surprise endings). Truman Capote, however, amateurishly overacts like he's in a school production, and other characters are corny exaggerations. The best laugh comes from a mute maid trying to scream, which is faint praise indeed.

Fans of old movies will enjoy the references to classics such as *Casablanca* (1942) and *To Have and Have Not* (1944). Unfortunately, as a comedy *Murder by Death* can't compare with Mel Brooks's laugh-out-loud genre spoofs. The only murder here is that it's an occasionally amusing way to kill ninety-four minutes.

ADDED ATTRACTION: More '70s Simon

Seven months before *Murder by Death*, Neil Simon scored with *The Sunshine Boys* (1975), a better movie that generates real comedy and emotion. Like the incompatible leads brilliantly played by Walter Matthau and Jack Lemmon in Simon's *The Odd Couple* (1968), Matthau and George Burns play opposites, here bickering ex-vaudevillians who reluctantly team up for a modern-day TV special. Richard Benjamin plays the hard-working agent who's trying to bring them together. Based on Simon's 1972 play, *The Sunshine Boys* movie earned multiple Oscar nominations (one for Simon's screenplay), plus a win for eighty-year-old Burns that made him the oldest Oscar-winning actor. Two years after *Murder by Death,* Simon parodied 1940s film noir with *The Cheap Detective* (1978). *Murder by Death*'s director Robert Moore and Peter Falk, again a trench-coated gumshoe, both returned, with a cast of comedic pros (including Madeline Kahn and Stockard Channing) joining in for a witty mashup of *Casablanca*, *The Maltese Falcon* (1941), diamonds, documents, and dames. It's a delightful feast for Bogart buffs and entertaining, inspired silliness for everyone else. While all these Simon-penned movies were box-office successes, they're all subordinate to his '70s masterpiece, *The Goodbye Girl* (1977).

Buffalo Bill and the Indians, or Sitting Bull's History Lesson

Released: June 1976
Director: Robert Altman
Stars: Paul Newman, Joel Grey, Geraldine Chaplin
Academy Awards: None

PREVIEW: Buffalo Bill stages his Wild West show but has trouble with a co-star, Sitting Bull.

NOW SHOWING: "There Ain't No Business Like Show Business"

Robert Altman's 1970s movies ranged from on fire to misfire. For every popular classic like *M*A*S*H* (1970), there was an eccentric oddball like *Quintet* (1979). *Buffalo Bill and the Indians, or Sitting Bull's History Lesson* (1976) falls somewhere in between. Average Altman, however, is still better than no Altman at all.

Paul Newman.

Here he examines stardom in a long story roped to 1885 (near the end of the Wild West) and a single setting (Buffalo Bill Cody's big circus-like theatrical production). After ornate tone-setting opening credits, the movie explores Cody's show both onstage and behind the scenes. Cody (Paul Newman, in a flamboyant wig) is the star, as he reminds everyone: riding a magnificent white steed, he's always introduced as "America's national entertainer," "America's national hero," or the "Monarch of the West." His "titanically momentous" show presents sharp shooters, trick riders, dramatic re-creations of frontier battles, and buffalo stampedes. Much of it is faked, but, according to Cody, it's "the finest spectacle in the history of the show business." What's interesting is how this nineteenth-century show parallels our own entertainment spectacles. Cody deals with temperamental actors, unrealistic wage demands, unhelpful yes-men, and fact-inventing publicists, but he also rakes in millions of dollars. "There ain't no business like show business," we're told. There sure ain't.

All of Altman's usual cinematic tricks are on display. He showcases big beautiful landscapes, but his roving camera also captures scenes with small actions in the backgrounds. The natural-sounding dialogue is seemingly improvised and often overlaps (a confused character even asks, "Are you listening to me? Excuse me, we're tryin' to have a conversation"). The diverse cast includes a legend (Burt Lancaster), an Oscar winner (Joel Grey), an Altman regular (Shelley Duvall), and some good, interesting choices (Geraldine Chaplin, Harvey Keitel).

Everything changes when Cody hires the great Sitting Bull, billed as "Killer of Custer." The proud, headstrong Sioux chief battles the jocular Cody over contracts, the nature of his act, even his sleeping arrangements. In frustration Cody fires him, rehires him, and, after Sitting Bull dies, replaces him with a lookalike. But that's typical of the mercurial showman. Profane and profound, Cody practices speeches in front of a mirror like a politician. He's also cheap, a heavy drinker, a liar, and unfaithful to his wife. "A man like that made this country what it is today," President Cleveland says admiringly of Cody. Ah, Altman's point, perhaps?

ADDED ATTRACTION: Team Altman

Fans who watch Robert Altman's movies closely will start seeing some familiar faces over and over again. Members of Team Altman include Rene Auberjonois, who had roles in four of the director's '70s movies from *M*A*S*H* (1970) to *Images* (1972); Elliott Gould and Michael Murphy, each with four roles from *M*A*S*H* to *Nashville* (1975); John Schuck, four roles from *M*A*S*H* to *Thieves Like Us* (1974); and three '70s roles each for Keith Carradine, Geraldine Chaplin, Corey Fischer, and Henry Gibson, among others. Team Altman's two MVPs, however, are both in *Buffalo Bill and the Indians*. Character-actor Bert Remsen plays a bartender in the movie, one of his *seven* appearances for Altman during the decade. Meanwhile, eight-four minutes into *Buffalo Bill and the Indians*, Shelley Duvall arrives as the First Lady to President Cleveland. She doesn't have many lines, and she's in the movie for only sixteen minutes, but this appearance kept alive her streak of significant roles (sometimes starring roles) in six of Robert Altman's movies during the 1970s, which are listed below. In 1979, production had already started on another Altman movie that was just over the horizon: *Popeye* (1980), starring Robin Williams as the title character and Duvall as Olive Oyl.

- *Brewster McCloud* (1970)
- *McCabe & Mrs. Miller* (1971)
- *Thieves Like Us* (1974)
- *Nashville* (1975)
- *Buffalo Bill and the Indians, or Sitting Bull's History Lesson* (1976)
- *3 Women* (1977)

The Omen

Released: June 1976
Director: Richard Donner
Stars: Gregory Peck, Lee Remick, David Warner
Academy Awards: One win (Best Music), plus one more nomination (Best Song)

PREVIEW: A boy may be at the center of scary events, so his father investigates his son's past.

NOW SHOWING: The Devil Made Him Do It

Modern viewers inured to movies with violent demonic possession might question all the fuss about *The Omen* (1976). But we remember sitting in a theater with everyone around us either holding their breath or gasping out loud. Maybe it's not as terrifying now, but in the '70s many people considered *The Omen* an instant horror classic.

The movie's obvious ancestor is *The Exorcist* (1973), the Best Picture-nominated landmark that transformed the horror genre. Compared to *The Exorcist*, which parades a revolting monster doing grotesque things, *The Omen* is relatively restrained. It scares but doesn't disgust: Damien (Harvey Stephens), the young Antichrist, doesn't turn into a hideous beast; we never see a horned demon or projectile vomiting; and except for a decapitation and a kitchen-utensil fight the killings are almost bloodless. In fact, most of the supernatural occurrences are explicable. A suicide, zoo animals overreacting to a car, Damien's tricycle bumping his mother over a balcony, a storm knocking a lethal lightning rod off a tower—all disturbing, but all possible without Satanic intervention.

Harvey Stephens.

The movie gives these dark events more gravitas by cleverly injecting solemn Biblical quotes and portentous omens (the word "omen," though, is never spoken). Intensifying the terror are effective supporting characters—the doomed priest who warns, the scarred priest who points, and especially the creepy nanny (Billie Whitelaw) who guards. One late scene even involves an exorcist.

The movie unfolds as a mystery, with Damien's father, Robert Thorn (Gregory Peck), and an inquisitive photographer (David Warner) investigating the truth about Thorn's adopted son. Their discovery scenes in the movie's second half are supremely scary, thanks to director Richard Donner's eerie settings and Jerry Goldsmith's Oscar-winning music. Theater audiences were riveted during the suspenseful cemetery scene that uncovers shocking skeletons; viewers shrieked when Thorn, silently snipping Damien's hair in a darkened room, is suddenly attacked. And who wasn't chilled by the last scene, when Thorn's demise leaves Damien smiling alongside the president?

Admittedly, there are plot holes 666-feet wide. If the photographer knew his light-streaked photos foretold deaths, why wouldn't he quickly take more of everyone, especially of himself? To protect his only son, Satan sends ... a dog? And an English nanny? That's all? The movie ignores any such objections and instead pushes ahead with the seriousness of its fast-moving story. While some critics mocked and resisted, audiences shuddered and surrendered to the power of *The Omen*.

ADDED ATTRACTION: Repossessed

Since they were both huge box-office hits, naturally *The Exorcist* and *The Omen* were followed by sequels. *Exorcist II: The Heretic* (1977) brought back Linda Blair but none of the original movie's other major stars or filmmakers (John Boorman took over for William Friedkin as director, and a bored Richard Burton stepped in as an investigating priest). With an utterly incoherent plot involving locusts and dull psychological nonsense, the so-bad-it's-bad *Exorcist II* is frequently called one of the worst sequels—actually, one of the worst *movies*—ever made. In contrast, *Damien: Omen II* (1978) is a far more satisfying follow-up to its predecessor because it doesn't abandon the first movie but instead extends it by making Damien a lethal teenager who comes to accept his unearthly powers. Just as Oscar-winner Gregory Peck had helped legitimize *The Omen* as a serious movie, so too do Oscar-winners William Holden and Lee Grant add weight to this solid sequel that's highlighted by several inventive horror sequences, especially a dramatic drowning under a frozen pond and a terrifying sequence involving a man clamped onto the front of a moving train.

The Outlaw Josey Wales

Released: June 1976
Director: Clint Eastwood
Stars: Clint Eastwood, Sondra Locke, Chief Dan George
Academy Awards: One nomination (Best Music)

PREVIEW: In the Civil War, vigilantes kill Josey Wales's family, so he rides out for revenge.

NOW SHOWING: Classic Clint

By the mid-1970s Clint Eastwood had already starred in numerous westerns as a laconic drifter who rides into problematic situations and solves them with his guns. His mysterious characters often had no backgrounds, sometimes not even names (in 1973's *High Plains Drifter*, he's simply "the Stranger"). *The Outlaw Josey Wales* (1976), a popular movie that Eastwood directed and stars in, dramatically departs from that formula and is now remembered as one of his great westerns.

The departures start immediately as Josey Wales (Eastwood), a hard-working Missouri farmer, is transformed into an outlaw. During the Civil War, a violent band of Union Army guerrillas roars onto Wales' property, kills his family, and incinerates his farm. Eastwood's characters are normally stoic, but here Wales cries as he buries his wife and son. He joins some rebellious Southerners, but when they surrender they're helplessly slaughtered. Wales kills some of the Northerners and escapes.

Having lost his family, Wales gradually builds a new one as people are attracted to his strength and leadership. Among them are quiet, pretty Laura (Sondra Locke)

Clint Eastwood.

and Lone Watie (Chief Dan George), whose deadpan delivery provides gentle comic relief. With these and other allies, Wales starts a new ranching life in Texas far from any pursuers. Unsurprisingly, Wales's past finds him; he's "not a hard man to track" because he "leaves dead men wherever he goes." Eventually bounty hunters and Union vigilantes arrive, leading to a bloody siege at the ranch.

Unlike other Eastwood westerns, there's real sensitivity in the characters. Wales doesn't win Laura with macho heroics; they slowly fall for each other during quiet moments together. Additionally, the movie's Indians aren't mindless savages and instead are more like the wise, reasonable Human Beings in *Little Big Man* (1970). Eastwood the director treats them with respect.

Eastwood went on to direct and star in more westerns, and an Eastwood-less sequel to *Josey Wales* followed in 1986. But *Josey Wales* real legacy might be Eastwood's Best Picture masterpiece, *Unforgiven* (1992). In both movies Eastwood plays a farmer who kills numerous enemies in a single confrontation, and immediately he's asked how he knew which one to shoot first. Both movies are beautifully filmed, and both confront the theme of inescapable violence. Eastwood himself understood how important *Josey Wales* was to his long career making westerns: on the movie's DVD special features he correctly calls it "one of the high points."

ADDED ATTRACTION: Home on Derange

The Outlaw Josey Wales premiered while two less-impressive westerns were still in theaters. *The Missouri Breaks* (1976) is a long, unsatisfying movie boasting two superstars, Marlon Brando as a bizarre man hunter who tricks his targets with clever conversations, and Jack Nicholson as a tough rustler who tries farming and falling in love before finally exacting vengeance. Brando enters thirty-six minutes in and either dazzles or annoys, depending on the viewer's tolerance for eccentric behavior (he belabors an Irish accent, acknowledges his bodily functions, laughs out of context, and even dresses in drag—it's like the mighty Brando is trying to see how much he can get away with before someone will dare to rein him in, which never happens). Director Arthur Penn had already succeeded with an unusual western, *Little Big Man*, but *The Missouri Breaks* is too peculiar and disjointed to match that classic's power and significance. Meanwhile, *The Duchess and the Dirtwater Fox* is a forgettable western comedy starring Goldie Hawn and George Segal as two scoundrels trying to abscond with $40,000 that Segal's character helped steal from a bank. The movie has scenic settings, several potentially humorous situations that go unfulfilled, Hawn's performances of bawdy musical numbers with an English accent, an incongruous pop song from Bobby Vinton, and, regrettably, almost no laughs.

Treasure of Matecumbe

Released: July 1976
Director: Vincent McEveety
Stars: Robert Foxworth, Joan Hackett, Peter Ustinov
Academy Awards: None

PREVIEW: Two nineteenth-century boys set out on a journey that will lead to buried treasure.

NOW SHOWING:
Raiders of the Lost *Treasure of Matecumbe*

A movie's best attribute shouldn't be its dramatic poster. Unfortunately, that's the case with *Treasure of Matecumbe*, Disney's well-postered summer adventure for 1976. Audiences never dug this buried-treasure yarn, though it's not a bad movie. After an incongruous soft-rock theme song, a family in post-Civil War Kentucky finds a map to gold buried in Florida. Two boys take up the quest, traveling via a Mississippi River sternwheeler and then a keelboat owned by a comical quack reminiscent of Professor Marvel in *The Wizard of Oz* (1939). Adding urgency is a thuggish gang chasing the boys and the treasure.

With an hour of the Mighty Mississippi and its colorful characters, there's plenty of *Huckleberry Finn* in *Treasure of Matecumbe*. Mid-movie a group of roughnecks erupts into a raucous dance evoking *Seven Brides for Seven Brothers* (1954), although the math is more like One for Seven. Joan Hackett plays a smart, feisty runaway bride who brings modern feminist energy to the boys' team. Moreover, some dark elements make this movie more daring than traditional Disney adventures, especially the KKK's sudden arrival for some cross-burning, lynching, and speechifying (derided as "Klan claptrap").

Disney balances any controversy with generally entertaining kid-centric storytelling. The boys are plucky and talented (one is a harmonica virtuoso), there's abundant wildlife, and the episodic obstacles (mosquitos, gators, a hurricane) are quickly overcome before the inevitable happy ending. Actually, with its elegant four-columned mansion, river boats, lively New Orleans section, creepy native masks, and cave-tomb with a skeleton, what this movie really reminds us of is Disneyland.

A week after *Treasure of Matecumbe*'s premiere, Disney released *Gus* (1976), an inane comedy about a mule that becomes an NFL kicker, thanks to a rulebook loophole. Naturally he leads his hapless team to the title with incredibly long field goals, which are accompanied by a dumb sound effect. The "miracle mule" wears a football helmet, flies alongside other passengers on commercial jets, sleeps in beds, and winks. When a nine-minute supermarket chase generates every pratfall from every cartoon ever made, a tyke sitting in a shopping cart laughs, showing the right audience for this silliness. Adults might be interested to see NFL star Dick Butkus acting, announcer Dick Enberg wearing a mule hat, and familiar TV stars collecting paychecks (look, Barney Fife! Ensign Parker! Lou Grant! Mr. Cunningham!). The final *two-minute* play signals the end of football as we know it.

ADDED ATTRACTION:
And the Oscar for Best Names Goes to …

Disney has always been good at creating fun character names. Remember Panchito Pistoles from *The Three Caballeros* (1944), and Launchpad McQuack from TV's *Duck Tales* (1987-1990)? Similarly creative names populated Disney's '70s movies (some came from the original stories the movies were based on, others were Disney inventions); here are fifteen from the decade, including one from *Treasure of Matecumbe*.

- *The Apple Dumpling Gang* (1975): Magnolia "Dusty" Clydesdale
- *Bedknobs and Broomsticks* (1971): Eglantine Price
- *Charley and the Angel* (1973): Leonora Appleby

- *Escape to Witch Mountain* (1975): Aristotle Bolt
- *Gus* (1976): Crankcase
- *Herbie Goes to Monte Carlo* (1977): Wheely Applegate
- *Herbie Rides Again* (1974): Willoughby Whitfield
- *Hot Lead and Cold Feet* (1978): Jasper Bloodshy
- *Pete's Dragon* (1977): Dr. Terminus
- *The Shaggy D.A.* (1976): Katrinka Muggelberg
- *Snowball Express* (1972): Double L. Dingman
- *The Strongest Man in the World* (1975): Kirwood Krinkle
- *Superdad* (1973): Cyrus Hershberger
- *Treasure of Matecumbe* (1976): Dr. Ewing T. Snodgrass
- *The World's Greatest Athlete* (1973): Buzzer Kozak

The Shootist

Released: August 1976
Director: Don Siegel
Stars: John Wayne, Lauren Bacall, Ron Howard
Academy Awards: One nomination (Best Art Direction)

PREVIEW: In 1901, an aging gunfighter arranges one final shoot-out against three villains.

NOW SHOWING: The Duke's Last Stand

Transitions. That one word summarizes the subject of *The Shootist* (1976), which is set in 1901 as the dusty cowboy era gives way to the modern electric age. Legendary gunfighter J.B. Books (John Wayne), who has killed thirty men and can "draw trouble like an outhouse draws flies," has become an anachronism: "To put it in a nutshell, you've plain plumb outlived your time," he's bluntly told. Books, however, is actually experiencing another kind of transition.

After a clever introduction that highlights Books' life with actual scenes from Wayne's old western movies, Books comes to Carson City, Nevada, for a second medical opinion, but the doctor there (James Stewart) only confirms the first opinion. Books is soon going to die a painful death from cancer. Rather than waste away, Books sets about doing the only thing he knows how to do, which is to kill bad guys ("I don't believe I ever killed a man that didn't deserve it," he announces confidently). The movie spans Books' last week as he prepares for a final shoot-out with the town's three villains.

Those around him go through transitions of their own. The boarding house's owner (Lauren Bacall) is initially repulsed by Books' dangerous presence, but she comes to admire and respect him. Her son, played by Ron Howard, learns you can't judge this Books by his cover, as he goes from mocking Books ("The old man ain't worth the bullet, he looks all tuckered out") to worshipping him and even avenging his death in the final gun battle. In *American Graffiti* (1973), Howard played an indecisive teenager; in *The Shootist* he transforms into a decisive man, valiantly firing three bullets into the traitorous bartender who has killed Books.

Ron Howard, Lauren Bacall, and John Wayne.

That Books is shot in the back parallels a similar scene in *The Cowboys* (1972), when a vicious lowlife guns down John Wayne as he's walking away. The entire theme of death gains significance when you realize that Wayne himself was fighting cancer and would die in 1979. *The Shootist* is his last movie, and he plays his role beautifully with a blend of quiet power, nobility and sensitivity (surprisingly he carries around a pretty little pillow and admits that he's "a dying man scared of the dark"). Few actors have been able to go out with such a dignified swan song, and few westerns are as moving and as good as *The Shootist*.

ADDED ATTRACTION: Classic Stars Who Died in the 1970s

John Wayne died in 1979 at age seventy-two. The following twenty-five actors and actresses, all of them fifty years old or more, and many of them legends from the Golden Age of Hollywood, also died during the decade. Their ages at their deaths, and the years they were born and died, are noted.

- Jack Benny, 80 (1894–1974)
- Joan Blondell, 73 (1906–1979)
- Charles Boyer, 78 (1899–1978)
- Walter Brennan, 80 (1894-1974)
- Lon Chaney Jr., 67 (1906-1973)
- Charlie Chaplin, 88 (1889–1977)
- Lee J. Cobb, 64 (1911–1976)
- Joan Crawford, 71 (1906–1977)
- Bing Crosby, 74 (1903–1977)

- Peter Finch, 60 (1916–1977)
- Betty Grable, 56 (1916–1973)
- Susan Hayward, 57 (1917–1975)
- Veronica Lake, 50 (1922–1973)
- Harold Lloyd, 77 (1893–1971)
- Fredric March, 77 (1897–1975)
- Groucho Marx, 86 (1890–1977)
- Zero Mostel, 62 (1915–1977)
- Merle Oberon, 68 (1911–1979)
- Mary Pickford, 87 (1892–1979)
- Paul Robeson, 77 (1898–1976)
- Edward G. Robinson, 79 (1893–1973)
- Rosalind Russell, 69 (1907–1976)
- Robert Ryan, 63 (1909–1973)
- George Sanders, 65 (1906–1972)
- Gig Young, 64 (1913–1978)

Burnt Offerings

Released: August 1976
Director: Dan Curtis
Stars: Oliver Reed, Karen Black, Bette Davis
Academy Awards: None

PREVIEW: A family rents a mansion where eerie experiences lead to a shocking, tragic climax.

NOW SHOWING: Low Flame

A family moves into a big old-fashioned rural building for a lengthy stay. The father has a typewriter in a writing room. He has nightmares and visions. He abuses his young son. The building is apparently controlling events. There's sudden violence at the end. The father dies, the mother lives. The last shot shows old photos of the building and its former inhabitants, including the father. What is this, *The Shining*? No, *Burnt Offerings* (1976), four years before Stanley Kubrick's horror classic. Unfortunately, *Burnt Offerings* is no classic. It's a slow haunted-house movie with only a few scary moments.

Ben (Oliver Reed), Marian (Karen Black), their son and Ben's elderly aunt (Bette Davis) rent a beautiful mansion for the summer. Upon arrival they're told about an unseen old woman upstairs who never leaves her room, and how "the house takes care of itself" and is "practically immortal." But for the next hour not much happens that's genuinely spooky. A light bulb doesn't work, dad plays too roughly with his son, clocks reset themselves to midnight—nothing memorably sinister, and the house is usually shown with soft, pretty lighting.

Marian's the one who becomes obsessed, possessed, and eventually overdressed. She visits the old lady's room daily, starts wearing vintage clothes and jewelry, and lets her hair go gray. In the movie's second half, after a near-death and a sudden death, Ben realizes the house is inexplicably rejuvenating itself. The big reveal comes when dad slowly enters the now-darkened house and confronts ... a lethal, scary someone (we're not saying). The house itself then dispatches someone else, and pictures of these newly deceased join the photo collection.

Sooooo ... the house is alive? It controls vines that curl around people's legs? Ben's recurring visions of a creepy suspect—all red herrings? Dan Curtis, director of the *Dark Shadows* TV show and movies, leaves these and other questions unanswered and most of the horror unexperienced. He does boast a cast with some pretty impressive credentials, however. Davis won two Oscars in her long career, landlord Eileen Heckart won one, Karen Black and Burgess Meredith were Oscar nominees, and Oliver Reed and Anthony James both played murderers in Best Picture winners, *Oliver!* (1968) and *In the Heat of the Night* (1967), respectively. While they all add gravitas to the proceedings, and while the mansion is undeniably atmospheric, *Burnt Offerings* still doesn't generate much heat.

ADDED ATTRACTION: Go Direct Yourself, Part One

Director Dan Curtis is actually in *Burnt Offerings*. In the last shot of family photographs, one black-and-white photo shows a stern-looking Curtis. Here are additional 1975-1977 movies in which the directors gave themselves small roles. We're not including leading roles, like when Mel Brooks starred in his own *High Anxiety* (1977). For a similar list of 1978-1979 movies, see the entry for *Saint Jack* (1979).

- *A Bridge Too Far* (1977): Richard Attenborough is the bearded "lunatic" seen fifty-five minutes into the movie.
- *End of the World* (1977): John Hayes is the driver of a T-bird that detonates.
- *Family Plot* (1976): Forty minutes in, Alfred Hitchcock's silhouette is seen behind the glass door at the Registrar of Births and Deaths office.
- *The Kentucky Fried Movie* (1977): Seven minutes in, John Landis is one of the crewmembers fighting the gorilla.
- *Oh, God!* (1977): Carl Reiner does a thirty-second bit on Dinah Shore's TV show.
- *Taxi Driver* (1976): The first time we see Cybill Shepherd (white dress, slow-motion), Martin Scorsese is sitting in the background, watching her pass by; later, he's the jealous husband who discusses his murderous plans in Travis's cab.
- *The Wind and the Lion* (1975): Forty-four minutes in, John Milius is the one-armed man next to a machine gun.
- *You Light Up My Life* (1977): Five minutes in, Joseph Brooks gives advice at a TV-commercial audition.

At the Earth's Core

Released: September 1976
Director: Kevin Connor
Stars: Doug McClure, Peter Cushing, Caroline Munro
Academy Awards: None

PREVIEW: Two explorers go into the Earth to caves where monsters rule over primitive people.

NOW SHOWING: Dig It

This movie really makes you appreciate *Star Wars* (1977). *At the Earth's Core* (1976) is closer to bad science-fiction movies of the 1950s (or the dopiest *Star Trek* TV episodes of the 1960s) than the state-of-the-art space epic that premiered just ten months later and quickly overwhelmed the late 1970s.

At the Earth's Core wastes no time revving up. Immediately two Victorian adventurers, a hearty American (Doug McClure) and an old-but-enthusiastic British professor (Peter Cushing) climb into the *Iron Mole*, a "high-calibration digging machine." Like a steampunk rocket angled downward into a rural hill, it bores toward "the bowels of the Earth." However, literally *one minute* into its journey, the ship becomes wildly uncontrollable. Knocked unconscious, both men awake to find themselves thousands of miles below the surface, like the ship navigated on its own. The men emerge into vast caverns with purple skies, oversized plants, and a pig-snouted "sub-human species" that dominates primitive English-speaking human slaves, a la the Morlock/Eloi relationship in H.G. Wells' *The Time Machine*. Ruling all are aggressive winged reptiles that stand uneasily, fly clumsily, and communicate telepathically. Naturally the two explorers lead a revolt that frees the slaves and defeats the monsters. Guiding the *Iron Mole* back home, the men somehow emerge right outside the White House.

That brief summary makes this nonsensical movie sound more coherent than it really is, but *At the Earth's Core* is still as diverting as a good, silly cartoon. There's plenty to giggle at, especially the ludicrous horned creatures that are obviously rubber-suited men stomping around like mini-Godzillas. McClure, looking a little soft, constantly smokes cigars, even while running for his life. Cushing will soon be a dignified Death Star commander in *Star Wars*; here he's a slightly daft professor who tries

Caroline Munro and Doug McClure.

to fend off monsters with his umbrella. Voluptuous Caroline Munro plays, as usual, a tanned princess in skimpy outfits (unfortunately she runs off and is out of the movie for thirty minutes), and the cave dwellers have awesome names like Hoojah the Sly One and Jubal the Ugly One. And when a fire-breathing dinosaur falls off a cliff, it hits bottom and explodes in a fireball. It's the stuff Saturday-matinee dreams are made of. While it may seem ridiculous now, back then *At the Earth's Core* was successful enough to keep alive the mini-streak of 1970s fantasy movies based on Edgar Rice Burroughs' novels (see "Added Attraction").

ADDED ATTRACTION: He's Doug McClure, You May Remember Him from Such Movies as …

Doug McClure's busy 1970s were highlighted by the four entertaining action/adventure movies directed by Kevin Connor. Bracketing *At the Earth's Core* were *The Land That Time Forgot* (1975) and *The People That Time Forgot* (1977), a fun double-feature based on more of Edgar Rice Burroughs' "lost world" books. Set in 1916, *The Land That Time Forgot* has McClure taking command of a German U-boat and finding an uncharted island populated by cave men and big fake-looking dinosaurs. Two years later, *The People That Time Forgot* brings Patrick Wayne and his rescue party to the island in search of the now-bearded McClure (who dies in this sequel); this time the usual prehistoric encounters are supplemented by the addition of a helium-chested cavebabe (Dana Gillespie). Despite crude special effects, both movies offer old-fashioned entertainment that's ideal for your inner ten-year-old. Finally, *Warlords of Atlantis* (1978) moves the *Earth's Core* conceit underwater for another fast-paced fantasy. This time the Victorian scientific investigation leads to a gigantic octopus, monsters, a crew mutiny, and a hostile Martian civilization ruled by … (wait for it) … long-legged Hollywood legend Cyd Charisse! Awesome! Good choice, but bad timing, however, because *The People That Time Forgot* and *Warlords of Atlantis* both came out after *Star Wars*, so both were instantly outdated and outclassed upon arrival.

The Front

Released: September 1976
Director: Martin Ritt
Stars: Woody Allen, Michael Murphy, Zero Mostel
Academy Awards: One nomination (Best Writing)

PREVIEW: To aid blacklisted writers in the 1950s, a man submits TV scripts as if he wrote them.

NOW SHOWING: The Unlikely Hero

The Front (1976) is an entertaining drama directed by an Oscar nominee, Martin Ritt, but everyone remembers this as being the first '70s movie Woody Allen starred in but didn't write or direct. During the decade there were only three years (1970, 1974, and 1976) when the prolific Allen didn't release one of his own movies; it was while he was writing his masterpiece, *Annie Hall* (1977), that he starred in *The Front*.

It's a noble effort worthy of Best Picture consideration. Allen is thoroughly convincing as the Damon Runyon-style character Howard Prince, a street-smart cashier and bookie in 1950s New York. Prince agrees to "front" for his struggling writer friends who've been blacklisted as Communists. Submitting their TV scripts as his own, he gets their work produced, and everybody (including Prince) gets paid. Complications arise when the "practically illiterate" Prince is suddenly asked to rewrite scripts with no help. Prince falls for a pretty script editor (Andrea Marcovicci) who mistakenly thinks he's a brilliant writer, and he befriends a blacklisted comedian (Zero Mostel) who tragically succumbs to despair (his sad death echoes the actual 1958 suicide of blacklisted actor Philip Loeb). Prince wrestles with his conscience before he is forced to testify to an investigating committee in the movie's dramatic climax. Intensifying the message is the participation of numerous stars and filmmakers, including Ritt and Mostel, who actually were blacklisted.

The Front is a significant departure for Allen. Casually amusing and expressing serious concerns, Prince is unlike the frantic, farcical characters Allen had usually played (his previous movie was 1975's hilarious *Love and Death*). The movie's poster emphasizes Allen's different persona by showing him in modern clothes and calling him "America's Most Unlikely Hero." In addition, Allen flagrantly curses in *The Front*, something he'd never done on-screen (he'll drop another F-bomb in 1991's *Scenes from a Mall*, and he'll really let the execrations fly in 1997's *Deconstructing Harry*). *The Front* is also much more somber than Woody's own movies up to this time. He can't stop being funny, obviously, and he seems to have injected some of his own jokes into the script (in a "proper" Connecticut family "the biggest sin was to raise your voice," but in his family "the biggest sin was to buy retail"). Here, though, his humor serves a higher cause. By effectively exposing the viciousness of McCarthyism, *The Front* becomes a powerful, important movie.

ADDED ATTRACTION:
The Front, Annie Hall, and *Manhattan*

The Front has several connections with two of Woody Allen's later classics from the '70s, *Annie Hall* (1977) and *Manhattan* (1979).

- Before *The Front*, Allen's characters didn't drink. For instance, in *Play It Again, Sam* (1972), his character even says his body "cannot tolerate alcohol," and a single sip of bourbon makes him pass out in a bar. Howard Prince casually drinks alcohol in *The Front*, something Allen's characters will do in both *Annie Hall* and *Manhattan*: he'll sip wine with Annie on her roof, and in *Manhattan*'s opening scene he's had so much to drink another character jokingly accuses him of being drunk.
- Near the end of *Annie Hall*, Alvy (Allen) and his date (Sigourney Weaver) are outside the Thalia Theater when they run into Annie (Diane Keaton) and her date, who is played by Walter Bernstein. Bernstein got an Oscar nomination for writing the screenplay for *The Front*.
- In *The Front*, Allen appears alongside actor Michael Murphy for the first time. Murphy would soon co-star in *Manhattan*.
- Blacklisting is incorporated into *Manhattan* when Allen's character chastises Murphy's character inside a classroom late in the movie and mentions "a Senate subcommittee," "naming names," and "informing on your friends."
- Several behind-the-scenes people worked on all three movies, including casting director Juliet Taylor and producers Robert Greenhut, Charles Joffe, and Jack Rollins (all four would work on dozens of Allen's later movies).

Marathon Man

Released: October 1976
Director: John Schlesinger
Stars: Dustin Hoffman, Laurence Olivier, Roy Scheider
Academy Awards: One nomination (Best Supporting Actor—Laurence Olivier)

PREVIEW: An innocent grad student is chased by a vicious Nazi who's been in hiding since 1945.

NOW SHOWING: Run for Your Life

Marathon Man (1976) is a thrilling sprint. Before the movie's mid-point we've witnessed deadly road rage, an exploding bomb, a bloody murder victim, an assassination attempt, and a violent mugging. All this, with an hour of dramatic chases and unforgettable torture scenes still ahead.

"There's something going on here that we don't know about," says a character; viewers could also say that, since they're kept off-balance by seemingly unrelated events. *Marathon Man* is about an elderly Nazi war criminal, Szell (Laurence Olivier), who's trying to abscond with stolen diamonds, and he thinks Babe, the long-distance-running title character (Dustin Hoffman), is in his way. Babe, however, isn't even aware that Szell exists for most of the movie. What happens when they meet is justifiably famous.

Hoffman was thirty playing twenty-two in *The Graduate* (1967); now he's a thirty-nine-year-old graduate student (inflation has affected more than age: in *The Graduate*

Dustin Hoffman.

Ben offers $20 to get a dime for a pay phone, here Babe swaps his Rolex watch). Fully committed to this dynamic role, Hoffman is convincing as a Hitchcock-style innocent who falls for a duplicitous dame (Marthe Keller) and struggles to survive his dangerous situation (committed? he's butt-naked in one scene). Roy Scheider, usually a street-smart cop, makes a French connection as Babe's mysterious, well-dressed brother in Paris who unintentionally leads Szell to Babe. A brutal dentist at Auschwitz, Szell has been hiding in Uruguay in a house full of skulls. Now "the most-wanted Nazi left alive" is in Manhattan and coming for Babe. Intelligent, charming, and sadistic, Szell is a great movie villain, and Olivier delivers one of his most memorable performances (ironically, he'd soon *hunt* Nazis in 1978's *The Boys from Brazil*).

It's impossible not to cringe when Szell performs raw dentistry on Babe. This three-minute scene succeeds through implication—deliberate pacing, Szell's calmly repeated "Is it safe?" question, high-pitched drill sounds—instead of images, which are rather tame (imagine the gory drill-on-tooth close-ups we'd get today). Almost as riveting is the movie's tense, unsettling seven-minute climax, when Babe finally traps and torments Szell until Szell's own avarice defeats him.

Utilizing the new Steadicam, director John Schlesinger moves the story along expertly. He also incorporates flashbacks and black-and-white footage from the 1960 Olympics to underscore Babe's lonely pursuit after he's been abandoned and betrayed. A blockbuster in 1976, the classy-and-compelling *Marathon Man* can still give your nerves a good workout.

ADDED ATTRACTION:
Black-and-White Movies, Part One

It's easy to remember the 1970s as a decade of neon colors and disco lights, but these 1975-1976 movies feature black-and-white cinematography, as *Marathon Man* does in a few scenes. For more black-and-white movies, see the entry for *Eraserhead* (1977).

BLACK-AND-WHITE MOVIES
- *Hester Street* (1975)

COLOR MOVIES WITH BLACK-AND-WHITE SEGMENTS
- *The Bad News Bears* (1976): The last shot is of the black-and-white team photo.
- *The Front* (1976): Black-and-white images fill the opening 1950s montage and are used again in the closing photo.
- *The Great Waldo Pepper* (1975): The opening and closing minutes show nostalgic black-and-white photos.
- *The Hindenburg* (1975): The first three minutes and the last dozen show old newsreels.
- *The Last Tycoon* (1976): The studio's screening room presents scenes from fictional black-and-white movies.
- *Midway* (1976): This color movie includes three minutes from the old black-and-white *Thirty Seconds Over Tokyo* (1944).
- *Network* (1976): Thirty seconds of rough bank-robbing footage are in black and white.
- *The Shootist* (1976): The first minutes show scenes from John Wayne's old black-and-white movies.
- *The Song Remains the Same* (1976): The powerful concert footage and fantasy scenes are interrupted by two minutes of black-and-white scenes showing the crime investigation after the band's hotel safe is burgled.
- *That's Entertainment, Part 2* (1976): The modern narrators (shown in color on MGM's backlot) present favorite clips from the studio's classic black-and-white musicals.

Car Wash

Released: October 1976
Directors: Michael Schultz
Stars: Richard Pryor, Franklyn Ajaye, George Carlin
Academy Awards: None

PREVIEW: A single humorous day in the lives of employees and customers at a busy L.A. car wash.

NOW SHOWING: Workin' at the Car Wash

Car Wash (1976) is often described as a Richard Pryor/George Carlin comedy, and indeed those two brilliant comics dominate DVD covers, even though they're in the movie for only eight and four minutes, respectively. Among the dozens of other performers who appear are Franklyn Ajaye (sporting the decade's biggest Afro), Garrett Morris from TV's *SNL*, Professor Irwin Corey, football star Otis Sistrunk, and the director's wife and son. It's fun picking out familiar faces from other movies: "Look, the lady from *Jaws*! A guy from *The Sting*! The *Animal House* singer! Those two die in *Predator* and *Scarface*!" In one of the best scenes, the Pointer Sisters show up and sing (great funk music fills the Grammy-winning soundtrack, and the theme song was a number-one hit). The eclectic cast is offbeat and entertaining—as one employee says toward the end, "There's been some weird people in here today."

Nearly everything takes place on a single day at the Dee-Luxe Car Wash near downtown L.A. Most of the characters are energetic employees who play pranks when they're not washing cars. Other characters come to get their cars washed or conduct other business (a hooker turns the bathroom into her personal dressing room for half the movie, for instance). Much of the comedy is juvenile—machines soaking a worker, a kid barfing inside a car, etc. Pryor (one long scene) and Carlin (several brief, seemingly improvised appearances) deliver laughs when they roll in, but the cleverest joke comes at dusk when three guys reprise the slaves' "quittin' time" bit from *Gone with the Wind* (1939). There are a few serious moments, too—some revolutionary talk, an arrest, an after-hours robbery—plus racist and profane language, but director Michael Schultz, who made the well-received *Cooley High* (1975), generally keeps things light, likeable and mainstream.

Richard Pryor.

So is it funny? Many viewers and critics thought so in 1976; we were frequently amused but waited in vain for the movie to soar. *Car Wash* is reminiscent of Robert Altman's ensemble movies, a comparison that's invited when the closing-credit announcements are almost exactly like the ones that conclude Altman's *M*A*S*H* (1970). While it's not great, *Car Wash* is still a fascinating cultural artifact that preserves the decade's "hang loose" and "get down" lingo, fast radio-DJ patter, imposing platform shoes, colorful leisure suits, awesome cars, and fifty-nine-cents-a-gallon gas prices. Those memories alone are worth the price of admission.

ADDED ATTRACTION: Pryor the Workin' Man

The two star comedians in *Car Wash* took different career paths after this movie came out. George Carlin narrated the oddball satire *Americathon* (1979) but was otherwise off the big screen until the late '80s. In contrast, Richard Pryor was in movies all decade long, including two 1977 comedies—*Greased Lightning* and *Which Way Is Up?*—made by *Car Wash*'s director, Michael Schultz. Pryor's best work, however, was in *Blue Collar* (1978), a tough, realistic crime drama co-written and directed by Paul Schrader, the screenwriter of *Taxi Driver* (1976). A year before *Norma Rae* (1979) enthusiastically advocated labor unions, *Blue Collar* shows that unions, when they're headed by the wrong people, can be just as harmful to employees as the bad management they're supposed to be confronting. In *Blue Collar*, three frustrated automobile-plant workers (Pryor, Harvey Keitel, and Yaphet Kotto) steal a ledger that reveals widespread corruption in their union. Their misguided attempt to execute a muddled blackmail scheme leads to violence and murder. Keitel and Kotto are strong, but it's Pryor, erupting with rage and profanities in most of his scenes, who is the mighty engine that powers this hard-hitting movie.

The Song Remains the Same

Released: October 1976
Directors: Peter Clifton, Joe Massot
Stars: Robert Plant, Jimmy Page, John Bonham
Academy Awards: None

PREVIEW: Fantasy sequences are mixed with footage of Led Zeppelin's concert performances.

NOW SHOWING: Stairway to Zeppelin

For years fans could experience Led Zeppelin only through their powerful live shows or epic albums. This band wasn't the Beatles, putting out feature-length movies and a cartoon TV show. Like remote gods coming down to play for the masses, Led Zeppelin was either onstage, on your turntable, or on holiday. Thus *The Song Remains the Same* (1976) is a valuable, if inconsistent artifact presenting these legendary heavy-metal pioneers in their prime.

The movie's main problem is evident immediately. It starts with a pretentious fantasy sequence about the band's *manager*, Peter Grant, who leads a 1930s-style gangland slaying that includes a werewolf and a silly decapitation. The movie then gathers the four band members one at a time from their British estates and delivers them to New York's Madison Square Garden.

John Bonham.

Thirteen minutes in, the concert commences with live footage compiled from three 1973 Garden performances. The eleven songs are supplemented with lighting effects, fog machines, and even explosions during the "Whole Lotta Love" finale. Some spacy visuals (a spinning camera, psychedelic color filters, etc.) create you-are-there-and-you-are-extremely-high effects, but mostly the routine camera work captures musician close-ups, wide-angle views of the stage, and shots of enraptured fans. The band is in its *Houses of the Holy* glory, but at this particular moment in time it's not at its best as it finishes a long, exhausting tour. Nevertheless, Jimmy Page's fingers fly; John Bonham's drums thunder; Robert Plant's kielbasa-stuffed pants thrust spasmodically and his hands flit about like he's signing; and versatile bassist/keyboardist John Paul Jones pretty much stays in the background. Regrettably, there's virtually no interaction with the audience, and the *twenty-nine-minute* "Dazed and Confused" is interminable, giving movie viewers time to go grab a bite.

Unfortunately, bizarre, self-indulgent fantasy sequences overlap the music: Jones with ghoulish horseback riders; Plant looking ridiculous with a sword and castle; Page climbing a mountain to meet Obi-Wan Kenobi; Bonham, more genuine as a regular guy on his farm and in various vehicles. We also get some backstage scenes, notably with Grant bullying the promoter, plus a black-and-white sequence involving a real robbery at the group's hotel. To devotees, interesting; to anyone else, inessential. Remove everything but the actual concert to get a solid musical keepsake for the time capsule. Sorry Zepheads, but for a better 1970s concert movie focused strictly on the music, *Ladies and Gentlemen: The Rolling Stones* (1974) still tops the charts.

ADDED ATTRACTION: More Music

Earlier that same year, two other movies showcased music very different from Led Zeppelin's majestic arena rock. *The Blank Generation* (1976) is a curious fifty-five-minute experiment that's possibly the decade's homeliest home movie. Grainy, jittery black-and-white footage shot inside New York nightclubs documents the city's emerging punk scene, giving musicologists early looks at Patti Smith, the Ramones, the Talking Heads, Blondie, and others. Because images were captured without sound, a rough soundtrack was added later. The visuals, however, aren't synchronized with the songs we're actually hearing, so we what we see compared to what we hear is way off, like we're watching very bad lip-syncing. Even if the results are amateurish, *The Blank Generation* is still compelling because of all the baby-faced stars we're seeing at the start of their careers. Meanwhile, *That's Entertainment, Part 2* (1976) modifies the pattern established in the popular 1974 original. Instead of eleven different stars as narrators, here two legends (Gene Kelly and Fred Astaire) briefly introduce joyous scenes from MGM's greatest movies, mostly musicals but some non-musicals, too (the Tracy/Hepburn movies, famous scenes with the Marx Bros., etc.). The new Kelly/Astaire numbers that were made for the movie look weak compared to the amazing clips (and some of the new rhymes they work into familiar songs are real groaners), but otherwise this is a worthy successor, which isn't something you can always say about sequels.

Carrie

(One of 1976's five **FAR-OUT** movies)

Released: November 1976

Director: Brian De Palma

Stars: Sissy Spacek, Piper Laurie, Nancy Allen

Academy Awards: Two nominations (Best Actress—Sissy Spacek; Best Supporting Actress—Piper Laurie)

PREVIEW: A shy high school girl uses telekinetic powers to destroy those who humiliated her.

FINE LINE: "It has nothing to do with Satan, mama. It's me. *Me*. If I concentrate hard enough, I can move things." (Carrie's response to her mother's accusations.)

CLOSE-UP: Did you catch the name of Carrie's school? Bates High, an obvious reference to Norman Bates, the deranged killer played by Anthony Perkins in *Psycho* (1960). See "Added Attraction" for another 1976 movie with *Psycho* connections.

NOW SHOWING: Scary *Carrie*

Carrie (1976) is a movie of firsts. In 1974 *Carrie* was the first of dozens of Stephen King novels to be published, and it was his first work to transition to the big screen (not yet famous, his name was misspelled as "Steven King" in *Carrie*'s trailer). For Brian De Palma, director of *Sisters* (1972) and *Phantom of the Paradise* (1974), *Carrie* represented his first real mainstream success. Playing the leading role of a socially awkward teenager, Sissy Spacek earned the first of six Oscar nominations in her long career. *Carrie* also scored an Oscar nomination for Piper Laurie, returning to the big screen after fifteen years away. The movie marks Amy Irving's, Betty Buckley's, and P.J. Soles' movie debuts, and it gave John Travolta a villainous part in the first hit of his nascent movie career.

Audiences in 1976 didn't care about notable firsts. What made *Carrie* a smash hit, and why it still delivers such a strong impact, is its tremendous fright factor. In the horror genre, cinematic atmosphere, not theatrical dialogue, makes a great movie, and in *Carrie* De Palma excels at creating and sustaining an atmosphere of impending terror. People don't remember lines from *Carrie*, just its indelible images. Viewers hold their breath as they watch the late scene when Carrie, soaked in blood after the prom massacre, slowly walks up the front steps of her house, its windows lit in orange, and cautiously enters rooms illuminated by hundreds of candles, knowing the lone, menacing inhabitant is lurking somewhere. Throughout the movie De Palma confidently blends dark themes (the disturbing religious rantings by Carrie's mother), universal emotions (every teen's feeling of being ostracized at school and misunderstood at home), apocalyptic imagery (the hellish red light as flames erupt around Carrie at the prom), scary music (shrieking violins reminiscent of *Psycho*), distinctive visuals (long tracking shots, split-screen), and some inspired casting (especially Spacek and Laurie) to create what was quickly recognized as a modern horror classic.

An unfortunate first begins the movie when shy, fragile Carrie has her first menstrual period while she's naked in a school shower, a sight that evokes derisive laughter from the other students (they won't be laughing when blood completely shrouds Carrie near the movie's end). Not only is this daring shower scene probably the first time menstruation is shown in a major movie, but the scene occurs right up front in the first four minutes, in slow-motion, and under bright lights. *Carrie*, we immediately realize, is going to be a different kind of horror movie.

Carrie responds to her taunting classmates with what's apparently the first exhibition of her strange gift—the ceiling light explodes. Soon she's making an ashtray fly off a desk and a cruel kid fall off his bike. But it's not just Carrie's ability that's important; it's Carrie herself, the sad victim who has "always been their scapegoat" and who is traumatized at home for things that aren't her fault (her mother, for example, blames Carrie for getting her period). No wonder this frightened, abused girl carries herself with closed-in body language and speaks with a timid voice, like something is always about to pounce on her. Because Spacek makes Carrie so convincingly lonely, vulnerable, and damaged, we can watch her claim revenge without judging her as a mindless monster.

Sissy Spacek.

The movie steadily builds in suspense through its first half as Carrie applies her mental ability to control objects. Grasping for understanding, she finds a real book by Max Freedom Long called *The Secret Science Behind Miracles* and reads a passage that defines telekinesis as "the ability to move or cause changes in objects by force of the mind," thus clarifying and naming her abilities for the audience. Early suspense becomes late shock when Carrie suddenly (and scarily) asserts her powers at full force, memorably destroying the school gym from the stage, causing a car to flip on the street, and finally sending a squadron of sharp kitchen implements flying at her deranged, dangerous mother. De Palma changes King's ending by limiting Carrie's destruction to the school, a car, and her house (the book has her destroying the entire town). De Palma also adds a famous heart-stopping coda in which Carrie suddenly reaches from the grave, a nightmarish scene perhaps developed from a much shorter hand-rising-from-the-river dream at the end of *Deliverance* (1972). De Palma, a flamboyant stylist to the end, adds flourishes to this whole last sequence to make it even more dreamlike and bizarre. Ninety-four minutes into the movie, note that as Sue (Amy Irving) walks forward on the sidewalk in slow-motion, the two cars far behind her are driving in reverse.

In Hollywood, *Carrie*'s impact was immediate. The bloody *Carrie* movie poster was quickly emulated by the poster for *Ruby* (1977), and it's shown fifty-nine minutes into David Cronenberg's *Rabid* (1977); *Jennifer* (1978), where a teen uses her psychic powers to get revenge on school bullies, is an obvious *Carrie* clone; and Carol Burnett's character actually mentions *Carrie* in Robert Altman's *A Wedding* (1978). A *Carrie* sequel, remakes, parodies and homages have appeared in movie theaters, on Broadway, and on TV for decades now. Stylish, intense, and still one of the few horror movies to get Oscar recognition, *Carrie* works as effectively on audiences now as it did then, and it always will so long as people experience, or can remember, feeling alienated as teenagers.

ADDED ATTRACTION: Psycho, Sweet Psycho

In November 1976, with *Carrie* starting its long successful run in theaters, another horror movie about a scary young girl premiered. *Alice, Sweet Alice* (aka *Communion*) is not the milestone that *Carrie* is, but director Alfred Sole effectively combines elements of scary classics into a tense slasher movie. Pre-teen Brooke Shields, in her big-screen debut, plays a schoolgirl who gets strangled eleven minutes into the story. For the next suspenseful hour everyone tries to discover who the killer is. Various clues make twelve-year-old Alice (Paula Sheppard) the likeliest suspect, especially because she and the killer both have an eerie mask and identical raincoats. Alice is similar to the wicked prankster in *The Bad Seed* (1956): she's a "weird little girl" with "deep-seated problems" who causes trouble at school and "has a knack of making things look like accidents." Alice is suspected again when someone in that same mask-and-raincoat combo stabs her aunt repeatedly. However, midway through the movie Alice disappears for twenty-six minutes, and while she's gone the real killer is revealed. Two more victims die before a shocking final scene that shows Alice at her creepiest. There's a lot of extended screaming and shrieking in this movie. Blood, too, as several close-up killings involve a big kitchen knife, just like in *Psycho* (1960); reinforcing the *Psycho* connection, eighty-six minutes into *Alice, Sweet Alice* we actually glimpse a *Psycho* poster, and a white 1957 Ford Custom features prominently in both movies. *Alice* goes farther than *Psycho* in terms of violence, however, especially when one victim has his teeth bashed in just before he's shoved from a building to his death.

Network

(One of 1976's five **FAR-OUT** movies)

Released: November 1976

Director: Sidney Lumet

Stars: Peter Finch, William Holden, Faye Dunaway

Academy Awards: Four wins (Best Actor—Peter Finch; Best Actress—Faye Dunaway; Best Supporting Actress—Beatrice Straight; Best Writing), plus six more nominations (Best Picture; Best Actor—William Holden; Best Supporting Actor—Ned Beatty; Best Director; Best Cinematography; Best Editing)

PREVIEW: To get higher ratings, network executives radically reformat their evening news.

FINE LINE: "All I want out of life is a thirty share and a twenty rating." (Diana Christiansen, admitting that she is "inept at everything, except my work.")

CLOSE-UP: Twenty-three minutes into *Network*, a woman on the programming team pitches three new shows. This scene reveals screenwriter Paddy Chayefsky's general opinion of TV, since all three shows lead with the same character—"a crusty but benign ex-Supreme Court Justice," "a crusty but benign police lieutenant," and "a crusty but benign managing editor."

NOW SHOWING: Number One in the Ratings

Other than *The China Syndrome* (1979), which showed a nuclear accident two weeks before the Three Mile Island accident actually happened, was any 1970s movie more prescient than *Network* (1976)? What seemed at the time to be a completely outrageous satirical premise has by now actually come to pass. *All the President's Men* (1976), the other contender for the title of "The Year's Most Intelligent Movie," elucidates the recent past; *Network* brilliantly anticipates the next forty years of American television.

Network starts by exploring the inner workings of a TV network, but by the end of the movie it's clear the "network" is really the mutual interdependence between all people and international conglomerates through the relentless exchange of dollars precipitated by television programming. *We* are the network, and television, we're literally told, "destroys everything." Thought, feeling, and "simple human decency" have been sacrificed in the name of television, especially the kind of reality TV (the "angry shows") that *Network* invents. "Woe is us, we're in a lot of trouble," an impassioned newscaster warns in the movie, "because less than three percent of you people read books! Because less than fifteen percent of you read newspapers! Because the only truth you know is what you get over this tube! ... This tube can make or break presidents!" That's in 1976; it's as startling as if a 1930s movie had accurately described the 1970s gas crisis.

Network's complicated story unfolds through three main characters: an idealistic head of the news division who rose from TV's early, innocent years, Max Schumacher (William Holden); an icy young programmer who is "television generation," Diana Christiansen (Faye Dunaway); and a silvered anchorman taking one last stab at significance, Howard Beale (Peter Finch). In the first three minutes, Schumacher and Beale are two drunken news-department buddies bandying ideas for better TV ratings, including a live suicide on national TV and ludicrous shows like *Terrorist of the Week*. Christiansen, a headstrong entertainment programmer, makes their sarcastic suggestions real. "The American people are turning sullen. They've been clobbered on all sides by Vietnam, Watergate, the inflation, the depression ... and nothing helps," she declares. "The American people want somebody to articulate their rage for them." Willing to "violate every canon of respectable broadcasting," she exploits Beale as "The Mad Prophet of the Airways" who forcefully inveighs "against the hypocrisies of our times." Punctuating his raving editorials is his famous command for all Americans to scream from their windows, "I'm as mad as hell, and I'm not going to take this anymore!" Soon, however, Beale really does become unstable as he hears voices and walks the streets in his pajamas. By the end of the movie, with his ratings slipping and his lectures about "dying democracy and dehumanization" too gloomy, inevitably Christiansen asks, "What would you fellows say to an assassination?" A stunning climax, and a ratings hit, are forthcoming.

Network pulls together various elements, including a terrorist group, corporate maneuverings, Schumacher's fling with Christiansen, and the break-up of Schumacher's marriage, with power and plausibility. Paddy Chayefsky nimbly constructed one of the decade's most audacious but perfect screenplays, and the movie won him his third screenwriting Oscar. *Network* whips from one show-stopping highlight to the next, among them Beale's first televised rant in which he says his signature phrase five times in a minute, inciting a city-wide cacophony; the three-minute seduction-and-bedroom sequence in which Christiansen starts talking nonstop on the beach and continues right through dinner and sex; and Schumacher's last confrontations with Christiansen in which he exposes her hollow soul. In some ways *Network*

Peter Finch.

is like Chayefsky's earlier Oscar-winner, *The Hospital* (1971), where George C. Scott's raging director of a dysfunctional hospital had screamed "We heal nothing!" out his office window and contemplated suicide. *Network* even anticipates Chayefsky's next hit, *Altered States* (1980), with its cosmic themes and elevated vocabulary (Chayefsky challenges *Network*'s viewers to keep up with rapid-fire dialogue that includes words like auspicatory, oraculate, misprision, peccant, immane, and adamantine, so study up). It's obvious that Chayefsky has done his homework; we sense his *Network* characters are speaking knowledgeably when they review Q scores, argue subsidiary rights, and mention people like Patty Hearst, Eric Sevareid, Mary Tyler Moore, and James Caan.

Director Sidney Lumet eschews an emotional music score and instead underlines the movie's drama with lighting and staging. For example, when the network head (Ned Beatty) lectures Beale about global commerce, the presentation in a darkened conference room comes out like an over-the-top hell-fire sermon. As Schumacher's betrayed wife (Beatrice Straight) sobs to her cheating husband, she turns from the camera, suggesting her raw pain would be too unbearable for us to see (think of it—in one of the movie's most riveting scenes, she's acting part of it with her *back*). Titanic performances are everywhere: Straight wins an Oscar, though she's in the movie for only about five minutes; Dunaway also wins as the cold-blooded Christiansen (asked about restaurants, she says she "will eat anything," and indeed she devours everyone in her path); Robert Duvall, no longer the quiet background *consigliere* from the *Godfather* movies, is a loud, abrasive executive. A master class in acting, *Network* is the only movie besides *From Here to Eternity* (1953) to have five Oscar nominations for its actors and actresses. *Network* should be treated reverently like that; profound and prophetic, daring and disturbing, it's one of the decade's great landmarks.

ADDED ATTRACTION: Famous Film Quotes

Network's "I'm mad as hell" line is ranked nineteenth on the American Film Institute's list called "AFI'S 100 Greatest Movie Quotes of All Time." Here are nine other famous quotes from 1975-1979 movies that made the AFI list. The 1970s, incidentally, have five quotes in the top thirteen, more than any other decade (only one other decade, the 1950s, has as many as three quotes in the top thirteen). AFI's number-one quote comes from *Gone with the Wind* (1939): "Frankly, my dear, I don't give a damn."

- AFI #8, *Star Wars* (1977): "May the Force be with you."
- AFI #10, *Taxi Driver* (1976): "You talkin' to me?"
- AFI #12, *Apocalypse Now* (1979): "I love the smell of napalm in the morning."
- AFI #35, *Jaws* (1975): "You're gonna need a bigger boat."
- AFI #55, *Annie Hall* (1977): "La-dee-da, la-dee-da."
- AFI #70, *Marathon Man* (1976): "Is it safe?"
- AFI #80, *Rocky* (1976): "Yo, Adrian!"
- AFI #82, *Animal House* (1978): "Toga! Toga!"
- AFI #86, *Dog Day Afternoon* (1975): "Attica! Attica!"

The Last Tycoon

Released: November 1976
Director: Elia Kazan
Stars: Robert De Niro, Tony Curtis, Robert Mitchum
Academy Awards: One nomination (Best Art Direction)

PREVIEW: In the 1930s, the head of a big movie studio becomes obsessed with a secretive woman.

NOW SHOWING: Stahr Search

After the box-office success of *The Great Gatsby* (1974), Paramount must have thought it had the formula knocked: put a hot star in an F. Scott Fitzgerald story about a doomed romance in glamorous surroundings, and watch those dollars flow in. Unfortunately, *The Last Tycoon* (1976) is so boring that many critics derided it, audiences ignored it, and the few viewers it had probably ran straight from *Tycoon* to saloon.

That's a shame, because this prestige picture had real potential. Two-time Oscar-winner Elia Kazan directed it (it's his last movie); nine months after his blood-soaked breakthrough in *Taxi Driver* (1976), Robert De Niro goes formal, wearing glasses, suits, and a tux as the well-spoken head of a 1930s movie studio; Hollywood heavyweights Robert Mitchum, Tony Curtis, Dana Andrews, and Jack Nicholson play important roles, and John Carradine and Anjelica Huston have cameos. The story follows smart, solemn Monroe Stahr (De Niro), a fictional Hollywood producer similar to MGM's Irving Thalberg (like Thalberg, Stahr is called a "boy wonder"). Stahr deals with studio troubles—a minor earthquake, labor issues, a disastrous director, a self-absorbed leading lady, a dashing actor with personal problems—while simultaneously obsessing over a mysterious beauty who's the only person *not* interested in movies. She's played by lovely-but-bland ex-model Ingrid Boulting, whose palette of dramatic colors runs the gamut from light-brown to beige. The fiery combustion of her and Stahr's scenes together could incinerate an entire postage stamp.

Fitzgerald died before he finished the novel, which stops after a fistfight between Stahr and Nicholson's character. Fitzgerald's notes suggest that half the story, including a murder and Stahr's plane-crash death, was still ahead. The fistfight comes late in the movie, and the lackluster ending has Stahr walking alone into a darkened sound stage. The best scenes come much earlier at the studio, where Stahr's movie screenings and interactions with executives ring true (*Gatsby* cagily concealed the hero's actual job, but *Tycoon* indulges in it). Thirty-eight minutes into the movie Stahr delivers a one-man-performance of an invented movie scene, and it's riveting. Also good is the ten-minute sequence matching De Niro against Nicholson, the only time these two titans are in the same feature film. And visually the movie is undeniably impressive. But big stars, Oscar-nominated visuals, and a few interesting moments can't rouse this 123-minute snoozarama. Stahr says movies are "my life"; *The Last Tycoon* is more like "my still-life."

ADDED ATTRACTION:
Nostalgia's Not What It Used to Be

Studios binged on Hollywood nostalgia in 1976. In addition to *The Last Tycoon*, other fictional movies about the early days of filmmaking included spring's *Won Ton Ton, The Dog Who Saved Hollywood* and winter's *Nickelodeon*. Directed by Michael Winner, *Won Ton Ton* tells the story of a Rin Tin Tin-style movie dog in the 1920s; Madeline Kahn stars, but the main fun is identifying the Hollywood legends who make cameo appearances (Dorothy Lamour, Ann Miller, Johnny Weissmuller, and many, many more fill a long, impressive list). Meanwhile, Peter Bogdanovich's *Nickelodeon* pairs Ryan O'Neal and Burt Reynolds in a stylish, affectionate comedy about the pre-1920s era when movies were short, silent, seat-of-the-pants productions. Of the two, *Nickelodeon* is better, but neither movie is exceptional, and neither was a hit. For some semi-biographical movies about *real* stars from yesteryear, see the entry for *Gable and Lombard* (1976).

Rocky

(One of 1976's five **FAR-OUT** movies)

Released: November 1976

Director: John G. Avildsen

Stars: Sylvester Stallone, Talia Shire, Burgess Meredith

Academy Awards: Three wins (Best Picture; Best Director; Best Editing), plus seven more nominations (Best Actor—Sylvester Stallone; Best Actress—Talia Shire; two for Best Supporting Actor—Burgess Meredith, Burt Young; Best Writing; Best Sound; Best Song)

PREVIEW: An unknown boxer gets a chance to prove himself in a bout with the heavyweight champ.

FINE LINE: "She's got gaps, I got gaps, together we fill gaps." (Rocky, giving Paulie a simple but eloquent rationalization for his relationship with Adrian.)

CLOSE-UP: Ninety-seven minutes into the movie, Rocky expresses his deepest feelings just before the fight. "All I wanna do is go the distance … I'm gonna know for the first time in my life, see, that I weren't just another bum from the neighborhood." Watch closely; for seventy seconds Stallone delivers his heartfelt lines without blinking.

NOW SHOWING: Gonna Fly Now

And boom! goes the dynamite. It took an explosive movie to defeat *All the President's Men* (1976), *Network* (1976), and *Taxi Driver* (1976) for Best Picture. But *Rocky* (1976) blew away those three classics to reign not only as Best Picture but also as the year's biggest box-office hit. At a time when America was exhausted by the Vietnam War and Watergate, *Rocky* provided a powerful blast of heart and hope by showing one man's noble fight to prove himself, not by winning, but by simply enduring against impossible odds. And while many other '70s movies were filled with cynical anti-heroes, violent shootings, noisy car crashes, R-rated lust and ugly profanity, the hero of *Rocky* wages his fight without guns, cars, sex scenes, and swearing. Rocky Balboa's struggle is old-fashioned, but his triumph felt like a breath of fresh air.

Hollywood had been making boxing movies for decades. The long list ranges from dramas starring William Holden, Errol Flynn, Kirk Douglas, and Paul Newman to comedies starring Charlie Chaplin, Danny Kaye, Mickey Rooney, and Elvis Presley. And there had already been two good boxing movies in the 1970s, *The Great White Hope* (1970) and *Fat City* (1972). All these movies, however, starred established, even iconic actors; *Rocky* cast a virtual unknown as its pugilist, so the movie's David-vs.-Goliath story of an underdog boxer challenging the world's heavyweight champion paralleled the real-life story of an underdog writer/actor trying to succeed in Hollywood. Sylvester Stallone talks in the DVD special features about the theme of "unrealized dreams" because people "didn't get that shot." That sounds like Stallone himself, since he could've sold his *Rocky* script for over a quarter-million dollars right when he was flat broke, but he held out until he could also star in it, deciding he had "to roll the dice" on his one big break. He did; it was. History.

With Stallone perfectly embodying the uneducated, self-effacing longshot, *Rocky* became a beloved, crowd-pleasing classic. How could anyone root against a totally guileless bruiser who helps local kids, talks to small pets, and counsels debtors as he collects their payments to a loan shark? Even when he wins the first bloody fight, he earns only $40.55 and walks home alone through trashy streets to his run-down room. Throughout the movie he's called a bum (he admits he's "at least half a bum"), and he's so humble that when he's offered a fight against the heavyweight champ, he turns it down. When he finally accepts this "chance of a lifetime," he sheepishly offers his only strategy: "I guess I'll have to do the best I can."

Sylvester Stallone.

Besides giving us an engaging hero to cheer for,

the movie presents an endearing love story that makes us jump to Rocky's side. He's the only one who sees something special in shy, fragile Adrian, and by the end she's blossomed from a meek wallflower into an attractive, vital ally (significantly, for awhile she's the only one who believes he might win). The way Stallone the screenwriter skillfully weaves a love story into his glove story is one of his best achievements.

Once the "novelty" match is set midway through the movie—the opponent is well-muscled champion Apollo Creed (Carl Weathers), a rhyming Muhammad Ali-style showman—Rocky begins training in earnest, further drawing the audience into his corner. While the confident Creed makes business deals, Rocky's up at 4:00 a.m., gulping down raw eggs and running alone in the dark. We're with him as he punches sides of beef in the meat locker, strains through one-arm pushups, and sprints up the seventy-two steps of the Philadelphia Museum of Art as the "Gonna Fly Now" music swells (these training scenes look authentic—not many actors could match Stallone's performance). All that's needed is the stereotypical last-second victory to complete the optimistic tale.

Here the movie upends our expectations. After a long, bloody fight in which announcers declare that Rocky has taken "a tremendous beating," both boxers "look like they've been in a war," and this has been "the greatest exhibition of boxing stamina in the history of the ring," the good guy ... fails? Yes, but like the lovable losers in *The Bad News Bears* (1976), the Bad News Bum wins respect, plus Adrian's love. We remember hearing thunderous cheers in the theater at the climax—the next time audiences had a rousing response like this, the Death Star was blowing up in *Star Wars* (1977).

Director John Avildsen won that year's Oscar for his daring choices. One of these was to use the just-invented Steadicam to run smoothly alongside Rocky as he trains and then to circle around the fighters in the ring, capturing views no spectator can get. In addition, Avildsen makes Philadelphia look grey, freezing, and bleak, like it's another opponent to beat (the story spans six cold weeks from mid-November to January 1st). He ends the movie by famously freezing the last shot at the absolute celebratory pinnacle of Rocky's life; then, surprisingly, as the credits roll he plays elegant orchestral music, not the martial-trumpets-into-battle theme, thus underlining the tender love story and the artfulness of this violent sport.

No wonder the character would live on, through sequels and as everyone's definition of an enthusiastic upstart. Rocky isn't just a boxer, or just a man. By now he's a folk hero. And *Rocky* isn't merely an exultant movie; it's durable mythology.

ADDED ATTRACTION: Rocky Junior

Sylvester Stallone made an underwhelming directing debut with *Paradise Alley* (1978), another movie about a violent sport (wrestling) that he wrote and stars in (he even belts out the theme song, something you've got to hear once—and only once—in your lifetime). Stallone improved with his next directorial effort, the inevitable *Rocky II* (1979). Again written by and starring Stallone, *Rocky II* starts moments after the first movie's final fight. Soon Rocky marries Adrian, blows his winnings, and fails as an actor in commercials, so he signs for a rematch with Apollo Creed. His half-hearted training borders on parody when he tries to get "demon speed" by comically chasing a live chicken around. Domestic melodrama takes over when Adrian has a baby (Rocky Junior) and goes into a coma, leaving Rocky to read aloud to her, write a poem, and pray beside her in the hospital. She awakens in time for him to restart his training, which means more one-arm pushups and another up-the-steps sprint, this time trailing a cheering army of kids. Superfight II incorporates slow-motion, more gore, and an exciting double-knockdown ending that puts both fighters on the canvas simultaneously and then draws out the ten-second count for fifty-five seconds before one of them finally staggers up to claim victory. As sequels go, it's no champ, but it's no bum, either.

Silver Streak

Released: December 1976
Director: Arthur Hiller
Stars: Gene Wilder, Jill Clayburgh, Richard Pryor
Academy Awards: One nomination (Best Sound)

PREVIEW: A passenger on board a train meets a woman and becomes entangled in a murder mystery.

NOW SHOWING: All Aboard!

If *Silver Streak* (1976) weren't so utterly enjoyable, it might be criticized for being too long and too absurd. Instead, *Silver Streak*, which was a box-office hit, is fondly remembered as an entertaining action/comedy/romance. Screenwriter Colin Higgins, who wrote *Harold and Maude* (1971), here reveals a playful affection for Alfred Hitchcock's movies. Imagine the sixteen-minute train sequence in Hitchcock's great *North by Northwest* (1959) as the basis for an entire thriller; that's *Silver Streak*, where a meek train passenger (Gene Wilder) is drawn into a murder mystery that doesn't end until the last stop. The two movies have much in common: both trains are headed to Chicago and make an unscheduled stop; Wilder plays George Caldwell, a name echoing Hitchcock's George Kaplan, who meets a pretty, flirty blonde (Jill Clayburgh) who's analogous to Hitchcock's Eva Marie Saint character; both women work for the villain; both leading men hold the murder weapon and are accused of murder; both movies have a British villain, a professor, and a biplane; both show a bad guy stepping on fingers to precipitate a fall. The villain's demise in *Silver Streak* recalls *Shadow of a Doubt* (1943), where Hitchcock's evildoer falls from one train into the path of another.

Typically Hitchcock's thrillers have a "MacGuffin," an elusive, desirable object. In *North by Northwest* it's microfilm, and in *Silver Streak* it's "the Rembrandt letters" that will expose art forgeries, but in both

Gene Wilder.

movies the excitement about finding the item is secondary to the fun of watching the characters have adventures. In *Young Frankenstein* (1974) and *The Adventure of Sherlock Holmes' Smarter Brother* (1975) Wilder's characters frequently yelled, but here he gives Caldwell sweet, intelligent charm. Clayburgh is a *femme* without the *fatale*, she's simply appealing. Richard Pryor enters midway through as a likeable thief who injects street-smart comedy into the movie; the show-stopping scene where he camouflages Caldwell so he can pass for black was always slightly uncomfortable yet is still indisputably funny (the strong Wilder/Pryor chemistry would continue in three more movies). The last main character is the train itself, a gleaming luxury ride through scenic vistas that's like one continuous train-travel commercial.

In the last ten minutes that train becomes a hurtling runaway. Surprisingly, it isn't stopped by some stereotypical just-in-time rescue and instead plows into the station for a glorious minute of slow-motion destruction. It's a terrific climax that even Hitchcock didn't dare try.

ADDED ATTRACTION: Hitchcock's Exit

Silver Streak, a pseudo-Hitchcock movie, is superior to that year's actual Hitchcock movie. *Family Plot* (1976) is supposed to be a fun thriller, but this talky movie offers little fun and, surprisingly for "the master of suspense," few thrills. The slow-to-unfold plot follows two couples working separate criminal schemes until their paths cross, leading to a weak final-act confrontation. Bruce Dern tries hard, Barbara Harris is engaging (as always), and the one exciting highlight—a '66 Mustang's three-minute careen down a mountain road—is tense and amusing, but everything else feels low-budget and lazy. There are lame coincidences, a ludicrous kidnapping in a packed church, and dumb mistakes, like a kidnapper stupidly opening a car door so her drugged victim can fall out right in front of a key witness. The final knowing wink into the camera isn't charming, it's unearned, and Hitchcock's last movie isn't delightful, it's tedious. For good '70s Hitchcock, see *Frenzy* (1972).

Bound for Glory

Released: December 1976

Director: Hal Ashby

Stars: David Carradine, Ronny Cox, Melinda Dillon

Academy Awards: Two wins (Best Cinematography; Best Music), plus four more nominations (Best Picture; Best Writing; Best Costume Design; Best Editing)

PREVIEW: Woody Guthrie ambles through the west and becomes known for his sincere folk songs.

NOW SHOWING: These Songs Are Your Songs

Bound for Glory (1976) is an accomplished two-hour movie that unfortunately stretches to two-and-a-half hours. A fictionalized version of Woody Guthrie's rise from aimless, unknown sign painter to American folk hero, the movie has scenes where little happens besides Guthrie (David Carradine) walking down highways, Guthrie singing softly, Guthrie walking through towns, Guthrie playing his harmonica quietly, Guthrie walking by fields, Guthrie strumming a guitar, and Guthrie walking some more. For variety, he sometimes rides on trains or in the back of trucks. Twenty-one minutes into the movie

David Carradine.

a colossal dust storm sweeps across the plains like a tidal wave, a sequence that's undeniably powerful, and later Guthrie gets into some fights, but these dramatic moments punctuate periods of relative inactivity that challenge viewers to stay engaged.

Bound for Glory has much to recommend, however. Throughout the movie the period details perfectly evoke time and place. Next, top billing in the opening titles goes to cinematographer Haskell Wexler, for good reason. Shot to emphasize the browns of the bleak, dusty Depression Era, his Oscar-winning images make viewers feel the temperature of the hot, dry air. A telling visual moment comes thirty minutes in when Guthrie abandons Texas for California: behind him the skies are brown, but ahead, where there's "everything a man needs," they're an optimistic blue.

The movie daringly presents a warts-and-all look at Guthrie's life. He hitches rides west with no goodbyes to his wife and kids, leaving behind only a brief, uninformative note. As he travels, he sleeps with other women; settling in Los Angeles, he brings his family out to join him and promptly leaves them again because he "can't stand to sit still." What's admirable about Guthrie is his sincere commitment to exploited field workers. He encourages them to unionize and constantly befriends hobos and laborers (Guthrie puts the "folk" in "folk music"). When he lands a lucrative radio show, he's told to stop singing his controversial, troublemaking songs, so he quits. Guthrie sings from the heart, not from the pocketbook.

Carradine brings quiet amiability and integrity to the role, perhaps a surprise for an actor fresh off *Death Race 2000* (1975) and *Cannonball!* (1976). Director Hal Ashby was in the middle of a run of memorable '70s hits that included *Harold and Maude* (1971) and *Coming Home* (1978), but unfortunately *Bound for Glory* is a noble effort that's easier to admire than to love.

ADDED ATTRACTION: Heartbreak County U.S.A.

Another important movie with its heart in the right place is *Harlan County U.S.A.* (1976), that year's Oscar-winner for Best Documentary. Like *Bound for Glory*, this raw, riveting movie examines the hard lives of common workers, here struggling

Kentucky coal miners who endure dangerous, unhealthy work conditions, shacks with no plumbing, poverty-level pay when company profits are up 170%, and unsympathetic bosses who treat employees "like animals." Director Barbara Kopple leans into these issues by interviewing oppressed workers and wives, and by showing the abusive "gun thugs" who suppress protests. Using archival black-and-white footage, minimal on-screen text, no flashy charts or animations, and no narrator, Kopple simply photographs people and events, including live gunfire and a heartbreaking scene of wailing family members who are in mourning after a young striker is murdered. Solemn folk songs about these actual events add power to the progressive message. Woody Guthrie would approve.

Freaky Friday

Released: December 1976
Director: Gary Nelson
Stars: Barbara Harris, Jodie Foster, John Astin
Academy Awards: None

PREVIEW: A mom and daughter magically switch bodies for a day and gain respect for each other.

NOW SHOWING: Use Your Inside Voice

Ten months after playing a twelve-year-old hooker in *Taxi Driver* (1976), Jodie Foster returned to her gentle Disney roots. She'd already been in two Disney movies, *Napoleon and Samantha* (1972) and *One Little Indian* (1973), but her most successful Disney effort this decade was *Freaky Friday* (1976), a lightweight romp that became a heavyweight hit and the inspiration for several remakes.

Foster plays Annabel, a thirteen-year-old suburban girl with big braces. She loves but contends with her mother (Barbara Harris), and the early scenes show their mild conflicts. Eleven minutes into the movie, they simultaneously say, "I wish I could switch places with her for just one day." After five seconds of colorful split-screen effects, "something really freaky" happens and they somehow exchange bodies for about eight hours (the only explanation is that it's Friday the Thirteenth). Mom's body, speaking in mom's outward voice, now has Annabel's mind, while Annabel's body and voice are controlled by mom's thoughts.

Director Gary Nelson keeps the comic potential low-key and family-friendly. Mom's adult body rides Annabel's skateboard and dances to rock music, while Annabel's young body wrecks classes at school and talks to her friends with mom's formal tone. Both characters play sports, mom's body impressively (because athletic Annabel is inside her) and Annabel's body disastrously (clueless mom is inside). The movie touches some slightly serious situations, as when mom (in Annabel's body) gets suspicious of her husband's sexy new secretary, or when Annabel (in mom's body) flirts with the neighbor boy, who thinks Annabel's mom is coming on to him. Before things get too complicated, the frantic finale arrives. During some whirlwind escapades Annabel and mom both wish for their own bodies again, inducing a quick return to normal. Twelve minutes of speeding cars, water-skis, and a hang-glider conclude with mom, daughter, friends, dad, boss, and vehicles all in the bay. Naturally, mom and daughter learn about themselves and gain new respect for each other.

Both actresses are excellent, but the energetic Harris has more to do and seems to have the best time. There's nostalgic fun seeing kids typing in a typing class, wearing puka shells, and carrying Pee-Chee folders (love Foster's final 1970s hair-do, too). Among the familiar comedic performers are John Astin and Ruth Buzzi, plus Charlene Tilton in her movie debut. It's not deep, but *Freaky Friday* has a good heart and nicely delivers its simple, positive message.

ADDED ATTRACTION:
The Shaggy Dog Learns New Tricks

Released concurrently with *Freaky Friday*, *The Shaggy D.A.* (1976) follows Disney's usual comedy formula. First, it updates an earlier movie (*The Shaggy Dog*, a black-and-white 1959 hit that was like a Disneyfied werewolf movie). Next, it shows an animal performing human tasks, similar to the football-playing mule in *Gus* (1976), among many other Disney farces. *The Shaggy D.A.* brings Wilby, the teen in the first *Shaggy* movie, into adulthood as a candidate for district attorney. A villainous rival gets ahold of the first movie's magic ring and transforms Wilby (Dean Jones) into a sheepdog at will, often when Wilby is being interviewed or making a speech. The car-driving, bike-riding, roller-skating sheepdog, a big pie fight, and inept ice-cream man Tim Conway generate some laughs. Distressingly, a dog-pound scene has dogs on the brink of being put down, but as per the Disney formula the dogs make their getaway (parents will smile to hear these dogs humorously imitating the voices of old-time stars such as Peter Lorre and Mae West). It's all inoffensive, slapsticky matinee fun for undemanding kids, and a dog-day afternoon for jaded adults.

King Kong

Released: December 1976
Director: John Guillermin
Stars: Jeff Bridges, Jessica Lange, Charles Grodin
Academy Awards: One win (Special Achievement Award for Visual Effects), plus two more nominations (Best Cinematography; Best Sound)

PREVIEW: Tragedy ensues when an oil company brings a huge ape from its tropic isle to New York.

NOW SHOWING: "Bringing in the Big One"

Remakes of earlier classics didn't fare too well in the early 1970s: *Lost Horizon* (1973), *The Great Gatsby* (1974), and *The Front Page* (1974) all opened to some less-than-stellar reviews. *King Kong* (1976) was similarly maligned by some critics, but it was also the decade's first remake to become a genuine blockbuster. Occasionally silly, and utilizing some un-special effects, *Kong* does offer entertaining adventure.

This *Kong* updates the 1933 original with 1970s sensibilities, so a greedy petroleum company, not an intrepid film crew, lands on the exotic island, and the brave hero (Jeff Bridges) is a vigorous long-haired paleontologist, not a rough sailor. Also modernized is the ravishing blonde (Jessica Lange), now a wanna-be actress who wears tight cut-offs, asks Kong his zodiac sign, and mentions *Deep Throat* (1972). In the original movie, early scenes showed the desperate search for an actress to star in a jungle movie; now Dwan (Lange) arrives in a life raft after a yacht accident. We also got different dinosaurs in the original, especially an impressive T. rex; disappointingly, this second movie musters one giant rubber snake. Some new sequences weren't in 1933's *Kong*, such as the long ocean crossing back to America with Kong a prisoner. And in 1976's gory, emotional climax, Kong scales a World Trade Center tower, not 1933's Empire State Building.

A slimy villain (Charles Grodin) starts off with pompous predictions, and tongue-in-cheek dialogue lightens the mood as the oil-hunters get underway; only an earnest, well-meaning stowaway (Bridges) anticipates any danger (Bridges works so hard to sell this character to viewers, he'd undoubtedly deliver and install it if he could). Fifty-three minutes in, the big guy arrives and takes

Jessica Lange.

over the movie. Close-ups of Kong's giant mechanical paw and his expressive face are effective, and his cheeks impressively puff out when he blow-dries Dwan after her bath. But Kong diminishes anytime he stands up, because he's obviously someone in an ape suit trying to look bow-legged and walk with a squat, lumbering gait. Even worse is the four-story Kong under the giant gasoline pump at 106 minutes. This Kong can only be glimpsed for a few split-seconds because he is so stiffly ludicrous.

Despite the flaws we see today, the movie received a special visual effects Oscar, and thrill-seeking audiences went ape and made it a king-size hit. *King Kong* may be a guilty pleasure, but it is a pleasure nonetheless.

ADDED ATTRACTION: Unnatural Wonders

Animals went crazy in the 1970s, growing in numbers or in sizes not seen since the sci-fi monster flicks that played in drive-in theaters throughout the 1950s (three good examples of those '50s favorites are 1953's *The Beast from 20,000 Fathoms*, about a defrosted dinosaur; 1954's *Them!*, about giant irradiated ants; and 1955's *Tarantula!*, about a huge laboratory-enhanced arachnid). In addition to *King Kong*, here are sixteen more examples from the '70s (not included are the decade's many Godzilla movies made in Japan).

- *Frogs* (1972): Various animals
- *Night of the Lepus* (1972): Rabbits
- *Bug* (1975): Cockroaches
- *Jaws* (1975): Shark
- *The Giant Spider Invasion* (1975): Spiders
- *Grizzly* (1976): Bear
- *Squirm* (1976): Worms
- *Food of the Gods* (1976): Various animals
- *Claws* (1977): Bear
- *Day of the Animals* (1977): Various animals
- *Empire of the Ants* (1977): Ants
- *Orca* (1977): Killer whale
- *The Pack* (1977): Dogs
- *Tentacles* (1977): Octopus
- *Piranha* (1978): Piranha
- *The Swarm* (1978): Bees

A Star Is Born

Released: December 1976

Director: Frank Pierson

Stars: Barbra Streisand, Kris Kristofferson, Gary Busey

Academy Awards: One win (Best Song), plus three more nominations (Best Cinematography; Best Music; Best Sound)

PREVIEW: A rock star with a failing career falls in love with a singer who is rising to stardom.

NOW SHOWING: Snore, or Adore?

Like another December blockbuster, *King Kong* (1976), *A Star Is Born* (1976) remakes an earlier classic movie, here the 1937 and 1954 versions about two movie stars, one a man who is falling and the other a younger woman who is rising. And like *Kong*, *Star* updates its familiar story into a '70s milieu, replacing traditional Hollywood-movie culture with modern sex-and-drugs-and-rock-'n'-roll excess.

John Norman Howard (Kris Kristofferson) is a debauched, unlikeable rocker whose career is already fading as the movie starts: he's hours late for concerts, forgets lyrics, insults crowds, destroys his stage with an impromptu motorcycle ride, shoot guns at interviewers, and is a spoiled jerk to everyone around him. Dropping in unannounced at a small nightclub, he hears Esther Hoffman, an unknown-but-talented singer (Barbra Streisand); he's impressed but is still a rude jackass, interrupting her act and getting into a fistfight. Howard takes over her career and steers her to stardom. Then, exactly halfway into the movie they marry. He plummets, cheats, and drinks; she soars and wins a Grammy. In previous versions, Howard's character obviously commits suicide, but in this *Star* Howard's intentions are more ambiguous when he crashes his Ferrari at 160 mph (is he suicidal, or just stupid?). High production values, nice '70s touches (roles for Gary Busey and Paul Mazursky, cameos by Tony Orlando and Rita Coolidge), and a bestselling soundtrack helped draw humongous audiences.

Non-Streisand fans might call this 140-minute movie *A Star Is Boring*. It's full of clichés (the silly romantic-candles-around-the-couple-in-the-bathtub scene, for instance) and predictable outcomes (Howard is so foolishly self-destructive, his death is inevitable). But Streisand fans will swoon. Dominating the movie, she's listed as executive producer, "musical concepts" creator, and co-composer of the Oscar-winning song, "Evergreen"; she performs magnificent full-length versions of songs (Howard performs snippets); her "incredible eyes," "beautiful mouth," and "sweet little ass" get complimented; she wears an impressive array of flattering costumes that are, as the credits note, "from her

Barbra Streisand.

closet" (there's one minute outdoors at their 88,000-acre ranch when she wears five different outfits, including hot pants and a 1930s-newsboy ensemble); and the movie ends with a reverential ten-minute close-up on her face as she belts out the powerhouse finale dressed in white. Streisand didn't write or direct, but under her influence the movie becomes *A Star Is Adored*. You probably already know whether or not you're in the target audience she was aiming for.

ADDED ATTRACTION:
Oscar Records Set During the 1970s

In the 1970s, all of the following movies and people set new Oscar records.

- First …
    … sequel to win Best Picture: *The Godfather: Part II* (1974).
    … horror movie nominated for Best Picture: *The Exorcist* (1973).
    … movie with its entire cast nominated for Best Actor: *Sleuth* (1972), Laurence Olivier and Michael Caine.
    … posthumous winner of an acting Oscar: Peter Finch, Best Actor, *Network* (1976).
    … actor/actress to win for Best Actor/Best Actress and also for Best Supporting Actor/Actress: Helen Hayes, Best Actress, *The Sin of Madelon Claudet* (1931); Best Supporting Actress, *Airport* (1970).
    … actor/actress to win consecutive Best Supporting Actor/Actress Oscars: Jason Robards, *All the President's Men* (1976) and *Julia* (1977).
    … woman to win an Oscar for Best Picture: Julia Phillips, one of the producers of *The Sting* (1973).
    … woman nominated as Best Director: Lina Wertmüller, *Seven Beauties* (1976).
    … composer to win for a song he/she performed in the movie: Isaac Hayes, "Theme from *Shaft*."
    … Oscar-winning actor/actress to win for composing a song: Barbra Streisand, "Evergreen."

- Most …
    … wins for a movie without winning Best Picture: eight, *Cabaret* (1972).
    … nominations for a movie with zero wins: eleven, *The Turning Point* (1977).

- Oldest …
    … winning actor/actress: George Burns (80), Best Supporting Actor, *The Sunshine Boys* (1975).

- Youngest …
    … winner in any competitive category: Tatum O'Neal (10), *Paper Moon* (1973).
    … Best Actor: Richard Dreyfuss (30), *The Goodbye Girl* (1977).
    … nominee for a competitive Oscar: Justin Henry (8), *Kramer vs. Kramer* (1979).

- Longest …
    … gap between the first and second Oscar for acting: thirty-nine years, Helen Hayes, *The Sin of Madelon Claudet* (1931) and *Airport* (1970).

- Shortest …
    … acting performance to win an acting Oscar: five minutes by Beatrice Straight, Best Supporting Actress, *Network* (1976).

Smokey and the Bandit

"What we have here is a total lack of respect for the law!"

Burt Reynolds
"Smokey and the Bandit"
Sally Field · Jerry Reed and Jackie Gleason
as Sheriff Buford T. Justice

Screenplay by JAMES LEE BARRETT and CHARLES SHYER & ALAN MANDEL
Story by HAL NEEDHAM & ROBERT L. LEVY · Music by BILL JUSTIS and JERRY REED
Directed by HAL NEEDHAM · Produced by MORT ENGELBERG · Executive Producer ROBERT L. LEVY
A RASTAR Production · A UNIVERSAL Picture · Technicolor® PG PARENTAL GUIDANCE SUGGESTED
Original sound track available exclusively on MCA Records & Tapes

1977

In Film

- Oscar for Best Picture: *Annie Hall*.
- Most Oscar wins (seven): *Star Wars*.
- Most Oscar nominations (eleven): *Julia* and *The Turning Point*.
- With *Annie Hall*, Woody Allen receives his first Oscar nomination (and first win) for writing a screenplay; he will eventually become the all-time record holder for most Oscar nominations (sixteen) and most wins (three) for Best Original Screenplay.
- Top-grossing movie: *Star Wars*.
- Top-grossing comedy: *Smokey and the Bandit*.
- Top-grossing horror or sci-fi: *Star Wars*.
- *Star Wars* supplants *Jaws* (1975) as the highest-grossing movie in history; it's the third time a '70s movie takes over as the all-time box-office champ (prior to *Jaws*, 1972's *The Godfather* had supplanted 1939's *Gone with the Wind*).
- *Oh, God!*, *Smokey and the Bandit*, and *Star Wars* launch new movie franchises.
- *Star Wars* introduces the computerized motion-controlled camera and wins the Oscar for Best Visual Effects.
- Average price for an adult movie ticket: $2.25.
- Five memorable actors: Woody Allen, Richard Burton, Richard Dreyfuss, Harrison Ford, John Travolta.
- Five memorable actresses: Anne Bancroft, Melinda Dillon, Diane Keaton, Marsha Mason, Vanessa Redgrave.
- Movie debuts: Dan Aykroyd, Tom Berenger, Beverly D'Angelo, Judy Davis, Brian Dennehy, Bo Derek, Mel Gibson, Steve Guttenberg, Tom Hulce, Helen Hunt, Meryl Streep, Sigourney Weaver, Robin Williams, directors Ron Howard, David Lynch, Ridley Scott.
- Deaths include Stephen Boyd, Sebastian Cabot, Richard Carlson, Charlie Chaplin, Joan Crawford, Bing Crosby, Peter Finch, Jean Hagen, Henry Hull, Groucho Marx, Zero Mostel, directors William Castle and Howard Hawks.

In America

- Jimmy Carter is sworn in as America's thirty-ninth president; one of his first actions is to pardon those who evaded the draft during the Vietnam War; later in the year he will establish a new cabinet-level department, the Department of Energy.
- In July a twenty-five-hour long blackout hits New York City.
- After a year-long crime spree in which he murdered eight New Yorkers, David Berkowitz, the "Son of Sam," is captured.
- Three years after construction began, the eight-hundred-mile-long Alaska pipeline delivers its first barrels of oil.
- Space news: The first space shuttle, *Enterprise*, makes its five suborbital test flights; NASA launches *Voyager I* and *Voyager II* to explore the outer solar system; American astronomers discover the rings of Uranus.
- Now open: Space Mountain at Disneyland in Anaheim, California; the first-ever Chuck E. Cheese's Pizza Time Theatre, in San Jose, California; *Beatlemania* on Broadway.
- Ted Turner's yacht *Courageous* wins the America's Cup.
- The Toronto Blue Jays and Seattle Mariners play their first major-league baseball games.
- Average price for a gallon of gas: Sixty-four cents.
- New technology: Apple II and Commodore PET ("Personal Electronic Transactor") personal computers, Atari 2600 home video game console.
- New cars: Chrysler LeBaron, Dodge Omni, Lincoln Versailles.
- New products: Chia Pet, Slim-Fast.
- Sports champions: Oakland Raiders at Super Bowl XI, Montreal Canadiens in hockey, Portland Trail Blazers in basketball, New York Yankees in baseball.
- Bestselling books include Jay Anson's *The Amityville Horror*, Wayne Dwyer's *Your Erroneous Zones*, Colleen McCullough's *The Thorn Birds*, J.R.R. Tolkien and Christopher Tolkien's *The Silmarillion*.
- Music: In April, Led Zeppelin plays to over 76,000 fans at the Pontiac Silverdome, a new indoor world record; in June, Elvis Presley plays his last concert; in October, three members of Lynyrd Skynyrd die in a plane crash; Bing Crosby and David Bowie sing together on a Christmas TV special; new albums include Fleetwood Mac's *Rumours*, Billy Joel's *The Stranger*, Steely Dan's *Aja*, the *Saturday Night Fever* soundtrack; new songs include Aerosmith's "Walk This Way," Debby Boone's "You Light Up My Life," Jimmy Buffett's "Margaritaville," Hall and Oates' "Rich Girl," Queen's "We Will Rock You."
- TV debuts: *Circus of the Stars*, *Eight Is Enough*, *Fantasy Island*, *The Love Boat*, *Roots*, *Soap*, *Three's Company*.
- Deaths include James M. Cain, Erroll Garner, James Jones, Guy Lombardo, Vladimir Nabokov, Elvis Presley, Freddie Prinze.

fun with Dick and Jane

Released: February 1977
Director: Ted Kotcheff
Stars: George Segal, Jane Fonda, Ed McMahon
Academy Awards: None

PREVIEW: Facing bankruptcy, a couple commits robberies to maintain its upscale lifestyle.

NOW SHOWING: See Dick and Jane Steal

The American Dream almost becomes the American Nightmare in *Fun with Dick and Jane* (1977). This satirical comedy spotlights a handsome yuppie couple who go to drastic lengths to hold onto their lavish lifestyle. Dick (George Segal) and his wife Jane (Jane Fonda) have the big house, big car, and big bills, but when he gets laid off they're on the brink of a big financial disaster and, horrors, having people think their garden looks bad. After failing to generate steady income (he takes a gig in an opera chorus, she tries modeling), and after bungling their attempts to collect food stamps and unemployment, they hit on a better solution: robbery. They start with small business but work up to stealing $200,000 from the corrupt company where Dick worked. The closing text announces an ending even happier than the one we've been expecting.

Overall the movie is lightly entertaining—too light, in fact, because we hoped for something more biting than this pleasant diversion. Segal and Fonda are well-matched, though, and keep the movie bubbling along. Having already made a dozen '70s movies, including *The Hot Rock* (1972) and *California Split* (1974), Segal was a busy star all decade long, and *Fun with Dick and Jane* fits right in with his other comedic successes. Fonda, of course, was a superstar, having won the Best Actress Oscar for *Klute* (1971). For her, *Fun with Dick and Jane* represents a nice comedic pause just before she accelerates with three powerful dramas: *Julia* (1977), *Coming Home* (1978), and *The China Syndrome* (1979).

Adding to the fun are the fashions that make this movie a veritable '70s museum. Some of the clothes, like Dick's bright striped bellbottoms and Jane's rolled-up jeans and boots, were awful even then (Fonda is already in her fitness mode, standing on her head and flaunting a bare midriff). Ed McMahon, normally Johnny Carson's second banana, here has a real role as a villainous executive. What's more, eight minutes into the movie a left-handed carpenter in a tank top is working in the

Jane Fonda and George Segal.

house: heeeeere's Jay, twenty-seven-year-old Jay Leno, making his big-screen debut. And dig this forward-thinking line: "Printed circuits ... collecting and storing information right here on mother Earth, that's the future." So while it's not a great movie, it's still enjoyable and somewhat relevant, which is probably why Jim Carrey and Téa Leoni tried a remake in 2005.

ADDED ATTRACTION: Fun with George and Timothy

Four months after *Fun with Dick and Jane*, George Segal starred in *Rollercoaster* (1977), a good summer movie that's part disaster blaster, part hunt-for-the-killer thriller. Originally this movie was shown in Sensurround, the theater-rattling sonic experiment that had already rumbled through *Earthquake* (1974) and *Midway* (1976). In *Rollercoaster*, Sensurround added volume to the dramatic roller-coaster scenes. There are many, obviously, especially some exciting front-of-the-coaster shots reminiscent of the exhilarating Atom Smasher ride shown in *This Is Cinerama* (1952). *Rollercoaster* wastes no time cranking up: immediately a bomber (Timothy Bottoms) plants a device that soon explodes and kills everyone on a roller coaster. More attacks on other coasters, extortion demands, and cat-and-mouse strategies fill the next hour. Segal plays a safety inspector who "thinks like the bomber" and figures out that the suspect is headed to California's sprawling Magic Mountain amusement park, which is where the last thirty-seven minutes take place. The calm, polite bomber will be chilling to some viewers but frustrating and even dull to others, since he's unemotional and reveals literally nothing about himself, not even his name. Note young Helen Hunt and Steve Guttenberg appearing in their first movie and seventy-two-year-old Henry Fonda collecting a three-minute paycheck. Fun '70s memories include popular L.A. radio-DJ Charlie Tuna and TV-personality Gary Franklin playing themselves and the pop band Sparks performing a mini-concert, but the nuttiest '70s bit comes in King's Dominion park in Virginia, where Segal's character wins a ring-toss game and is awarded ... a ten-pack carton of cigarettes!

Slap Shot

(One of 1977's five **FAR-OUT** movies)
Released: February 1977
Director: George Roy Hill
Stars: Paul Newman, Michael Ontkean, Strother Martin
Academy Awards: None

PREVIEW: New players, and a new attitude, elevate a losing small-time hockey team to the top.

FINE LINE: "Bring the kids! We got entertainment for the whole family!" (The announcer, speaking during an especially bloody hockey fight.)

CLOSE-UP: Eleven minutes into *Slap Shot*, Reggie (Paul Newman) asks, "Who are these guys?" That's virtually the same line Newman says repeatedly in *Butch Cassidy and the Sundance Kid* (1969). In both movies, George Roy Hill was the director, and Strother Martin plays important supporting characters.

NOW SHOWING: Miracle on Ice

A losing team, led by an unconventional hard-living coach, gets a skillful addition to its young roster and becomes competitive. Ah, the lovable comedy *The Bad News Bears* (1976), right? Well, yes, but that's the PG-rated kids' version of this plot. *Slap Shot* (1977) is the R-rated adult version. It's raunchy, violent, funny, and terrific.

Slap Shot presents the final season of a fictional minor-league hockey team, the Charlestown Chiefs. Frustrated by the lame public-relations stunts they have to participate in (such as community fashion shows), motivated by rumors that the team may fold, and ignited by the mid-season arrival of three spirited, hard-nosed goons, the Chiefs start to win. Soon they become "rags-to-riches Cinderella contenders," and they even reach the championship game. Along the way there are scrapes with the law, broken relationships, and lots of male bonding.

What makes *Slap Shot* special is its harsh realism. Sports movies from earlier in the decade—*Le Mans* (1971), *The Longest Yard* (1974), *Rocky* (1976)—had been making strides toward more realistic depictions of their culture and competitions, but *Slap Shot* makes a giant leap. Baseball and football fans have movies they cherish and watch over and over—for hockey fans, this is the one they claim. It's not a movie for the easily offended, as the unedited locker room talk flows naturally and descriptively, just like we all assume it does when the athletes are together with the cameras and microphones turned off. Then there's the bloody violence, which may shock viewers, though the blood-letting is no worse than what happens in *Rocky*. Still, there are so many gory fistfights on the ice that the actual puck action almost feels like it's interrupting the game. Brawls erupt during pre-game warm-ups, move into the stands, and involve everyone from coaches and refs to the team's fans, boss and announcer. There are war movies with less violence than what's shown close-up in *Slap Shot*.

What makes the movie *really* special is Paul Newman. He's in nearly every scene as Reggie Dunlop, the old-school player/coach who still has a boyish streak in him. When the three thuggish Hanson brothers join the team and energize the players and the crowds, Dunlop embraces a "whole new attitude" of violence, even putting a bounty on another player. It's thrilling to watch this legendary fifty-two-year-old actor do his own skating, rumble with opponents, and get his handsome face pummeled. Mentoring the young, uneducated players (he calls most of them "kid"), Dunlop also imparts wisdom, works some schemes, and applies some sly psychology, in a way anticipating Kevin Costner's role in another sports classic, *Bull Durham* (1988). Newman convincingly embodies the influential coach everyone wishes they had.

Perhaps the biggest surprise is that the hard-hitting *Slap Shot* was written by a woman, Nancy Dowd, who based the movie on her brother's hockey experiences. Her first feature film, *Slap Shot* immediately catapulted her to a major career milestone, an Oscar for co-writing *Coming Home* (1978). Some of Dowd's most touching scenes in *Slap Shot* show how the wives and girlfriends suffer. Often left alone as

Paul Newman.

their men travel, they console each other, and they drink. No surprise is veteran director George Roy Hill. Is there anything he couldn't do? Previously he'd made a landmark western—*Butch Cassidy and the Sundance Kid* (1969)—and a memorable science-fiction movie—*Slaughterhouse-Five* (1972)—and an Oscar-winning crime comedy—*The Sting* (1973). With *Slap Shot* he captures the sport's power and speed by putting the camera right on the ice, sometimes at puck level so that it skims along for the ultimate hockey close-up.

The wild finale begins with Dunlop's pre-game speech that in hindsight seems prophetic, like it could apply to non-sports areas (music? politics?) as well: "Violence is killin' this sport. It's draggin' it through the mud. If things keep up the way they are, hockey players will be nothing but actors, punks!" He decides he wants to play a clean final game, but his Chiefs, now established as the "toughest team in the Federal League," is soon on its way to what looks like a blow-out loss. Though crowd-pleasing brutality resumes in the second period, it takes an outrageous four-minute striptease on center ice to bring home the unexpected victory and the not-totally-happy ending.

Controversial at the time for its raw language and ferocious fisticuffs, *Slap Shot* still found its appreciative (and mostly male) audience. It has risen in stature over the decades and is now often hailed as one of the best sports movies of all time. For Newman's fans, *Slap Shot* is a must-see, if only to watch their hero walk around in heart-patterned boxer shorts, flaunt wildly colored slacks and casual leather suits, dance to Leo Sayer's "You Make Me Feel Like Dancing," and cruise in a bitchen Pontiac GTO. The vocabulary, behavior, and fashions of his remarkable character are radical departures for the cool, beloved actor who had played an affable charmer in *Butch Cassidy and the Sundance Kid*. But the two characters do have something in common. Butch sensed the familiar days of the Old West were coming to an end (the newly reinforced bank, the arrival of the bicycle, etc.), and similarly Reggie Dunlop knows retirement is near for any athlete with graying hair. Big changes are coming for both characters, but at least in their last battles they go out with their guns blazing.

ADDED ATTRACTION: Movie Marquees, 1975-1977

Slap Shot's closing parade passes a theater where *Deep Throat* (1972) is playing. Here are other 1975-1977 movies where a marquee, or an actual clip, announces another real movie. For more movie marquees, see the entry for *A Little Romance* (1979).

- *Alice, Sweet Alice* (1976): Eighty-six minutes into this slasher movie, the poster for *Psycho* (1960) is visible.
- *Annie Hall* (1977): Alvy and Annie meet at a theater to see *Face to Face* (1976) but end up seeing *The Sorrow and the Pity* (1969); a flashback shows a Wisconsin theater and *The Misfits* (1961); Alvy carries black soap past a poster for *Children of Paradise* (1945); Alvy drives past L.A. marquees showing *The House of Exorcism* (1975) and *Messiah of Evil* (1973); near the end, Alvy runs into Annie outside *The Sorrow and the Pity*.
- *Cooley High* (1975): Midway through, the guys watch *Mothra vs. Godzilla* (1964).
- *The Day of the Locust* (1975): *The Buccaneer* (1938) is playing at Grauman's Chinese Theatre.
- *Dog Day Afternoon* (1975): A marquee reading *A Star Is Born* (perhaps the 1954 version) appears in the first two minutes.
- *Escape to Witch Mountain* (1975): In this Disney movie, the kids go to see Disney's *Snow White and the Seven Dwarfs* (1937).

- *The Front* (1976): *Mogambo* (1953) is playing at Radio City Music Hall.
- *The Great Waldo Pepper* (1975): Waldo takes Mary Beth on a date to see *The Son of the Sheik* (1926).
- *Hustle* (1975): The main characters see *A Man and a Woman* (1966).
- *The Last Remake of Beau Geste* (1977): Includes a three-minute mirage of *Beau Geste* (1939).
- *Nickelodeon* (1976): Includes scenes from *The Birth of a Nation* (1915).
- *Silent Movie* (1976): Seventy-six minutes into this Mel Brooks movie, a theater displays posters for Brooks's *Young Frankenstein* (1974).
- *The Song Remains the Same* (1976): Led Zeppelin is driven past a Manhattan marquee displaying *The Stepford Wives* (1975) and *The Godfather: Part II* (1974).
- *Taxi Driver* (1976): Six minutes in, Travis drives past *The Texas Chain Saw Massacre* (1974) and *Return of the Dragon* (1974). Later he takes Betsy to see *Sometime Sweet Susan* (1975), with *The Eiger Sanction* (1975) playing across the street.
- *W.W. and the Dixie Dancekings* (1975): Five minutes in, *The Sun Also Rises* (1957) plays at a drive-in.

Airport '77

Released: March 1977
Director: Jerry Jameson
Stars: Jack Lemmon, Lee Grant, James Stewart
Academy Awards: Two nominations (Best Art Direction; Best Costume Design)

PREVIEW: After a 747 crashes into the sea, rescuers try to save the survivors trapped inside.

NOW SHOWING: Fasten Those Seatbelts

Trailing the Best Picture-nominated *Airport* (1970) was the ludicrous *Airport 1975* (1974), one of the main inspirations for the classic airline-disaster parody, *Airplane!* (1980). One more sequel would've permanently grounded the entire series, but fortunately *Airport '77* (1977), though not great, was strong enough to keep the *Airport* legacy aloft.

This time out, thieves steal a 747 that's carrying priceless art, but while trying to fly away they clip an oil rig and crash into the sea. The jet teeters on a submerged shelf for the next hour as the survivors struggle inside (a la 1972's *The Poseidon Adventure*) while the Navy mounts a rescue operation outside. Unlike its two predecessors, which have few fatalities and land their damaged craft safely, *Airport '77* kills off many of the passengers and loses the jet.

Airport 1975 sprinkled some campy TV stars among its cast, but *Airport '77* stays serious. As per the disaster-movie formula, various movie legends are in peril, including Joseph Cotton, Olivia de Havilland, and Christopher Lee, with James Stewart safely monitoring events from shore. The new action hero in the Charlton Heston role is Jack Lemmon, wearing a moustache and working hard as the pilot-turned-frogman who aids the underwater rescue. George Kennedy, the gutsy crowd-pleasing mechanic in *Airport*, has minimal impact as a consultant. As expected, there are contentious relationships, loving couples, pretty girls, cute kids, a terrific crash sequence, and a sappy song. Disaster fans eagerly jumped on board, which could mean only one thing. One more sequel.

With *The Concorde ... Airport '79* (1979), the *Airport* series finally crashes and burns. When the *Concorde* is attacked in midair, the supersonic airliner does two 360-degree rolls and flies inverted so the pilot can fire diversionary flares out the window (huh?). There's more drama when the brakes fail during the landing. Everybody temporarily deplanes and, incredibly, re-boards to continue the trip as if nothing happened. Evidently the passengers haven't suffered enough, because sabotage forces a final emergency landing in the snow. Kennedy's character is now the heroic pilot, and the supporting cast is a weird blend of respected stars such as Mercedes McCambridge and Cicely Tyson with TV lightweights like Charo and Jimmie Walker (who flies high by sneaking a mid-flight reefer). And somehow, after three previous *Airport* movies, the special effects have gotten *worse*. *Airport '79* is everything you'd expect from a dumb disaster movie, and less.

ADDED ATTRACTION: Bermuda Angle

Airport '77's movie poster mentions the Bermuda Triangle, and one of the hijackers quickly mentions that region just as he's about to fly the plane so low it won't be picked up on radar screens, but actually the movie has no eerie occurrences. The Bermuda Triangle connection was intentional, however, because Charles Berlitz's bestselling book, *The Bermuda Triangle* (1974), had already made the Triangle a hot '70s topic. After several low-budget Mexican movies and TV movies capitalized on the sudden interest, Sunn Classic Pictures, makers of popular documentaries like *In Search of Noah's Ark* (1976), contributed *The Bermuda Triangle* (1979). Historical re-creations, stock footage, and pseudoscientific commentary cover centuries of Triangle-related events, starting with strange sightings by Columbus, continuing with the missing planes of Flight 19 (the World War Two planes recovered at the start of 1977's *Close Encounters of the*

Third Kind), and ending with twenty minutes of UFO sightings. In between are dramatic depictions and crackpot discussions of "weird haze," an "anti-gravity tunnel," "a time-warp," "a space-window," "the fabled continent of Atlantis," and "the immense energy of the stars … stored in a powerful crystal." Ridiculous? Patently. Lucrative? Undeniably, as the movie drew impressive audiences, proving that you don't have to make a lot of sense to make a lot of money. Somewhere P.T. Barnum was smiling.

The Many Adventures of Winnie the Pooh

Released: March 1977
Director: John Lounsbery, Wolfgang Reitherman, Art Stevens
Stars: Sebastian Cabot, Sterling Holloway, Paul Winchell
Academy Awards: None

PREVIEW: Pooh bear and his friends have various gentle adventures in the Hundred-Acre Wood.

NOW SHOWING: Walt Disney's Wonderful World of Pooh

Parents couldn't ask for a more perfect children's movie than *The Many Adventures of Winnie the Pooh* (1977). Its beautiful world is safe and polite, its child-like characters are honest and loyal, and their problems are simple and innocent. Compare this gentle movie to Disney's other animated movie that year, *The Rescuers*, a frantic adventure with menacing alligators, chilling vampire bats, pirate skulls, and a raging adult shooting at a young girl. They're so different they could be from different studios.

Like Disney's *Davy Crockett, King of the Wild Frontier* (1955), *Many Adventures* packages together three short theatrical features that had already been released separately. The twenty-five minute cartoons—*Winnie the Pooh and the Honey Tree* (1966), *Winnie the Pooh and the Blustery Day* (1968), and the Oscar-winning *Winnie the Pooh and Tigger Too* (1974)—appear in *Many Adventures* chronologically, with new animated sequences smoothing the transitions between stories. We also see A. A. Milne's actual book, and this is where the animators really started to experiment. As the book is being read aloud (Sebastian Cabot, in his final role before his

Winnie the Pooh.

death, is the kindly narrator), the illustrations on the pages come alive and move delightfully across the text; thus Pooh jumps from page to page, the wind blows letters sideways from their sentences, and the rain washes soggy words to the bottom.

In the first section, *Honey Tree*, Pooh, "a bear of very little brain," eats so much honey that he gets stuck in Rabbit's front door, and the others try to extricate him. Next comes *Blustery Day*, the best of the three sections. After a wonderful scene when Piglet blows away like a kite, the stormy night leads to Pooh's three-minute nightmare about Heffalumps (elephants) and Woozles (weasels), an imaginative sequence reminiscent of the famous four-minute "Pink Elephants on Parade" number from *Dumbo* (1941). Tigger, a bundle of "bouncy trouncy flouncy pouncy fun fun fun fun fun" exuberantly voiced by Paul Winchell, stars in the third section, *Tigger Too*, where he so annoys the others with his destructive bouncing that they try to change his ways.

A final two-minute chapter sends Christopher Robin off to school. It's a poignant coda that adults can watch with nostalgic feelings for a world that was easy to enjoy and free of violence and sarcastic insults. Sweet without being cloying, *The Many Adventures of Winnie the Pooh* is an endearing, enduring treat.

ADDED ATTRACTION: Recog-gonize These Words?

Disney's regular tunesmiths, Richard M. Sherman and Robert B. Sherman, contributed the whimsical songs to *The Many Adventures of Winnie the Pooh*. As they often did, the Shermans incorporated silly words and rhymes—"rumbly in my tumbly," "heave-age, ho-age, go-age"—into their playful lyrics. This was one of the Shermans' staple techniques for making their music memorable. Previously they had used unusual words and rhymes in songs such as "Higitus Figitus" for *The Sword in the Stone* (1963), "Supercalifragilisticexpialidocious" for *Mary Poppins* (1964), and "Substitutiary Locomotion" for *Bedknobs and Broomsticks* (1971), to name just three of many examples. Indeed, all of *The Many Adventures of Winnie the Pooh* is filled with child-friendly nonsense words, especially once Tigger shows up nine minutes into the second section, *Winnie the Pooh and the Blustery Day*. His unique phraseology includes two ways of pronouncing "ridiculous"—"ricky-diculus" and "ri-dic-cour-ous"—and he manages to expand "recognize" into the four-syllable "recog-gonize."

Eraserhead

Released: March 1977
Director: David Lynch
Stars: Jack Nance, Charlotte Stewart, Judith Anna Roberts
Academy Awards: None

PREVIEW: A weird man experiences a series of awkward encounters and dark, peculiar visions.

NOW SHOWING: Pointed, or Pointless?

What to make of *Eraserhead* (1977)? Unpleasant and incomprehensible, it was initially dismissed but gradually became a hit on the midnight-movie circuit, which is where we first caught it ("caught it," not "got it," because *Eraserhead* defies "getting"). Other unique cult movies like *The Rocky Horror Picture Show* (1975) are sweetly adorable compared to the ugly, jarring, nightmarish *Eraserhead*. It shows a disfigured woman, smiling as she stomps on live creatures; a chicken grotesquely oozing, in close-up; and the decade's most nauseating death scene. *Eraserhead* is like a test: how much can you tolerate before disgust or confusion overwhelms you? Many writers strive for artistic cred with deep interpretations and fawning appreciations, but every time we've seen *Eraserhead*, we've immediately felt like taking a bath. In bleach.

Hard as it is to watch, *Eraserhead* is even harder to describe. Since there's virtually no plot, you could probably run much of the movie backwards, and it would make as much sense. Basically an awkward loner with an ill-fitting suit, pocket protector, and shock-treatment hair stumbles through his shabby life, converses stiffly with various people, has dark, symbolic visions, and deals with a baby that's so repulsive "they're still not sure it *is* a baby." Only about nineteen minutes, or 21% of the movie, include spoken words. *2001: A Space Odyssey* (1968) is another challenging movie with minimal dialogue, but that masterpiece still manages to tell its complicated story. *Eraserhead* has no story to tell. It strings together strange, surreal episodes with undeveloped, often unidentified characters. Where some viewers see brilliance and black comedy, others see madness and horror.

Jack Nance.

If the meaning is intentionally obscured, the technique is clearly impressive, especially considering the movie's miniscule budget. *Eraserhead* is filled with mesmerizing black-and-white images, and layered sounds create a suitably oppressive industrial environment. Everything coheres into a singular experience, even if that experience isn't coherent. David Lynch, in his debut feature film, is credited as producer, writer, director, editor, sound-effects and special-effects creator, and production designer. *Eraserhead* is truly his personal statement, and it put Lynch on the path to his great, more accessible *Blue Velvet* (1986). But does future success make a creepy early experiment a landmark? Or good? Or even watchable? Viewers will have to decide for themselves. But be warned: like some extreme avant-garde paintings and disturbing performance art, *Eraserhead* is impossible to forget, though you may wish you could.

ADDED ATTRACTION:
Black-and-White Movies, Part Two

These 1977-1979 features include black-and-white images, as *Eraserhead* does. For more black-and-white movies, see the entry for *Marathon Man* (1976).

BLACK-AND-WHITE MOVIES
- *Eraserhead* (1977)
- *Manhattan* (1979)

COLOR MOVIES WITH BLACK-AND-WHITE SEGMENTS
- *The Black Stallion* (1979): Thirty seconds of newsreel footage shows horse races.
- *A Bridge Too Far* (1977): It opens with old black-and-white war footage.

- *Days of Heaven* (1978): Vintage photographs open the movie.
- *The World's Greatest Lover* (1977): Sprinkled throughout are black-and-white clips from fictional silent movies.
- *The Jerk* (1979): Steve Martin's character watches in horror as he's shown a minute-long "cat juggling" sequence.
- *The Last Remake of Beau Geste* (1977): Two black-and-white sections include a silent movie.
- *Looking for Mr. Goodbar* (1977): Opening minutes show urban-nightlife photos.
- *Martin* (1978): A modern-day vampire has frequent visions of various meetings and rituals.
- *Midnight Express* (1978): A last minute of black-and-white photos.
- *Movie Movie* (1978): Two of the three sections are in black and white.
- *Norma Rae* (1979): The opening minutes include black-and-white photos of young Sally Field.
- *The One and Only* (1978): Black-and-white photos show the main character as a child.
- *Same Time, Next Year* (1978): Historical photos mark the transitions as the movie moves from 1951 to 1977.
- *Wise Blood* (1979): The opening minutes show black-and-white Southern scenes.

Black Sunday

Released: April 1977
Director: John Frankenheimer
Stars: Robert Shaw, Bruce Dern, Marthe Keller
Academy Awards: None

PREVIEW: Terrorists plan an explosive attack at the Super Bowl, but the FBI is on their trail.

NOW SHOWING: Touchdown!

An underappreciated thriller, *Black Sunday* (1977) had the misfortune to come out in the same spring season as *Star Wars* (1977). All those audiences zooming to a galaxy far, far away missed a first-rate movie.

Borrowing from the real-life massacre at the 1972 Munich Olympics, *Black Sunday* tells a long, no-nonsense story about Palestinian terrorists striking America "where it hurts them most, where they feel most at home." Where would that be, do you think, sitting in church? Enjoying family dinner? Nope, attending a football game. We watch the terrorist team, led by a beautiful, calculating woman (Marthe Keller), make plans to detonate explosives from a blimp flying over the jam-packed stadium where the Super Bowl is being played. For two months the terrorists go from Beirut to California to Florida, carefully gathering and testing the materials for their attack. They're a ruthless bunch who live by a "you either kill or you get killed" credo.

On their trail is the FBI, aided by an Israeli national (Robert Shaw) who's called "the Final Solution" because he "takes things to their ultimate conclusion, and beyond."

Halfway through the movie the plot and the target become clear, and from there the story accelerates with suspenseful chase scenes, especially an exciting pursuit through Miami streets. Soon the actual Dallas Cowboys and Pittsburgh Steelers de-plane, the president (a Jimmy Carter lookalike) arrives, and the FBI makes final efforts to protect the stadium. Game footage is then intercut with a riveting helicopter-vs.-blimp aerial duel. Pandemonium results when the blimp finally reaches the field, and the last twelve minutes play out to an explosive conclusion.

There's much to recommend in any movie that effectively combines a political thriller with a disaster epic with the Super Bowl. (It's a real game, by the way, Super Bowl X on January 18, 1976, with famous players, actual plays, commissioner Pete Rozelle, and the musical entertainers Up with People.) What's more, the great John Williams has composed another of his dramatic scores, and Bruce Dern is excellent as a disturbed ex-POW who's more complicated and sympathetic than the cowardly killer Dern played in *The Cowboys* (1972). After more than two hours of build-up, the actual attack is a little diminished, with quick cuts and crowd reactions covering for the absence of a full-size blimp inside the Orange Bowl. Nevertheless, *Black Sunday*, like Pittsburgh in the big game, is a winner.

ADDED ATTRACTION: Iron Man

As *Black Sunday* premiered in early 1977, theaters were already showing another brawny movie, this one a fascinating documentary about bodybuilders. *Pumping Iron* stars Arnold Schwarzenegger, who had made a primitive debut in *Hercules in New York* (1970) and earned good notices as the co-star of the quirky comedy/drama *Stay Hungry* (1976). Here he's the reigning Mr. Olympia preparing for the 1975 title. Early in the movie he's charismatic and loquacious as he helps younger competitors, makes public appearances like the future politician he'll eventually become, and enthusiastically discusses his motivations by graphically comparing bodybuilding to sex. Once shy Lou Ferrigno is introduced, the movie darkens. "The largest bodybuilder ever," Ferrigno lives at home and is so obsessed with beating Schwarzenegger that he chants the champ's name as he trains. Schwarzenegger, meanwhile, laughingly boasts how he easily psyches out challengers so they can't win, and indeed the final contest almost seems unnecessary. Extensive footage shows these massive athletes blasting through "the pain barrier" to sculpt their granite-like bodies in the gym, and the informal scenes include an amusing bit where a strongman picks up a car to help it negotiate a tight parking space.

3 Women

Released: April 1977
Director: Robert Altman
Stars: Shelley Duvall, Sissy Spacek, Janice Rule
Academy Awards: None

PREVIEW: Personalities and situations get rearranged when a young woman comes out of a coma.

NOW SHOWING: Modern Art

Like *Images* (1972), Robert Altman's little-seen psychological thriller, *3 Women* (1977) is a strange movie that flopped with audiences. Some critics call it a masterpiece because, if nothing else, Altman goes full Altman, presenting surreal images and arresting characters with no clear narrative or resolution. Altman's enigmatic story is like an intense but ambiguous dream.

The title's three women are really closer to two-and-a-half women, because the sullen painter Willie (Janice Rule) arrives well after the other two and barely speaks. Pinky (Sissy Spacek) is a playful new employee at a California geriatric center. She blows bubbles in her Coke, spins in a wheelchair, and childishly goofs around. Millie (Shelley Duvall) is Pinky's older, more mature mentor. Both women are from Texas, both have the first name Mildred. Pinky studies and copies Millie, calling her, "the most perfect person I ever met," even though Millie, who drives with her dress always caught in the car door, is quietly mocked by neighbors.

The movie seems to be building to second-half suspense involving switched identities, like it's veering into *Vertigo* (1958) territory. That sort of happens midway through when Pinky bangs her head and lapses into a coma. When she revives, she's changed. She doesn't recognize her parents, she doesn't want to be called Pinky, and she's more assertive and obnoxious. Millie, meanwhile, becomes more submissive and confused. Transitions fill the last fifteen minutes: Pinky has a long, eerie dream, Willie's baby is stillborn, and her lecherous husband suffers an unseen "terrible accident." In the final scenes, Pinky calls Millie "my mom," Millie looks like a stern matron and calls Pinky "Millie," and Willie calls Pinky "baby" and says she's just had a dream. Outside is a pile of tires where, perhaps, Willie's husband is buried, though the ending invites interpretations.

It doesn't all make sense, but dreams and avant-garde movies don't have to. The possibility that identities are merging or switching is reinforced by all the doppelgangers—actual twins, twin beds, two diaries, a pair of cops, a pair of delivery drivers, the husband's job as a stunt double, etc. Altman underscores the hypnotic elements by lingering on nightmarish images of hideous erotic art and shooting *through* water, sometimes literally through an aquarium or with waves rising and falling across the screen. It all means ... something. Beautifully acted by Spacek and Duvall, *3 Women* is weirdly mesmerizing, if ultimately undecipherable.

ADDED ATTRACTION: Guests at *A Wedding*

Altman's next movie was *A Wedding* (1978). Like *Nashville* (1975), it's a satirical comedy/drama with a huge ensemble cast of diverse stars, here including Desi Arnaz Jr., Carol Burnett, Geraldine Chaplin, Howard Duff, Mia Farrow, Lillian Gish, Lauren Hutton, and Nina van Pallandt. A more accurate movie title would be *A Reception*, because the wedding ceremony led by a stumbling bishop concludes in the first twelve minutes. The remaining action is mostly confined to a large house for a chaotic celebration that begins and ends with sudden deaths. Gossip, flirtations, news that the groom has impregnated the maid of honor, a tornado, and drugs swirl up the subplots before the fatal finale. As usual in Altman's movies, his technique is interesting and the cast seems to be improvising the occasionally amusing dialogue. However, the meandering vignettes are uneven, and the ending feels forced. Critics in 1978 were divided, and modern viewers who RSVP to *A Wedding* might consider it only a mild diversion.

Annie Hall

(One of 1977's five **FAR-OUT** movies)

Released: April 1977

Director: Woody Allen

Stars: Woody Allen, Diane Keaton, Tony Roberts

Academy Awards: Four wins (Best Picture; Best Actress—Diane Keaton; Best Director; Best Writing), plus one more nomination (Best Actor—Woody Allen)

PREVIEW: Two people fall in love in New York, but then one has the chance to move to California.

FINE LINE: "I guess that's pretty much now how I feel about relationships. You know, they're totally irrational and crazy and absurd, but I guess we keep going through it because most of us need the eggs." (*Annie Hall*'s last line, delivered as traffic moves past Lincoln Center and Alvy walks away, alone for one of the only times in the movie.)

CLOSE-UP: *Annie Hall* has three unique split-screen scenes. In the first, Alvy and Annie stand to the side and comment as they observe her earlier relationship with a long-haired actor. Later, the genteel dinner with the Halls is next to a raucous dinner in a different location with the Singers—Allen's breakthrough is having the two split-screen families actually interact with each other. Finally, Annie and Alvy are almost back-to-back as they use similar words to discuss with their analysts their "three times a week" sex life (he: "Hardly ever"; she: "Constantly!").

NOW SHOWING: Lurve Story

The decade's most daring romantic comedy culminated Woody Allen's swift surge from novice movie clown to innovative movie artist. Allen's previous movies, from the chaotic-but-hilarious *Take the Money and Run* (1969) to the more polished *Sleeper* (1973), had advanced his technique and expanded his ambitions. *Love and Death* (1975), an intelligent, delightful costume comedy, firmly established him as a gifted writer/director/actor in full command of his powers. Allen's next movie, *Annie Hall* (1977), would be his masterpiece.

Modern viewers who underappreciate *Annie Hall* are ignoring its 1970s context. A major hit that charmed audiences and critics, it collected Oscars in the Best Picture/Actress/Director/Writing categories, becoming one of the few comedies to win for Best Picture and putting Allen in the pantheon of filmmakers to win for both writing and directing. It influenced women's fashions and inspired subsequent movies like *When Harry Met Sally...* (1989). People who've never seen *Annie Hall* have probably heard some of its lines ("the only cultural advantage is being able to make a right turn on a red light," "la-de-da," etc.). And for adults who lamented that movies changed forever when *Star Wars* (1977) premiered a month later and ushered in the era of teen-oriented sci-fi blockbusters, *Annie Hall*, with its in-the-know cultural references and thoughtful examination of contemporary relationships, towers like a shining beacon of sophistication. It's as smart, funny, and poignant as comedy gets.

Amazingly, the final movie is not at all the one Allen and co-writer Marshall Brickman started with. Numerous critiques and biographies discuss *Annie Hall*'s radical transformation from inception to completion: the title, for instance, was *Anhedonia* (the inability to experience happiness) until studio executives requested something less esoteric; originally Alvy (Allen) and Annie (Diane Keaton) investigated a murder; settings would've included the Garden of Eden, Hell, and Nazi Germany; scenes with Alvy's first love (played by young Brooke Shields), with basketball-playing philosophers, and with conversant Times Square signs never made it in. Overall this eclectic movie was going to be a stream-of-consciousness assortment of scenes, images, and stand-up delivery that illuminated the random inner life of Alvy's active mind, a cinematic variation on James Joyce's *Ulysses*.

While *Annie Hall* doesn't include all these experiments, it's still audaciously unconventional. Consider the movie's inverted chronologies. In the opening monologue, Alvy describes his feelings for Annie before we even know who she is. When Annie arrives eight minutes into the movie, she and Alvy are obviously deep into their relationship, though their actual tennis-court introduction is still sixteen minutes away. Later the movie jumps around to flashbacks of Alvy's first wife, to Annie's "first big romance," to Alvy's second marriage, to Alvy's nascent joke-writing career, and to Alvy's childhood, all followed by a flash forward to his encounter with Annie a year into the future. In the last moments, flashbacks present snippets from sixteen different scenes we've already witnessed, but even these flashbacks are out of chronological order.

The story of the Annie/Alvy romance is told in such an unusual way that Allen seems to be trying to see how much innovation he can get away with. For instance, in the first three minutes, Alvy reveals the ending ("Annie and I broke up"). Other movies—*Double Indemnity* (1944), *Sunset Boulevard* (1950), *Lolita* (1962)—had done something similar, but immediately giving away the ending was still an uncommon storytelling technique (naturally, in Allen's modern romantic comedy there's no happy-ever-after climax, another daring choice). Next, the two male leads, Alvy and Rob (Tony Roberts), both call each other Max (are nervous/neurotic Alvy and calm/confident Rob two sides of one person?). One conversation adds subtitles to lay bare unspoken insecurities.

Diane Keaton and Woody Allen.

A twenty-four-second cartoon includes Alvy as a main character. Alvy talks to Annie's "spirit" when it leaves her body. And 1970s Rob questions 1945 Tessie during a flashback. Besides these conspicuous inventions, subtle creative flourishes fill the movie: six minutes in, we watch eighty seconds of the two Maxes walking toward us on East Sixty-Sixth Street, the men barely discernible at first but their friendly conversation gradually revealing their distinct personalities. Strangers tell Alvy where Annie's living and offer advice ("Love fades!"). Alvy invents new words for love ("lurve," "luff"). His white-on-black opening and closing credits have no musical accompaniment. There's even an alternate ending that shows play rehearsals with a happier resolution for the bittersweet story we've been watching, enabling audiences to contemplate what might've been for the likeable characters they've enjoyed for ninety minutes.

Annie Hall represents a major advance for Allen's own on-screen persona. Usually he played costumed characters in comical situations; here he's wearing his own casual clothes, he acts like a regular (if witty and paranoid) person, and he's immersed in psychoanalysis and serious relationships, not silly slapstick and zany heroics. Additionally, Allen's in New York for most of the movie, where he'll stay for his next milestone, *Manhattan* (1979), and for much of his movie career.

More importantly, *Annie Hall* signals Allen's rejection of farcical comedy for melancholic drama. Anti-Semitism, the intellectual life (represented by New York) vs. hedonistic abandonment (L.A.), and the inefficacy of modern romantic love are just three of the movie's dissertation-worthy topics. He'd push his serious concerns to laughless extremes in his next movie, *Interiors* (1978). But it's the marvelous balance of timeless jokes and relatable emotions that makes *Annie Hall* Allen's most beloved movie. Applying a word Shelley Duvall's character says three times, it's transplendent.

ADDED ATTRACTION: Looking for Diane Keaton

Diane Keaton made a daring selection for her next movie. Instead of playing another adorable ditz, which would've been an easy, popular choice, Keaton went extremely dark for *Looking for Mr. Goodbar* (1977), an uneven but harrowing drama that ends with her brutal murder by a knife-slashing maniac. Keaton is amazing as a first-grade teacher who descends from a tacky affair with a jerky married professor to a grim life of singles bars, sordid pick-ups, and drugs. Bravely, she doesn't pull any punches and is fully committed to this raw character who goes topless and engages in casual sex with virtual strangers. And as in *Annie Hall*, there's an interesting little connection to *The Godfather* (1972), the classic movie that Keaton was in: *Annie Hall* has an early scene where Alvy complains that while he's been waiting for her to arrive at the movie theater he's been forced to talk "with the cast of *The Godfather*," and early in *Looking for Mr. Goodbar* she's shown with *The Godfather* novel in the bar where she first sees the live-wire lover played by Richard Gere.

Smokey and the Bandit

Released: May 1977
Director: Hal Needham
Stars: Burt Reynolds, Jerry Reed, Sally Field
Academy Awards: One nomination (Best Editing)

PREVIEW: Two pals have adventures as they try to drive 1800 miles in just twenty-eight hours.

NOW SHOWING: "That's a Big Ten-Four"

As car-revvin' entertainment, *Smokey and the Bandit* (1977) is a winner. It's got a barely-there plot (two friends, a long-distance-driving challenge, now GO!), and it's mostly a series of highway sprints away from frustrated cops, but audiences were so charmed by the movie's good-natured spirit they made it a blockbusting smash.

Burt Reynolds drives the movie. A huge movie star in his swaggering prime, the forty-one-year-old Reynolds is handsome Bo "Bandit" Darville, a "bodied-up smooth-talkin' thing" workin' a tight-jeans-cowboy-hat-and-moustache combo. It's Reynolds at full Reynolds, which we'd know just by the sound of his signature high-pitched cackling laugh (we counted eight separate cackles). At one point he confidently smiles directly into the camera because this cocky rascal *knows* the audience likes him. Surrounding him are appealing co-stars, particularly Sally Field, adorable in her first of four movies with Reynolds. Known at the time for sitcoms and TV movies, she plays a chatty runaway bride and is clearly on her way to movie stardom. Good-ol'-boy Jerry Reed is Bandit's truck-driving pal, providing affable support and singing the movie's jaunty songs.

Burt Reynolds.

Admittedly, the movie has flaws big enough to drive a Peterbilt through. The comedy is adolescent, every cop is hopelessly inept, and the main pursuer (Jackie Gleason) is such a nonstop-over-the-top-blowing-his-top volcano that his angrified act gets tiresome. Modern audiences must overlook non-PC jokes, especially one about punching a wife in the mouth. Also, the last double-or-nothing bet seems doomed from inception: a 2100-mile Atlanta-Boston roundtrip ÷ eighteen hours = an average of 116 mph, in a Cadillac, not a muscle car, and imagine the traffic. And was Coors the official sponsor? (Coors, "to celebrate in style," seriously? The real winner was Pontiac: Trans-Am sales surged after this movie.)

Fans aren't running the numbers, though. They're enjoying the screeching tires, impressive stunts like the show-stopping slow-motion-car-over-the-river jump, and especially the amiable company, everything that makes *Smokey and the Bandit* a fun, rollickin' ride.

Six months later Reynolds starred in another macho movie, *Semi-Tough* (1977). He'd been a football player before in *The Longest Yard* (1974), a darker movie with beatings and death. *Semi-Tough* was promoted as a sexy gridiron comedy with Reynolds (again #22) and Kris Kristofferson as playboys and Jill Clayburgh as their mutual friend. Unfortunately, there's surprisingly little game action, a tedious satire on New Age gibberish takes over, and this disjointed, unfunny movie is semi-tough to sit through.

ADDED ATTRACTION: Muscle-Car Movies

Dig *Smokey and the Bandit*'s black 1977 Pontiac Firebird Trans-Am? Buckle up for these other 1970s movies that feature some of the era's most powerful muscle cars.

- *Aloha, Bobby and Rose* (1975): Chevrolet Camaro
- *Brewster McCloud* (1970): Plymouth Road Runner
- *Coming Home* (1978): Shelby GT 500
- *Convoy* (1978): Chevrolet Chevelle
- *Corvette Summer* (1978): Chevrolet Corvette
- *Diamonds Are Forever* (1971): Ford Mustang
- *Dirty Mary Crazy Larry* (1974): Dodge Charger
- *The Driver* (1978): Ford Galaxie
- *Eat My Dust!* (1976): Chevrolet Camaro
- *Foxy Brown* (1974): Dodge Charger
- *The Getaway* (1972): Chevrolet Impala
- *Gone in 60 Seconds* (1974): Ford Mustang
- *Grand Theft Auto* (1977): Dodge Charger
- *Old Boyfriends* (1979): Pontiac Trans-Am
- *Phantasm* (1979): Plymouth 'Cuda
- *The Seven-Ups* (1973): Pontiac Ventura Custom
- *Shaft's Big Score!* (1972): Plymouth Sebring
- *Stingray* (1978): Chevrolet Corvette
- *Two-Lane Blacktop* (1971): Pontiac GTO
- *The Unholy Rollers* (1972): Dodge Charger
- *Vanishing Point* (1971): Dodge Challenger

Star Wars

(One of 1977's five **FAR-OUT** movies)
Released: May 1977
Director: George Lucas
Stars: Mark Hamill, Harrison Ford, Carrie Fisher
Academy Awards: Seven wins (Best Editing; Best Art Direction; Best Costume Design; Best Visual Effects; Best Music; Best Sound; Special Achievement Award for Sound Effects), plus four more nominations (Best Picture; Best Director; Best Supporting Actor—Alec Guinness; Best Writing)

PREVIEW: Rebels try to strike back against the galaxy's evil Empire and its ultimate weapon.

C-3PO and R2-D2.

FINE LINE: "Just you reconsider playing that message for him! … No, I don't think he likes you at all. … No, I don't like you either." (C-3PO, the fussy, anxious droid, conversing with intrepid little R2-D2, whose beeps and chirps follow 3PO's lines; their friendly bickering makes them the movie's droll comedy team.)

CLOSE-UP: *Star Wars* has the best proper nouns since *The Lord of the Rings* books (interestingly, some of the *Star Wars* names get multiple pronunciations: Leia is spoken in the movie as both "Lay-yuh" and "Lee-yuh," the planet Alderaan as "Alda-ran" and "Alda-ron," and at different times Han rhymes with both "Ron" and "Ran"). In keeping with the movie's fun spirit, we offer this name-game challenge. Of the following ten names, nine are characters or places in the first *Star Wars* movie (the names are either spoken or are listed in the credits); one name is of a small fish found in the Atlantic Ocean near South America. Can you find the fish? If the Force is with you, you'll pick one, and it'll be correct.

- Blenny
- Dantooine
- Dodonna
- Greedo
- Kessel
- Porkins
- Tarkin
- Tatooine
- Tiree
- Yavin

NOW SHOWING: "Here's Where the Fun Begins"

Like Mickey Mouse and the Beatles, *Star Wars* (1977) was a transcendent pop-culture game-changer. For people all around the world, of all ages and intellect, it was love at first flight. *Jaws* (1975) comes close, but really there was no other theatrical experience equivalent to *Star Wars* in the 1970s, and maybe never before either. Fans revere *Gone with the Wind* (1939), *The Sound of Music* (1965), and *The Godfather* (1972), yet nobody collects the complete set of Tara action figures or attends annual conventions dressed like the Von Trapp family or sleeps in Don Corleone-themed pajamas. But things like this existed for *Star Wars*; as Han Solo (Harrison Ford) declares during an exciting chase, "Here's where the fun begins."

Any fan of '70s movies is probably already up to light speed on the good-rebels-vs.-bad-Empire story. Even people who've never even seen the movie know who Darth Vader is and recognize Leia's hairstyle. So let's consider *how* this glorious movie does what it does. First, it draws on familiar themes and situations. In *Star Wars*, elements from old-fashioned Flash Gordon serials, traditional westerns, classic hero-rescuing-a-princess fairy tales, the Arthurian knights-and-swords-and-sorcery legends, and more are updated into imaginative settings. Just two specific examples: "hyperspace" appeared in the much-admired *Forbidden Planet* (1956); "here's where the fun begins," Han's comment as the *Millennium Falcon* races away from Tatooine with Imperial cruisers close behind, is the same exact line spoken near the end of *King Solomon's Mines* (1950), a Best Picture nominee. Thus the new *Star Wars* story, even with all its unusual creatures and environments, already has the built-in nostalgia of something fondly remembered. Additionally, we easily identify with Luke (Mark Hamill), the protagonist who's literally a farm boy on what looks like the American plains. Luke feels isolated and stifled—what teen hasn't shared his desire to see new horizons? The movie gradually supplies him with appealing allies: Leia, fearless, smart, and pretty (not a vapid, ravishing bombshell); Han, a swashbuckling, charismatic renegade; Chewie, the best family pet ever; Ben, the wise mentor everyone wishes they'd had.

Darth Vader (David Prowse) and Princess Leia (Carrie Fisher).

These engaging characters appeared after the late-'60s assassinations and the early-'70s Vietnam turbulence. In those traumatic years many movies were dark, violent, cynical dramas propelled by fallible heroes who didn't achieve happy outcomes (1971's *The French Connection* is a prime example). Then, a year before *Star Wars*, a surprising hit lifted the national mood, and was named Best Picture for doing it. *Rocky* (1976) was a feel-good dynamo about a likeable underdog, but its sensitive love story and bloody climax made it a movie for adults. *Star Wars* similarly celebrated the exultation of great old movies, but it aimed younger. Practically fizzing with confidence and energy, it takes viewers on a kid-friendly roller-coaster ride through outer space, with no serious love story putting on the brakes. Yes, there are many deaths (including Obi-Wan Kenobi, Luke's two incinerated relatives, all life on the planet Alderaan, and everyone on the Death Star), but there's no blood. All the back story that's needed is in the prefatory text crawl; after that, we're immediately immersed into the whiz-bang action, and everything we see simply exists, as if lightsabers and Jawas and the rough-and-ready *Millennium Falcon* (the galactic equivalent of a beat-up 1950s hot rod) have always been around and were waiting to be filmed. The easy-to-follow chronological narrative, the quickly explained Force that adds a touch of philosophical gravitas, the satisfaction of seeing young spirited rebels triumphing over the oppressive Empire, the visual storytelling, the humorous touches ("Will someone get this walking carpet out of my way?"), the rousing music, the ingenious sounds and the razzle-dazzle effects brought out the cheering child in everyone.

Star Wars' influence was profound and lasting. Quickly becoming the all-time biggest moneymaker, the movie redefined May as the start of the summer season and established writer/director George Lucas as a powerful mogul. As a social movement, *Star Wars* totally reinvented the concept of movie merchandising and made its had-to-have toys more profitable than the movie itself; it added "may the Force be with you" to the vernacular; it introduced new computer technology to the filmmaker's toolbox; it launched successful sequels, new subsidiaries (ILM, LucasArts, THX, etc.), and even a Disneyland ride.

After countless viewings we've accumulated a sandcrawler full of observations and questions. For instance, can't stormtroopers shoot straight? Han is accurate while running away and firing one-handed over his shoulder, and Leia closes her eyes ninety-three minutes into the movie and still blasts a distant target. Also, soon after the *Millennium Falcon* uses hyperspace to reach a far-off rebel base, the Death Star arrives—did it too zoom through hyperspace? (2016's *Rogue One* finally gives a clear answer.) "The target area is only two meters wide"—the metric system, who knew? Voices and choices: James Earl Jones (the sonorous vocals for Darth Vader) wasn't listed in the original credits, Luke's Aunt Beru is apparently dubbed, and Leia (Carrie Fisher) starts (but doesn't finish) the movie with a mild English accent ("stah systems will slip through your fingahs"). Veteran viewers may recall the movie's simpler title in 1977: initially it was just *Star Wars*, not *Episode IV—A New Hope*, which was added for later re-releases, as were new scenes, including Han and Jabba the Hutt's confrontation in Mos Eisely. And be sure to watch the amusing blooper that occurs seventy-nine minutes into the movie when four stormtroopers enter a control room and the trooper on the right conspicuously bonks his head on the door frame.

None of these trivial discrepancies or questions make us exclaim "I have a bad feeling about this," which both Luke and Han say in the movie. *Star Wars* is both an epic accomplishment and stupendous entertainment. Like Luke's Death Star-destroying "great shot," it's "one in a million."

ADDED ATTRACTION: Vehicle Names

Star Wars introduces one of the most famous spaceships in movie history, Han Solo's awesome *Millennium Falcon*. Here are twenty-one more vehicles with distinct names in movies from the 1970s.

The Millennium Falcon.

FLYING
- *Alien* (1979): *Nostromo*
- *The Black Hole* (1979): *Palomino*
- *Dark Star* (1974): *Dark Star*
- *Gray Lady Down* (1978): *Neptune*
- *The Hindenburg* (1975): *Hindenburg*
- *The Island at the Top of the World* (1974): *Hyperion*
- *Meteor* (1979): *Hercules*
- *Moonraker* (1979): *Moonraker 6*
- *Silent Running* (1972): *Valley Forge*
- *Star Trek: The Motion Picture* (1979): *Enterprise*
- *Unidentified Flying Oddball* (1979): *Stardust*

SAILING/SUBMERSIBLE
- *Death on the Nile* (1978): *Karnak*
- *The Dove* (1974): *Dove*
- *Jaws* (1975): *Orca*
- *Juggernaut* (1974): *Britannic*
- *King Kong* (1976): *Petrox Explorer*
- *Lucky Lady* (1975): *Lucky Lady*
- *The Neptune Factor* (1973): *Neptune II*
- *Orca* (1977): *Bumpo*
- *The Poseidon Adventure* (1972): *Poseidon*
- *The Spy Who Loved Me* (1977): *Liparus*

The Deep

Released: June 1977
Director: Peter Yates
Stars: Jacqueline Bisset, Nick Nolte, Robert Shaw
Academy Awards: One nomination (Best Sound)

PREVIEW: Danger follows two scuba-diving tourists who find underwater treasure and drugs.

NOW SHOWING: Wading into *The Deep*

" … and the Oscar for Best Tee-Shirt goes to … Jacqueline Bisset, *The Deep* (1977)." Indeed, Bisset's wet tee dominates *The Deep*'s first ten minutes and is still the main thing anybody remembers. That can't be good for a big-budget underwater adventure movie.

Nevertheless, audiences made *The Deep* one of 1977's top-ten hits. So what were they responding to? With *Jaws 2* (1978) still a year away, *The Deep* was the classiest approximation of *Jaws* (1975) so far; that link was intentional, since the posters looked similar, both movies were based on popular Peter Benchley novels, both starred Robert Shaw, and both had sharks. Additionally, summer audiences may have been treating the movie like a mini-vacation. *The Deep* is shallow escapist entertainment long on beautiful Bermuda settings and enticing activities (moped rides, scuba diving, rum drinking) and short on interesting character development (we never learn what the two main tourists played by Bisset and Nick Nolte do for a living, or why Shaw is so grouchy). Wanna get away? See *The Deep*.

Jacqueline Bisset.

Additionally, *The Deep* throws in every '70s movie danger possible except for aliens and a vomiting demon: a lunging moray eel, swarming sharks, a sinister drug gang, a killer brandishing a churning outboard motor, spear guns, dynamite explosions, a truck-vs.-moped chase, kidnapping, voodoo, and more. Despite all this commotion, *The Deep* actually feels a little tedious. For one thing, forty-five minutes are spent underwater, where dialogue is minimal and movements naturally slow down. Next, the story itself is uninvolving. Exploring a sunken wreck, two tourists find some treasure and bottles of medicinal morphine. Shaw plays a local expert who helps them recover more of what they've found. The morphine attracts a drug lord who wants to do the ol' morphine-into-heroin-into-street-sales conversion. (Where would '70s movies have been without heroin? It's in movies as disparate as *The French Connection*, *The Godfather*, *Lady Sings the Blues*, *Live and Let Die*, *Lenny*, *Who'll Stop the Rain*, and *The Rose*, to name a quick seven in chronological order.) *The Deep* dog-paddles to its implausible ending without much tension and none of *Jaws*'s wit.

The scenery, including stunningly beautiful Bisset and handsome, fit Nolte, is the real star. Shaw is the same curmudgeon he was in *Jaws*, only now he has the irritating habit of constantly calling Nolte "boy" and Bisset "girl." We kept expecting Nolte to feed him to the eel.

ADDED ATTRACTION: Howard's Start

Premiering the same week as *The Deep* was another summer success. *Grand Theft Auto* (1977) was Ron Howard's directorial debut, a result of a deal he'd cut with producer Roger Corman: if Howard starred in Corman's *Eat My Dust!* (1976), he'd get to direct. Both movies are silly and innocuous, and together they'd be a fun drive-in double-feature. In *Eat My Dust!* Howard, egged on by a foxy blonde in hot pants (Christopher Norris), races around rural California in a stolen Camaro. Police cars (duh), buildings, chicken coops, shopping carts, and more get destroyed by various cars that leap, sink, flip, spin, plummet, and crash, somehow while incurring zero injuries to the passengers. In *Grand Theft Auto* a year later, Howard and his rich fiancée (Nancy Morgan) elope to Las Vegas in her dad's Rolls-Royce, with family, cops, helicopters, reward hunters, mobsters, Marion Ross from TV's *Happy Days*, and Howard's real-life dad and brother in pursuit. "We've got a cockamamie circus on our hands," says Howard's character in the midst of all the vehicular mayhem. Indubitably.

The Hills Have Eyes

Released: June 1977
Director: Wes Craven
Stars: Susan Lanier, Robert Houston, Martin Speer
Academy Awards: None

PREVIEW: A family is stranded in the desert and repels a group of attacking mutant cannibals.

NOW SHOWING: *The Hills Have Eyes* ... and Teeth

Middle-class Americans venture into the wilderness and are attacked by sick locals. Sound like *Deliverance* (1972)? That's the polished, star-driven version of this story. *The Hills Have Eyes* (1977) is a savage, ultra-low-budget take on that same basic concept.

Though it's disturbing, this movie's raw, primal horror resonated with enough viewers for it to become a drive-in hit.

The Hills Have Eyes starts with a big family driving through the California desert and getting a warning to "stay on the main road," because in the desolate hills there's "nobody you'd wanna meet." Naturally, they immediately get lost and their car breaks down. Director Wes Craven creates a creepy atmosphere of grim isolation: buzzards circle, a tarantula crawls too close, unseen things run through the darkness, bushes shake. We also hear ominous stories about a twenty-pound baby "hairy as a monkey" that grew from "devil kid" to "devil man." Soon this demented grown-up monster appears, along with the rest of his feral brood. All of them badly need showers, decent clothes, and dental work. Freakiest of all is Michael Berryman, the misshapen baldy who's featured on the movie's forbidding poster.

The territorial mutants turn out to be sadistic cannibals who kidnap the family's "tenderloin baby" and literally eat grandpa. By the end of the terrifying night a dog has been gutted, and two of the stranded women have been shot to death. The next day the young survivors use some ingenuity, an axe, and a knife to retaliate. It's all extremely violent and alarming, but thankfully good (not good taste) does triumph. In the last scene, one of the stranded family members slays his attacker, and as he stares at the corpse the screen goes blood red and the end credits follow. So what happens next? The survivors are still stranded in the desert, they've blown up their trailer that had the food, supplies, and CB radio, and their broken-down car is out of gas. Oh, and they've got a baby with them. Good luck with that!

The movie has a kind of tacky appeal, it has Dee Wallace as one of the family members (she'll soon star in 1981's *The Howling*, 1982's *E.T.*, and 1983's *Cujo*), and it's more professional than director Craven's earlier rough-and-ready slasher movie, *The Last House on the Left* (1972). Craven's steady development would take him to his horror classic, *A Nightmare on Elm Street* (1984).

ADDED ATTRACTION: Drive-In Demise

Even as *The Hills Have Eyes* was playing, another low-budget horror movie was scaring the summer drive-in crowd. Tobe Hooper, director of *The Texas Chain Saw Massacre* (1974), followed up that influential slasher classic with *Eaten Alive* (1977), which is even more disturbing than its title suggests. The main setting is a dilapidated backwoods hotel run by Judd (Neville Brand), a mumbling maniac who makes Norman Bates look like Mr. Rogers. During one night people somehow keep arriving at Judd's dank hellhole, and his hospitable response is to attack them with a scythe and feed them to his alligator. Hooper underlights everything, incorporates eerie sound effects, and includes a chase through dark woods a la *Chain Saw Massacre*, but the results are more lurid than terrifying. The interesting cast includes Carolyn Jones, Robert Englund, and Marilyn Burns, the pretty girl who barely survived Hooper's previous movie and proves again she's one of the best screamers in the business. In 1977 drive-in audiences could also see a horror movie that was actually *set* at a drive-in. *Drive-In Massacre*, a no-budget gorefest that's only seventy-four minutes long, shows an unseen swordsman slashing and beheading moviegoers as they sit in their cars. The police shoot the suspect but ... oh no, he's the wrong killer! As the "senseless bloodbath" is about to continue, the movie abruptly ends with an official announcement that "there is a murderer loose in the theater!" Quick, everybody get dressed! Start your cars! Drive for your lives!

The Rescuers

(One of 1977's five **FAR-OUT** movies)

Released: June 1977

Director: John Lounsbery, Wolfgang Reitherman, Art Stevens

Stars: Bob Newhart, Eva Gabor, Geraldine Page

Academy Awards: One nomination (Best Song)

PREVIEW: Two mice fly from New York to the bayou so they can rescue an imprisoned young orphan.

FINE LINE: "Faith is a bluebird you see from afar. It's for real and as sure as the first evening star. You can't touch it, or buy it, or wrap it up tight, but it's there just the same making things turn out right." (The wise cat Rufus, consoling Penny when she doubts that she'll ever be adopted.)

CLOSE-UP: The interior of the Rescue Aid Society's headquarters is first viewed at almost six minutes into the movie (it'll reappear seventy minutes later). Inconspicuously mounted on the back wall to the left of the society's big blue banner is the "clock"—a Mickey Mouse watch with a brown leather band!

NOW SHOWING: A Rave for *The Rescuers*

Ask someone to list the biggest box-office hits among Disney's animated movies from 1937 up to 1979, and it's doubtful that *The Rescuers* (1977) will get a mention. But this underrated charmer was indeed one of the studio's all-time major blockbusters. After the amusing but slightly disappointing *Robin Hood* (1973) and the cartoon-compilation *The Many Adventures of Winnie the Pooh* (1977), *The Rescuers* brought back the strongest elements of the studio's greatest animated adventures. Compelling drama, not Hanna-Barbera-style slapstick gags, drives the story: the movie has action, suspense, interesting heroes, a terrific villainess, a heart-warming finish, good songs, and some gorgeously animated sequences. It's the best animated movie of the 1970s. Significantly, *The Rescuers* was Disney's twenty-third animated feature but the first to inspire a sequel, *The Rescuers Down Under* (1990). It would also be the last Disney animated movie to be nominated for an Oscar for over a decade, a streak finally broken by *Who Framed Roger Rabbit* (1988).

Unlike previous Disney movies that had started with the pages of a traditional story book being turned or a parade of characters marching through the opening credits, *The Rescuers* jumps right into the plot even as the credits roll. Lovely oil-painting-like images thrust viewers into the story of Penny, a young girl in undefined peril on the bayou, who tosses a message in a bottle into the water. Storm-tossed seas deliver the bottle to New York's East River. In Manhattan the Rescue Aid Society, made up of mice, reads Penny's pleading message and sends two representatives, the elegant, confident Miss Bianca (voiced by Eva Gabor) and the quiet, reluctant Bernard (Bob Newhart) to go rescue her.

Their investigation leads them to "a sleazy pawnshop" and a raging redhead with a volatile temper named Madame Medusa (Geraldine Page). She recklessly drives off like Cruella De Vil in *101 Dalmatians* (1961), heading to the Devil's Bayou, where Penny is being held. The mice, meanwhile, avail themselves of the Albatross Air Service; now a third of the way into the movie, things take off, literally and figuratively, with the arrival of Orville, the goggled albatross that straps them to his back and flies them through the city's concrete canyons and under the Brooklyn Bridge at sunset. A beautiful three-minute flight over scenic landscapes, past rainbows, and through the blue evening sky follows, a wonderful sequence reminiscent of the memorable flight to Neverland in *Peter Pan* (1953).

In the bayou the captors' fiendish plot—to send little Penny into a deep cave to retrieve the fabulous Devil's Eye, "the world's largest diamond"—is revealed. After some indoor chases involving alligators, brooms, and a gun (including a clever scene with the mice inside a pipe organ), nighttime falls on the bayou. When Penny starts to lose hope, Shelby Flint sings the lovely Oscar-nominated ballad, "Someone's Waiting for You."

Penny and her rescuers finally descend into that dark cave in the last third of the movie. Echoing the cave scenes inside Disneyland's iconic Pirates of the Caribbean ride, this great five-minute sequence has pirate skulls, skeletons, cutlasses, treasure, and a dangerous escape through turbulent waters. "A rip-snortin' fight" back on the surface leads to a satisfying Disney ending that unites the diamond with the Smithsonian, Penny with new parents, and the mice with ... a sequel? Sure seems like it when they get another message and Orville carries them aloft in the last scene.

What Miss Bianca excitedly anticipates at the very end—"Adventure! Thrills! Intrigue! Travel! Exotic places! Oh come on, darling, let's go!"—basically summarizes *The Rescuers*. It's got everything audiences could want in an entertaining animated adventure, including a roster of impressive artists. Carrying over from *Robin Hood* were six of Walt's legendary "nine old men," the great animators Ollie Johnston, Milt Kahl, Eric Larson, John Lounsbery, and Frank Thomas, plus director Wolfgang Reitherman.

Of the voice actors and actresses, Bob Newhart and Eva Gabor are perfect for their mice roles (he's his usual hesitant, under-stated self, she's sweetly alluring). However, it's powerful Geraldine Page who steals every scene as the imperious Madame Medusa. This volatile character ranks among the best of Disney's animated villains. Avaricious and strong-willed, wearing heavy makeup, big green earrings, and distinctive short hair, she bears some similarity to Cruella De Vil in *101 Dalmatians*, but Medusa is not as cruel as that sadistic puppy-killer. Joe Flynn, a stalwart of Disney's live-action comedies, voices Medusa's rotund henchman, Snoops (it's a posthumous screen credit for Flynn, who died before the movie was finished). Missing is Phil Harris, who had co-starred in *The Jungle Book* (1967), *The Aristocats* (1970), and *Robin Hood*; the absence of his relaxed, folksy voice showed that *The Rescuers* was a shift away from the jocularity of those earlier movies.

Also notable in *The Rescuers* is the move toward

Madame Medusa.

feminism. Not only does the female mouse lead the rescue effort, but Penny herself tries to effect an escape, and she delivers the movie's message that "faith makes things turn out right." This isn't *The Jungle Book*, where all the major characters are male, or *The Aristocats*, where the aristocratic Duchess needs O'Malley the alley cat to save her and her family, or *Robin Hood*, where Maid Marian is barely in the movie's second half. "It's not like the old days when it was a man's world," announces the society's chairman ten minutes into *The Rescuers*. Right on.

ADDED ATTRACTION: The Love Machine

Two days after *The Rescuers* came out, Disney released an inoffensive live-action comedy, *Herbie Goes to Monte Carlo* (1977). Dean Jones had starred in *The Love Bug* (1968) and then skipped the first sequel, *Herbie Rides Again* (1974), but he returned for *Monte Carlo*. His character, Jim, acknowledges this long gap, though he doesn't mention the woman he married at the end of *The Love Bug*. In fact, he's now single. *C'est la vie*. This third Herbie derby really does go to Monte Carlo for the Trans France Race. The scenery is *magnifique*, with lots of beautiful aerial shots tracking the cars as they race through the French countryside. As always Herbie, the lively VW who's "kinda like a person," steals the show. In addition to battling sleek race cars, Herbie's got a baseball-sized diamond stashed in his gas tank, thanks to two bumbling thieves (bumbling thieves—is there any other kind in a Disney comedy?). But the race and the diamond aren't what give this fun movie its distinctive charm. Herbie makes his most daring emotional leap ever by falling in love with Giselle, a "luscious little Lancia" that is evidently female (cars have genders, who knew?). Like a smitten teen Herbie revs up and shows off, popping wheelies, bouncing, spinning, flicking his windshield wipers, and playing romantic music on his radio. Before their first date, he even takes a shower in a fountain and snags her some flowers. All these distractions make Herbie fall behind in the race, but he successfully finishes with a gravity-defying sprint. Criminals are caught, the diamond is returned, couples are united. Jim gets Diane (Julie Sommars), an angry rival driver for the first fifty-six minutes until she softens and admits that she's been "a little uptight." Incredibly the bug-eyed Wheely (Don Knotts) gets the race's slinky trophy girl. And twice the audience gets the sentence "no one would believe this." *Exactement*.

New York, New York

Released: June 1977
Director: Martin Scorsese
Stars: Liza Minnelli, Robert De Niro, Barry Primus
Academy Awards: None

PREVIEW: In 1945, two talented musicians get married, but their careers and lives separate.

NOW SHOWING: "Start Spreading the News"

What a pedigree this movie has. Martin Scorsese, hot off *Taxi Driver* (1976), is the director; Liza Minnelli and Robert De Niro, two stars who had already won Oscars, play the leads; the great music includes new songs by the legendary team of Kander and Ebb; and this big-budget movie has an impressive technical polish. Yet somehow *New York, New York* (1977) misfires. What happened?

Two words: Jimmy Doyle. Obnoxious and pushy, Doyle (De Niro) incorrectly thinks he's charming, just like De Niro's abrasive Jake La Motta character does in *Raging Bull* (1980). *New York, New York* starts with this conceited jerk relentlessly pestering a "spirited filly" named Francine (Minnelli) in 1945. Doyle is a saxophone player who argues at his audition, but once Francine, a talented singer, joins him, they're hired together. Singing the standards in fabulous costumes, Minnelli is truly in her element, and she elevates the movie.

Liza Minnelli and Robert De Niro.

Illogically, a romance ensues, even though Jimmy's a "five-star pain in the ass" (he's called a pain in the ass four more times). His arrogant marriage proposal (there's yelling, a broken window, and a suicide attempt) is uncomfortable to watch. Soon Jimmy is bossing everybody around, flinging tables, engaging in shouting matches, and even getting abusive with his wife. Midway through the movie she announces she's pregnant and leaves their tour to return to New York. Cad that he is, Jimmy continues the tour without her and has an affair. Then, the same day Francine delivers the baby, Jimmy splits for good, later opening his own jazz club. With Jimmy out of the movie for seventeen minutes, Francine, now a movie star, performs a glittering medley reminiscent of the long "Broadway Melody" number in *Singin' in the Rain* (1952). She finally belts out the movie's show-stopping theme song (which amazingly wasn't nominated for an Oscar), and in the last scene she stands Jimmy up, finally deciding she's had enough of his act.

So it's appropriate that there's no happy ending. This dark movie takes the template of old-fashioned romantic musicals, including the stylized, colorful sets, and adds a volatile, unlikeable male lead, downbeat emotions, intense conflict, realistic improvised dialogue, and a climax in which the two stars separate. Unfortunately, the mix of old-time artifice and gritty realism doesn't jell. Despite the showy musical numbers (staged by Scorsese), audiences never warmed to this lumbering two-and-a-half hour movie. It's an ambitious disappointment.

ADDED ATTRACTION: *New York, New York* Who's Who

Even viewers who don't like *New York, New York* have to admit that it's got an interesting supporting cast.

- **Diahnne Abbott**: Robert De Niro's real-life wife in 1977, in *Taxi Driver* (1976) she played the employee at the counter inside the adult movie theater that Travis Bickle patronizes. In *New York, New York*, she's the sultry "Honeysuckle Rose" singer in the Harlem Club 114 minutes into the movie.
- **Clarence Clemons**: Famous as the saxophone player in Bruce Springsteen's E Street Band. In *New York, New York*, he has several scenes as a trumpet player in a jazz combo.

- **Sydney Guilaroff**: The legendary hair stylist for hundreds of movies from the 1930s to the 1990s. Guilaroff plays Francine's hairdresser in *New York, New York*.
- **Jack Haley**: Liza Minnelli's real-life father-in-law, he played the Tin Man in *The Wizard of Oz* (1939). He plays the emcee at the testimonial dinner 136 minutes into *New York, New York*.
- **Casey Kasem**: The popular host of *American Top 40*, a long-running nationally syndicated radio show. Kasem is shown as a DJ 145 minutes into the movie and introduces an instrumental version of "New York, New York."

Sorcerer

Released: June 1977
Director: William Friedkin
Stars: Roy Scheider, Bruno Cremer, Francisco Rabal
Academy Awards: One nomination (Best Sound)

PREVIEW: Four men make a perilous journey through the jungle in trucks carrying explosives.

NOW SHOWING: *Sorcerer* Casts a Spell

Sorcerer (1977) had the misfortune to come out thirty days after *Star Wars* (1977), which meant record-setting audiences were zooming to a fascinating galaxy far, far away rather than venturing into a harsh South American jungle. Luckily we caught *Sorcerer* during its brief run at Westwood's majestic National Theatre, and we can attest to the grip it held on its sparse audience. Given a chance, William Friedkin's movie is riveting.

The basic story—four desperate men cautiously drive two trucks carrying about-to-explode nitroglycerin through rugged mountains—could be enjoyed by watching only the second half. *Sorcerer* is like *Jaws* (1975) that way; once the trucks get rolling, viewers can ride along like they could once the *Orca* headed out to sea. Friedkin's storytelling is so pure, so visceral, he limits the movie's second-half dialogue and still makes the adventure thoroughly engrossing. Two back-to-back thirteen-minute sequences are especially harrowing: a tense inch-by-inch struggle to maneuver the trucks across a dilapidated wooden bridge during a raging storm, and the ingenious effort to clear an obstacle from the path. Both artistic triumphs, either one would be the highlight of another action movie.

Even without considering the competition from *Star Wars*, it's understandable why audiences might've avoided *Sorcerer*. First, despite the title (which is the name on one of the trucks) and a glimpse of a demonic stone face, there's nothing sorcerer-ish or supernatural going on, perhaps a disappointment for anyone expecting something like Friedkin's *The Exorcist* (1973). Next, it takes sixty-three minutes to get the trucks underway. What's more, English isn't even spoken for the first sixteen minutes, so it's all subtitles until Roy Scheider appears. Because he's the movie's only well-known actor, *Sorcerer* doesn't have Hollywood star power working its crowd-pleasing magic. And though we can admire their skills and bravery, these grim, amoral criminals aren't likeable.

Friedkin fans will recognize elements from his previous movies. A la *The French Connection* (1971), the first sequence shows an anonymous assassination in a foreign country. Strong visuals, atmospheric instrumental music (here by synthesizer-based Tangerine Dream), and men in gritty, dangerous situations all evoke Friedkin's previous masterpieces. With its last scene of long-forgotten hit-men arriving to claim final retribution, *Sorcerer* delivers a brutally pessimistic message that's similar to *The French Connection*'s fruitless pursuit: unsympathetic fate just might intervene at any moment to negate best efforts and intentions. In the dark world of *Sorcerer*, everybody's doomed.

ADDED ATTRACTION: Friedkin's Follow-Up

After *Sorcerer* failed to summon audiences, director William Friedkin conjured up an amusing crime caper that has no deaths, no bloodshed, and no heart-racing tension. *The Brink's Job* (1978) tells the true story of petty thieves in Boston who go from bumbling through small-scale heists, especially a comical break-in at a candy factory, to pulling off what's called "the crime of the century" at the Brink's headquarters in January 1950. These endearing shmoes manage to escape with over two-million dollars, but they barely get to celebrate because the gang members soon turn on each other, the FBI closes in with "the largest criminal roundup in history," and eventually prison sentences are handed out. The gloomy mood of the last half-hour lightens when the neighborhood celebrates the guys as local heroes. *The Brink's Job* boasts Oscar-nominated art direction that effectively captures the period and an interesting cast highlighted by Peter Falk as the brains of the outfit, but being neither laugh-out-loud funny nor deviously clever the movie is more diverting than essential.

MacArthur

Released: June 1977
Director: Joseph Sargent
Stars: Gregory Peck, Dan O'Herlihy, Ed Flanders
Academy Awards: None

PREVIEW: The main military victories and political defeats of the famous American general.

NOW SHOWING: *Patton* 2.0

Comparisons are inevitable between *Patton* (1970) and *MacArthur* (1977). Some of the crew is the same, including composer Jerry Goldsmith, and so is the plot structure, starting with a rousing opening speech by a military legend to a military audience. As in *Patton*, *MacArthur* soon follows its speech with an early military defeat, continues with impressive World War Two triumphs that incorporate actual war and newsreel footage, and ends with a forced retirement for political reasons. Each movie spotlights a controversial, glory-seeking general who favored attack over defense, quoted literature, and staged his beach landings to make sure he looked good for the cameras. *MacArthur* even mentions General Patton, who is "fighting his seesaw tank battles" in Africa while General MacArthur is in the Pacific. It's also rumored that George C. Scott was offered both roles.

MacArthur asserts itself in some important ways, however: *Patton* covers the years 1943-1945, whereas *MacArthur* ambitiously goes beyond World War Two to Korea in the early 1950s, to American politics of that decade, and to MacArthur's famous "old soldiers never die, they just fade away" retirement speech. *Patton* shows its vigorous general shooting at enemies with his own pistols; *MacArthur* has its general pointing at maps, never pointing with (or even carrying) guns. Brilliant strategy, sheer will, and bombastic speeches are MacArthur's main weapons.

In one vital way *MacArthur* is very similar to *Patton*: the strength of each movie is the star's commanding performance. In *MacArthur* Gregory Peck is compelling as a powerful speaker and dignified leader devoted, as he reminds us repeatedly, to "duty, honor, country." As his ego overtakes his judgement (a theme present in *Patton*), this "American Caesar" dares to challenge American presidents (President Truman sarcastically calls him "His Majesty" before orchestrating his ouster). These political confrontations are clear and fascinating.

Unfortunately, budget limitations kept the filming

Gregory Peck.

on domestic locations (whereas *Patton* was shot in Europe and North Africa). Moreover, *MacArthur*'s supporting cast isn't as imposing as *Patton*'s, which boasted Oscar-winner Karl Malden as General Bradley (in contrast, eight minutes into *MacArthur*, we're supposed to take Russell Johnson, already familiar as the Professor on TV's *Gilligan's Island*, seriously as an admiral). Ultimately *MacArthur* the movie isn't as remarkable as MacArthur the man, though it is still a solid biography. Only when it's compared to the epic *Patton*, one of the great war movies of all time, does *MacArthur* seem significantly diminished.

ADDED ATTRACTION: Tora! Tora! *Midway*!

Just as *MacArthur* echoes the Oscar-winning *Patton*, *Midway* (1976) applies a formula well-established by the Oscar-winning *Tora! Tora! Tora!* (1970). Both *Midway* and *Tora!* begin with long lead-ins that present strategies on both sides of a famous World War Two aerial attack by the Japanese against a Pacific island. After an hour of decoded messages and discussions, each battle is then fought with zooming planes, burning ships, and all-star casts (in *Midway*, the last names include Heston, Fonda, and Mitchum). Some big differences between the movies: *Midway*'s Japanese officers speak English (so no subtitles), *Midway* has an unnecessary romantic subplot, and, since it coincided with 1976's Bicentennial celebrations, *Midway* ends with a rousing American victory (*Tora!* recreates Pearl Harbor, and you know how that ignominious day ended). Also, *Midway* was initially released with Sensurround, the theater-shaking audio experiment introduced by *Earthquake* (1974) and about to end with *Rollercoaster* (1977). Disappointingly, while *Midway* includes actual combat footage, the movie cheats by excerpting other war movies, including three minutes of *Thirty Seconds Over Tokyo* (1944) and many battle scenes pulled directly from *Tora! Tora! Tora!*, which had come out just six years earlier and so wasn't exactly ancient history. *Midway* is watchable, but, compared to its more focused, better-made predecessor, it's a second-rate spectacle.

The Spy Who Loved Me

Released: July 1977
Director: Lewis Gilbert
Stars: Roger Moore, Barbara Bach, Curt Jurgens
Academy Awards: Three nominations (Best Art Direction; Best Song; Best Music)

PREVIEW: Agent James Bond teams up with a Russian agent to track down two missing submarines.

NOW SHOWING: "Why'd You Have to Be So Good?"

Of Roger Moore's four 007 movies in the Double-Oh-Seventies, his best was his third, *The Spy Who Loved Me* (1977). Its lackluster predecessor, *The Man with the Golden Gun* (1974), had followed just a year after *its* predecessor, *Live and Let Die* (1973), and both seemed relatively insignificant compared to nearly every previous Bond movie. By comparison, almost three years and an enormous budget were invested in *Spy*, which required the construction of the world's largest sound stage. *Golden Gun* has pistol shots in a funhouse; *Spy* detonates two nuclear bombs. *Spy* gambled big and triumphs spectacularly.

While it's punctuated with humorous quips, *Spy* has a welcome gravitas that's lacking in the other, campier Bond movies of the 1970s. As usual there's a long pre-credits sequence that jumps from submarines to bedrooms to an amazing ski stunt. Then, instead of the typically bombastic theme song, the credits roll to Carly Simon's seductive hit, "Nobody Does It Better." Pursuing leads on two missing submarines, Bond goes to Egypt and teams up with a smart, alluring Russian counterpart, Agent XXX (Barbara Bach), sparking "a new era of Anglo-Soviet cooperation." The elegant villain is Stromberg (Curt Jurgens), "one of the richest men in the world" with one of the best henchmen in the entire Bond series, the massive metal-mouthed Jaws (Richard Kiel). Stromberg's got a fabulous marine lab, an oil tanker for capturing submarines, and a mad Captain Nemo-like obsession: after using the subs as his "instruments of Armageddon" to destroy New York and Moscow, "global destruction will follow" and he'll create "a new and beautiful world beneath the sea." Not if Bond has anything to say about it.

Roger Moore and Barbara Bach.

Visually, this is the richest Bond movie since *You Only Live Twice* (1967). Bond goes from Egypt's desert to Sardinia's coast, where a scenic chase ensues. Initially that chase puts Bond in a sleek white Lotus on winding mountain roads, but he then plunges the car into the water and converts it into a terrific missile-firing min-sub. Stromberg's enormous submarine pens and amazing amphibious lab are dazzling, as are the movie's women (among them is the majestic Caroline Munro, a bikinied bad girl killed off too quickly). In addition to the epic entertainment, we even get to hear the names of M (Miles) and Q (Major Boothroyd). For the decade's most polished Bond thrills, nobody does it better than *The Spy Who Loved Me*.

ADDED ATTRACTION: The Long Side of Midnight

In mid-'77 there was another romantic thriller in theaters alongside *The Spy Who Loved Me*. Both were based on books: *The Spy Who Loved Me* takes its title—but almost nothing else—from Ian Fleming's 1962 novel, while *The Other Side of Midnight* closely follows Sidney Sheldon's 1973 bestseller. Like the book, *The Other Side of Midnight* is a steamy World War Two tale of an American flyer (John Beck) who callously abandons his loving Parisian fiancée (Marie-France Pisier) and marries an innocent American girl (Susan Sarandon). *La parisienne* then sleazes her way through shallow relationships with older men to attain wealth and power so she can get her flyboy back (he may be a rat, but he's *her* rat). After a lusty reconciliation, they decide to murder his wife. Trashy and insipid to many viewers, and indefensibly long (165 minutes!) to almost everybody, the movie does offer all the sex, melodrama, glamorous lifestyles, and Oscar-nominated costumes that fans of Jacqueline Susann's and Harold Robbins' soapy stories could want, and thus it actually became a modest box-office success. Unfortunately, *The Other Side of Midnight* wasn't the hit that 20th Century Fox expected because it had the misfortune to come out two weeks after a movie that immediately conquered the galaxy: *Star Wars*.

The Last Remake of Beau Geste

Released: July 1977
Director: Marty Feldman
Stars: Marty Feldman, Ann-Margret, Michael York
Academy Awards: None

PREVIEW: Two brothers enlist in the French Foreign Legion and have adventures in the desert.

NOW SHOWING: Blazing Camels

After the success of Mel Brooks's *Blazing Saddles* (1974) and *Young Frankenstein* (1974), studios quickly produced more movie-genre spoofs, some of them directed by Brooks or alumni of his movies. To name just two examples, Gene Wilder wrote/directed/starred in the Sherlock Holmes send-up *The Adventure of Sherlock Holmes' Smarter Brother* (1975), and a year later Brooks himself parodied silent movies in *Silent Movie* (1976). Joining them in mid-1977 was *The Last Remake of Beau Geste*, an anarchic comedy co-written by/directed by/and starring Marty Feldman, veteran of both *Young Frankenstein* and *Smarter Brother*. His isn't the funniest comedy mentioned so far (Brooks's two '74 classics still rule), but it's among the most inventive.

As with all genre parodies, the more you know about the earlier movies, the more you'll enjoy the modern jokes told about them. Feldman's movie loosely follows *Beau Geste* (P.C. Wren's 1924 novel and William Wellman's 1939 movie) while making happy changes to the plot (Wren and Wellman both kill off the two leads, for instance). Feldman is Digby Geste and Michael York plays his dashing brother, Beau, in early twentieth-century England. After a priceless sapphire disappears, both men end up in Morocco as French Foreign Legionnaires. Arab attacks on their desert fort, a brutal sergeant, and a twist to the missing-gem mystery are familiar elements carried over from previous versions.

Feldman's comedy includes inspired sight gags (different styles of peg legs for different events), some clever jokes ("Gentlemen, synchronize your hourglasses, we leave in exactly seventy-thousand grains of sand"), and some funny repeated lines (an old man who's constantly "alive and dying"). Feldman really gets ambitious when he goes for *Blazing Saddles*-style meta-comedy with characters who know they're in a movie: "You can't just desert, you'll miss the rest of the story"; a newspaper-headline shot is announced as "another movie cliché"; a character reads the subtitles displayed below him. Feldman also includes a three-minute black-and-white silent movie, a Busby Berkeley-style dance number, TV's Ed McMahon ("We interrupt this important battle to bring you the news"), and a commercial from used-camel-salesman "Honest Hakkim." Feldman's most innovative moment comes when Digby has a mirage and he joins Wellman's 1939 movie to talk with Gary Cooper; Carl Reiner and Steve Martin later turn this brilliant three-minute idea into a whole movie, *Dead Men Don't Wear Plaid* (1982). Not everything works, but enough does to make *The Last Remake of Beau Geste* an entertaining diversion.

ADDED ATTRACTION: Wilder's *Greatest Lover*

Between Feldman's *The Last Remake of Beau Geste* and Mel Brooks's Hitchcock spoof *High Anxiety* (1977), another comedy parodied a movie genre, though it isn't as funny as the other two. Gene Wilder produced/wrote/directed/composed the song for/and starred in (whew!) *The World's Greatest Lover* (1977), a take-off on 1920s silent movies. Wilder plays a nervous Milwaukee baker who enters a Hollywood contest to find the next Rudolph Valentino. The always-delightful Carol Kane plays his wife (that same year Kane was in *Valentino*, Ken Russell's drama starring Rudolf Nureyev as the screen idol). For a movie set in the silent era, *The World's Greatest Lover* is awfully screechy, with Wilder frequently yelling like he did throughout *Young Frankenstein* (Dom DeLuise, playing a studio head, is just as noisy). Juvenile slapstick, obvious gags, and slide whistles displace sophisticated wit, though the scene of the couple's sprint through a "sex by numbers" manual is pretty good. Wilder finishes with romantic sweetness, but it's too late. Nevertheless, audiences swooned for this *Lover* and made it a hit.

Orca

Released: July 1977
Director: Michael Anderson
Stars: Richard Harris, Charlotte Rampling, Will Sampson
Academy Awards: None

PREVIEW: A sailor battles a killer whale that wants revenge for the death of its mate and baby.

NOW SHOWING: *Jaws* Too

Several seafaring adventures tried to fill the gap between *Jaws* (1975) and *Jaws 2* (1978). Not only did these mediocre copycats fall well short of the original *Jaws*'s artistry and success, they weren't even as good as its waterlogged sequel. One of these *Jaws*titutes was *Orca* (1977), aka *Orca: The Killer Whale*. The movie borrows plenty from *Jaws*, including opening moments of underwater sounds, images from the beast's point of view, a long chase with the quarry leading its pursuers out to sea, and an out-of-the-water leap that tilts the creature's human nemesis back to his doom. Richard Harris plays an arrogant captain, Nolan, who mocks a young scientist, here played by Charlotte Rampling, the same way that *Jaws*'s old-school shark hunter, Quint (Robert Shaw), mocked the brash young Hooper (Richard Dreyfuss). As in *Jaws*, *Orca*'s ancient mariner is on his last voyage, while the youngster lives to research another day.

A key difference between the two movies is that *Orca*'s orca has a specific motivation. *Jaws*'s great white was an "eating machine" that mindlessly gulped down anything nearby, behaving just like, y'know, a shark. *Orca*'s killer whale, we're told, has human-like emotions, "a profound instinct for vengeance," and intelligence that "may even be superior to man." The orca targets Nolan after it watches him harpoon and string up its pregnant mate. Then the screaming fetus graphically tumbles onto the boat, a nightmarish scene that could permanently scar impressionable viewers. With the audience now rooting for the male orca, it stalks Nolan, kills his crew one by one, destroys his seaside house, and starts a devastating dock fire. Feeling remorseful, but with "no choice but to fight," Nolan follows the orca to the polar ice. There the orca gets its *Moby Dick*-like revenge, a legitimate connection to make since Herman Melville actually gets a shout-out.

One of the movie's flaws appears in the first two minutes, when shots of orcas at sea are interrupted by insert shots of orcas in a Marine World tank. This awkward mix continues throughout, and it doesn't take an ichthyologist to see the obvious difference. Later problems include an unrealistic romance and a turgid closing love song. Bo Derek has little to do in her movie debut, besides proving that the orca is a leg man. *Orca* isn't the decade's worst sea saga, but there are reasons why this killer-whale-of-a-tale floundered at the box office.

ADDED ATTRACTION: Lost at Sea

Other ocean-going movies that soon trailed in *Jaws*'s wake included *The Jaws of Death* (1976) and *Tentacles* (1977). *The Jaws of Death*, aka *Mako: The Jaws of Death*, presents sharks as friends, not foes, and has more action on land than in the water. Richard Jaeckel plays a loner who wears a magic medallion that makes him "a member of the shark clan," enabling him to communicate with sharks and swim safely among them. Betrayed when he loans sharks to a callous scientist and an unscrupulous businessman, he feeds his human enemies to his underwater friends, but he too becomes shark bait when his medallion comes off. "Crazy" is the appropriate last line. Thirty-one minutes into the movie, watch for a girl wearing the decade's widest bellbottoms, and then, at seventy-four minutes, note the mustachioed cop: he's played by Luke Halpin, formerly the youthful star of the 1960s *Flipper* movies and TV series. Meanwhile, *Tentacles* has slightly better production values and much bigger names, including two-time Oscar-winner Shelley Winters, Oscar-winning director John Huston, and the venerable Henry Fonda (he plays the head of an unethical underwater-construction company called Trojan, hopefully its motto is something like The Company That Protects You). Bad dubbing for the movie's Italian actors, an underwhelming "giant" octopus that terrorizes the California coast, a bizarre motivational talk given to two heroic orcas, and a blurry final fight sink this dumb *Jaws* wannabe.

Empire of the Ants

Released: July 1977
Director: Bert I. Gordon
Stars: Joan Collins, Robert Lansing, John Carson
Academy Awards: None

PREVIEW: Giant ants terrorize, and even indoctrinate, people in a Florida beach community.

NOW SHOWING: A Bug's Life

The big-bug sci-fi movies of the 1950s—especially the Oscar-nominated *Them!* (1954)—got revived in the mid-'70s with new variations on familiar themes. *Empire of the Ants* (1977) is one of the movies that helped exterminate this ant-iquated subgenre for the rest of the decade.

Empire of the Ants was directed by Bert I. Gordon, the master of low-budget drive-in flicks about normal-size creatures that become gigantic; his *The Food of the Gods* (1976) included giant chickens, rats and wasps. *Empire of the Ants* starts with a solemn narrator and footage of real ants carrying things, a la the Oscar-winning documentary *The Hellstrom Chronicle* (1971). Then comes the time-tested cause of all ant problems, whether it's a real-life picnic or a horror movie: someone doesn't properly clean up a mess, here a drum of radioactive waste that washes onto a Florida beach and breaks open. Naturally ants come to feast, start growing, and off to B-movieland we go.

Enhancing the fun is Joan Collins, starring as a deceitful developer who takes ten suckers on a tour of a soon-to-be-badly-constructed beach community. She's a shyster, but she's also an awesome employer, telling her handsome assistant, "You're so terrific in the sack that it almost justifies the excessive salary that I have to pay you." As ant-icipated, a third of the way into the movie the ants, now bigger than cows, appear in full shriek-and-attack mode. There's no ant-idote, only escape, so the rest of the movie shows the group fleeing through nearby swamps. The end gets surreal by showing a supersized colony inside a sugar factory, where the queen ant converts humans, including Collins, into mindless slaves by spraying them. For Collins the real horror had to be enduring the entire movie in a single outfit ... that gets torn! Nooooooo!

Schlocktastic movies are made memorable by unintentionally hilarious lines, like this gem, mid-movie among ants and carnage: "All we wanted was to enjoy what was left of our life. Is that bad?" Inexplicably the movie kills off a pretty girl way too early; did Gordon learn *nothing* from *The Poseidon Adventure* (1972)? The ant-agonized ants themselves are shown in a mix of live footage projected around the cast and artificial ant heads for close-up attacks. Nothing works, making this movie *Empire of the Can'ts*: it can't intrigue us, can't scare us, and can't make us watch it one more time.

ADDED ATTRACTION: Monster Mash

Because there's never a can of Raid around when you need one, three more 1975-1977 movies featured big bugs. In *Bug* (1975), thumb-size incendiary "firebugs" rise from the ground after an earthquake. The bugs evolve, create patterns that spell actual English-language words on the wall (wow, smart bugs!), and grow to the size of shrieking seagulls. Patty McCormack, the wicked girl in *The Bad Seed* (1959), is one of the victims in this disturbing movie. Next, *The Giant Spider Invasion* (1975) is a laughable cheapie that was surprisingly popular, despite having only one "giant spider" (actually a car that's covered with fur and moving insect legs) that arrives via a crashed meteorite. The goofy sheriff, Alan Hale Jr., says "Hi, little buddy!" a la TV's *Gilligan's Island*, and he seriously brings up a popular 1975 movie to explain how scary the spider is: "Did you ever see that movie *Jaws*? Well it makes that shark look like a goldfish!" No it doesn't. *Damnation Alley* (1977) is a better movie that unleashes a nuclear holocaust and sends survivors on a long, dangerous driving trip from California to New York in big armored vehicles. Along the way Jan-Michael Vincent goes out on his own and encounters some huge scorpions in the desert, but he simply speeds his motorcycle around them. It's tough to be a bug.

The Kentucky Fried Movie

Released: August 1977
Director: John Landis
Stars: Evan Kim, Neal Thompson, Bill Bixby
Academy Awards: None

PREVIEW: Various stars make cameo appearances in a wild collection of skits and short films.

NOW SHOWING: Pick Up Some *KFM*

Anthology movies had been around long before the 1970s. Notable examples include the star-studded *Tales of Manhattan* (1942), *O. Henry's Full House* (1952) with Marilyn Monroe, and Gene Kelly's *Invitation to the Dance* (1956). By 1977 the '70s had already produced a half-dozen anthology movies spanning Neil Simon's *Plaza Suite* (1971) and Disney's *The Many Adventures of Winnie the Pooh* (1977). Mid-decade, *The Groove Tube* (1974) was a raunchy, often hilarious anthology that led to another fun, frantic comedy collection, *The Kentucky Fried Movie* (1977).

A zany, rude, and uneven mix of anarchic skits and short movies, *The Kentucky Fried Movie* was the low-budget academy where comedy masterminds John Landis, Jim Abrahams, David Zucker, and Jerry Zucker perfected their craft. Landis would direct *Animal House* the next year, and in 1980 Abrahams and the Zuckers would create *Airplane!* Their brash, irreverent styles are already in evidence in *The Kentucky Fried Movie* via bits ranging in length from just a few seconds to a thirty-two-minute martial arts showpiece called *A Fistful of Yen* that somehow ends like *The Wizard of Oz* (1939). Various 1970s commercials and movie topics get spoofed, including blaxploitation flicks such as 1973's *Cleopatra Jones* (here called *Cleopatra Schwartz*), disaster epics (*That's Armageddon*), and amplified movies like *Earthquake* (1974) that used Sensurround (enhanced here into the hands-on Feel-A-Round).

Some of the skits are a little distasteful (a Kennedy-assassination board game called Scot Free), some are inspired (the *Zinc Oxide and You* send-up of old-fashioned educational films for kids), and some feature lots of nudity (the coming attraction called *Catholic High School Girls in Trouble*). But always, if you don't like one sketch, the next one is just minutes away, because director Landis keeps the pace moving. Watch for the many celebrity cameos, which include Donald Sutherland, Bill Bixby, George Lazenby (he was James Bond in 1969), Henry Gibson from TV's *Laugh-In*, Tony Dow from TV's *Leave It to Beaver*, horror-movie expert Forrest J. Ackerman, Stephen Stucker (later a scene-stealer in *Airplane!*), and even the writing team itself in several scenes. One curiosity is the credit for singer Stephen Bishop, who makes his acting debut as "Charming Guy." What's curious is that in his next movie, *Animal House* (1978), he'll be "Charming Guy with Guitar"; in *The Blues Brothers* (1980), he's the "Charming Trooper"; in *Twilight Zone: The Movie* (1983), the "Charming G.I." Now that's what we call typecasting!

ADDED ATTRACTION: Evel Knievel Retrieval

In the summer of '77, another distinctive movie with interesting casting was *Viva Knievel!* (1977). George Hamilton had already played the famous motorcycle stuntman in a fictionalized bio-pic, *Evel Knievel* (1971). That one had an entertaining vitality to it, some of it gained from Hamilton's passionate portrayal of the reckless daredevil, and the rest from dramatic footage of Knievel's actual stunts and crashes. Co-written by John Milius, the movie has the shameless self-promoter make such solemn pronouncements as "Fear is not a word in my vocabulary" and "I am the last gladiator in the new Rome." The wheels came off the Evelcycle in 1977 when the real Evel Knievel moved from the track to the big screen. He plays himself in *Viva Knievel!* alongside Gene Kelly (sadly, not in any kind of musical role, but as an angry alcoholic), Lauren Hutton, Red Buttons, Leslie Nielsen, Frank Gifford, and more. Identified in this hagiography as "the greatest and bravest showman in the world," Knievel shows us his softer side by delivering toys and inspiration to orphans. Unfortunately, at times he also comes across as a surly jerk, and Knievel is such a wooden actor that his part could've been played by a six-foot elm tree. The ludicrous plot has drug-lord Nielsen trying to knock off Knievel in Mexico so he can smuggle drugs back to America in Knievel's truck, but our Cheesy Rider turns the tables in a five-minute desert chase highlighted by a motorcycle leap *onto* (not over) a moving vehicle. Almost everything in *Viva Knievel!* is big: the motorcycle ramps, the cars, the sideburns, the shirt collars, the plot holes, the unintended laughs ... weren't the '70s awesome?

Julia

Released: October 1977
Director: Fred Zinnemann
Stars: Jane Fonda, Vanessa Redgrave, Jason Robards
Academy Awards: Three wins (Best Supporting Actress—Vanessa Redgrave; Best Supporting Actor—Jason Robards; Best Writing), plus eight more nominations (Best Picture; Best Actress—Jane Fonda; Best Supporting Actor—Maximilian Schell; Best Director; Best Editing; Best Cinematography; Best Costume Design; Best Music)

PREVIEW: Two friends go separate ways in the 1930s; one writes plays, the other fights Nazis.

NOW SHOWING: Judging *Julia*

One of the decade's most well-crafted movies, *Julia* (1977) showcases bravura performances. Under the direction of Fred Zinnemann, already a two-time Oscar winner for Best Director, the movie earned Oscar nominations for Jane Fonda, Vanessa Redgrave, Jason Robards, and Maximilian Schell (Redgrave and Robards won). Though the movie is named after Redgrave's character, it's really about Fonda's. She plays Lillian Hellman, who wrote the memoir *Julia* is based on. Those are Lillian's narrated thoughts we're hearing, her memories we're seeing.

Lillian and Julia are teenage best friends who separate as young adults in the 1930s but stay devoted to each other. Throughout the movie, scenes instantly shift, as memories do, from present to past, so that adult Lillian will suddenly recall sailing or hiking with Julia when they're both young (those dreams eventually become nightmares). Following Julia's advice to "work hard, take chances, be very bold," Lillian becomes "the toast of the town" in 1934 when her first play, *The Children's Hour*, becomes a Broadway hit; Julia, meanwhile, starts medical school in Oxford but soon relocates to Austria. As Julia's politics get more radical, she's severely beaten up by Nazis, who are becoming an obvious menace.

Fifty-four minutes in, the story dramatically changes: heading to a theater festival in Moscow, Lillian is asked (via a letter from Julia) to smuggle $50,000 into Berlin, where it will be used as bribes to help Jews and "political people" fight back against the Nazis. The second half of the movie is dominated by shadowy European train stations and nerve-wracking train travel as Lillian finds a new courage inside herself and endures all kinds of suspenseful espionage to complete the dangerous trip. Lillian and Julia

Vanessa Redgrave and Jane Fonda.

finally enjoy a touching, but brief, reunion; Julia now has a baby named Lillian, but she has also lost a leg and is much plainer than her always-glamorous friend. Despite all the darkness in their lives and in the world, their genuine, lasting affection for each other shines through. Lillian leaves and later learns that Julia has been murdered by Nazis. Lillian unsuccessfully tries to find the baby, and she is also shut out by Julia's family, leaving her in the last shot the way we saw her in the first shot: alone, fishing quietly in a small boat. It's a heart-wrenching story beautifully told, with exquisite French and English locations perfectly evoking the look and feel of the period.

ADDED ATTRACTION: Star Debuts

Forty-one minutes into *Julia*, Meryl Streep makes her big-screen debut as "Anne Marie" (her first line ever: "Lillian, it was beautiful"). Here are fifteen other future cinema superstars, many of them eventual Oscar winners, whose first movies came out in between 1975 and 1979.

- Jamie Lee Curtis: *Halloween* (1978)
- Carrie Fisher: *Shampoo* (1975)
- Richard Gere: *Report to the Commissioner* (1975)
- Ed Harris: *Coma* (1978)
- Helen Hunt: *Rollercoaster* (1977)
- Michael Keaton: *Rabbit Test* (1978)
- Diane Lane: *A Little Romance* (1979)
- Jessica Lange: *King Kong* (1976)
- Bill Murray: *Next Stop, Greenwich Village* (1976)
- Liam Neeson: *Pilgrim's Progress* (1978)
- Patrick Swayze: *Skatetown, U.S.A.* (1979)
- John Travolta: *The Devil's Rain* (1975)
- Sigourney Weaver: *Annie Hall* (1977)
- Robin Williams: *Can I Do It 'Till I Need Glasses?* (1977)
- Debra Winger: *Slumber Party '57* (1976)

Oh, God!

Released: October 1977
Director: Carl Reiner
Stars: John Denver, George Burns, Teri Garr
Academy Awards: One nomination (Best Writing)

PREVIEW: Nobody believes an ordinary man who says God has given him vital messages to spread.

NOW SHOWING: And Lo, There Was a Divine Comedy

Oh, God! (1977) is a delightful charmer that blends warm humor with gentle wisdom. The simple story has God (George Burns) appearing in human form to Jerry (John Denver), an ordinary assistant manager at a Burbank supermarket. God gives Jerry nice, reassuring messages and nudges him to share them with the world. When he does, everyone doubts Jerry's sanity, so he's ridiculed, fired, and even dragged into court. God occasionally reappears to encourage him and work some minor miracles (to prove a point he makes it rain inside Jerry's AMC Pacer, for instance), but mainly Jerry struggles alone.

Larry Gelbart earned an Oscar nomination for his screenplay, which is both smart and funny (no surprise from the creator of TV's brilliant *M*A*S*H*). Director Carl Reiner, reining in the chaos that made *Where's Poppa?* (1970) so unpleasant, keeps this movie calm and tasteful. His best decisions were in the casting. Eighty-one-year-old George Burns is ideal as "Big G" (what God jokingly calls himself) who carries a business card that simply reads "God." Throughout, Burns underplays the role with an informal, matter-of-fact delivery that perfectly matches Gelbart's dry humor. Here's God admitting a mistake: "Avocados. Made the pit too big. ... A few things I got right. I put summer before winter, didn't I?" And on the creation of the world in six days: "To tell you the truth, I thought about it for five days and did the whole job in one. I'm really best under pressure." Testifying for Jerry, God swears to tell the truth, "So help me Me." The movie is filled with wonderful lines like these, but God also repeatedly imparts important words: "I set the world up so it can work. Only it's up to you. You can't look to me to do it for you." The movie's other big success is Denver. A novice actor appearing in his first and only '70s movie, his innocent confusion nicely balances Burns' optimistic confidence. Teri Garr, appealing as always, is the pretty, sweet, and perplexed wife, a character similar to the one she'll play a month later in *Close Encounters of the Third Kind* (1977).

Teri Garr and John Denver.

Clever cultural references—Reiner's *The Dick Van Dyke Show* on a background TV, Reiner himself on Dinah Shore's TV show, references to the 1969 Mets and *The Exorcist* (1973)—add to the fun. *Oh, God!* will restore your faith in good family comedies.

ADDED ATTRACTION: You Light Up My Turntable

Another wholesome movie in theaters that autumn was the clichéd melodrama *You Light Up My Life* (1977). Laurie (Didi Conn) is a struggling actress/comedian who endures humiliating Hollywood jobs before finally becoming a New York recording star. While her desire to stay true to her career goals is commendable, Laurie herself is not entirely admirable. For instance, she goes home with a total stranger after he gives her an out-of-the-blue kiss in a restaurant, even though her own wedding is just days away. However, she learns her lesson the hard way, and for most of the last thirty minutes she's hurt and disappointed before her big "I gotta depend on myself" speech. The movie is most famous for its Oscar-winning song, heard in different forms a half-dozen times and sung here by Kacey Cisyk (with Conn earnestly lip syncing). The movie-song-becoming-a-hit-song concept wasn't new, obviously: previous '70s movies that launched new hit songs include *Shaft* (1971), *Live and Let Die* (1973), and *The Way We Were* (1973). But *You Light Up My Life*, while not a very good movie, led to Debby Boone's version of the song, which became the decade's biggest-selling record. Conn, pouring on the charm and vulnerability, quickly graduated to another movie with a hit theme song of its own, *Grease* (1978).

Pete's Dragon

Released: November 1977
Director: Don Chaffey
Stars: Helen Reddy, Jim Dale, Mickey Rooney
Academy Awards: Two nominations (Best Song; Best Music)

PREVIEW: A boy and his often-invisible pet dragon go to a small town and soon run into trouble.

NOW SHOWING: Pet Sounds

In the late 1970s Disneyland updated its amazing Main Street Electrical Parade to include a dazzling thirty-eight-foot-long dragon. Did everyone recognize it as the likeable title character from *Pete's Dragon* (1977)? Maybe not, because this movie wasn't the blockbuster Disney hoped for. It has its devoted fans, however, and can be watched today as an underrated triumph of Disney animation.

Like *Mary Poppins* (1964) and *Bedknobs and Broomsticks* (1971), *Pete's Dragon* is a big-budget musical that brilliantly mixes live-action with animation; and like those two earlier movies, *Pete's Dragon* has a running time of well over two hours (different versions cut the time to around ninety minutes). The movie opens with young Pete (Sean Marshall) being chased through the

Mickey Rooney, Helen Reddy, and Sean Marshall.

woods by scraggly hillbillies (Shelley Winters is the dentally challenged mama). He's aided by Elliott, a wonderfully emotive animated dragon who's the world's largest, friendliest pet. Elliott understands English and responds with grunts and clicky noises; he also flies, breathes fire, turns invisible, dances, and plays tic-tac-toe. Pete escapes to a quaint fishing village in New England (California's central coast, actually) where Nora (Helen Reddy) takes him into her lighthouse. Everything's fine until villainous Dr. Terminus (Jim Dale) tries to chop up Elliott for medicinal ingredients. In the action-packed finale, Elliott saves the day, naturally, but the perfect Disney ending is tempered by his sad, sudden departure.

Some of the animated scenes are truly impressive, as when Pete tosses real apples into Elliott's mouth, and especially the two times when Elliott uses a claw to catch Pete's teardrop. The catchy Oscar-nominated music includes the lovely "Candle on the Water" and the cheery "Brazzle Dazzle Day," both sung by Helen Reddy, at the time one of the world's most popular singers. Draggin' the movie toward silliness are some hyperactive cast members, especially Mickey Rooney, whose over-the-top mugging suggests he's trying to win the Oscar for Best Supporting Ham. And for a Disney movie, there sure is a lot of alcohol: for instance, the jolly "I Saw a Dragon" number involves an entire saloon, the Lampie and Hoagy characters are comical drunks, and Hoagy is told, "I can't stand you when you're sober ... get yourself a good stiff drink!" Even Elliott is given alcohol, with comically woozy results. Generally, however, *Pete's Dragon* is heart-warming and sweet. Kids will really be entertained, and only a cantankerous adult could totally resist its abundant charms.

ADDED ATTRACTION: Weird *Wizards*

In contrast to the traditional Disney animation in *Pete's Dragon*, Ralph Bakshi, famous for the X-rated *Fritz the Cat* (1972), went psychedelic (and PG) with his animated *Wizards* (1977). Reminiscent of *The Lord of the Rings*, this fantasy epic presents "an everlasting battle for world supremacy fought between the powers of Technology and Magic." Blackwolf, a "mutant wizard," is a familiar dictator: his symbol is the swastika, he says "*Sieg Heil*," he's called "Führer," and his dark army uses World War Two tanks and planes. Meanwhile, Avatar, a "kind and good wizard," leads sword-carrying fairies and elves on a quest to stop him. Bakshi's trippy visuals blend Saturday-morning-style cartoon characters, detailed comic-book art, landscapes echoing Roger Dean's album art for Yes, old movies that have been heavily stylized to look animated, and even actual documentary footage of Hitler and Nazis. Add in Susan Tyrrell's expressive narration, plus the sexiest fairy woman ever, some

Necron in Wizards.

gentle rock instrumentals, and hip humor, and you've got a strange, entertaining brew. One of the characters is similar to J.R.R. Tolkien's weird Gollum creature; Bakshi's next movie would actually be *The Lord of the Rings* (1978), an ambitious attempt to compress Tolkien's three-volume story into two animated parts. Unfortunately, this 132-minute first movie drew mixed reviews, so the second part never got made, leaving the story hanging midway through Tolkien's second novel in the trilogy, *The Two Towers*. Somewhere somebody might still be wondering if Frodo ever destroyed that darn ring.

The Turning Point

Released: November 1977
Director: Herbert Ross
Stars: Anne Bancroft, Shirley MacLaine, Mikhail Baryshnikov
Academy Awards: Eleven nominations (Best Picture; Best Actresses—Anne Bancroft, Shirley MacLaine; Best Supporting Actor—Mikhail Baryshnikov; Best Supporting Actress—Leslie Browne; Best Director; Best Writing; Best Editing; Best Cinematography; Best Art Direction; Best Sound)

PREVIEW: Two former rivals review the life choices that took one of them from a ballet career.

NOW SHOWING: Dance Fever

Preceded by megahits like *Smokey and the Bandit* and *Star Wars*, and followed by *Close Encounters of the Third Kind* and *Saturday Night Fever*, *The Turning Point* (1977) offered a sophisticated alternative to 1977's car-chase/sci-fi/disco-dancing spectaculars. *The Turning Point* tells a relatively quiet story about relationships and career decisions in the ballet world. If the names Baryshnikov and *Gisselle* mean something to you, and if the prospect of thirty-two minutes (25% of the movie) of beautifully filmed ballet performances entices, then this is your movie.

"Turning point" has a literal ballet meaning, but it also refers to momentous past decisions made by Emma (Anne Bancroft) and DeeDee (Shirley MacLaine), formerly rival ballerinas who are now in their forties. Emma clings to her legendary ballet career but knows she must soon transition from onstage to backstage (Bancroft poses in ballet costumes but doesn't really dance in the movie). DeeDee, meanwhile, long ago surrendered career for family. DeeDee's daughter, Emilia (Leslie Browne), faces the "fork in her road" when she's invited to leave Oklahoma for ballet opportunities in Manhattan. All the characters work through their decisions and resentments with dignified conversations, with one wild exception: late in the movie Emma and DeeDee confront each other in a bar and take the fight outside, where their riveting nine-minute scene turns ridiculously violent. It's the best catfight between two famous actresses since the titanic Carol Burnett vs. Geraldine Page championship bout in *Pete 'n' Tillie* (1972).

Everything about *The Turning Point* is smart and refined. Even the many affairs are handled tastefully: the tender sex scene between Emilia and the ballet company's playboy incorporates ballet's expressive arm movements. Director Herbert Ross presents the actual ballet scenes with wide shots as if we're sitting in the audience, so we can see all the dancers and can fully appreciate Mikhail Baryshnikov's astonishing athleticism when he seemingly flies across the stage (his minute-long solo in *Le Corsaire* and the final six-minute *pas de deux* with Browne are glorious).

At the 1978 Oscars ceremony, *The Turning Point* tied with *Julia* for the most nominations, eleven (though it also set a dubious record for earning the most Oscar nominations with zero wins). Additionally, *The Turning Point* was the only '70s movie to have two Best Actress nominations. While *The Turning Point* isn't for all audiences, it's an intelligent, well-made movie for anyone who relishes superb acting and sublime movement.

ADDED ATTRACTION: Dancing Duo

While two science-fiction classics, *Star Wars* and *Close Encounters of the Third Kind*, were obvious blockbusters, 1977 was also a year with good dance movies. In addition to *The Turning Point* and *Saturday Night Fever*, which were both box-office hits, two other movies explored the terpsichorean world. *Roseland* is from producer Ismail Merchant and director James Ivory, whose elegant productions like *A Room with a View* (1985) and *Howards End* (1992) would later earn multiple Oscar nominations. Their sad, sweet *Roseland* presents three romantic tales set in Manhattan's nostalgic Roseland dancehall. One vignette has young Christopher Walken as a gigolo working three different dance partners. Meanwhile, *The Children of Theatre Street* was a nominee for 1977's Best Documentary Oscar (it lost to *Who Are the DeBolts? And Where Did They Get 19 Kids?*, an inspiring look at a family with nineteen adopted children, some of them disabled). Narrated by Grace Kelly, the joyous *Theatre Street* follows Russian ballet students who endure difficult training to become elite dancers.

Close Encounters of the Third Kind

(One of 1977's five **FAR-OUT** movies)

Released: November 1977

Director: Steven Spielberg

Stars: Richard Dreyfuss, Melinda Dillon, Teri Garr

Academy Awards: Two wins (Best Cinematography; Special Achievement Award for Sound Effects Editing), plus seven more nominations (Best Supporting Actress—Melinda Dillon; Best Director; Best Editing; Best Art Direction; Best Visual Effects; Best Music; Best Sound)

PREVIEW: Ordinary people have some extraordinary experiences with spaceships and aliens.

FINE LINE: "They can fly rings around the moon. But we're *years* ahead of 'em on the highway." (An elderly Indiana citizen who has just watched small alien ships skim past him down the road.)

CLOSE-UP: In early scenes, tiny lights move silently across the night sky, perhaps to indicate that aliens are already here, and they're watching. For example, fourteen minutes into the movie, young Barry runs outside and looks back at his house. For four seconds a white dot of light moves in the starry sky from the center of the screen toward the upper-left quadrant. At sixteen minutes, a panoramic shot of the Indiana blackout includes a small red light moving from left to right in the center of the night sky. Three minutes later, Roy Neary drives his truck from left to right across the screen. Far above him in the upper-left corner, a white dot is apparently following him.

NOW SHOWING: Good Heavens

Though they both came out in 1977 and both use revolutionary special effects, think how different the decade's two most famous sci-fi movies are. *Star Wars*, filled with alien worlds, strange creatures, and lots of weaponry, is a wild, rambunctious adventure that opens *in media res* with impressive spaceships shooting at each other, kills literally millions of people when the Death Star detonates the populated planet of Alderaan, includes the gruesome fiery deaths of Luke's Uncle Owen and Aunt Beru, and closes with the exhilarating annihilation of the Death Star. In stark contrast, *Close Encounters of the Third Kind* (1977), which was released six months after *Star Wars*, takes place entirely on Earth, has no gunfire or human deaths, opens with a scene of parked World War Two planes, mentions Disney's *Pinocchio* (1940) and shows a Daffy Duck cartoon, and closes with what looks like a glittering chandelier majestically floating to the heavens. Both movies were massively popular hits, obviously, but if the first one blows your mind with thrills, the second one warms your heart with wonderment. When we watched *Close Encounters* in a theater twice during its first week of release, both times the audience was so utterly spellbound for the last twenty minutes you could have heard a lightsaber drop.

Close Encounters was director Steven Spielberg's follow-up to his first mega-milestone, *Jaws* (1975). As in that exciting adventure, ordinary citizens in *Close Encounters* confront something extraordinary that's glimpsed for most of the movie and is then finally unveiled in the last act. But nobody in *Close Encounters* is running away, as they were in *Jaws*. Everyone, from a lone child in a field to the power-company employees in their trucks to the scientists with their instruments, is running toward the unknown, fearlessly inviting the aliens, as one old-timer's sign reads, to "stop and be friendly." The unknown in *Close Encounters* isn't terrifying, as it was in so many past sci-fi movies that were dominated by ominous flying saucers and ray-gun-wielding bugheads. Spielberg's mesmerizing spaceships are like twirling toys or holiday ornaments (a toddler even yells out "ice cream!" as they fly past). His benevolent, unarmed aliens aren't grotesque monsters; bathed in ethereal light at the end, most of them are the same size as human children.

As powerful as *Close Encounters* is, somehow its eight Oscar nominations didn't include one for Best Picture. Maybe the Academy was all science-fictioned out, as if that year's Best Picture nomination for *Star Wars* fulfilled some sci-fi allotment. More likely, the middle section of *Close Encounters* kept it out of 1977's pantheon. Everyone admires the opening sequences that effectively build up the story and suspense with UFO sightings and strange occurrences. The early scenes in the Mexican desert, and alongside the cautious air-traffic controllers, and with Roy Neary (the Indiana everyman played by Richard Dreyfuss) in his truck underneath a probing spaceship, and of the mother (Melissa Dillon) and son terrified by whatever is trying to get inside their house, are all truly masterful. And few viewers could complain about the final rendezvous at Devils Tower, Wyoming that goes from one marvelous reveal to another. In between, however, are scenes that show how the close encounters are affecting Neary, and these did indeed draw criticism. For awhile this beautiful sci-fi classic almost turns silly as Neary constructs a room-size Devils Tower model inside his house. While bewildered neighbors stare, Neary defiantly yanks plants from his garden, tosses bricks through an open window, tussles with a garbage man over a garbage can, releases penned ducks, sprawls across the family station wagon and lands in the street in his bathrobe. Amusing it may be, and a daytime contrast to the nighttime suspense it may provide, but this section feels like it's from a Disney comedy.

Melinda Dillon and Richard Dreyfuss.

Besides that quibble, after many, many viewings over the decades we've generated a few other questions. The title, for instance—why isn't it ever explained in the movie what a close encounter of the first, second, or third kind is? Not everyone knows that the term comes from J. Allen Hynek's *The UFO Experience: A Scientific Inquiry*, a 1972 book that defines the three "kinds" as, essentially, a UFO sighting, physical evidence, and alien contact. Next, how does the mother ship, which dwarfs twelve-hundred-foot-tall Devils Tower, rise *up* from *behind* the monument? Where has it been all this time? And when this enormous vessel finally lifts off, why aren't Air Force jets in pursuit? How could they not be tracking something that immense and slow? Earlier the air-traffic controllers monitored an alien craft on radar as it approached a passenger jet—why isn't the mother ship on somebody's radar? Most troubling of all is Neary's rushed decision to leave with the aliens. He's a father abandoning his young children—is he a hero as he ascends the ramp, or a louse? Have his close encounters driven him to madness? Given more time to think about it, would he still make that choice? Parents, would you do what he does?

Questions and debates on any of these topics don't diminish the movie one bit. We've been major fans since we first watched *Close Encounters of the Third Kind* with rapt admiration and tried to do what believers have been doing since it first came out: thinking up adjectives. Amazing, astonishing, astounding, awe-inspiring ... and those are just the A's.

ADDED ATTRACTION: The First "Special Edition"

Director Steven Spielberg said in a 2001 "Making of" DVD interview that he hadn't been able to finish the movie the way he had wanted to. Rather than make a sequel, he instead asked to "recut certain scenes" and "shoot a few more sequences." Thus, three years after the original movie, what is possibly the first "special edition" of a contemporary movie arrived in theaters. Though it adds seven minutes of new scenes, the 132-minute second movie is actually three minutes *shorter* than the original because it deletes ten minutes, notably the press conference where Bigfoot gets mentioned and half of the long sequence where Roy Neary builds a Devil's Tower replica inside his house. As for what's been added to *Close Encounters of the Third Kind: The Special Edition* (1980), here are seven of the new embellishments.

- 14 minutes into the *Special Edition*:
  Three minutes of the Neary family at home, highlighted by a miniature-train wreck (this scene lasts only thirty seconds in the theatrical version).
- 24 minutes:
  As Neary drives across rural Indiana, a large spaceship shadow intersects his route.
- 26 minutes:
  Just before a spaceship disappears around the corner, it hovers for six seconds in front of a large McDonald's billboard.
- 31 minutes:
  A ship, the *Cotopaxi*, rests in Mongolia's Gobi Desert.
- 61 minutes:
  An overwhelmed Neary sits fully clothed in the shower.
- 123 minutes:
  Neary enters the mother ship. For the next three startling minutes, he gazes in awe at the marvelous sights.
- 130 minutes:
  The closing credits end with a minute of "When You Wish Upon a Star" from *Pinocchio* (1940).

The Goodbye Girl

Released: November 1977
Director: Herbert Ross
Stars: Richard Dreyfuss, Marsha Mason, Quinn Cummings
Academy Awards: One win (Best Actor—Richard Dreyfuss), plus four more nominations (Best Picture; Best Actress—Marsha Mason; Best Supporting Actress—Quinn Cummings; Best Writing)

PREVIEW: An actor arrives in New York and has to share an apartment with a mother and daughter.

NOW SHOWING: Simon Sez

There's something magical about *The Goodbye Girl* (1977). Significantly, of the dozens of movies that Neil Simon wrote, *The Goodbye Girl* is his only Best Picture nominee.

Working from Simon's greatest script, the movie's three stars give career-best performances: Marsha Mason (Paula, the wounded, cautious title character); Richard Dreyfuss (Elliot, the offbeat actor); and Quinn Cummings (Lucy, Paula's precocious ten-year-old daughter who "was born twenty-six"). Working like a veteran comedy team, all three performers earned Oscar nominations. The trio is thrown together when Elliot shows up at Paula and Lucy's New York apartment, which he's sublet for three months, and circumstances force them all to stay. His "too-weird" personality initially generates hostility until he manages to bond with Lucy, which brings Paula and him together romantically.

Throughout, Dreyfuss is an energetic force of nature who blends charisma, accents, rapid-fire lines, frustration, and sensitivity into a lovable, fully realized character. An acting dynamo, he sings, impersonates Bogart, and performs Shakespeare's *Richard III* as a gay Richard in a career-milestone performance that would make him, at thirty years old, the youngest Best Actor winner ever. And this was with Dreyfuss' other blockbuster movie, *Close Encounters of the Third Kind*, newly arrived in theaters as *The Goodbye Girl* opened. Director Herbert Ross was also having a November to remember: released two weeks apart, *The Turning Point* and *The Goodbye Girl*, both directed by Ross, would both be nominated for Best Picture.

Simon's word wizardry is enchanting, as always, but *The Goodbye Girl* isn't exactly groundbreaking. It works its spell via the mismatched-leads conceit he'd used successfully in *The Odd Couple* (1968) and *The Sunshine Boys* (1975). What's more, it's soon obvious that Paula and Elliot, two quick-witted theater people, will end up together (not so obviously, they'll be on separate coasts). Quinn Cummings follows the path carved by Tatum O'Neal (who actually gets a mention) in *Paper Moon* (1973), so Lucy already feels familiar. Additionally, that sugary soft-rock theme song might make your teeth ache. On the other hand, the fun pop-cultural details are dy-no-mite: the Elton John and Fonzie posters, shout-outs for Al Pacino, Bette Midler, *The Exorcist*, *Company*, *Police Woman*, and more.

Audiences back then embraced *The Goodbye Girl* and made it an enormous hit. With this movie and multiple-Oscar-winner *Annie Hall* in theaters within a few months of each other, 1977 stands as the decade's best year for romantic comedies.

ADDED ATTRACTION: Two "Big" Mysteries

Richard Dreyfuss' next movie was *The Big Fix* (1978). Wearing a curly perm, a moustache, and a wrist cast, he plays a former '60s activist who's now got kids, an ex-wife, and a routine job as a private investigator. The lightly comedic tone of the first forty-two minutes, which involve a missing-persons search, suddenly darkens when the investigator's girlfriend is murdered. As the convoluted mystery introduces political dirty tricks and hit men, the charming private eye becomes a tough guy who punches out a rival and kills a bad guy, though he's still sensitive enough to cry and sing to his children. Dreyfuss is undeniably appealing, and the lost-ideals theme is affecting, but *The Big Fix* wasn't a big success. Neither was another "Big" crime-solving movie from 1978, *The Big Sleep*. Robert Mitchum reprises his world-weary Philip Marlowe character from *Farewell, My Lovely* (1975), which was a better Raymond Chandler adaptation. *The Big Sleep* moves Chandler's L.A. setting to modern London, gives James Stewart and Joan Collins small roles, includes the always appealing Candy Clark as the sexy but villainous young daughter, uses flashbacks to help clarify the famously labyrinthine plot, and adds nudity. While this new interpretation is intriguing, it still falls short of the iconic 1946 original with Humphrey Bogart and Lauren Bacall.

Saturday Night Fever

Released: December 1977
Director: John Badham
Stars: John Travolta, Karen Lynn Gorney, Donna Pescow
Academy Awards: One nomination (Best Actor—John Travolta)

PREVIEW: A frustrated disco dancer decides to break away from his dead-end life in Brooklyn.

NOW SHOWING: Hot Stuff

Like most viewers, we remember *Saturday Night Fever* (1977) as the decade's iconic dance movie. Seeing it again, we're struck by how little dancing *SNF* actually has. Guess how many minutes dance-superstar John Travolta spends on the lighted floor. Half the movie, fifty-nine minutes? Maybe 25%, thirty minutes? Try 12% of the movie, just fourteen minutes, in a musical where he doesn't sing a note. Travolta is spell-binding when he's dancing, obviously; sexy, athletic, and graceful, he's truly "the king out there," and his riveting two-and-a-half-minute solo midway through is a show-stopper. It's in the other 104 minutes when *Saturday Night Fever* gets ugly.

For much of the movie, Travolta's character, Tony, is contemptible. He and his moronic friends are all around nineteen, live at home, admittedly have no future, and blow their meager wages on clothes and Saturday nights at the local disco. Worst of all, they're overt racists and misogynists who casually use vile language and exhibit awful behavior toward minorities and women. While he has some nice moments at home and at work, Tony is ridiculously vain. And he repeatedly says unprintable words. Worst of all, he attempts rape. But a sudden death, romantic rejection, and growing awareness that dancing is "a short-lived kinda thing" motivate Tony to abandon Brooklyn despair for a Manhattan reboot. By recognizing the limitations of his aimless, macho lifestyle and struggling to escape it, he manages to become an endearing, sympathetic character. Both strutting and sensitive, Travolta gives a dazzling Oscar-nominated performance. Who else could've done everything he does in *SNF*?

For all the gritty melodrama, it's the music and moves that dominate. Maybe now *SNF* seems almost like a parody, but back then it was a vivid, hugely popular celebration that took disco mainstream, and for a while the glossy soundtrack was the all-time biggest-selling record. Some favorite movie moments: the hair dryer and Vitalis

Karen Lynn Gorney and John Travolta.

Super Hold beside Tony's bed; his passionate "will you just watch the hair" plea at dinner; the DJ's "I like that polyester look" compliment; and all the '70s idols identified on posters or in conversation (Al Pacino, David Bowie, Joe Namath, and more). Briefly defining what was hot, *Saturday Night Fever* wasn't merely a movie, it was a cultural phenomenon. Today, despite the archaic attitudes around it, that energetic dance floor still looks like fun. As Tony says twice in the movie, "Can you dig it? I knew that you could."

ADDED ATTRACTION: Disco Dracula

Director John Badham followed *Saturday Night Fever* with another stylish success. *Dracula* (1979) revamps the ancient bloodsucker into a sexy seducer played by Frank Langella, whose lean physique and thick black hair actually make him resemble Travolta. As in his Tony-nominated performance in the Broadway play, Langella eschews the usual fangs and exotic accent in favor of a hypnotic, charismatic portrayal. Badham's romantic presentation retains expected elements—Renfield, Mina, Lucy, Van Helsing, the famous "children of the night" quote—but de-emphasizes the horror. Dracula's head-first climbs down walls and a two-minute post-bite hallucination are among the visual highlights. This was 1979's second major Drac attack; earlier, *Love at First Bite* was an amusing spoof with George Hamilton as a comical count who hits modern New York discos looking for Susan Saint James. With TV stars and references to TV shows and TV commercials, it's a little TV movie-ish, but audiences went batty and made it a surprising hit.

Candleshoe

Released: December 1977
Director: Norman Tokar
Stars: Jodie Foster, David Niven, Helen Hayes
Academy Awards: None

PREVIEW: An L.A. tomboy lies her way into an English manor so she can look for hidden treasure.

NOW SHOWING: *Candleshoe* Caper

After her roles as a twelve-year-old Manhattan hooker in Martin Scorsese's violent *Taxi Driver* (1976) and a thirteen-year-old suburban girl in Disney's amiable *Freaky Friday* (1976), Jodie Foster played a fourteen-year-old tomboy in another wholesome Disney comedy, *Candleshoe* (1977). This one is noteworthy because it's Foster's last '70s movie for Disney after three previous successes (1972's *Napoleon and Samantha* and 1973's *One Little Indian* preceded *Freaky Friday*), and in fact it's her last movie of any kind for the decade. Happily, the one she goes out with is also one of her most appealing.

Casey (Foster) starts the movie as a streetwise orphan in Los Angeles. A "bellicose," tough-talking, petty thief who's been to a "correctional institution," she's not exactly a sympathetic character. Two crooks pay her to pose as a long-lost English granddaughter who will live in Candleshoe, a majestic English manor, just long enough to discover where a pirate treasure has been stashed away. Once there she meets a butler (David Niven), the old lady of the manor (Helen Hayes, in her last role), and four kids who have been rescued from a children's home. "This place is a nut house," she scornfully declares. Casey stays tough and independent—"I got me. Listen, if you don't hand it out, you don't have to worry about not getting it back"—and nobody gets along with her, at first anyway.

As per her agreement Casey does try to pursue the clues to the hidden treasure, but when the crooks show up and get rough with her she switches sides and becomes nicer, especially after she realizes that Candleshoe is being sold and the kids are going to be sent away. Before the climax, an antique car frantically chases a train and everyone is involved in a slapstick battle inside the manor, with confident Casey now uniting and motivating the kids like a team captain who gets everyone to contribute. If you can't predict who gets the treasure or where Casey ends up living, then you haven't seen many Disney movies. Let's just say that in the poignant final scene Casey admits to crying for the first time in her life. This entertaining family movie shows off lots of beautiful English scenery, presents Foster at her youthful best, and has a supporting cast of capable old pros, especially Niven, who seems to be having a great time playing four different roles.

ADDED ATTRACTION: Two Candlestars

Candleshoe's two venerable legends, Helen Hayes and David Niven, are also in other 1970s Disney movies. After making the popular *Herbie Rides Again* (1974), Hayes starred in a lackluster comedy-caper, *One of Our Dinosaurs Is Missing* (1975), as a feisty English nanny. Peter Ustinov plays a comical Chinese spy who steals a museum's dinosaur skeleton in a search for missing microfilm. The light martial arts action was perhaps intended to keep current with the decade's kung fu trend. Compared with director Robert Stevenson's Oscar-winning epics, *Mary Poppins* (1964) and *Bedknobs and Broomsticks* (1971), this silly movie is a *disappointasaurus*. Fans of *Star Wars* (1977) may recognize that the dinosaur skeleton in *One of Our Dinosaurs Is Missing* is the same one sprawled across a Tatooine sand dune. Niven, meanwhile, gets top-billing in *No Deposit No Return* (1976), though he's barely in the movie. He's the rich grandfather of two precocious kids who get kidnapped by bumbling crooks (Darren McGavin, Don Knotts). Mild mayhem ensues when rival criminals appear, a pet skunk repeatedly escapes, and slapstick gags are unleashed. Knotts is his usual bug-eyed, anxious self, while Barbara Feldon is the worried working mom who learns that "you can't raise kids by long-distance!" The typical long, frantic Disney car chase leaves police cars demolished. Children probably would've enjoyed this tedious movie more if it weren't 112 minutes long, which is at least twenty minutes too many.

High Anxiety

Released: December 1977
Director: Mel Brooks
Stars: Mel Brooks, Cloris Leachman, Harvey Korman
Academy Awards: None

PREVIEW: The new administrator at an unusual psychiatric institute gets framed for murder.

NOW SHOWING: The Highs and Lows of *High Anxiety*

Mel Brooks's 1977 Christmas present to his fans was another of his entertaining movie parodies. He'd already spoofed westerns with *Blazing Saddles* (1974), old horror movies with *Young Frankenstein* (1974), and silent movies with *Silent Movie* (1976). Brooks goes after Alfred Hitchcock's thrillers in *High Anxiety* (1977), with uneven results.

Mel Brooks.

As usual on his movies, Brooks is all-in: he produced, co-wrote, directed, and stars in High Anxiety, and he also wrote and sings the theme song. He plays Dr. Richard Thorndyke— the name referencing Roger Thornhill in Hitchcock's *North by Northwest* (1959)—an eminent psychiatrist who's the new administrator at a prestigious psychiatric institute. Investigating suspicious case histories, Thorndyke gets falsely accused of murder (again, *North by Northwest*) and goes on the run with the help of a seductive "Hitchcock blonde" played by Madeline Kahn. After solving the mystery while atop a tower straight out of *Vertigo* (1958), they finish the movie on their honeymoon.

Brooks's Hitchcock homages are sometimes inspired (the clever shower scene) and sometimes included just for Hitchcock's devotees without being humorous. Brooks parodies a few other movies too—the broomstick-holding villainess evokes the witch in *The Wizard of Oz* (1939), and the metal-mouthed assassin is like the Jaws character in *The Spy Who Loved Me* (1977). Some of the best bits don't involve Hitchcock at all, as when a disguised Brooks and Kahn bluff their way through an airport.

Since it's a Mel Brooks movie, there's naturally a wonderful musical number, this time with Brooks crooning in a lounge like Frank Sinatra. And as always he's got a terrific supporting cast, here led by two veterans of his earlier movies, Cloris Leachman (as a sadistic nurse with a faint moustache and two torpedoes busting through her shirt) and Harvey Korman.

But since it's a Mel Brooks movie, some of the comedy falls flat. Brooks might be a better supporting character than a lead; after all, Gene Wilder starred in both *Blazing Saddles* (with Brooks in hilarious supporting roles) and *Young Frankenstein* (with no Brooks at all), and both of those are funnier. Kahn's awesome talent is squandered (she doesn't enter the movie until its forty-eighth minute), and the lowbrow scenes with a stereotypical flasher, the patient who thinks he's a dog, and an obscene phone call are just dumb. *High Anxiety* doesn't have the madcap lunacy of his previous hits, but above-average Brooks is still enjoyable.

ADDED ATTRACTION:
The Brooks / Hitchcock Connection

Forty-one minutes into *High Anxiety*, Richard Thorndyke hears the name Mr. MacGuffin. "MacGuffin" was Alfred Hitchcock's term for a desirable item (money, microfilm, etc.) that incites a movie's action. Sixty-five minutes in, Thorndyke asks to meet "at the north by northwest corner." Here are nine more connections between *High Anxiety* and various Hitchcock movies.

- 7 minutes into the movie:

  Dr. Thorndyke replaces the recently deceased administrator of a psychiatric institute. Early in *Spellbound* (1945), Dr. Edwardes replaces the retiring director of a mental hospital.

- 14 minutes:

  Looking over the balcony, Thorndyke imagines that he's falling into a spinning background.

  In *Vertigo*, Scottie dreams that's he's falling into a spinning background.

- 16 minutes:

  The camera moves to the closed dining-room window and breaks through the glass. In the opening scene of *Psycho* (1960), the camera moves to an open hotel window and continues into the room.

- 38 minutes:

  A doctor drives at night in the rain, squinting and panicking.

  In *Psycho*, Marion drives at night in the rain, squinting and looking for a place to stop.

- 46 minutes:

  The bellboy attacks Thorndyke in the shower with a rolled-up newspaper.

  In *Psycho*, a mysterious figure attacks Marion in the shower with a knife.

- 64 minutes:

  Thorndyke holds the murder weapon and is falsely accused of killing someone inside the hotel lobby.

  In *North by Northwest*, Thornhill holds the murder weapon and is falsely accused of killing someone inside the United Nations building.

- 66 minutes:

  As Thorndyke sits on a park bench, pigeons gather on the background play structure and eventually bomb him.

  In *The Birds* (1963), as Melanie waits outside the school, crows gather on the background play structure and eventually attack her.

- 75 minutes:

  Thorndyke is attacked in a phone booth below the southern end of the Golden Gate Bridge.

  In *Vertigo*, Scottie follows Madeleine to this same location, where she jumps into the bay.

- 84 minutes:

  Thorndyke climbs the stairs of a tower to rescue a helpless victim at the top.

  In *Vertigo*, Scottie takes Judy up the stairs of a similar tower.

When in Southern California visit UNIVERSAL STUDIOS TOUR
AN MCA COMPANY
It was the Deltas against the rules... the rules lost!
DELTA HOUSE
COLLEGE
NATIONAL LAMPOON'S®
ANIMAL HOUSE
A comedy from Universal Pictures
THE MATTY SIMMONS - IVAN REITMAN PRODUCTION
"NATIONAL LAMPOON'S ANIMAL HOUSE" Starring JOHN BELUSHI · TIM MATHESON · JOHN VERNON · VERNA BLOOM
THOMAS HULCE and DONALD SUTHERLAND as JENNINGS · Produced by MATTY SIMMONS and IVAN REITMAN
Music by ELMER BERNSTEIN · Written by HAROLD RAMIS, DOUGLAS KENNEY & CHRIS MILLER
Directed by JOHN LANDIS · Song "ANIMAL HOUSE" Composed and Performed by STEPHEN BISHOP
A UNIVERSAL PICTURE TECHNICOLOR®
Original sound tracks on MCA Records & Tapes
National Lampoon's Animal House Movie Book at Newsstands and Bookstores
R RESTRICTED
Under 17 requires accompanying Parent or Adult Guardian
© 1978 UNIVERSAL CITY STUDIOS INC
ALL RIGHTS RESERVED

1978

In Film

- Oscar for Best Picture: *The Deer Hunter*.
- Most Oscar wins (five): *The Deer Hunter*.
- Most Oscar nominations (nine): *The Deer Hunter* and *Heaven Can Wait*.
- With *Heaven Can Wait*, Warren Beatty becomes the first person since Orson Welles to earn acting, directing, producing, and screenwriting nominations in the same year (Welles did it with 1941's *Citizen Kane*).
- *Coming Home* becomes one of the few movies to win Oscars for both Best Actor (Jon Voight) and Best Actress (Jane Fonda).
- Top-grossing movie: *Grease*.
- Top-grossing comedy: *Animal House*.
- Top-grossing horror or sci-fi: *Superman*.
- *Grease* becomes the highest-grossing movie musical in history.
- *Attack of the Killer Tomatoes!*, *Halloween* and *Superman* launch new movie franchises.
- Average price for an adult movie ticket: $2.35.
- Five memorable actors: Warren Beatty, Gary Busey, John Hurt, Jon Voight, Christopher Walken.
- Five memorable actresses: Dyan Cannon, Jill Clayburgh, Jane Fonda, Geraldine Page, Maggie Smith.
- Movie debuts: Karen Allen, Kevin Bacon, Cheech & Chong, Billy Crystal, Jamie Lee Curtis, Harry Hamlin, Daryl Hannah, Ed Harris, Michael Keaton, John Malkovich, Christopher Reeve, Mary Steenburgen, Alfre Woodard, directors Warren Beatty and Robert Zemeckis.
- Deaths include Charles Boyer, John Cazale, Dan Dailey, Robert Shaw, Gig Young, cinematographer Geoffrey Unsworth, directors Mark Robson and Ed Wood, producer Jack L. Warner, screenwriters Leigh Brackett and Michael Wilson.

In America

- President Carter hosts secret peace talks between Egyptian President Anwar Sadat and Israeli Prime Minister Menachem Begin, resulting in Camp David Accords.
- Severe blizzards in the eastern United States kill over a hundred people and cause hundreds of millions of dollars in damage.
- California's landmark Proposition 13 dramatically reduces property taxes.
- San Francisco politicians George Moscone and Harvey Milk are assassinated.
- The Jonestown murders and mass suicides leave over nine-hundred people dead in Guyana.
- New York gangsters pull off the multi-million-dollar Lufthansa heist at JFK International Airport, an event depicted in the movie *Goodfellas* (1990).
- The nationally syndicated comic strip *Garfield* debuts.
- Average price for a gallon of gas: Sixty-eight cents.
- New technology: LaserDisc players, Space Invaders arcade game, WordStar word-processor program.
- New cars: AMC Concord, Ford Fairmont, Honda Prelude, Mazda RX-7, Toyota Supra.
- New products: Cabbage Patch Kids, Chipwich, Coors Light, Hungry Hungry Hippos board game, Reese's Pieces, Simon memory game, Speak & Spell.
- Sports champions: Dallas Cowboys at Super Bowl XII, Montreal Canadiens in hockey, Washington Bullets in basketball, New York Yankees in baseball.
- Bestselling books include Christina Crawford's *Mommie Dearest*, James Fixx's *The Complete Book of Running*, Ken Follett's *Eye of the Needle*, John Irving's *The World According to Garp*, M.M. Kaye's *The Far Pavilions*, Stephen King's *The Stand*, James Michener's *Chesapeake*, Herman Wouk's *War and Remembrance*.
- Music: The Blues Brothers debut on TV's *Saturday Night Live*; the Sex Pistols break up; new albums include Kenny Rogers' *The Gambler*, Rod Stewart's *Blondes Have More Fun*, the Rolling Stones' *Some Girls*, the Who's *Who Are You*, Warren Zevon's *Excitable Boy*, soundtracks for the movies *FM*, *Grease*, and *The Last Waltz*, and debut albums by the Cars, Devo, the Police, and Van Halen; new songs include the B-52s' "Rock Lobster," Andy Gibb's "Shadow Dancing," Billy Joel's "My Life," Dolly Parton's "Here You Come Again," Barbra Streisand and Neil Diamond's "You Don't Bring Me Flowers," Donna Summer's "Last Dance," the Village People's "Y.M.C.A."
- TV debuts: *Battlestar Galactica*, *Dallas*, *Diff'rent Strokes*, *The Incredible Hulk*, *Mork & Mindy*, *Taxi*, *20/20*, *WKRP in Cincinnati*.
- Deaths include Edgar Bergen, Joseph Colombo, Bob Crane, Hubert Humphrey, Margaret Mead, Keith Moon, Louis Prima.

Coma

Released: January 1978
Director: Michael Crichton
Stars: Geneviève Bujold, Michael Douglas, Richard Widmark
Academy Awards: None

PREVIEW: A doctor learns that a hospital is routinely killing patients for a secret purpose.

NOW SHOWING: Wake-Up Call

A top-notch thriller and a box-office success, *Coma* (1978) is a cerebral movie that blends science and suspense. What it shows—a hospital's secret plan to murder patients so their organs can be harvested and sold for huge profit—at first seems implausible, but the narrative is so taut and the presentation is so realistic that *Coma* might make viewers think of hospitals the same way *Marathon Man* (1976) makes viewers think of dentist chairs. In both places, scary and unexpected outcomes are definitely possible.

Coma was directed by sci-fi master Michael Crichton, who had been thrilling audiences all decade long as the writer and/or director of smart, entertaining movies like *The Andromeda Strain* (1971) and *Westworld* (1973). As always, Crichton challenges the audience with abstruse technical terminology, but he keeps the main plot direct and uncluttered so we never lose the main thread. That plot involves a conspiracy, so *Coma* fits right in with some of the decade's other hit movies about corrupt institutions, such as *Three Days of the Condor* (1975), *All the President's Men* (1976), and *Capricorn One* (1978), though here it's fictional Boston Memorial Hospital, not a governmental agency, that's effecting a malevolent plan.

Coma also fits right in with the '70s feminist surge, since the hero is actually a heroine, an intrepid young doctor (Geneviève Bujold) who relentlessly investigates the sudden death of her healthy-but-pregnant friend. She eventually turns from a determined detective into a strong action hero who crawls in tight spaces and sprints through darkened hospital hallways during a tense ten-minute chase (Crichton was always good at chases, as he proved in *Westworld*). The paranoia builds to a gripping climax with the doctor herself on the lethal operating table while her boyfriend (Michael Douglas) struggles to help. The ending arrives with a whimper, not a bang, but it's a quiet, effective payoff.

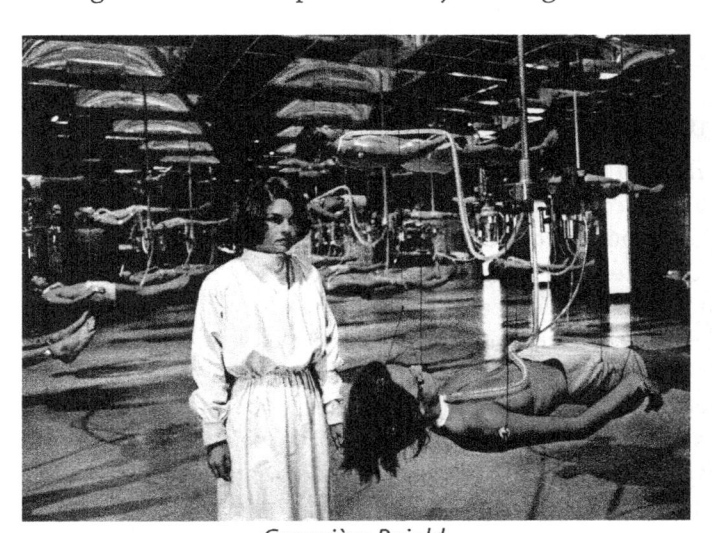

Crichton's visuals are impressive, especially in the secret facility where scores of comatose patients are dramatically

Geneviève Bujold.

suspended in midair, a sci-fi scene that frighteningly expands the conspiracy to gigantic proportions (Elizabeth Ashley plays an administrator like she's one of the chilling Stepford Wives). Crichton stages the villain's monologue about medicine being a "great social force" as a twisted sermon, and he includes some horror, too, especially in a pathology lab where a technician uses a meat slicer to get thick, perfect brain cutlets. See? We told you this movie was cerebral.

ADDED ATTRACTION: All Aboard the Gain Train

Two additional features add to *Coma*'s appeal. First, there's the interesting supporting cast, including Tom Selleck and Ed Harris (making his movie debut) in small roles. Another attraction is the medical authenticity, which makes the movie more believable and compelling. Screenwriter/director (and actual MD) Michael Crichton always was a stickler for details, obviously. He got the details right in his next hit, too, a terrific movie he wrote and directed that's based on his own 1975 novel. Unlike his techno-thrillers, *The Great Train Robbery* (1978) is a classy caper movie set in 1855. Crichton knows his Victoriana: everything from men's clubs to vocabulary seems accurate. A roguish trio—Sean Connery at his most charming, Donald Sutherland with a British accent, and seductive Lesley-Anne Down—attempts a daring robbery of a gold shipment from a train chuffing across England. The first hour is a methodical pursuit for four keys that will make the robbery possible. The last fifty minutes include Connery's dazzling ten-minute stunt atop the moving train and a tense climax as the police close in on him and he tries for one final daring escape. Crichton's verbal japes (like the invitation Down gets to join the train's "Fifty-Mile-An-Hour Club") add a lighthearted touch to this exciting tale.

The Betsy

Released: February 1978
Director: Daniel Petrie
Stars: Laurence Olivier, Tommy Lee Jones, Robert Duvall
Academy Awards: None

PREVIEW: Family members fight to control the company making a new car, the economical Betsy.

NOW SHOWING: Running on Fumes

Months before TV's *Dallas*, and years before *Dynasty*, *The Betsy* (1978) brought audiences into the lusty world of a rich, conniving, dysfunctional family. Here the wealth isn't from oil, it's from cars. Everyone is connected to a fictional car-manufacturing company headed by a headstrong eighty-six-year-old patriarch who's determined to build the Betsy, a new compact "people's car" that "the world will never forget" because it'll be safe, pollution-free, and economical (it gets sixty miles per gallon of gas, an important feature during the oil-depleted '70s when electric and hybrid cars were still science-fiction dreams). Unfortunately, not all of the family members support the Betsy, so there's infighting for control of the company. Complicating the business dealings are extra-marital affairs, divorces, blackmail, assassinations, arson, a gay son, a Mafia connection, and suicide. We get skinny-dipping scenes, steamy sex scenes, split-screen scenes, flashback-to-the-1930s scenes, racing-car scenes, private-jet scenes, explosion scenes, party scenes, and Sir Laurence Olivier enjoying a quickie-with-the-maid scene.

If it all sounds trashy and excessive, well, it is. However, *The Betsy* is still watchable, thanks to the fabulous East Coast mansions, the magnificent vintage cars from the 1920s and '30s, some eye-popping costumes and flower arrangements, and a few fun '70s trends, like a racquetball game, a '71 Ford Pinto (in a car chase!), and mammoth mid-'70s luxury cars. Then there's the all-star cast. Besides Sir Laurence (who goes full Hormel, hamming it up with an indeterminate American accent), there's Robert Duvall in a pencil-thin moustache, Tommy Lee Jones as a racer/designer, stylish Katharine Ross, and seductive Lesley-Anne Down among the many who keep this glamorous pot boiling. Interestingly, some of these actresses will later be regulars on the popular TV soap operas that *The Betsy* seems to have inspired, including *Dallas* (Lesley-Anne Down), *Dynasty* (Kathleen Beller), *The Colbys* (Katharine Ross), and *The Bold and the Beautiful* (Down again).

The one star that's conspicuously absent is the actual Betsy itself. After two hours of discussion about this revolutionary new car and some quick test-track shots, we finally get a good look during the end credits. Big whoop: it's a modified 1975 Lancia, an undistinguished little two-door coupe (picture a blue Ford Maverick). Painted in big curling letters on both doors is the car's name, a bizarre aesthetic choice that makes this ordinary-looking car even less appealing. Maybe it was smart to delay the reveal until theater audiences were filing out.

ADDED ATTRACTION: The Greek Cartoon

Three months after *The Betsy*, *The Greek Tycoon* put a fictional spin on the real-life Aristotle Onassis/Jackie Kennedy relationship. The movie's Theo Tomasis (Anthony Quinn) and Lizzie Cassidy (Jacqueline Bisset) resemble their celebrated counterparts, and many situations parallel actual events: he's a silver-haired Greek shipping tycoon whose son dies in a plane crash, her handsome husband becomes president and is assassinated next to her by a bullet to the head, etc. Neither main character is very likeable; he's a coarse, lusty billionaire who manipulates everyone around him, especially his mistresses, while she's America's laziest woman, always lounging around or shopping ("I just want everything," she announces). The Theo/Lizzie marriage is prefaced by formal negotiations (she commits to ten bedroom visits per month, and he promises a hundred-million-dollar payout if he dies first). This opera gets even soapier on their wedding day when Theo's ex-wife arrives, Theo slugs his son, Theo announces *on his wedding night* that he'll soon be sleeping with his old flame, and he flings a vulgar word at Lizzie when she finally throws him out. Their relationship sinks to physical brawling and yelling, she calls him an "animal" and a "clown," and she cringes when he wants to get romantic. The tawdriness of *The Greek Tycoon* is balanced by extravagant glamour, and this is probably why audiences made the movie a moderate box-office success. Spectacular scenery, a truly luxurious yacht, and plenty of well-dressed hedonists make *The Greek Tycoon* an early version of TV's popular *Lifestyles of the Rich and Famous*.

Coming Home

(One of 1978's five **FAR-OUT** movies)

Released: February 1978

Director: Hal Ashby

Stars: Jon Voight, Jane Fonda, Bruce Dern

Academy Awards: Three wins (Best Actor—Jon Voight; Best Actress—Jane Fonda; Best Writing), plus five more nominations (Best Picture; Best Supporting Actor—Bruce Dern; Best Supporting Actress—Penelope Milford; Best Director; Best Editing)

PREVIEW: When a disabled Vietnam vet falls for a soldier's wife, all their lives are changed.

FINE LINE: "I'm here because I'm trying to tell people, man, if we wanna commit suicide, we have plenty of reasons to do it right here at home. We don't have to go to Vietnam to find reasons for us to kill ourselves." (Luke, speaking from his wheelchair after being arrested for trying "to stop any others from going to Vietnam.")

CLOSE-UP: Two-thirds of the way through the movie, Jon Voight's and Jane Fonda's characters go to a matinee. The movie they buy tickets for is *2001: A Space Odyssey* (1968), with showtimes at 1:00, 4:00, 7:00, and 10:00 (it's a long movie). The theater is also displaying a poster for *In the Heat of the Night* (1967), which was awarded the Oscar for Best Picture on April 10, 1968. Both of these would've been in theaters in 1968, the year in which *Coming Home* is set. The ticket price isn't shown, but they probably paid about $1.25 each, the average adult-admission price that year.

NOW SHOWING: "There's a Choice to Be Made Here"

Hal Ashby directed many notable movies in the 1970s, including *Harold and Maude* (1971), *Shampoo* (1975), and *Bound for Glory* (1976). But *Coming Home* (1978) is probably his finest achievement. The movie isn't perfect—the ending still feels ambiguous and unresolved—but there are such moving performances, and the subject matter is so authentic and compelling, that *Coming Home* stands with the Best Picture of 1946, *The Best Years of Our Lives*, as one of the two or three best movies ever made about the aftermath of war.

Technically, *The Best Years of Our Lives* and *Coming Home* aren't war movies, and neither one includes any actual battle footage. Instead, these are movies about people profoundly changed by war, both physically and mentally, who then have to readjust to life in America. *The Best Years of Our Lives* was released a full year after World War Two ended, and the war is definitely over as the movie starts; in contrast, *Coming Home* premiered about five years after the Vietnam War's conclusion, but it is actually set at the end of the 1960s as the war was intensifying. Whereas *The Best Years of Our Lives* had Homer (Harold Russell) struggling to find self-esteem and love back home despite having lost both his hands in combat, *Coming Home* has Luke (Jon Voight) fighting the overwhelmed hospital staff and the local recruitment office while he's permanently paralyzed from the waist down. Formerly the captain of the football team, he's turned bitter and become embarrassed by his frustrating life on a table and in a bed. Meanwhile, Bob (Bruce Dern) is a gung-ho Marine, a dedicated lifer who is only really comfortable around other soldiers. Between Luke and Bob is Sally (Jane Fonda), Bob's devoted wife.

It's Sally who takes over the story by going through the biggest transformation. Resigned to her role as a military wife, we see her bored dissatisfaction as she has routine sex with Bob, but she supports him right up until he goes to

Jon Voight and Jane Fonda.

Vietnam. Once Bob is gone, she starts gradually reinventing herself with a rented beach house, a flashy Porsche, and a new volunteer position at the V.A. hospital. There she meets Luke, whose consistent anger forces him to initially reject her innocent advances (she recognizes him because they went to school together). Eventually they move to real friendship and intimacy, with Sally exploring a reckless hairstyle (see "Added Attraction"), casual hippy-ish clothes, and new ways to make love.

Though her outlook has been broadened and her acceptance of the war has evolved, Sally remains loyal to Bob. When he finally comes home, damaged and distant, she hopes to make a new life for them both, and so she gently pushes the empathetic Luke to the sidelines. The movie ends without clear resolutions and with the three characters separated. Luke tells a high school audience about the horrors and futility of war, breaking down as he describes the anguish and guilt he lives with now and reminding the students that "there's a choice to be made here" before they blindly enlist; Bob, after furiously confronting his wife with a loaded gun, takes off the wedding ring he promised he would never remove, strips naked, and swims silently into the ocean, perhaps, some have speculated, to commit suicide; and Sally, her hair long and bushy, is last seen pushing a grocery cart to the market and walking in through the Out door.

Perhaps this indecisive ending is Hal Ashby's way of saying that these problems don't go away, that the effects of war are sometimes inconclusive and unresolvable. Throughout he handles his issues compassionately, preferring subtlety and tenderness over the kind of violent, nightmarish scenes that punctuated the year's other big war movie, *The Deer Hunter*. Sally, notice, never does make any anti-war speeches, even as her stiff lifestyle relaxes and she has to confront the tormented veterans around her.

Ashby portrays his complex characters sensitively, but he is also brave and unflinching. For instance, the breakthrough scene of intimate sex between a man and a woman when one of them is disabled: Fonda and Voight aren't unknown actors groping under shadowed covers in some low-budget indie production, they're major Hollywood stars shown in full light, up close, and in an important high-profile movie. Ashby dares to explore their actions and feelings. Later, the emotional statements Luke makes to his audience about his battlefield memories and his post-war feelings are haunting and moving. Dern's character is seething inside and is unable to articulate his feelings, so when he finally unleashes his rage to Sally ("What I am saying issss, I do not belong in this house! And they're saying that I do not belong over there!") he becomes a frightening hurricane of raw emotion (no longer in the over-the-top sadistic-villain role he often played in movies, Dern is a potent, sympathetic presence here). And just as he used music so effectively in *Harold and Maude*, Ashby brings together epic songs that showcase the musical giants of the late 1960s, everyone from the Rolling Stones, Beatles, and Buffalo Springfield to Dylan, Hendrix, and Steppenwolf. The performances, the skillful production, the period details and the effective music all join together into a powerful, memorable movie. For anyone who grew up in the '60s, or who went to war, *Coming Home* might feel real, true, and, well, like coming home.

ADDED ATTRACTION: Sally's Changing Hairstyles

Twenty-two minutes into *Coming Home*, we see Sally's yearbook photo, presumably taken while she was in high school in the 1950s. The photo reveals that she was straightening her hair even then; tellingly, her yearbook comment about "the one thing she'd want on a desert island" is a conservative, traditional choice: "a husband." However, as Sally's feelings and alliances change throughout the movie, her hairstyles change too.

- 7 minutes-38 minutes into the movie:

    Sally's hair, straightened and brushed away from her face, is a conservative, matronly "hair helmet" perfect for the wife of a career military man.

- 38-57 minutes:

    With her husband overseas, Sally blows out her hair so that waves and curls fall to her face. Luke immediately notices and says happily, "You changed your hair! … It's very nice!"

- 57-89 minutes:

    Sally straightens her hair again when she flies to meet her husband in Hong Kong. She wears a scarf and a Chinese hat during the trip and keeps this conservative hairstyle until she returns and sleeps with Luke.

- 89 mins-125 minutes:

    Sally returns to the curled, reckless look and wears a flower in her hair. When she picks up her husband at the airport, the very first thing he says to her contrasts the enthusiastic compliment Luke had given her earlier: Bob stares accusingly and blurts, "What the hell did you do to your hair?" "I've stopped straightening it," she calmly replies.

An Unmarried Woman

Released: March 1978
Director: Paul Mazursky
Stars: Jill Clayburgh, Alan Bates, Michael Murphy
Academy Awards: Three nominations (Best Picture; Best Actress—Jill Clayburgh; Best Writing)

PREVIEW: After her unfaithful husband leaves, a woman rebuilds her life and relationships.

NOW SHOWING: Reality Show

In late 1977 and early 1978, strong, modern women were leading characters in diverse movies like *The Turning Point*, *The Goodbye Girl*, and *Coma*. The best woman's role of the year, maybe of the *decade*, came in *An Unmarried Woman*. Erica, a complex urban woman who discovers herself throughout this penetrating movie, is in every scene and is brought to such vivid life by Jill Clayburgh that she seems like a real person.

Nearly everything goes Erica's way for the first twenty-five minutes. She has a sixteen-year-long marriage to a successful, loving husband, a smart teenage daughter, close friends, and a rewarding job in an art gallery. Life is so wonderful that Erica giddily dances solo through her scenic Manhattan apartment.

Problems, however, are looming (obviously, since the title isn't *A Permanently Married Woman*). Erica's friend declares, "There's no such thing as total honesty, not with men," and Erica's husband, Martin (Michael Murphy) says he's "fantasizing about changing my life." When he sobs through his pitiful confession that he's in love with another woman, Erica is so shocked she throws up.

From then on she struggles with anger, confusion and depression as she reboots her life. Interestingly, and realistically, her effort isn't always noble. Burning with a short fuse, she overreacts and argues with her daughter, and she responds profanely when a man merely says hello. Later she assertively invites herself into a friend's bed for casual sex.

Midway through the movie Erica meets Saul (Alan Bates), a compassionate artist, and she's finally capable of exploring (but not committing to) a romantic relationship. She's also ready to get her own apartment and confidently reject Martin when he comes crawling back. Lugging a colorful parasail-size painting alone down a SoHo street in the memorable ending, Erica emerges as a willful, independent woman who's symbolically transforming into a winged butterfly before our eyes. We know she'll get that unwieldy painting home.

Writer/director Paul Mazursky tells this sophisticated story almost entirely through intelligent, sometimes amusing, often intimate dialogue, which is kept up-to-the-minute with references to *Star Wars* (1977), Jane Fonda, Barbra Streisand, and TV's *Kojak*, plus '70s trends like jogging, singles bars, and Leo Sayer songs. Making the movie especially relevant was America's surging divorce rate, which in 1978 terminated 51% of marriages, the highest percentage yet. Adult audiences responded and made *An Unmarried Woman* a major hit. For Mazursky and the astonishing Clayburgh, it's a career-defining triumph.

ADDED ATTRACTION: Oscars Yes, Tops No

In the daring '70s, major Oscar-nominated actresses like Jill Clayburgh could go topless in major Oscar-nominated movies like *An Unmarried Woman*. That simply didn't happen in movies from earlier decades. Here are eleven other Oscar-winning and Oscar-nominated actresses who were topless (or even naked) in 1975-1979 movies (in the list, Melanie Griffith, Helen Mirren, and Susan Sarandon earned their wins and nominations after the 1970s; the other actresses had wins and nominations in or before the 1970s).

- Julie Christie: *Demon Seed* (1977)
- Candy Clark: *The Big Sleep* (1978)
- Melinda Dillon: *Slap Shot* (1977)
- Faye Dunaway: *Network* (1976)
- Jane Fonda: *Coming Home* (1978)
- Melanie Griffith: *Night Moves* (1975) and *Smile* (1975)
- Sondra Locke: *The Gauntlet* (1977)
- Diane Keaton: *Looking for Mr. Goodbar* (1977)
- Helen Mirren: *Caligula* (1979)
- Susan Sarandon: *Pretty Baby* (1978)
- Sissy Spacek: *Carrie* (1976)

The Fury

Released: March 1978
Director: Brian De Palma
Stars: Kirk Douglas, John Cassavetes, Amy Irving
Academy Awards: None

PREVIEW: A government conspiracy wants to control young adults who have psychic abilities.

NOW SHOWING: *Carrie*, Part Two

At the climax of *The Fury* (1978), the villain shudders ... and blows up. This fifteen-second blast is fifty percent longer than the awesome Death Star explosion near the end of *Star Wars* (1977) and way bloodier (imagine a blood-filled Death Star detonating and shooting out a gore-gusher that propels a human head toward the camera). Director Brian De Palma uses multiple angles and fast cutting to create one of the decade's truly spectacular movie deaths.

That in-your-face explosion is the most famous scene in this stylish but inconsistent movie. *The Fury* mixes several stories—one about a government conspiracy to weaponize psychic young adults who have "raw ability" with "the power of an atomic reactor," another about a father's search for his kidnapped son who is one of those young psychics, and one more about a girl who's struggling to understand her unique telekinetic abilities. Government agents, father, son, and girl unite for a suspenseful finale that includes weirdly glowing eyes, freaky levitation, and gruesome hemorrhages ("fury," meaning unleashed psychic power, is graphically shown, but the word itself is never uttered).

De Palma had already struck movie gold with another movie about telekinesis, *Carrie* (1976). He strikes bronze with *The Fury*, a lesser but still solid achievement. Working here with a bigger budget than what he had on *Carrie*, plus actual locations in Israel, a John Williams score, and a starry cast headed by Kirk Douglas, De Palma directs the movie within an inch of its life, mixing overhead shots, moving cameras,

Amy Irving.

slow-motion, special effects, eerie sounds, and gallons of blood into over-the-top but, in its best moments, exciting horror. Sixty-two-year-old Douglas is a not-quite-convincing overemoting action star who wears a tight bathing suit and in one silly scene becomes a master of disguise. John Cassavetes, a glowering, devilish conspirator often filmed in shadows, isn't in the movie much. Carrie Snodgress, Oscar-nominated star of *Diary of a Mad Housewife* (1970), returns to the big screen after an eight-year hiatus, and Daryl Hannah makes her movie debut as a student twenty minutes in.

Carrie-ing the movie is Amy Irving, who actually was in *Carrie*. She's excellent as the gifted girl who evolves from early confusion to full control; like Carrie White, she finally turns into Madame Fury and exacts supernatural revenge by inducing the bad guy's big ka-boom. She's subtle and effective as everyone and everything around her gets outrageous.

ADDED ATTRACTION: They Spit on Your Movie

Another 1978 movie that ends with a woman's fierce revenge is *I Spit on Your Grave* (1978). Originally called *Day of the Woman*, this low-budget flick is a harrowing endurance test: how much disturbing brutality can you take before you're sickened? Beautiful Jennifer (Camille Keaton, a distant relative of Buster's) retreats to a bucolic cabin to write a novel, but four sleazy rubes viciously assault her. The shocking, repulsive rape scenes of "total submission," with Keaton naked and ridiculed throughout repeated attacks, never seem to end and are almost unwatchable; *Straw Dogs* (1971) also had a gang rape, but at least that one scene didn't sadistically continue for a half-hour. Jennifer somehow survives the savagery and eventually exacts bloody revenge on all four assailants in violent ways: she hangs one, fatally castrates another, cleaves a third with an axe, and dices the last with a motor boat's propeller. As she races away in the boat at the end, the audience will feel like it needs a shower after witnessing so much stark ugliness presented with amateurish acting and crude production values. Several countries banned this movie, some protesters picketed theaters, a few disgusted major critics called it the worst or most offensive movie ever, and viewers still debate its limited merits. The titular "I," by the way, was a busy person in '70s movies. At least eleven different movies start their titles, as *I Spit on Your Grave* does, with "I." "I" sure has diverse interests: for every nice-sounding title like *I Love My Wife* (1970) and *I Wanna Hold Your Hand* (1978), there's another one like *I Drink Your Blood* (1970) and *I Eat Your Skin* (1971). I caramba.

Gray Lady Down

Released: March 1978
Director: David Greene
Stars: Charlton Heston, David Carradine, Stacy Keach
Academy Awards: None

PREVIEW: The U.S. Navy mounts a major rescue operation to save the crew of a sunken submarine.

NOW SHOWING: In the Deep Blue with *Gray Lady Down*

A worthy addition to the disaster genre, *Gray Lady Down* (1978) is a fluff-less movie. Whereas another ocean-going epic, *The Poseidon Adventure* (1972), was swollen with subplots, *Gray Lady Down* is stripped to a plausible core: the rescue of submerged crewmembers after their nuclear sub collides with a ship and plummets a quarter-mile down. It's a straightforward saga told with actual vessels (especially the impressive Deep Submergence Rescue Vehicle) and real rescue techniques, as the end credits remind us (the "DSRV is today a reality," "capable of rescuing men from U. S. submarines in any of the world's oceans"). An earlier maritime-disaster movie, *The Neptune Factor* (1973), had already used a small sub to rescue the crew trapped in a damaged undersea lab, but that plodding story sank into absurdity once monstrous tropical fish appeared. *Gray Lady Down* is Best Picture material by comparison.

Gray Lady's collision comes in the first ten minutes, and for once Charlton Heston, playing the bearded, arrogant captain, isn't the hero, as he was in other '70s movies like *Airport 1975* (1974). In fact, he's apparently the cause of the accident, since he's accused of "grandstanding" toward port by keeping his sub on the surface just because he's about to retire and wants to show off. The lesson here is the same one in earlier disaster movies: if this genre has taught us anything, it's that any vessel making a first or last voyage is doomed. Consider the maiden-voyage/retiring-captain disaster in all *Titanic* movies; *The Poseidon Adventure*'s last-voyage scenario; the airship's first passenger flight to America in *The Hindenburg* (1975); the inaugural flights of the jets in *Airport '77* (1977) and *The Concorde ... Airport '79* (1979); the maiden journey of *The Big Bus* (1976); and *Gray Lady Down*'s retirement-bound captain. Announce it's a first or last voyage for you or your vessel, and you might as well signal mayday before you leave port.

Anyway, as Navy ships speed to the crash site, the sub keeps sliding even deeper, complicating any rescue attempt. The imperiled crew provides its own stress relief by watching *Jaws* (1975) with no sound and hilariously improvising new dialogue (note some of the sailors making their movie debuts: Christopher Reeve, soon everyone's *Superman*, and Michael O'Keefe, the main caddy in 1980's *Caddyshack*). Eventually the tense rescue is made possible by a maverick submariner (David Carradine) who nobly wedges his tiny experimental vessel under the sunken sub to prevent it from slipping into the abyss. Well done, sir.

ADDED ATTRACTION: Last Disasters

The realism and tension that make *Gray Lady Down* effective both fly away in *The Swarm* (1978), a big-budget disaster movie that unintentionally plays like a parody. Irwin Allen, producer of the Best Picture-nominated *The Towering Inferno* (1974), directed this overlong flop about an immense swarm of mutant, extremely venomous killer bees that beesiege Texas. Numerous you-can't-bee-serious situations—the bees derail a train?—and beezarre last-act solutions—the military deliberately torches the entire city of Houston?—are too unbeelievable for the impressive all-star cast (Michael Caine, Henry Fonda, and various past Oscar winners) to overcome. Bee prepared for formulaic melodramas (a pregnancy, adorable elders in a romantic triangle), beemusing hallucinations of a giant bee, and some beeyond-bad dialogue. Whereas *The Swarm* is Blah with a capital Bee, *Attack of the Killer Tomatoes!* (1978), an ultra-low-budget parody with a no-name cast, is just as energetic as its exclamation-pointed title suggests (just like a later parody, 1980's *Airplane!*, which *Killer Tomatoes!* seemingly influenced). The movie opens with wacky credits and zooms through a nation-wide invasion by tomatoes (some of them the size of cars), tossing in goofy musical numbers along the way. Silly, saucy, and occasionally hilarious, *Killer Tomatoes!* isn't for all tastes (it's like the old song, "you say tomato, I say tomahto …"), but enough people laughed to make it a cult hit and to warrant several sequels.

Pretty Baby

Released: April 1978
Director: Louis Malle
Stars: Brooke Shields, Susan Sarandon, Keith Carradine
Academy Awards: One nomination (Best Music)

PREVIEW: In 1917, a mother and her twelve-year-old daughter are prostitutes in New Orleans.

NOW SHOWING: End of the Innocence

Wary audiences welcomed *Pretty Baby* (1978) with folded arms. This daring movie eventually became a modest box-office success, and it was praised by critics who lavished attention on the images that accurately capture life inside a New Orleans whorehouse in 1917. But the elephant in this bedroom has always been the movie's core subject, conceived by screenwriter Polly Platt and controversial French director Louis Malle (making his first American film): a prostitute leads her twelve-year-old daughter into the profession. Mom is even there as her virginal daughter is paraded on a tray in front of clients and her deflowering is auctioned off for $400. Upset viewers leveled savage criticism at *Pretty Baby*, and some countries banned it altogether. It's safe to say this movie wouldn't be made today.

The closest comparison to *Pretty Baby* is *Lolita* (1962), but when Stanley Kubrick filmed Vladimir Nabokov's scandalous novel he upped Lolita's age from twelve to fourteen and he cast fifteen-year-old Sue Lyon in the role. In *Pretty Baby*, not only is the character twelve, she's played by an actual twelve-year-old, Brooke Shields (she's shown naked, but thankfully her sexual experiences aren't shown at all). *Taxi Driver* (1976) also has a twelve-year-old hooker (in a supporting role), but Iris's parents want to reclaim her, not auction her.

Viewers may find *Pretty Baby* pretty boring, especially in the second half. While it's a well-made movie, and its atmospheric music earned an Oscar nomination, the novelty of its decadent world wears off. Living in the whorehouse, Violet (Shields) is an illiterate child who skips rope, sometimes acts bratty, and casually walks in on couples

Brooke Shields and Susan Sarandon.

having sex. Susan Sarandon plays the frustrated mother with bigger dreams, but she disappears midway through the movie to get married and returns only at the very end to take Violet away so she can be "raised right." Keith Carradine is a thirtyish photographer who marries Violet until mom arrives and puts her in prim schoolgirl clothes. Meanwhile, the whores feign interest in their mostly older clientele and help each other, which in one scene means applying a swift hammer to the head of a drunk, obstreperous hothead with a gun.

Other '70s movies that broke new ground for profanity, violence, or sex were soon eclipsed by movies that were even more extreme. Not *Pretty Baby*, which for all its tasteful craftsmanship might be more disturbing than ever to modern audiences.

ADDED ATTRACTION: Mae Day

As in *Pretty Baby*, age is usually the first topic when the conversation turns to *Sextette* (1978), a preposterous vanity project that might make you question the entire system of free enterprise. Eight-five-year-old Mae West embarrassingly reprises the kind of sexy, smirking role she had played over *forty* years earlier (during the Great Depression, people), only now she's shown in ultra-soft focus with lovers less than half her age. Pretentiously flinging innuendos and recycled lines ("Come up and see me sometime"), West is slow and stiff in her glamorous gowns as, unfathomably, various handsome men, including George Hamilton and Tony Curtis, vie for her affection. Ear-numbing musical numbers—Dom DeLuise belts out the Beatles' "Honey Pie," future-007 Timothy Dalton talk-sings "Love Will Keep Us Together" and keeps a straight face for the line, "Young and beautiful, your looks will never be gone" as West preens nearby—drag this kitschy disaster closer to a painfully long skit in an awful TV variety show. Campy comedy scenes with Beatle Ringo Starr (doing an exotic accent), rocker Keith Moon (as a flamboyant designer), and Jimmy Carter and Don Corleone impersonators just seem desperate. West was a humdinger back around the time when fire was discovered, and devout fans might magnanimously applaud their queen, but to paraphrase one of her golden oldies, "When I'm good, I'm very good, but when I'm bad, I'm in *Sextette*."

Rabbit Test

Released: April 1978
Director: Joan Rivers
Stars: Billy Crystal, Joan Prather, Alex Rocco
Academy Awards: None

PREVIEW: The first pregnant man becomes famous and meets world leaders before the delivery.

NOW SHOWING: Prognosis Negative

After successful predecessors like Elaine May's *The Heartbreak Kid* (1972) and Joan Micklin Silver's *Hester Street* (1975), plus the first Best Director Oscar nomination for a woman (Lina Wertmüller, 1976's *Seven Beauties*), three more women directed their first feature films in 1978. First up was spring's *Rabbit Test*, an inept comedy directed and co-written by comedienne Joan Rivers. Billy Crystal gamely plays a twenty-four-year-old virgin who has sex with a virtual stranger on an arcade table. He inexplicably gets pregnant and somehow delivers—spoiler alert!—a baby girl (there's no clarification about how any of this is possible, and we never see the baby, though the birth does indeed happen). It's a quantity-over-quality movie cramming in as many Mel Brooks-style one-liners and sight gags as possible (there's even a Brooksian musical number). Unfortunately, the funny bits can be counted on one hand, and the remaining stream of juvenile jokes, insulting racist cracks, and dumb quips generates more cricket sounds than laughs. Even Crystal cringes at one offensive line and says, "That's awful." If you ever wanted to see your TV friend Paul Lynde play a racist doctor who swears, or see Billy Crystal wear a huge moustache, or hear incest jokes, here's your chance. There's more fun picking out the cameos: Imogene Coca (a gypsy), Michael Keaton (a bespectacled sailor), Elvis's girlfriend Linda Thompson (a sexy bus passenger), Roddy McDowall (in drag), and even Rivers herself (a panicky nurse), among others. Crass, amateurish and awkward, *Rabbit Test* fails.

Claudia Weill's *Girlfriends* (1978) is Best Picture material by comparison. This warm, intelligent gem feels, unlike *Rabbit Test*, totally genuine, as if it's showing real people going through actual experiences. Melanie Mayron is thoroughly engaging as a struggling New York photographer whose roommate leaves to get married. As her professional situation improves, Mayron's character adjusts to life alone, finds romance, and even has a flirtation with a much older man. Instead of loud, intense drama, *Girlfriends* offers quiet sensitivity and offbeat charm.

December brought Jane Wagner's *Moment by Moment*, a major flop that pairs John Travolta and Lily Tomlin (who look like twins in this movie) in an unconvincing May/December romance set in sunny Malibu. Travolta, of course, was hot off of *Saturday Night Fever* (1977), and in one scene Tomlin's character even asks, "I wonder if you have a fever." Critics and audiences turned a cold shoulder to this tepid movie.

ADDED ATTRACTION: One-Hit Wonders

For Joan Rivers, Joan Tewkesbury, and Jane Wagner, the feature films discussed above are the only ones they ever directed (though all of them did enjoy long television careers, with Rivers and Wagner winning Emmy Awards). Likewise, everyone listed below made a single '70s movie and then never directed another theatrically released feature.

- Saul Bass: *Phase IV* (1974)
- Jackie Cooper: *Stand Up and Be Counted* (1972)
- Robert Culp: *Hickey & Boggs* (1972)
- Philip D'Antoni: *The Seven-Ups* (1973)
- Dennis Donnelly: *The Toolbox Murders* (1978)
- Charles Eastman: *The All-American Boy* (1973)
- Bob Einstein: *Another Nice Mess* (1972)
- Berry Gordy: *Mahogany* (1975)
- James William Guercio: *Electra Glide in Blue* (1973)
- Larry Hagman: *Beware! The Blob* (1972)
- Jerome Hellman: *Promises in the Dark* (1979)
- Leonard Kastle: *The Honeymoon Killers* (1970)
- Remi Kramer: *High Velocity* (1976)
- Ernest Lehman: *Portnoy's Complaint* (1972)
- Jack Lemmon: *Kotch* (1971)
- Barbara Loden: *Wanda* (1970)
- Thomas McGuane: *92 in the Shade* (1975)
- Dalton Trumbo: *Johnny Got His Gun* (1971)

The Last Waltz

Released: April 1978
Director: Martin Scorsese
Stars: The Band, Bob Dylan, Eric Clapton
Academy Awards: None

PREVIEW: With various stars joining in, the Band says goodbye with a glorious final concert.

NOW SHOWING: Rock Show

Launched by *Woodstock* (1970) and highlighted by documentaries starring the Beatles, the Rolling Stones, Led Zeppelin, and the Who, the 1970s were amazing years for documentaries about rock music. Widely acclaimed as the best of them all is *The Last Waltz* (1978), the only one of the decade's rockumentaries directed by a household name. Thanks to *Mean Streets* (1973), *Alice Doesn't Live Here Anymore* (1974), and *Taxi Driver* (1976), Martin Scorsese was already on the short list of top young directors. *The Last Waltz* revealed what became obvious in his later documentaries like *Shine a Light* (2008) and in such features as *Goodfellas* (1990): Scorsese's incomparable flair with classic rock.

In *The Last Waltz* Scorsese brings his cinematic artistry to the final live concert by the Band, the revered five-piece group that had backed Bob Dylan and had scored numerous hits, including "The Weight" and "Up On Cripple Creek." The concert was held on Thanksgiving in 1976 at San Francisco's beloved Winterland, a large ballroom glamorously decorated for this show with glittering chandeliers and theatrical curtains. Many songs are followed by filmed interviews with musicians, so actual concert footage fills about 60% of the movie. The Band plays on every song, often helped by famous friends, including several—Clapton, Dylan, Ringo—recognizable by one name. Everyone joins the all-star finale, and the movie ends with the Band performing an instrumental waltz.

There are a few oddities: the movie's first song is actually the concert's encore; strangely, three numbers were shot in a Hollywood studio; and two completely out-of-place poets give readings. Most everything else, however, is overwhelmingly impressive. This may be the best-lit, best-filmed music documentary *ever* (several accomplished cinematographers contributed, including Oscar-winner Vilmos Zsigmond). It's clear from Scorsese's well-timed close-ups of musicians smiling and signaling to each other that everyone's having fun, even the normally dour Dylan. The occasionally humorous interviews, conducted by Scorsese, explore everything from the group's early years to "women and the road."

Most of all, there's the music. With no fan interviews (the crowd is barely seen), and with no psychedelic light shows or stage explosions, the concert scenes focus on the remarkable musicians and memorable songs. Favorite moments include the rollicking "Further on Up the Road," with Robbie Robertson and Eric Clapton trading guitar solos. *Ah, those were the days.* For fans of this era, *The Last Waltz* is essential viewing, listening, and reminiscing.

ADDED ATTRACTION: Prince Charming

Martin Scorsese's follow-up to *The Last Waltz* was another compelling documentary made in a completely different style. In *American Boy: A Profile of Steven Prince* (1978), Scorsese daringly eliminates glossy visuals to present pure, unadorned storytelling. Basically he aims a camera at twenty-eight-year-old Steven Prince, feeds him topics, and then lets this natural-born raconteur riff for fifty-five minutes, with brief home-movie clips inserted between the stories. Prince had played Easy Andy, the persuasive gun dealer in Scorsese's *Taxi Driver*, a distinctive role that doesn't even get mentioned. Instead, Prince recalls being in a house with a nine-hundred-pound gorilla, a neighborhood boy getting electrocuted, his own heroin addiction while he was Neil Diamond's road manager, and killing a thief with six shots from a .44 Magnum. One riveting anecdote has Prince grabbing a Magic Marker, drawing a target on a girl who has overdosed, and plunging an adrenaline shot into her chest with "a stabbing motion," elements that seem to have been incorporated directly into a famous scene in Quentin Tarantino's *Pulp Fiction* (1994).

The Buddy Holly Story

Released: May 1978

Director: Steve Rash

Stars: Gary Busey, Don Stroud, Charles Martin Smith

Academy Awards: One win (Best Music), plus two more nominations (Best Actor—Gary Busey; Best Sound)

PREVIEW: Rock pioneer Buddy Holly goes from Lubbock, Texas to national stardom in the 1950s.

NOW SHOWING: Oh Boy!

The 1970s were good years for music bios. After powerful, sometimes harrowing movies like *Lady Sings the Blues* (1972), *Leadbelly* (1976), and *Bound for Glory* (1976), *The Buddy Holly Story* (1978) took a different biographical approach. By far the shortest of these four movies, *Buddy* has the least conflict and the most joy. Refreshingly, its hero doesn't abuse substances, chase women, or go to jail. He even turns down champagne for Coke and Dr. Pepper. Buddy Holly (Gary Busey) is simply a talented Texas kid who's determined to make his own special music, and we root for him all the way.

At the start of the movie Holly is a gawky nineteen-year-old playing lively shows in the local skating rink to indifferent listeners who are soon invigorated by his exciting new sound. Most people, however, don't understand him: his church calls his "jungle music" "un-Christian," "un-American," and "a threat to our morals"; his parents counsel him to find "something to fall back on in case things don't work out"; his girlfriend advocates college; and a record producer demands that he play "hillbilly" music. Holly resists them all.

Gary Busey.

Everything changes once Holly and his band reach New York. Quickly he gets a hit record, a lucrative contract, and TV appearances, with only minor speed bumps on his race to the top. Along the way Holly meets his wife, discovers his signature horn-rimmed glasses, overcomes tensions within the band, and takes time to fix a kid's guitar. Perhaps not everything happened exactly like this (it's the Buddy Holly *story*, after all), but Holly comes across as history's nicest rock star.

Two things propel this movie: the music and Gary Busey. A dozen Holly classics ("Peggy Sue," "Oh Boy!," etc.) are performed, especially in two showpiece concerts. Midway through, Buddy Holly and the Crickets become the first white group to play Harlem's Apollo Theatre, and their exuberant set wins over the hostile crowd. The movie's climax is Holly's thrilling ten-minute final concert with an orchestra (closing text then announces that twenty-two-year-old Holly died in a plane crash later that same night). Busey passionately commits to the role and delivers a confident, energetic, star-making performance. Impressively, that's really him singing and playing.

In the late '70s Linda Ronstadt and Bruce Springsteen were among those reintroducing audiences to Holly's songs. *The Buddy Holly Story* provides an entertaining look at the man behind that timeless music.

ADDED ATTRACTION: More Music Movies

The hits kept comin' in early 1978 via two more music-themed movies aimed at totally different audiences. *FM* is about cool radio personalities who rebel against uncool corporate executives by barricading themselves inside their station and broadcasting commercial-free music. An awesome rock soundtrack led by Steely Dan's seductive theme song, Linda Ronstadt and Jimmy Buffett's concert performances, and Tom Petty's cameo almost redeem this unexceptional comedy. We fondly recall that when

FM played in L.A. it was preceded by a delightful novelty: one of the first elaborately produced music videos, Elton John's "Ego." Meanwhile, *Thank God It's Friday* is a much-maligned, very silly comedy trailing in the disco-dance steps of the great *Saturday Night Fever* (1977). Though it's garish and dated, *TGIF* does offer a dancing Columbia logo at the beginning, Jeff Goldblum and Debra Winger in early supporting roles, crazy costumes, and performances by the Commodores and Oscar-winner Donna Summer. So was either of these movies as good as *The Buddy Holly Story*? That'll be the day.

Big Wednesday

Released: May 1978
Director: John Milius
Stars: Gary Busey, William Katt, Jan-Michael Vincent
Academy Awards: None

PREVIEW: Three surfing buddies in the early 1960s have to confront adult responsibilities.

NOW SHOWING: Big Changes, *Big Wednesday*

Another of the teen movies that followed in the wake of the spectacularly successful *American Graffiti* (1973) was *Big Wednesday* (1978). Like that earlier classic, *Big Wednesday* is initially set in 1962, when three buddies enjoy the last years of their independent youth, with a rock-and-roll soundtrack accompanying their crazy antics. Carefree days are filled with surfing, nights are devoted to beach cuties and beer-soaked parties, and always the adult responsibilities are delayed as long as possible.

Known for robust adventure movies like *The Wind and the Lion* (1975) and *Conan the Barbarian* (1982), director John Milius deals here with more sensitive coming-of-age themes about nostalgic innocence confronting adult traumas. The three surfers, played believably by tanned, lean, athletic young actors (Gary Busey, William Katt, and Jan-Michael Vincent), struggle to accept the onset of maturity. When all three are called by their draft boards midway through the movie, two of them go to wild extremes to avoid military service, but the other enlists. One of them impulsively marries and abandons a Mexican girl in Tijuana, another one has a child with his girlfriend but resists serious employment. One becomes a drunk and a "screw-up," and their mentor loses everything and becomes homeless. A mutual friend's death in Vietnam sobers all of their attitudes. Ultimately they come to accept that "nobody surfs forever."

Gary Busey, Jan-Michael Vincent, and William Katt.

Whereas *American Graffiti* immersed audiences in the culture of cruising, *Big Wednesday* beautifully captures the world of surfing at a time when Malibu was largely undeveloped and low-budget surf documentaries played in small local venues. Milius knows this life because he personally lived it back in the day (a photo in the opening credits shows him with his surf buddies). He lovingly photographs the ocean with nostalgic reverence and showcases the sublimely skilled surfers as if they're heroes. Not only is the wave footage spectacular, a real-life legend, Gerry Lopez, is spotlighted and mentioned several times. Everything aims to a titanic finish when the biggest swell in memory, "like nothing anybody has ever seen," offers a monumental challenge that the three friends can't resist and can't conquer.

As the *Big Wednesday* trailer says, it's "the story of a generation, of every generation," which is why the movie, a flop in its initial release, has become something of a cult classic. Like surfing itself, *Big Wednesday* isn't for everybody, but those who know, identify, or remember will always love it.

ADDED ATTRACTION: No Pants Lance

Big Wednesday is divided into five sections, each beginning with a title shown over majestic vistas of sea and sky: "The South Swell, summer 1962" (the first 37 minutes); "The West Swell, fall 1965" (37-70 minutes); "The North Swell, winter 1968" (70-90 minutes); "The Great Swell, spring 1974" (90-98 minutes); and "Big Wednesday" (98-120 minutes). Early in that second section, forty-eight minutes into the movie, a poster on the wall of a surf shop shows a surfer along with the caption, "No Pants Lance." This was the nickname of a real-life Malibu madman named Lance Carson, an accomplished surfer who famously mooned crowds and pulled outrageous pranks on and off the beach during the 1960s. *Big Wednesday*'s co-screenwriter, Dennis Aaberg, was friends with Carson and used some of their wild-and-crazy escapades in a short story called "No Pants Mance," which was published in *Surfer* magazine in 1974. Aaberg and John Milius later incorporated some of Carson's antics into the *Big Wednesday* screenplay (the Leroy character played by Gary Busey seems to be the closest match to Carson). No Pants Lance even gets a shout-out sixty-two minutes into *More American Graffiti* (1979) when a hippie up in San Francisco makes the off-hand comment that he "used to know a surfer named Lance, his name was No Pants Lance."

Capricorn One

Released: June 1978
Director: Peter Hyams
Stars: James Brolin, Elliott Gould, Brenda Vaccaro
Academy Awards: None

PREVIEW: A failed mission to Mars leads to a major conspiracy and a hunt for three astronauts.

NOW SHOWING: Final Score—
Capricorn One, NASA Zero

In a decade that brought the Pentagon Papers, Watergate, and surges of Bigfoot sightings and alien abductions, big conspiracies propelled a wide range of vivid movies.

Sam Waterston, James Brolin, and O.J. Simpson.

Joining an impressive group that included *Soylent Green* (1973), *The Parallax View* (1974), and *Three Days of the Condor* (1975) was *Capricorn One* (1978), which used a well-known event as a springboard for fast, crowd-pleasing action.

Conspiracy theorists had long doubted the veracity of the 1969 lunar landing by noting that the public's only awareness of this event came from NASA's own announcements, from scratchy TV broadcasts, and from alleged "moon rocks." According to the theorists, NASA had tried but failed to land a man on the moon; to keep its budget from being cut, NASA then faked the entire mission and orchestrated a massive cover-up. *Capricorn One* runs with this idea. When a mission to Mars fails, NASA stages a landing in a hangar in the American desert and adds phony broadcasts from the crew, interviews with anxious wives, and even a message from the president.

This bifurcated movie starts with a fascinating set-up and ends with thrilling chases. Director Peter Hyams launches his story quickly: the elaborate conspiracy starts seven minutes into the movie, and soon a NASA leader (Hal Holbrook) is explaining everything at the Martian stage set. The three astronauts, however, refuse to play along. They escape from captivity (a little too easily), separate in the desert, and try to reach civilization with menacing military helicopters close behind. Also pursuing them is a curious journalist (Elliott Gould, approximating his rumpled, sarcastic characters in 1973's *The Long Goodbye* and 1974's *California Split*). Sniffing around some suspicious occurrences, he too becomes a target. Along the way Woodward, Bernstein, a "second gunman in the Kennedy assassination," and Patty Hearst all get mentions.

Impressive camera work intensifies the action. There's a terrific runaway-car sequence through Houston streets, wide shots in the open desert to underscore the astronauts' peril, a cool vultures-into-helicopters mirage, and a thrilling helicopters-vs.-biplane chase. Telly Savalas is a hoot as a cranky pilot, but O.J. Simpson, clearly the weak acting link among the astronauts, isn't given much to do besides dying.

Obviously NASA's plan has flaws—seriously, hundreds of employees are supposed to take NASA's secret to their graves? Fortunately, there's enough realism and excitement to make *Capricorn One*, if not one giant leap in popular entertainment, then a good strong step.

ADDED ATTRACTION: "A Sucker's Tour"

Following two weeks behind *Capricorn One* was another movie about a failed government plan. *Go Tell the Spartans* (1978) is based on an actual suicide mission that sent American soldiers in Vietnam to a position at first considered "vital" but then immediately deemed unimportant once they met resistance. Throughout the movie, confusion and disillusionment reign: the soldiers can't distinguish their allies from their enemies, and the assignment to kill Communists seemingly requires the soldiers to kill women and kids. The cigar-chomping major (Burt Lancaster) calls their futile efforts "a sucker's tour, going nowhere, just round and round in circles." There aren't any Rambo-style heroes or clear victories here, and the deaths aren't glorious—when Lancaster's character is surprisingly killed two-thirds of the way through the movie, his body is left to lie in the open, stripped of its clothes. *Go Tell the Spartans* is an unsentimental movie with rough language and beheadings, but it all feels authentic, despite being filmed on a tight budget in California instead of Southeast Asia. After the last battle, final text reminds us that we're watching "advisors" in 1964, foreshadowing the grim Vietnam years ahead. The movie's title, incidentally, comes from a sign the soldiers read above a French graveyard: "Stranger, when you find us lying here, go tell the Spartans we obeyed their orders." A reference to the doomed Battle of Thermopylae in 480 B.C., the words could be taken as a warning that obeying senseless orders (as the American soldiers in the movie are doing) can lead to certain death. It also suggests that France's decade-long failures in Vietnam are about to be repeated by the United States.

Grease

(One of 1978's five **FAR-OUT** movies)
Released: June 1978
Director: Randal Kleiser
Stars: John Travolta, Olivia Newton-John, Stockard Channing
Academy Awards: One nomination (Best Song)

PREVIEW: High school seniors share exciting and emotional experiences before graduation.

FINE LINE: "Sandy, you just can't walk out of a drive-in!" (Danny's exasperated plea as Sandy leaves him "stranded at the drive-in.")

CLOSE-UP: "Who knows ... among you young men there may be a Joe DiMaggio, a President Eisenhower, or even a Vice-President Nixon." (From the principal's address to the graduating seniors. This is one of the movie's only topical lines; theater audiences chuckled at the Nixon reference, since he'd resigned in 1974 and by 1978 had become a national joke.)

NOW SHOWING: *Grease* Was the Way We Were Feeling

Grease is an example of a critic-proof movie. Like *The Rocky Horror Picture Show* (1975) and other campy classics, *Grease* can be disparaged, but it can't be dismissed. In 1978

Grease was the number-one movie at the box office, passing *The Sound of Music* (1965) to become the highest-grossing movie musical in history (a ranking eclipsed by 1991's *Beauty and the Beast*). "Grease is the way we are feeling," sings Frankie Valli in the theme song. Audiences enthusiastically agreed.

For anyone wondering why *Grease* was and still is so popular, we have two words: John Travolta. Travolta wasn't just a movie star back then, he was a cultural Pied Piper. He danced, and people followed. From the disco world of *Saturday Night Fever* (1977) to the '50s nostalgia of *Grease* (1978), and later to the western styles of *Urban Cowboy* (1980), Travolta turned fashions and music into national trends (it's a good thing Travolta never played a chainsaw-wielding psycho in these years, who knows what kind of mayhem would've swept the country). Travolta isn't in every scene, and he sings only one solo, but he so completely dominates *Grease* that you can't take your eyes off him whenever he's around.

Nostalgia for the 1950s and early '60s was already a thing by 1978, thanks to movies like *American Graffiti* (1973), *Let the Good Times Roll* (1973), and *The Buddy Holly Story* (1978), and to successful TV shows like *Happy Days* and *Laverne & Shirley*, which were both enjoying long runs. Usually copycat TV shows *follow* popular movies, but *Grease* actually echoes *Happy Days*: both star leather-clad tough guys (Travolta's character, Danny, and TV's Fonzie); *Grease*'s Putzie character mimics TV's Potsie; *Grease* and 1970s *Happy Days* episodes have characters named Danny, Sandy, and Eugene; and *Grease*'s co-stars Jeff Conaway and Didi Conn actually appeared on *Happy Days* in 1975. One last similarity: the stars playing teens weren't teens, something especially noticeable in *Grease*. In the year *Grease* came out, Stockard Channing was thirty-four and Olivia Newton-John was thirty, and both are playing high school students. Channing is actually seven months older than Fannie Flagg, who's playing the school nurse. Channing's not the oldest "teen" of the '70s (early in 1975's *Capone*, forty-five-year-old Ben Gazzara plays nineteen-year-old Al Capone), but c'mon, at thirty-four she's old enough to have a kid of her own in high school.

Grease does make major departures from *Happy Days*' formula for lightweight entertainment. It doesn't show friendly, supportive parents, and among the stronger situations is a scene of a teen couple about to have unprotected sex in a car, leading them to deal later with a possible pregnancy. Additionally, some of the language and lyrics ("Greased Lightning," especially) are perhaps too racy for children. None of these things is truly objectionable, of course. Critics looking for real flaws have plenty to work with. Stretched thin from the first day of school in September to graduation the following June, the episodic plot strings together

Olivia Newton-John and John Travolta.

clichéd high school settings and scenes like it's running down a checklist of teen movies: beach romance, classroom cutups, malt shoppe conversations, dance contest in the gym, one-on-one car race, etc. Events zip by with little explanation, as when Sandy (Newton-John) tells Danny why she's in California instead of Australia: "We had a change of plan," and the topic never comes up again. Additionally, the broad humor is forced and idiotic. Characters laugh hysterically at each other's lame jokes and witless pranks, and the movie wears out trite sayings like "that's my name, don't wear it out" and "you're cruisin' for a bruisin'." There's plenty of bullying, too, usually when nerdy Eugene or tough-girl Rizzo (Channing) appears. Many viewers love Rizzo because she's "sassy," but often she's merely cruel, like when she literally kicks Sandy into the trash cans while Sandy sings the joyful "Summer Nights."

The preceding paragraphs risk paralysis by analysis, because when the music starts, the movie soars. "Summer Nights" is delirious fun; Travolta goes full Elvis for the show-stopping "Greased Lightning"; in the all-school "Born to Hand Jive" dance number, Travolta flashes the kind of sexy, swaggering moves he flaunted in *Saturday Night Fever*, here in cool black clothes instead of iconic white; at the drive-in Travolta sings the heartfelt "Sandy" with nutty concession-stand commercials showing behind him; and who doesn't smile when he jump-starts "You're the One That I Want" with "I got chills, they're multiplyin'!" It's Newton-John's beautiful, countryish "Hopelessly Devoted to You," however, that brought the movie its only Oscar nomination.

The best way to enjoy *Grease* is to go with the opening credits, which are presented as a children's cartoon. Treat the movie as a juvenile celebration of energetic characters who are exactly what one girl says they are: "We *are* adolescent!" Don't overthink the bewildering climax when Sandy finally caves in to peer pressure, abandons her wholesome good-girl image, and transforms into a seductive vixen with a cigarette, teased hair, tight clothes, and a glowering stare. And just embrace the inevitable happy ending that repeats a cheery line—"We'll always be together"—twelve times in a row and shows the car getting airborne. The people are caricatures, the movie nonsensical. To be fair, *Grease* isn't trying to be *Cabaret* (1972), an artistic, truly great movie musical. It's trying to be an endearing, entertaining summertime hit. Like it or not, at that it succeeds gloriously.

ADDED ATTRACTION: Broadway Babies

The original Broadway production of *Grease* earned a Tony Award nomination as 1972's Best Musical. Three other late-'70s movies were similarly based on Broadway shows that were nominated for or won the Tony for Best Musical: 1977's *A Little Night Music* (based on the 1973 musical, the Tony-winner); 1978's *The Wiz* (1975, Tony-winner); and 1979's *Hair* (1968, Tony-nominee). The most unusual of these is *The Wiz*, the only musical directed by Sidney Lumet, who had helmed powerful dramas like *Serpico* (1973). Long and extravagant, *The Wiz* reimagines *The Wizard of Oz* story by making all the characters black, funkifying the music, and moving everything to modern New York. Since Dorothy is played by thirty-four-year-old Diana Ross, the character has changed from a hopeful young Kansas girl to a twenty-four-year-old Harlem teacher. Who cries. A lot. Critics and audiences were severely underwhelmed. Michael Jackson makes a memorable movie debut as the Scarecrow, Richard Pryor is a sad, frightened Wizard, a few songs generate energy, and there's plenty to look at (the enormous sets and creative costumes earned Oscar nominations), but overall *The Wiz* isn't exhilarating, it's exhausting.

Jaws 2

Released: June 1978
Director: Jeannot Szwarc
Stars: Roy Scheider, Lorraine Gary, Murray Hamilton
Academy Awards: None

PREVIEW: A small-town sheriff confronts a menacing shark that is hunting just off the coast.

NOW SHOWING: Second Helpings

Jaws 2 is a competent action/adventure that would have a better reputation if it weren't following in the wake of *Jaws* (1975), one of history's most influential movies. *Jaws 2* continues with some of the same *Jaws* characters, especially Chief Brody (Roy Scheider); the same fictional New England beach town, Amity; and even some of the same lines (again Mrs. Brody asks, "Wanna fool around?"). Not present are *Jaws* director Steven Spielberg, Matt Hooper (the charismatic scientist who phones in that he's "presently in the Antarctic Ocean" and is unavailable), and Quint, the rough fisherman who's long since been digested.

Like *Jaws*, *Jaws 2* starts with undersea sounds and a sneak attack, but this movie makes the shark more visible. *Jaws* delayed the full reveal until the eighty-first minute, but *Jaws 2* shows the beast just twenty-two minutes in. When Brody tells Amity's leaders that another rogue shark is lurking, they foolishly prefer the "boating accident" theory disproved in *Jaws* (evidently they never saw that movie). This second shark explodes a boat, sinks a helicopter, and terrorizes some occasionally obnoxious teens in sailboats. Brody comes to their rescue and goes *mano-y*-sharko in the blazing finale. It's no *Jaws* (what is?), but *Jaws 2* still has some bite to it.

With sharks, orcas, a giant octopus, and other big aquatic killers already starring in sea-going horror movies, by mid-1978 producer Roger Corman figured it was time to downsize. Hence, *Piranha*, director Joe Dante's cult classic about small fish with huge appetites. This lively movie entertains by not taking itself seriously. The cast, including sci-fi/horror veterans like Kevin McCarthy and Barbara Steele, plays it straight, but over-the-top situations and tongue-in-cheek lines (a newscaster: "Terror, horror, death—film at eleven!") edge toward smart parody. An opening nighttime attack on swimmers, waterline shots, and efforts to stifle bad publicity all nod to *Jaws*, and a Jaws arcade game is actually shown seven minutes in (*Piranha*'s topless girls are un-*Jaws*-like, though). The story involves a secret military project that's mutating piranha into

Piranha.

river-destroying weapons for the Vietnam War. Accidentally released into a Texas river, they bring bloody carnage to a summer camp and water park, killing many more people than *Jaws*'s shark does. While the jittery, quick-moving fish aren't seen in full, their flashing teeth, the eerie churning sounds, and the gory results provide effective jolts. Wit, style, scares—this is a B-movie done right.

ADDED ATTRACTION: Gone Fishin'

Late 1978 brought more submerged horror, but in *Barracuda* the title fish barely appears. An absent predator almost became an issue in *Jaws 2*, because the shark made its big appearance early in the movie and then disappeared for the next forty-five minutes as civic politics took over the story. At least the shark returned to literally chew up the scenery in the last act. In *Barracuda*, toothy barracudas are present in the movie but don't appear at all in the last thirty-seven minutes. That's a problem when a movie about killer fish doesn't have any live killer fish in its last third. *Barracuda* starts like any other low-budget *Jaws* clone, using lots of *Jaws* tricks (a fictional coastal town, bloody sea attacks, washed-up remains, a diligent small-town sheriff, fish-POV shots, etc.), plus a cast of unknowns. It becomes a serious land-based ecological thriller when college students investigate chemical-plant pollution and expose a deadly cover-up that leads to a surprisingly downbeat ending. Despite the menacing fangs lunging from the movie's poster and the expectations raised by the title, guns and hypoglycemia do the most damage. It's as if *Jaws* started with the shark and really did end with lethal boating accidents. *Barracuda*'s schizophrenic story desperately needs barracuda, either the ferocious predator or Heart's classic song.

Heaven Can Wait

Released: June 1978
Directors: Warren Beatty, Buck Henry
Stars: Warren Beatty, Julie Christie, James Mason
Academy Awards: One win (Best Art Direction), plus eight more nominations (Best Picture; Best Actor—Warren Beatty; Best Supporting Actor—Jack Warden; Best Supporting Actress—Dyan Cannon; Best Director; Best Writing; Best Cinematography; Best Music)

PREVIEW: When an angel brings a man to Heaven prematurely, he's given a new life back on Earth.

NOW SHOWING: Here Comes Mr. Beatty

Heaven Can Wait (1978) is a winning update to *Here Comes Mr. Jordan* (1941), the classic comedy about Joe Pendleton, a boxer yanked prematurely into Heaven and sent back to Earth. *Heaven Can Wait*'s Joe Pendleton is now a modern pro quarterback played by Warren Beatty. Pendleton rides his ten-speed on L.A.'s twisty mountain roads and appears to be heading toward a fatal crash, at which point an overanxious rookie angel (Buck Henry) plucks Pendleton from this life and ships him to the next one (the trip involves a white, unbordered space with tule fog and a supersonic *Concorde* about to depart). Pendleton's "fantastic reflexes," however, actually would've enabled him to avoid the oncoming vehicle, so he's been taken prematurely. And he's not happy about it, especially with his team challenging for the Super Bowl.

A senior angel (James Mason) arrives to calm Pendleton and give him the chance to return to Earth in a different body. After considering various options, he settles on a handsome millionaire (what a sacrifice!), moves into an elegant mansion, does some good deeds, and falls for a pretty environmental activist (Julie Christie). Pendleton manages to make it to the Super Bowl after all and finds himself in a win-win situation, leading his team to victory and then getting the girl in a quiet, sentimental ending. Everything's handled with a breezy confidence reminiscent of the sophisticated romantic comedies of Hollywood's Golden Age.

Beatty, the rebel behind the revolutionary *Bonnie and Clyde* (1967) and the daring *Shampoo* (1975), went conservative and mainstream with *Heaven Can Wait*. He produced, co-directed (with Buck Henry), co-wrote (with Elaine May), and stars in this inoffensive, big-budget delight that's so highly polished it should be waxed annually to preserve the shine. Charming, handsome, and a good enough athlete to convincingly play a football star, Beatty is "looking awful good," as he's described six times in the movie. The starry ensemble cast includes past Oscar winners and nominees (Christie, Mason, Dyan Cannon, Vincent Gardenia) who are all wonderful here. Watching Cannon and Charles Grodin together is like watching two aerialists perform a high-wire act.

Audiences couldn't wait and made this attractive fantasy one of 1978's top money-makers. Additionally, *Heaven Can Wait*, surrounded by *Grease* and *Foul Play*, was the centerpiece of an impressive trifecta of stylish throwbacks to old-fashioned movies—all were released within a six-week period, and all became summer blockbusters.

ADDED ATTRACTION: A High Ol' Time at the Movies

The total inverse of the refined, Oscar-nominated *Heaven Can Wait* came out later that summer. With a low budget, a seemingly ad-libbed script, and goofy vignettes instead of a cohesive plot, *Up in Smoke* (1978) is about as unserious as movies get, yet it became a serious box-office success. That's because of the good-natured interplay between Cheech Marin and Tommy Chong, who'd been perfecting their anti-establishment comedy act in clubs and on records all decade long. In their first of many movies, they're, duh, two bumbling slackers searching for dope (Chong's character is actually named Anthony Stoner). Next they drive a van "constructed entirely of high-grade marijuana" from Tijuana to Hollywood. Then they win the "Rock Fight of the Century" by singing "Earache My Eye" (their 1974 hit) with Cheech in Mickey Mouse ears, a pink tutu, and argyle knee socks.

Cheech Marin and Tommy Chong.

Instead of carefully crafted jokes, there's mostly just amiable improvised banter that inserts the word "man" into virtually every sentence, sometimes twice. Cops are unhip nitwits, an Asian reporter is named Toyota Kawasaki, a partygoer accidentally snorts lines of Ajax cleanser and freaks out, the boys smoke a joint the size of a soda can ... juvenile hijinks like these create an eighty-six-minute buzz that can be pretty funny despite your better judgement. Suitably relaxed viewers armed with enough munchies will give it the highest praise.

Sgt. Pepper's Lonely Hearts Club Band

Released: July 1978
Director: Michael Schultz
Stars: The Bee Gees, Peter Frampton, George Burns
Academy Awards: None

PREVIEW: To save Heartland, Sgt. Pepper and his band must recover their stolen instruments.

NOW SHOWING: ♫ Picture Yourself ... Hit by a Train in a Station ♫

As his *Saturday Night Fever* and *Grease* movie soundtracks soared to the top of the charts in the '70s, producer Robert Stigwood turned to the bestselling album of the '60s, the Beatles' *Sgt. Pepper's Lonely Hearts Club Band*. The Beatles had disbanded in 1970, but thanks to popular solo records and reunion rumors the group was still a vivid presence. Stigwood's *Sgt. Pepper's Lonely Hearts Club Band* (1978) was intended to return audiences to the Fab Four's heyday via flashy updates of their songs by current superstars like Peter Frampton and the Bees Gees. A splendid time was guaranteed for all.

That preceding paragraph attempts to answer the what-were-they-thinking question most viewers ask after enduring this travesty. Possibly the decade's worst major movie, *Pepper* weakly apes a genuinely entertaining Stigwood production, *Tommy* (1975). *Tommy*'s songs, however, tell a cohesive story that had already been worked out satisfactorily on the Who's double album; *Pepper* clumsily shoehorns totally unrelated Beatles songs from five different Beatles albums—*Revolver*, *Sgt. Pepper*, *Magical Mystery Tour*, *Abbey Road*, and *Let It Be*—into a moronic live-action cartoon that skids desperately through a patched-together plot made from disparate elements. One-dimensional characters have names like Strawberry Fields, Mr. Kite, and Mr. Mustard, proper nouns drawn from three different LPs (what, no Eleanor Rigby, Penny Lane, or Rocky Raccoon?). We do learn a little about the unusual Sgt. Pepper himself, because the movie opens with a recap of the sarge's life from 1918 up to his sudden heart-attack death on August 10, 1958. So there's that.

Frampton and the brothers Gibb perform many of the songs, and at least they're real singers. The mockery starts eleven minutes in when

The Bee Gees (Robin Gibb, Barry Gibb, Maurice Gibb) and Peter Frampton.

eighty-two-year-old George Burns strums an electric guitar and talk-sings "Fixing a Hole," followed soon by Donald Pleasence, wearing a glittery-jacket-cowboy-hat-wig combo, growling through "I Want You (She's So Heavy)." Like a bad TV variety show with embarrassed musicians trying to "act" in mindless skits and non-singing actors trying to "sing" pop songs, it all goes nowhere man.

To show we're not Blue Meanies, here are some positives: Earth, Wind & Fire and Aerosmith acquit themselves creditably, the puffed-up hair and outrageous costumes are amusing, the Sunset Strip's venerable Tower Records gets a scene, and the finale's fun cameos include Carol Channing, Tina Turner, Donovan, Helen Reddy, Wolfman Jack, and more. Otherwise, this movie is a dumb day in the life.

ADDED ATTRACTION: Screen Songs

Studios already had a long history of naming movies after popular songs (1954's *White Christmas*, for example) when three early-'78 movies were released with musical titles. Informalizing "I Want to Hold Your Hand," April's *I Wanna Hold Your Hand* was the entertaining debut by Robert Zemeckis, the future Oscar-winning director of *Forrest Gump* (1994). In this fast, fun tribute to the Beatlemania that greeted the Fab Four's 1964 arrival in New York, four teenage girls have hectic Plaza Hotel adventures while trying to glimpse the Beatles, and then everybody bugs out to the TV studio for the group's landmark appearance on *The Ed Sullivan Show*. Slapstick, chases, and seventeen Beatles songs fill this energetic movie. A month later, *Harper Valley P.T.A.* was a dippy comedy expanding on Tom T. Hall's and Jeannie C. Riley's hit song about a feisty single mom who exposes small-town hypocrisies. Vivacious Barbara Eden gets Harper Valley Payback To All by embarrassing her accusers with well-planned pranks, like turning three live elephants loose inside a house. Jail time? No, veil time, as she ends up marrying the town's handsome millionaire. Next, rugged Kris Kristofferson and well-tanned Ali MacGraw rolled in with *Convoy*, based on C.W. McCall's novelty hit that incorporated CB-radio slang. Sam Peckinpah's jumbled, tedious chase movie has a pretentious rebels-vs.-mean-sheriffs story and clichéd slow-motion fights and crashes, but big summer audiences still came along for the ride.

Foul Play

Released: July 1978
Director: Colin Higgins
Stars: Goldie Hawn, Chevy Chase, Dudley Moore
Academy Awards: One nomination (Best Song)

PREVIEW: An innocent woman falls for the cop who is protecting her as a murder scheme unfolds.

NOW SHOWING: The Woman Who Knew Too Much

Foul Play (1978) was a huge audience-pleasing hit and one of the year's best date movies. Stylish, inoffensive and likeable, it's got attractive stars, a nice mix of comedy, romance, and action, mild violence without the bloodshed, and playful sexual humor without the sex.

If all this sounds like one of Alfred Hitchcock's classic 1950s movies, that's no accident. Writer/director Colin Higgins had already scored big with his script for *Silver*

Streak (1976), an affectionate, well-made variation on Hitchcock's *North by Northwest* (1959). Here, in his first directorial effort, he fills an elaborate assassination plot (to kill the Pope, no less) with many allusions to Hitchcock's movies, including a San Francisco setting, a MacGuffin (a roll of film kick-starts the story), an innocent character drawn into intrigue, and, from *Vertigo* (1958), a spinning

Chevy Chase and Goldie Hawn.

screen and characters named Scotty and Ferguson. Higgins adds his own eccentricities, such as an albino, fanciful character names like Scarface, Rupert Stiltskin, Mrs. Monk and Mrs. Venus (this is starting to sound like a board game), plus a fast, funny car sequence that races up and down San Francisco's hills and a humorous scene of old ladies misspelling profanities on a Scrabble board. Hitchcock would approve.

Higgins' Hitchcock blonde is played by Goldie Hawn, who's thoroughly adorable as the guileless girl entangled in murder. She's not a helpless victim, however, so she orchestrates her own escapes. Chevy Chase, getting his first major role, is her co-star, though he's in only about half the movie. Famous as a klutz on TV's *Saturday Night Live*, he immediately knocks over all the glasses on a serving cart in his first scene. Later he tumbles from a dock into San Francisco Bay. Chase is generally appealing and amusing, though he's unconvincing as an authoritative police lieutenant. Dudley Moore is the one who delivers the movie's riotous laughs. He plays a hapless pervert who converts his apartment into a sexed-up disco at the push of a button.

Foul Play is definitely of its time, showing off '70s artifacts (a VW Super Beetle convertible, Barry Manilow songs, a singles bar) and groovy attitudes (a friend advises Hawn's character, "Let's see some skin ... shake your booty, take some chances ... drag yourself into the '70s"). But it's the '70s by way of the '50s. With some sparkling moments, occasional farce, and light suspense, *Foul Play* is an entertaining update to old-fashioned movie fun.

ADDED ATTRACTION: The Mild Mild West

Also in theaters that July was *Hot Lead and Cold Feet* (1978), one of seven live-action adventure/comedies the Disney Studios released between its two big-budget special-effects showcases, *Pete's Dragon* (1977) and *The Black Hole* (1979). Several familiar Disney veterans worked on this sunny western, including director Robert Butler and co-stars Jim Dale and Don Knotts. Their collaboration produced a pleasing, if unrealistic and noisy movie featuring typical Disney ingredients: a few moments of light peril, cute kids, mild romance, and a happy ending. *Hot Lead and Cold Feet* starts with an old man (Jim Dale) bequeathing his businesses and riches to whichever of his two sons (both also played by Dale) wins a dangerous race involving mountains, river rapids, and horse-drawn wagons. Fifty minutes into the movie the race finally starts, and quickly it's obvious that someone is rampantly cheating (since it's a Disney movie, two orphans help reveal the villain). Farcical pratfalls, inaccurate gunplay, and comical fights ensue before everything works out for the brothers, the orphans, the town, and the good-versus-evil theme. The last scene points to a non-existent sequel set in "Cactus Ridge" with two sisters, "Calico Kate and Wildcat Winnie." Playing an inept sheriff a la his role on TV's *The Andy Griffith Show*, Knotts steals the movie with four hilarious duels against a mangy outlaw.

Animal House

(One of 1978's five **FAR-OUT** movies)

Released: July 1978

Director: John Landis

Stars: John Belushi, Karen Allen, Tom Hulce

Academy Awards: None

PREVIEW: At a small college in 1962, misfit members of a frat house go against a hostile dean.

FINE LINE: "Fat, drunk, and stupid is no way to go through life, son." (Dean Wormer, counseling a student he is expelling.)

CLOSE-UP: Ninety-four minutes into the movie, Dean Wormer is in the parade stands accepting the "ceremonial gold-plated whistle." Look at the upper-left section of the screen: for about thirty seconds, one of the elders sitting there is uncontrollably blinking and grinning.

NOW SHOWING: Welcome to the Jungle

It may be hard for modern audiences who are seeing *Animal House* (1978) for the first time (particularly if that first time is with an edited TV version) to understand this movie's significance and status. Yes it's rude, and crude, and sometimes totally juvenile, just like its main characters. But anyone who saw this in theaters in 1978 has to concede that it generated the most and the loudest laughs of any movie of the decade, except possibly *Blazing Saddles* (1974). *Animal House* wasn't merely a smash-hit movie; it was a game-changing landmark.

Unlike that earlier Mel Brooks classic, which gave audiences hilarious scenes but few characters they could really identify with, *Animal House* (formally titled *National Lampoon's Animal House*) is filled with people we all knew, or maybe were ourselves once. The dorks and drunks at Delta, the smug preppies at the rival Omega House, the confident smooth-talking stud, the nervous naïve freshmen, the condescending pretty girls who mock the chubby and the uncool, the one groovy professor on campus—for many viewers this movie could've been called *The Way We Were*.

For all the wild debauchery and crazy antics, at the heart of the movie is a traditional "us vs. them" story vaguely like the one in *M*A*S*H* (1970), where spirited anti-establishment characters assembled, drank, partied, challenged staid authority, and finished with a big rousing team effort (the *M*A*S*H* football game, the *Animal House* parade). *M*A*S*H*, however, had a cruel streak that *Animal House* replaces with sweetness. The hip doctors in *M*A*S*H* tortured and drummed out those they decided didn't belong; the cool Deltas in *Animal House* acknowledge the shortcomings of the feebs in their fraternity, but they still include them in their schemes.

The story takes place in 1962 at a fictional small-town college (the movie was shot at the University of Oregon) where the misfit members of a defiantly nonacademic and relentlessly party-oriented frat house challenge the conservative fraternity system and fight back against the uptight dean who wants to shut them down. Along the way the carefree Deltas enjoy various sexual escapades, wild road trips, and destructive debauches. After they're all expelled, they make an anarchic last stand by totally ruining the town's homecoming parade. As in *American Graffiti* (1973), another great comedy about small-town friends in 1962, most of the Delta House characters look out for each other. The older Deltas generally encourage the newbies, roommates cheer each other on, the patient girlfriend is endlessly supportive of her frat fella, and the seven-year college man Bluto rallies the troops with shouts of "food fight!" and an inspirational speech about the Germans bombing Pearl Harbor. You'd want to hang out with the guys from either movie.

John Belushi.

Ah, Bluto. John Belushi, the *Saturday Night Live* star, begins his big-screen career by going to the bathroom out in the front yard in his first-ever movie scene. After this daring debut, Belushi proceeds to walk away with the picture (and the cover of *Newsweek* magazine). He doesn't have a lot of lines, but he's got the expressive eyebrows, the knowing smile, the bouncy moves, and the can't-take-your-eyes-off-him presence of the master silent comedians. But he wasn't the only break-out star. To name just four: Tim Matheson quickly starred in *1941* (1979), Karen Allen (making her movie debut) went on to co-star in *Raiders of the Lost Ark* (1981), Kevin Bacon (another movie debut) later danced his way to stardom in *Footloose* (1984), and director John Landis, fresh off of *The Kentucky Fried Movie* (1977), soon had another hit with *The Blues Brothers* (1980). Landis wisely lets the expressive personalities of his young *Animal House* stars carry many of the scenes, as when Bluto hilariously loads up his cafeteria tray with free food and Otter (Matheson) pulls off a super-cool seduction of the dean's wife, two highlights that happen without any dialogue at all.

The *Animal House* influence rippled through the culture and through Hollywood. *Newsweek* magazine put it on the cover (October 23, 1978), a TV series quickly followed (see "Added Attraction"), the rowdy '60s anthem "Louie Louie" made a comeback, for awhile college students everywhere threw toga parties, and in the late '70s you couldn't go a day without hearing someone quote one of the movie's many famous lines (does "double-secret probation" sound familiar?). Brilliantly, the great Elmer Bernstein composed a serious music score that contrasted the raunchy comedy, a strategy quickly adopted by other filmmakers. And look for the cameos, including two of the writers (Doug Kenney, playing the dorky Stork, and Chris Miller, a card player); the real-life wives of Belushi (Judith is his dance partner at the toga party) and Stephen Furst (as Flounder he asks the store cashier, played by Lorraine Furst, for marbles near the end); and singer/songwriter Stephen Bishop (he's the cheesy folk singer whose guitar is smashed by the annoyed Bluto in the stairway; Bishop also composed and performs the doo-wop song played over the closing credits).

It's all done with a cocky confidence and in a shaggy who-cares style that doesn't worry too much about details, so don't get worked up over the anachronisms (the '70s cars occasionally on view, or the Kingsmen's 1963 version of "Louie Louie" that's heard in the movie). And don't even start with complaints about the outrageous anything-goes sense of humor that undoubtedly offends some viewers. The Deltas are having too much fun to care.

ADDED ATTRACTION: From Big Screen to Little Screen

The most successful comedy at the box office in 1978, *Animal House* was quickly made into a TV series (the show couldn't duplicate the movie's lightning-in-a-bottle popularity and lasted only season). Here are a dozen big-screen-to-little-screen transitions for 1975-1979 movies.

1970-1979 Movie Year, Starring...	**Later TV Show (Years), Starring...**
Animal House (1978), John Belushi	*Delta House* (1979), Josh Mostel
The Bad News Bears (1976), Walter Matthau	*The Bad News Bears* (1979-1980), Jack Warden
The Black Stallion (1979), Mickey Rooney	*Adventures of the Black Stallion* (1990-1993), Mickey Rooney
Breaking Away (1979), Dennis Christopher	*Breaking Away* (1980-1981), Shaun Cassidy
Cooley High (1975), Glynn Turman	*What's Happening!!* (1976-1979), Ernest Thomas
Foul Play (1978), Chevy Chase	*Foul Play* (1981), Barry Bostwick
Harper Valley P.T.A. (1978), Barbara Eden	*Harper Valley P.T.A.* (1981-1982), Barbara Eden
House Calls (1978), Walter Matthau	*House Calls* (1979-1982), Wayne Rogers
Logan's Run (1976), Michael York	*Logan's Run* (1977-1978), Gregory Harrison
Moonrunners (1975), James Mitchum	*The Dukes of Hazzard* (1979-1985), Tom Wopat
The Omen (1976), Gregory Peck	*Damien* (2016), Bradley James
Time After Time (1979), Malcolm McDowell	*Time After Time* (2017), Freddie Stroma

The Driver

Released: July 1978
Director: Walter Hill
Stars: Ryan O'Neal, Bruce Dern, Isabelle Adjani
Academy Awards: None

PREVIEW: A detective tries to snare the getaway driver who speeds clients from their heists.

NOW SHOWING: Riding with *The Driver*

Had this book been called *Coolest. Movies. Ever.*, *The Driver* (1978) would rate a chapter. This movie is too cool for character names: borrowing an idea from another cool, chapter-worthy movie, *Two-Lane Blacktop* (1971), everyone's identified simply by profession—The Player, The Connection, etc.—or physical trait—including Glasses, Teeth, and Frizzy. And it's too cool for lots of yakking and personal history: the emotionless Driver (Ryan O'Neal) speaks only 332 words, twelve fewer than Steve McQueen speaks in *Le Mans* (June 1971), another *Coolest. Movies. Ever.* entry.

Cars are the stars of these movies, and this is where *The Driver* shifts into top-gear coolness. It's got three amazing car scenes—an opening six-minute sprint through downtown L.A. (The Driver's Ford Galaxie leaves a trail of destroyed police cars), The Driver's skillful demolition of the Mercedes he's commandeered inside a parking garage, and a final ten-minute pursuit into a vast warehouse where his Chevy pickup plays "chicken" with a Trans-Am. You don't watch this movie, you buckle up, hang on, and smell burned rubber.

Ryan O'Neal and Isabelle Adjani.

The rest of the movie is a moody noir-style crime caper as The Driver, who freelances as the getaway driver on robberies, handles double-crossing lowlife clients and evades a trap set by The Detective (Bruce Dern). The Driver is nicknamed Cowboy, an outlaw connection reinforced when he whips out an old-fashioned pistol to win a fast-draw duel. Considering he made his bones as a sensitive loverboy in *Love Story* (1970) and a humorous star in *What's Up, Doc?* (1972) and *Paper Moon* (1973), O'Neal is surprisingly convincing as a laconic tough guy.

Some scenes seem derivative: the pistol-in-a-woman's-mouth threat echoes *Beyond the Valley of the Dolls* (1970), and the tense train search comes straight from *The Getaway* (1972). We'll also concede that director Walter Hill's minimalist style isn't everyone's cup of ethyl (most 1978 critics dissed *The Driver*). But we've always thought this exciting movie, hurtling along in ninety-one minutes, qualifies as an underrated classic of its kind.

"I'm on a streak," says The Driver, but unfortunately for O'Neal that streak temporarily ended here. Late that year he moped through *The Snoozer* ... uh, *Oliver's Story*, a melodramatic *Love Story* sequel with Candice Bergen as an assertive heiress helping Oliver get over his late wife. He can't, they split up in Hong Kong, and Ollie's again alone, though more socially conscious, when this dull, uncool story finally runs out of gas.

ADDED ATTRACTION: Drive-In Drivers

When *The Driver* hit theaters, two other car-chase movies were already screeching across summer screens. June's *Corvette Summer* was Mark Hamill's follow-up to *Star Wars* (1977). He plays a shaggy-haired high-schooler who uses the Force ... of his thumb to hitchhike to Las Vegas in search of a stolen Corvette. Spirited Annie Potts and an exciting muscle-car chase await in this above-average teen adventure. Released three weeks later, *Stingray* mixes guns, cars, dopey comedy, and rollicking country music into an oddly entertaining drive-in diversion. Drug dealers hide cash and stash inside a bitchen Corvette that two innocent guys happen to buy. Villains, cops, and hillbillies then pursue the 'Vette around St. Louis, leading to some high-speed chases and impressive stunts. The highlights, though, are every scene with Sherry Jackson, who consistently invigorates the movie as a tough-talking punch-throwing gun-toting gang leader. *Playboy* Playmate Sondra Theodore plays a leggy hitchhiker who fills the Corvette with eye candy for the last thirty minutes.

Annie Potts and Mark Hamill.

Eyes of Laura Mars

Released: August 1978
Director: Irvin Kershner
Stars: Faye Dunaway, Tommy Lee Jones, Brad Dourif
Academy Awards: None

PREVIEW: A fashion photographer has psychic visions of her associates as they are murdered.

NOW SHOWING: The Eyes Have It

John Carpenter co-wrote a great 1978 movie: *Halloween*, the horror milestone he also directed. Earlier that year he co-wrote *Eyes of Laura Mars* (1978), an Irvin Kershner-directed psychological thriller that's both daring and disappointing. The title character (Faye Dunaway) is a Manhattan fashion photographer who has psychic visions of the actual in-progress murders of her co-workers. Throughout the movie her visions get increasingly clear and graphic until at the end she's basically watching a movie starring herself. The lieutenant on the case (Tommy Lee Jones) goes from disbelief to a serious investigation to a romance with Mars until the psycho and the psychosis are revealed in a fast wrap-up.

Faye Dunaway.

Those final revelations shouldn't be a surprise, since the red herrings—Mars' grungy ex-con chauffeur, her drunken ex-husband, etc.—all get killed off one by one. What's more, the killer's motivations are explained halfway through the movie by someone who seems to know a little too much about these topics. "Your work," this person tells Mars, "is promoting porno and decadence," and the killer "has a mission to clean up the world." The "work" being referred to is Mars' controversial "violent and sexy" photography that puts erotic models amidst guns, car crashes, corpses, and flames. Unfortunately, it's never clear why the killer murders everyone around Mars when *she's* the one he's after. Nor do we understand anything about her sudden psychic gift. This is one of those movies where it's better not to raise too many questions (don't mention the mismatch between Oscar-winning superstar Dunaway, fresh off 1976's *Network*, and relative-nobody Jones, for instance).

Unless you love disco music and forceful songs by Barbra Streisand (her "Prisoner" theme song opens and closes the movie), the pleasures here are visual. Mars' visions are subjective shots from the killer's viewpoint, leading to interesting scenes where she watches *herself* being stalked (the last confrontation in front of multiple mirrors is especially impressive). In addition, unlike *The French Connection* (1971) and other '70s movies that make New York look grim and gritty, *Laura Mars* spotlights fabulous, flamboyant glamour, so in a way the movie is like a bridge between two other thrillers set in fashion-conscience big cities, *Blow-Up* (1966) and *American Gigolo* (1980).

Had it been more suspenseful and less obvious, *Laura Mars* might've been an eye-popping classic. Instead, we're left to imagine the possibilities had this material been in Alfred Hitchcock's hands, or Carpenter's.

ADDED ATTRACTION: Murder on the *Karnak* Express

In theaters simultaneously with *Eyes of Laura Mars* was a more traditional mystery, *Death on the Nile* (1978). Borrowing the formula of its successful predecessor, *Murder on the Orient Express* (1974), *Nile* is similarly based on a 1930s Agatha Christie novel, and it likewise puts an all-star cast of passengers (including Bette Davis, David Niven, and Maggie Smith) in a confined space for an exotic trip. When a passenger is murdered aboard the Nile steamer *Karnak*, detective Hercule Poirot (Peter Ustinov) applies his "little gray cells" to solve this and subsequent killings (with its five victims, the movie's title should've been pluralized into *Deaths on the Nile*). As with *Orient Express*, we see flashbacks to key events (including five different views of the first shooting), and we watch as Poirot gathers everyone together and brilliantly untangles the intricate crimes. As a character says, it's "a splendid piece of detecting." Sumptuous Egyptian locations and Oscar-winning costumes help make this a pleasurable (though long) voyage. This was an especially timely movie because the record-setting "Treasures of Tutankhamun" exhibition was concurrently touring American museums, and Steve Martin's goofy "King Tut" song was riding high on the charts (Tut gets mentioned in the movie, as does *Orient Express*). Another Christie mystery, this one based on a real event in her life, followed five months later. In *Agatha* (1979), Vanessa Redgrave plays the shy novelist and Dustin Hoffman is an American journalist trying to find Christie when she inexplicably disappears for eleven days in 1926. Critics generally applauded the movie's elaborate conjecture and stylish production.

Interiors

Released: August 1978
Director: Woody Allen
Stars: Geraldine Page, Diane Keaton, Maureen Stapleton
Academy Awards: Five nominations (Best Actress—Geraldine Page; Best Supporting Actress—Maureen Stapleton; Best Director; Best Writing; Best Art Direction)
PREVIEW: A family is torn apart when the father announces he's leaving and will soon remarry.

NOW SHOWING: Into *Interiors*

With *Interiors* (1978), Woody Allen made one of the decade's most daring career moves. Already nationally famous from dozens of TV appearances, recognized as the writer/director/star of hilarious comedies, and a recent two-time Oscar winner for *Annie Hall* (1977), Allen decided to temporarily abandon comedy and veer off in a serious new direction. How serious? *Interiors* ends with a mother's suicide in front of her daughter.

That "serious new direction" was right off a cliff for viewers who consider *Interiors* a pretentious failure. Some failure: it earned five Oscar nominations, drew gushing accolades from important critics, and turned a modest profit. In *Interiors*, Allen defiantly abandons his comedic strengths for an austere, humorless story with long dialogue-filled scenes, no musical soundtrack, and little action. Three upper-class sisters cope with their father's announcement that he's leaving their mother, Eve (Geraldine Page). To everyone's horror, he rushes into marriage with a younger "vulgarian," Pearl (Maureen Stapleton). Eve is so overwhelmed by these speeding developments that she walks into the sea, a tragic climax echoing *A Star Is Born* (1954).

Some familiar elements make *Interiors* recognizable as a Woody Allen movie, even though he's not in it (it's the first one he wrote but didn't appear in). The characters are well-to-do New Yorkers, several of them are writers, there's a role for Diane Keaton (appearing in her fifth movie written by Allen, she plays a published poet who's married to a novelist), and a character lives a shallow life in Los Angeles, all ingredients remixed from Allen's earlier light confections. Allen's own obsession with Ingmar Bergman movies, hinted at in his earlier comedies—the white-on-black credits, for instance—is manifested in *Interiors* with Bergman-like themes and compositions (see the arrangement of the sisters in the final profile shot). Some of Allen's artistic ambitions get a little heavy-handed: icy Eve wears bland colors, while lively Pearl bursts in wearing bright red.

Interiors isn't to every taste, but it's still an admirable experiment. And as somber as *Interiors* is, there's some hope at the end that the sisters will move past grief to calmer, happier lives. If its gravity makes possible exquisite comedy/drama blends like *Manhattan* (1979), *Hannah and Her Sisters* (1986), and *Crimes and Misdemeanors* (1989), then *Interiors* represents a vital hinge in Allen's career. After this transition, anything would be possible in the forty movies Allen would make over the next forty years.

ADDED ATTRACTION: Errors in the Credits

Interiors' closing credits list casting director Juliet Taylor as "Juilet" and say the Producers gratefully "ackowledge" various organizations. Here are other '70s movies with conspicuous mistakes in the opening titles or closing credits.

- *Annie Hall* (1977): Closing credits, Christopher Walken's last name is spelled "Wlaken."
- *The Buddy Holly Story* (1978): Closing credits, Ritchie Valens is "Richie."
- *Horror Express* (1973): Opening credits, Christopher Lee is "Cristopher."
- *Jaws of Death* (1976): Opening credits, Jennifer Bishop is "Jenifer."
- *Klute* (1971): Throughout the movie Jane Fonda's character calls herself Bree Daniels, but the closing credits list "Daniel."
- *The Life and Times of Judge Roy Bean* (1972): Opening credits, Jacqueline Bisset, one of the movie's stars, is "Bissett."
- *Macon County Line* (1974): Opening and closing credits, Leif Garrett (the future pop star) is "Lief."
- *Magnum Force* (1973): Closing credits, Clint Eastwood's character, the iconic and well-known Harry Callahan, is "Calahan."
- *Manhattan* (1979): Closing credits, Mark Linn-Baker, shown performing Shakespeare in the Park, is "Mary Linn Baker."
- *Wizards* (1977): Closing credits, Mark Hamill, star of *Star Wars* (1977), is "Hamil."
- *White Lightning* (1973): Closing credits, Diane Ladd is "Lad."
- *Wise Blood* (1979): Opening credits, the movie's director is spelled "Jhon" Huston, though this may be intentional.

Days of Heaven

Released: September 1978
Director: Terrence Malick
Stars: Richard Gere, Brooke Adams, Sam Shepard
Academy Awards: One win (Best Cinematography), plus three more nominations (Best Costume Design; Best Sound; Best Music)

PREVIEW: In 1916, two lovers pose as siblings and try to swindle a rich farmer who may be dying.

NOW SHOWING: Fields of Dreams

You don't watch *Days of Heaven* (1978), you experience it. Slowly flowing with ravishing, dream-like imagery, this bold movie rivals Stanley Kubrick's luminous *Barry Lyndon* (1975) as the decade's most artful cinematic achievement. Both movies express visual beauty through new camera technology, which for director Terrence Malick was the mobile Panaglide camera that enabled him to move smoothly and intimately through scenes; watch the couple walking in a shallow river twenty-six minutes into the movie to see how the camera circles their conversation. In addition, Malick, often filming in soft, crepuscular light (the late-afternoon "magic hour"), creates lush, romantic panoramas of pastoral fields and sunsets that are suitable for framing.

Richard Gere and Brooke Adams.

Like *Barry Lyndon*, *Days of Heaven* is lavishly praised for its technique but is sometimes criticized for its story. In early twentieth-century Chicago, Bill (Richard Gere) accidentally kills his boss and flees with his girlfriend, Abby (Brooke Adams), and his teenage sister, Linda (Linda Manz), to Texas, where Bill and Abby get low-paying jobs as field hands. Posing as brother and sister, they concoct a scheme whereby Abby marries their dying employer (Sam Shepard) to inherit his riches. The farmer comes to suspect that Bill and Abby are "a pair of con artists," Bill kills him, and there's one more escape before the inevitable conclusion. While this melancholic tale has the possibility of lots of tension and character development, it's told in cold, sporadic bursts so that Malick can return to his painterly images. By focusing on poetic presentation, Malick subordinates what could have been an involving story, giving the audience sensations to absorb instead of emotions to feel.

Days of Heaven has much in common with *Badlands* (1973), Malick's impressive, more powerful debut. Exactly the same length, both movies have a romantic couple involved in crime and a doomed male lead; both have natural, stream-of-consciousness narration by a girl in the movie (at times Linda's impassive observations seem totally random); both movies closely examine nature (Malick loves to linger on landscapes, animals, and wind over water or fields); and both have wistful music. Startling drama, however, drives *Badlands*; *Days of Heaven* is muted, contemplative. A quick killing opens the movie, later there are vigorous scenes of a locust plague and wildfire, and Bill eventually dies violently, but in between are leisurely periods with little dialogue and unrelated actions. *Days of Heaven* is easy to admire but harder to love.

ADDED ATTRACTION: Movie Technology in the 1970s

The history of movies parallels the history of movie technology. Long before the 1970s, movies advanced in step with developments in sound and color, among other technological achievements. In 1978 *Days of Heaven* became the first movie made using the new Panaglide camera for fluid handheld shots. Here are other technological advances in the '70s and the movies that introduced them, as well as important changes in theater design.

- 1971
  With an eight-story screen, the first permanent IMAX theater debuts in Toronto. Dolby noise-reduction system (*A Clockwork Orange*).
- 1973
  CGI, Computer-Generated Imagery (*Westworld*).
- 1974
  Sensurround audio system (*Earthquake*).
- 1976
  Steadicam camera-stabilizing mount (*Marathon Man*).
- 1977
  Computerized motion-controlled camera (*Star Wars*).
- 1979
  Crowning the surge of new multi-screen theaters, what was at the time the world's largest multiplex theater (eighteen screens) opens in Toronto.

The Boys from Brazil

Released: October 1978
Director: Franklin J. Schaffner
Stars: Gregory Peck, Laurence Olivier, James Mason
Academy Awards: Three nominations (Best Actor—Laurence Olivier; Best Editing; Best Music)

PREVIEW: Using Hitler's cells, the infamous Josef Mengele clones ninety-four duplicates.

NOW SHOWING: Raising *The Boys from Brazil*

Various movie titans in the cast and crew united for *The Boys from Brazil* (1978). The result is a serviceable thriller that starts out well but eventually disintegrates.

Based on the book by Ira Levin, who also wrote the novel that became *The Stepford Wives* (1975), the movie presents a unique idea "that carries with it the hope and the destiny of the Aryan race": the infamous Nazi doctor Josef Mengele (Gregory Peck) has used samples of Adolf Hitler's blood and tissue to clone ninety-four boys with Hitler's "infinitely superior" characteristics (all the clones have straight black hair, piercing eyes, and bad attitudes). Because "every social and environmental detail would have to be reproduced" to shape these boys into actual Hitlers, Mengele has all their surrogate fathers murdered at the same age when Hitler's own father died. Of course, this begs the question, how will Mengele replicate World War One, imprisonment, and other important experiences that molded *der Führer*? Aren't they also required to get another Hitler?

The Boys from Brazil never addresses that thorny issue. Instead, the movie plays out like a mystery that has the audience and Mengele's nemesis, Ezra Lieberman (Laurence Olivier), piecing together the sinister plot. After Lieberman figures everything out, he finally has his long-awaited confrontation with the diabolical doctor in a Pennsylvania farmhouse, but it's anti-climactic to watch Peck and Olivier, two legendary actors with a combined age of 133, wrestle on the floor, biting and scratching each other. Eventually, Lieberman seems to protect the boys by destroying the list with their identities, as if he is taking to heart something he'd said earlier: "Who would believe such a preposterous story?"

Behind the scenes, director Franklin J. Schaffner, who made *Planet of the Apes* (1968) and *Patton* (1970), and his go-to composer, Jerry Goldsmith (who gets an Oscar nomination here), give the story style as it moves around its international locations. Peck and Olivier both speak with heavy accents; Peck, almost always dressed in white, is alternately charming and growly as the monstrous Mengele, while Olivier is more feeble and whispery as the elderly Nazi hunter. Critics were divided over whether these were excessive or powerful performances (Olivier got an Oscar nomination as Best Actor). Viewers might also be divided: some will consider the plot's basic conceit ludicrous, while others may think it's prescient, especially as human cloning gets closer to becoming a reality.

ADDED ATTRACTION: Goin' Downhill

The first week of October 1978 was a busy time for scenery-chewing stars in underwhelming movies. Just days after *The Boys from Brazil* opened, *Goin' South* offered a respite from Nazi-hunting drama with an amiable comedy about a western outlaw rescued from the hangman's noose by a prudish woman who needs help with her nascent gold mine. It's a stylish movie with a good set-up, atmospheric music, scenic landscapes, and Mary Steenburgen, who's utterly beguiling in her first movie. Unfortunately, the movie slows in the second half and is never quite as funny as it thinks it is. You'd expect the brief description "occasionally amusing" would've been "consistently hilarious" for any late-'70s movie with John Belushi in it, considering how he dominated *Animal House* (1978). But nooooo, he's given almost nothing to say or do, and he mostly just stands around ready—but never able—to bust out. The director, Jack Nicholson, overindulges his spirited star, also Nicholson, whose manic over-the-top performance combines endless mugging with a strange vocal delivery that suggests extreme nasal congestion.

Jack Nicholson.

Midnight Express

Released: October 1978
Director: Alan Parker
Stars: Brad Davis, John Hurt, Randy Quaid
Academy Awards: Two wins (Best Writing; Best Music), plus four more nominations (Best Picture; Best Supporting Actor—John Hurt; Best Director; Best Editing)

PREVIEW: An American is caught smuggling drugs and is thrown into a dreadful Turkish prison.

NOW SHOWING: Pain Train

The Deer Hunter (1978) was named Best Picture, but some viewers consider that year's *Midnight Express* a better movie. Whereas *The Deer Hunter* is a sprawling (some say occasionally boring) three-hour epic, *Midnight Express* is a fast-moving two-hour tension machine. Based on real events, the movie, unlike *The Deer Hunter*, starts quickly—nine minutes in, young Billy Hayes (Brad Davis, in his movie debut) is arrested at a Turkish airport for smuggling drugs—and intensifies relentlessly as he endures the tortures inside a nightmarish prison. Some of the scenes are almost as harrowing as *The Deer Hunter*'s Russian roulette gunplay, especially when Hayes violently attacks one of his tormentors, bites off his tongue, and spits it out in slow-motion. Like another of the decade's famous prison movies, *Papillon* (1973), *Midnight Express* is grim, powerful, and unforgettable.

Though he's resilient, Hayes is too imprudent to be truly sympathetic. Inside the airport he's the guiltiest-looking smuggler ever, his eyes darting as he nervously sweats and chomps gum. Slipping away in a marketplace, he's so noisy and conspicuous that he's apprehended in two minutes. When he's allowed to make a courtroom statement, he stupidly delivers a profane, insulting speech, and to nobody's surprise he's immediately handed a harsher-than-expected thirty-year sentence. The prison tunnel he helps dig goes nowhere and is soon discovered, leading to more punishments. Clearly Hayes isn't good at this. He does pay the awful price for his decisions and, like the lifer in *Papillon*, loses his strong, handsome looks and becomes a haggard wreck. Spending all but fourteen minutes of this movie in brutal captivity will do that.

Midnight Express follows the well-worn path established by earlier prison movies—crime/capture/captivity/escape—but it has its own intense style. Director Alan Parker, whose previous movie, *Bugsy Malone* (1976), was for kids, here evokes constant menace by keeping scenes dark, even showing deep shadows outside in the daytime. Especially innovative is Giorgio Moroder's score, which provides a propulsive digital thrum that enhances the dread and weirdness surrounding Hayes. *A Clockwork Orange* (1971), *Tommy* (1975), and *Sorcerer* (1977) had successfully used synthesizers, but *Midnight Express* is the first synthesizer-scored movie to win the Best Music Oscar.

Some critics have challenged the movie's invented scenes and the over-the-top portrayals of sadistic Turkish guards. Fair enough, but then again *Midnight Express* isn't a documentary. It is now what it's always been, a bold and disturbing experience.

Brad Davis.

ADDED ATTRACTION: A Year of Prison

American studios made more prison movies in 1978 than in any other year of the decade. Besides *Midnight Express*, the best of the rest is *On the Yard*, a well-acted, above-average drama that blends interesting and poignant stories about four cons, one of them well-played by John Heard. Another spring release, *Mean Dog Blues*, echoes *Cool Hand Luke* (1967) and even stars *Luke*'s George Kennedy as the hard-hearted villain who ends up ... sobbing uncontrollably? Wow, didn't see that coming. The otherwise-predictable story has a wrongly convicted man trying to escape from a prison farm and its vicious dogs. Summer's *Seabo* (aka *Buckstone County Prison*) is a crude, violent movie with a lone-wolf bounty hunter, corrupt prison officials, and manhunts for escaped prisoners. Last but least, *They Went That-A-Way & That-A-Way* is a dismal December "comedy" written by and starring Tim Conway. Inept cops go undercover in a prison, leading to tired slapstick and, for the audience, ninety-five minutes of hard labor.

Halloween

Released: October 1978
Director: John Carpenter
Stars: Jamie Lee Curtis, Donald Pleasence, Tony Moran
Academy Awards: None

PREVIEW: A masked killer relentlessly stalks teenagers as they babysit on Halloween night.

NOW SHOWING: What Will You Be for *Halloween*?

Halloween (1978), the late-'70s horror classic, is deceptively simple. Here's your story: a motiveless murderer stalks and slays small-town teens on Halloween. But director John Carpenter brings so much innovative artistry to the telling that *Halloween* inspired decades of sequels and imitators, making it one of the most influential horror movies ever.

One of *Halloween*'s tricks is its invocation of other thrillers. Playing Laurie, the main teen, is Jamie Lee Curtis, whose mother, Janet Leigh, was the doomed Marion Crane in *Psycho* (1960); furthering the *Psycho* link is *Halloween*'s Dr. Sam Loomis, a character named after Marion Crane's lover in *Psycho* (Dr. Loomis is played by Donald Pleasence, previously a prominent James Bond villain; Pleasence is *Halloween*'s "star" and gets top billing, though he's in only 20% of the movie). Next, *Halloween*'s creepy theme music echoes "Tubular Bells," the familiar instrumental from *The Exorcist* (1973). As in *Jaws* (1975), *Halloween* opens with a point-of-view sequence of a predator targeting a lone, almost-naked girl. And in the first fifteen minutes we get a stormy night and scary topics like "monster movies," "a haunted house," and "the boogeyman." By connecting us to the past, Carpenter skillfully prepares us for future terrors.

Jamie Lee Curtis.

Nick Castle as Michael Myers.

The murderer's single-minded tenacity intensifies the fear. Michael Myers is never *not* pursuing and killing, making him more like *Jaws*'s relentless shark. Silent, expressionless behind his pasty-white mask, and utterly remorseless, Myers is given no rational motivation for his malevolence (sequels will later clarify Myers' relationship to Laurie). Like some kind of supernatural creature he's called "it," "the evil," and, in the end credits, "The Shape." Myers seemingly materializes and disappears at will, and even when he's stabbed in the neck, eye, and abdomen with sharp implements and then shot point-blank six times, he never makes a sound and pauses only briefly. Myers can't be reasoned with, understood, or stopped. He's the incarnation of primal, universal nightmares.

Carpenter's confident, intelligent delivery of the horror influenced the entire genre. His wide-screen compositions put characters in a foreground corner so we can watch Myers approach from the opposite background corner. Rooms are often lit either in an eerie blue or, for Halloween, in orange (furniture and drapes are orange, too). And in a decade surging with feminism, his terrified heroine fights back.

Fright fans loved it then and made *Halloween* one of the highest-grossing independent movies ever. Even today, *Halloween* is still a treat.

ADDED ATTRACTION: *Dawn* Phenomenon

With *Halloween*, *Damien: Omen II*, and *Piranha*, 1978 was a juicy year for horror movies. Director George Romero, famous for his game-changing zombie movie *Night of the Living Dead* (1968), released two juicefests back to back. In the spring, Romero sank his teeth into vampire lore with *Martin*, a disturbing, underrated movie made on a low-budget with a no-name cast. *Martin* wastes no time—during the opening credits a modern-day young man, Martin (John Amplas), sedates an anonymous woman on a train, has his way with her passive body, slices her with a razor blade, and then drinks her blood. While there are vampire tropes throughout—garlic, bloodsucking, the repeated name Nosferatu and "the Count"—Martin himself is more psychopathic murderer/rapist than classic vampire (he casts reflections and is fine out in the sunlight). Next, Romero really cut loose with his masterful *Dawn of the Dead*, which wasn't widely released in America until April 1979. Unlike *Halloween*, which creates shadowy suspense without spilling gallons of blood, *Dawn of the Dead* revels in brightly lit in-your-face gore. As in his *Night of the Living Dead*, an unidentified plague generates gruesome zombie hordes that relentlessly stalk the living. The difference between the two movies is quickly apparent: *Dawn* has an exploding head, severed limbs, and flesh-ripping close-ups in just the first ten minutes. Most of the action takes place in a

Pennsylvania shopping mall, where the zombies feast to disgusting, stomach-churning extremes as gentle mall music plays around them. *Dawn* adds loopy humor into the bloody mix with some unexpected zombies (a nun, a Hare Krishna), sight gags involving a mall blood-pressure machine, and even a pie fight. Inventive, intense, and hugely successful, *Dawn*'s spawn includes many sequels, copycats, and parodies.

The Deer Hunter

(One of 1978's five **FAR-OUT** movies)

Released: December 1978

Director: Michael Cimino

Stars: Robert De Niro, Christopher Walken, John Cazale

Academy Awards: Five wins (Best Picture; Best Support Actor—Christopher Walken; Best Director; Best Editing; Best Sound), plus four more nominations (Best Actor—Robert De Niro; Best Supporting Actress—Meryl Streep; Best Writing; Best Cinematography)

PREVIEW: Three friends struggle to cope with their horrific experiences in the Vietnam War.

FINE LINE: "See this? This is this. This ain't something else. This is this." (Michael, holding up a bullet and trying to articulate something important to Stan, though nobody really understands his message. Throughout the movie, characters struggle to express themselves verbally, as shown in the three scenes with phone calls—Mike and Nick each hang up before completing their calls, and Steven quickly gets off the phone when Michael surprises him with a call.)

CLOSE-UP: Who's the father of Steven and Angela's baby? As he's leaving the wedding forty-eight minutes into the movie, Steven (John Savage) confesses that he "never really did it with Angela" (Rutanya Alda). Standing nearby, Stan (John Cazale) mutters something to Mike (Robert De Niro) and then says, "You didn't know that about Angela, huh? ... I happen to know it's true." Is Stan gossiping about himself? Or Nick (Christopher Walken)? Consider that later Nick (still in Vietnam) inexplicably sends thousands of dollars to Steven (back in America)—is that money for Nick's own baby? And note Nick's funeral: the last woman to leave is Angela, holding her blonde baby.

NOW SHOWING: Walking Wounded

Ten years after 1968's Tet Offensive, and five years after 1973's cease-fire agreement, Hollywood was finally ready to dive deep into the murky waters of the Vietnam War. Between 1970 and 1977, movies from the lightweight *Norwood* (1970) to the brutal *Taxi Driver* (1976) had leading characters who were Vietnam veterans, but there were far more movies about World War Two—*Patton*, *Kelly's Heroes*, *Catch-22*, *Tora! Tora! Tora!* (all 1970), *Midway* (1976), *MacArthur* (1977)—than there were about Vietnam. That changed in 1978 when February's *Coming Home*, June's *Go Tell the Spartans*, and December's *The Deer Hunter* confronted Vietnam head-on.

Though it wasn't planned this way, *The Deer Hunter* powerfully blends elements of the other two. *Go Tell the Spartans* is a grim retelling of a disastrous battle, while *Coming Home* shows damaged soldiers returning from Vietnam. *The Deer Hunter* divides into three sections that cover some of the same territory of its two predecessors. The sixty-eight-minute first section slowly reveals personalities and relationships in a small Pennsylvania town in the late 1960s. It's a rough, simple place where men shoot pool, women drink beer, and everyone bowls. Emotions are expressed physically: a drunken father slaps his adult daughter, a boyfriend slugs his girlfriend when a stranger makes a pass, and men frequently tackle each other.

After opening scenes of hellish flames and cacophony inside a steel factory, men gather in a local bar and soon attend a twenty-seven-minute wedding that doesn't end until one of them is naked on an outdoor basketball court. Five friends then take a short hunting trip that further defines their characters. Concurrent with the wedding is the farewell to three of the men who have enlisted and are headed to Vietnam. Strong, quiet Michael (Robert De Niro) is admired by everyone; Nick (Christopher Walken) is a boyish, likeable diplomat; and Steven (John Savage), bossed by his mother and marrying a woman who's pregnant by an unnamed man, is the most vulnerable. After an hour in their company we *know* these people.

In a first-act bar scene Nick declares, "I hope they send us where the bullets are flyin', the fightin's the worst." That regrettable wish comes true in the forty-two-minute second section. Set in the early 1970s, this section has a totally different rhythm from the first. Immediately we're thrust into violent conflict. Vietnam is introduced with orange explosions and an enemy callously tossing a grenade into a children's hiding place. Captured and held in semi-submerged rat-infested cages, Michael, Nick, and Steven are forced to play Russian roulette while their captors bet on the deaths. These fourteen minutes are almost unbearable to watch. True to form, "Mighty Mike" steels himself with such ferocious determination that were he to click on a bullet instead of an empty chamber, the bullet would surely bounce off his iron skull. Naturally it's Mike who orchestrates the escape plan, leads the others to safety, and literally carries the broken Steven on his back.

Robert De Niro.

The third seventy-three-minute section shows how the three friends cope with their life-changing experience. It's now 1975, with Michael home, Steven hospitalized, and Nick A.W.O.L. in Saigon. Michael returns to locate Nick, a tragic journey that requires him to travel on a small boat past more flames and into a terrible place for a final heartbreaking game of Russian roulette.

While the movie has moments of almost unparalleled intensity, *The Deer Hunter* has not been universally revered. Bored viewers disparage the extremely deliberate first act and the movie's overall 183-minute length. Others bemoan the seemingly racist attitude toward the

Christopher Walken.

Vietnamese soldiers and civilians, all presented as either perverse sadists or predatory vipers. Some challenge the veracity of the Russian roulette scenes, and they do strain credibility—would anyone hand a loaded gun to a desperate enemy sitting right next to him? Fictional these roulette scenes may be, but they symbolically condense war's horror into unforgettable bursts. (Do viewers who criticize the movie because Russian roulette wasn't really played with prisoners also lament the anachronistic presence of two 1976 songs, "Drop Kick Me, Jesus" and "Tattletale Eyes"? *The Deer Hunter* delivers raw emotion, not precise historical documentation.) Finally, the controversial ending, in which the Clairton friends quietly sing "God Bless America" around a table, is open to interpretation. Is co-writer/director Michael Cimino being sincere or cynical with this late display of patriotism?

We can acknowledge all these issues and still recognize *The Deer Hunter* as a monumental achievement. Its excesses are redeemed by Vilmos Zsigmond's stunning cinematography and the young cast (maybe the best ensemble since 1972's *The Godfather*, another long classic that opens with a wedding). Looking back, *The Deer Hunter* seems almost destined to win the Best Picture Oscar: the great John Cazale, who died before this movie was released, made only five movies, and every single one was nominated for Best Picture; Walken was in two consecutive Best Picture winners (1977's *Annie Hall* and this one); and Meryl Streep had so far been in only one other movie, *Julia* (1977), another Best Picture nominee. Add De Niro, and this dramatic cast could topple mountains.

The Deer Hunter is like an epic novel that immerses you into a richly detailed world populated by fully developed characters. Even though it's challenging, flawed, and at least a half-hour too long, it must be seen and respected. Other war movies can impress, inspire, or affect; this one haunts.

ADDED ATTRACTION: Longest and Shortest Best Picture Nominees

The long and the short of the Oscar nominees for Best Picture in the 1970s. None of these movies really challenges the all-time record-holders for the longest Best Picture nominee—*Cleopatra* (1963), originally 248 minutes—and the shortest—*She Done Him Wrong* (1933), sixty-six minutes.

Longest (Year)	Minutes
The Godfather: Part II (1974)	202
The Emigrants (1972)	192
Barry Lyndon (1975)	185
Nicholas and Alexandra (1971)	183
The Deer Hunter (1978)	183
Fiddler on the Roof (1971)	179
The Godfather (1972)	175

Shortest (Year)	Minutes
Cries and Whispers (1973)	91
Annie Hall (1977)	93
Five Easy Pieces (1970)	98

Superman

(One of 1978's five **FAR-OUT** movies)

Released: December 1978

Director: Richard Donner

Stars: Christopher Reeve, Margot Kidder, Gene Hackman

Academy Awards: One win (Special Achievement Award for Visual Effects), plus three more nominations (Best Editing; Best Music; Best Sound)

PREVIEW: Kal-El travels from Krypton to Earth and becomes Superman with superhuman powers.

FINE LINE: "Lois, Clark Kent may seem like just a mild-mannered reporter, but listen, not only does he know how to treat his editor-in-chief with the proper respect, not only does he have a snappy, punchy prose style, but he is, in my forty years in this business, the fastest typist I've ever seen." (Editor Perry White explaining to Lois Lane why he has hired Clark Kent.)

CLOSE-UP: First seen seven minutes into the movie, Jor-El wears a black turtleneck with a glowing "S" emblem on his chest. This doesn't really make sense, since the name Superman won't exist until Lois Lane (Margot Kidder) invents it on Earth ninety-two minutes into the movie. Superman himself also has an "S" on his chest when we first see him at the forty-seven-minute mark.

NOW SHOWING: Superduperman

Adjust your expectations when you watch *Superman* (1978). Come for cartoonish, episodic action and nutty caricatures, not an iconic drama with compelling characters, and you'll have fun. This is a movie to eat popcorn by.

Powered by one of the decade's biggest budgets, the extravagant action ambitiously sprawls across Superman's origin story and the first thirty years of his life. This enormous show-biz spectacle is presented by various Hollywood legends and esteemed performers, from co-screenwriter Mario Puzo (of *Godfather* fame) down to the small roles played by Glenn Ford, Trevor Howard, and Susannah York. *Superman* never lacks for amazements. Just brains. The huge lapses in logic are more powerful than a locomotive.

The first twenty-three minutes are dominated by a white-wigged Marlon Brando as Superman's father, Jor-El, on the far-off planet of Krypton. Krypton is moments from total destruction when Jor-El puts his infant son, Kal-El, into a tiny spacecraft and launches it toward Earth. Kal-El's "dense molecular structure" gives him immense strength and speed; when he crash lands in America as a three-year-old toddler, he immediately lifts up a car. The Kents bring him to their Smallville farm, call him Clark, and raise him to age eighteen (Jeff East plays the teenager, though Christopher Reeve supplies his dubbed voice). Clark eventually heads north to the frozen Arctic, where he creates his crystal Fortress of Solitude. For twelve years he studies the lessons from "six known dimensions" and "the twenty-eight known galaxies." He emerges forty-seven minutes into the movie at age thirty as Christopher Reeve, flying in his bright blue-and-red Superman costume.

From here the movie becomes an episodic series of Superman's astonishing exploits in Metropolis as he fights "for truth and justice and the American way," all while his alter ego, Clark Kent, is a clumsy, mild-mannered newspaper reporter with his hair parted on the other side. Superman snatches a fired bullet (proving he is truly "faster than a speeding bullet"), catches a plummeting helicopter, and rescues Air Force One before it crashes. He even retrieves a cat from a tree and gently hands it to a grateful little girl. It's so enjoyable watching him perform all these feats, which are delivered by Oscar-winning special effects, that viewers may forget to ask where Clark's normal business clothes go when he miraculously transforms into his Superman outfit in midair.

He also flirts with plucky Lois Lane (Margot Kidder), and midway through the movie Superman takes Lois for a five-minute night flight. Unfortunately, this beautiful sequence, one of the most romantic dates ever, is ruined for some viewers when she recites to herself like she's a smitten teen talking the lyrics to a corny love song.

An hour in, the movie introduces the villain, the "fiendishly gifted" Lex Luthor (Gene Hackman). Luthor's "crime of the century" pairs a nuclear missile with "the greatest real-estate swindle of all time," and he almost pulls it off. At the two-hour mark the missile detonates, creating instant mayhem throughout California. Superman races everywhere, even diving deep into the Earth to push the collapsed San Andreas Fault back into position. The one thing he can't do in time is save Lois. And this is a problem.

Twice already Jor-El has warned his son not "to interfere with human history." But five minutes after the nuclear explosion, Lois is smothered to death by falling rock. Superman arrives, ten seconds too late. Enraged, he zooms into the atmosphere, where Jor-El's voice reminds him *four more times* that "it is forbidden" for him to change history. Superman does anyway. Rapidly flying around the entire planet, he somehow makes it reverse its rotation, which supposedly reverses time by a few minutes. Rocks roll back uphill, a dam reconstructs itself, and Lois is still alive. Superman then flies down to assist her.

We were among the audience members grumbling "yeah, right!" during this ridiculous sequence. Even if Superman *can* reverse time, why doesn't he do it to stop the missile on the launch pad, or to avert a previous war, or to interrupt Lee Harvey Oswald, or to prevent an infinite number of other tragedies? Instead, he uses this

Christopher Reeve.

gift to rescue an Earth girl he likes. And having done it once, why doesn't he keep doing it? There's not much time left in the movie to contemplate such matters. Superman flies off and immediately lands inside a prison yard, holding Lex Luthor and his henchman. No exciting scenes of their capture, no audacious last stand by Luthor—what a let-down.

Despite its faults, *Superman* was one of the decade's top money-makers. One big reason was Superman himself, the previously unknown Christopher Reeve. Strong and square-jawed, he definitely looks like the Man of Steel. More than that, he brings heroic conviction to Superman and charming sweetness to Clark Kent (unfortunately Clark's habit of frequently readjusting his glasses—nineteen times, twice in only four seconds—gets to be a distraction). Overrated is Brando, who's in about 10% of the movie but gets top billing (evidently he never bothered to learn the name of his own planet, since he insists on pronouncing it "Krypt'n," though it's "Kryp-tawn" to everyone else). Hackman, the other big name, plays his villainous part for easy laughs.

What nobody ever criticizes is the music. John Williams's famous theme is one of the decade's great, instantly memorable anthems. The producers obscure it with thirty-one "whooshes" as the opening credits zoom into space, but thankfully the theme is heard full-force at the end and leaves audiences cheering. And that's really the movie's legacy: flawed but fun, *Superman* is super entertainment that compels audiences to watch, smile, and cheer. The three 1980s sequels with Reeve, indeed every subsequent superhero movie starring various Batmans, Spidermans, Avengers, and even new Supermans, can trace their origins to 1978, the year when audiences really saw a man fly.

ADDED ATTRACTION: Luthor the Genius

Like most evil geniuses (and James Bond villains), Lex Luthor doesn't wait around to watch his adversary die once he's trapped him, which inevitably gives the hero time to escape. Nor can Luthor resist describing his entire plan in detail to Superman (having bought up low-priced desert land in the eastern half of California, Luthor has rerouted a nuclear missile that will detonate at the San Andreas Fault, theoretically dumping the western half of California into the ocean and turning his desert holdings into beach-front property). Showing how the movie is often humorous, Luthor's fanciful post-nuclear-blast map of the "new West Coast" with his prime real estate includes communities called Teschmacher Peaks, named after the anatomical assets of his voluptuous assistant (Valerie Perrine), plus Marina del Lex, Luthorville, Lex Springs, and Lexington, with Costa del Lex along the new shoreline. The goofy assistant Otis (Ned Beatty) has added Otisburg (with a backwards "s") to the map, but Lex makes him erase it.

California Suite

Released: December 1978
Director: Herbert Ross
Stars: Jane Fonda, Michael Caine, Maggie Smith
Academy Awards: One win (Best Supporting Actress—Maggie Smith), plus two more nominations (Best Writing; Best Art Direction)

PREVIEW: Four different relationship stories, each one set inside the Beverly Hills Hotel.

NOW SHOWING: The Simon Hotel, Part Two

Seven years after *Plaza Suite* (1971), *California Suite* (1978) moved the same concept—different relationship stories set in one location—to the West Coast. Whereas *Plaza Suite* confined the action to Suite 719 in Manhattan's Plaza Hotel, *California Suite* expands things by telling four stories, not three, and taking over several rooms, not just one, inside the Beverly Hills Hotel, where Claude Bolling's light jazz and David Hockney's paintings enhance the sophisticated environment. Like its predecessor, *California Suite* is uneven, but the key to this *Suite* is the powerhouse cast. Simon's hotel is worth checking into.

In the first segment, an acerbic New Yorker played by Jane Fonda wrangles for custody of her teenage daughter with her ex-husband (Alan Alda), whose new California girlfriend has "blonde hair, blonde teeth, blonde life." The conversation is smart, funny, and insightful. "You're worse than a hopeless romantic," says Fonda's character, "you're a hopeful one" ("hopeful romantic" later turns up in 1984's *Romancing the Stone*). Occasionally shown in a bikini, Fonda looks super-fit, like she's ramping up for the mega-successful *Jane Fonda's Workout* book and video coming soon.

Maggie Smith and Michael Caine.

The nicest segment, the one that puts the "sweet" in *Suite*, presents two British stars as a long-time married couple. Maggie Smith plays an actress in town for the Academy Awards, with Michael Caine as her devoted, and bi-sexual, husband. Filled with delightful banter between two great pros, the conversations are lovely, funny, and ultimately bittersweet (in the movie Smith's character doesn't take home the Oscar, but Smith herself actually won as Best Supporting Actress).

The funniest bit has Walter Matthau, back from *Plaza Suite*, with a drunk call-girl passed out in his room just as his wife (Elaine May) shows up. Lots of good, smart silliness ensues, Matthau is hilarious, and May is wonderful as always. The movie's last and noisiest section pairs two couples who get into some dopey slapstick complications over room arrangements. Despite the presence of two legendary comedians, Bill Cosby and Richard Pryor, this is the weakest of the four segments and feels like it belongs in a different movie.

Like *Plaza Suite*, *California Suite* was based on Neil Simon plays, as were five more 1970s movies, among them *The Sunshine Boys* (1975) and *Chapter Two* (1979). Add in the five movies he wrote directly for the screen, including *The Goodbye Girl* (1977), and the '70s become a highly Simonized decade.

ADDED ATTRACTION: Same But Different

Amazingly, when *California Suite* hit theaters, Alan Alda was already co-starring in another comedy set in a single location. Based on Bernard Slade's play, *Same Time, Next Year* pairs Alda with Ellen Burstyn in a warm, romantic story about two people who meet in 1951 at a Mendocino inn, quickly fall in love, and continue to meet in the same room every year for the next twenty-six years, though both have spouses and kids elsewhere. With historical photographs marking transitions, the movie visits their 1956, 1961, 1966, 1972, and 1977 rendezvous, so we see them going through radical changes—at different times she's a hippie and a successful businesswoman, while he goes from an ultra-conservative suit to groovy love beads. Pregnancy, deaths and current social issues impact their trysts. At times Alda is overemotional and consumed by guilt, while Burstyn (who got an Oscar nomination) stays more restrained throughout. Both performances are excellent, as they would have to be in a smart, sensitive movie with essentially a two-person cast.

Every Which Way But Loose

Released: December 1978
Director: James Fargo
Stars: Clint Eastwood, Sondra Locke, Geoffrey Lewis
Academy Awards: None

PREVIEW: A bare-knuckle fighter drives from L.A. to Denver to locate a woman he barely knows.

NOW SHOWING: Clint Goes *Every Which Way But Loose*

After the thunderous success of *Rocky* (1976), more boxing movies jumped into the ring. There were three in 1978 alone—*Matilda*, about a boxing kangaroo (read those words as "a guy-in-a-kangaroo-costume who boxes"); *Movie Movie*, a nifty parody of an old-fashioned double bill that has a humorous boxing section called "Dynamite Hands"; and Clint Eastwood's *Every Which Way But Loose* (1978).

Of this trio, *Every Which Way But Loose* was by far the box-office champ, though initially it was a risky project for Eastwood. A silly, episodic comedy, the movie presents Eastwood as a brawling trucker who undertakes a California-to-Colorado search for a pretty girl he's just met. In the 1960s, the most notorious film that had presented Eastwood as something other than his usual sullen cowboy was *Paint Your Wagon* (1969), in which he played a gentle farmer who sang sappy ballads (that bomb sound you just heard was "Kablooey!"). Nevertheless, *Every Which Way But Loose* became Eastwood's biggest '70s hit. It has some *Rocky*-like elements: Eastwood's character, Philo, has a sensitive side, a la Rocky Balboa;

Clint Eastwood.

he fights alongside sides of beef inside a meat-packing plant, the same setting where Rocky had trained; and Philo surprisingly loses the final clash of the titans, as Rocky did. If you're going to borrow from an earlier movie, the Best Picture-winning megahit *Rocky* is a good one to emulate.

Every Which Way But Loose shares even more with *Smokey and the Bandit* (1977), including a good-ol'-boy sidekick, a scene-stealing animal (here a brewski-guzzling jukebox-operating orangutan), a spirited girl picked up along the road (Sondra Locke), a truck running over some motorcycles, and country-western music. Scenes of bowlin', fishin', shootin' and chasin', settings in motels and bars, plus Ruth Gordon as a foul-mouthed shotgun-wielding old lady and generous servings of knuckle sandwiches really help make *Every Which Way But Loose* a crowd-pleasin' favorite. Especially if those crowds crave cartoony antics, such as Philo's Tarzan yell in the woods and villainous bikers who are dumber than Eric Von Zipper's idiotic gang in mid-'60s beach movies. There's even a snippet of the music from Eastwood's *The Good, the Bad and the Ugly* (1966) for comic effect. Refreshingly, Eastwood smiles a lot in the movie, a nice change for him. Occasionally shirtless, he still looks great too, especially for forty-eight. Unfortunately, the girl makes a monkey out of Philo, leaving the man with his orangutan.

ADDED ATTRACTION: Every Which Way But Abstruse

Clint Eastwood's two movies immediately before *Every Which Way But Loose* successfully update the straightforward formula of his earlier hits. "Cold bold Callahan with his great big .44" returns in *The Enforcer* (1976), the decade's highest-grossing Dirty Harry movie. As in *Dirty Harry* (1971) and its solid first sequel, *Magnum Force* (1973), Eastwood plays Inspector Harry Callahan, a "Neanderthal" trying to do his righteous job despite the legal restraints imposed on him. After a terrific car-meets-liquor-store sequence underscores Callahan's renegade belligerence, he's given a surprising partner—a woman (Tyne Daly), who eventually earns Callahan's begrudging respect. They're a good cinematic team (Callahan's more humorous than ever), but the main plot about a murderous revolutionary group isn't as intense as *Dirty Harry*'s riveting hunt for a cackling psycho. As usual, Callahan mouths off to superiors, gets suspended, and violently takes the law into his own hands. Director James Fargo uses San Francisco locations well, especially in a final eleven-minute assault on Alcatraz. Next for Eastwood was *The Gauntlet* (1977), the last of six '70s movies he directed. As he escorts a witness from Las Vegas to Phoenix, Eastwood's character, a heavy-drinking cop, is beaten, shot, and double-crossed, but at least this time he gets the girl (Sondra Locke). Entertaining action sequences include one with Eastwood racing through the desert on a chopper to elude a helicopter (our favorite *Gauntlet* transportation is a classic Hughes Airwest DC-9 that taxis into an early scene, the "flying banana" is totally appealing). During the movie thousands of rounds of gunfire cause the complete collapses of a car, a bus, and even, amazingly, a house, making *The Gauntlet* the winner of 1977's Most Bullets Award.

Invasion of the Body Snatchers

Released: December 1978
Director: Philip Kaufman
Stars: Donald Sutherland, Brooke Adams, Jeff Goldblum
Academy Awards: None

PREVIEW: Alien spores drift into San Francisco and turn the locals into creepy "pod people."

NOW SHOWING: "You're Next"

Remakes of classics are often derided—*The Wiz* (1978), anyone?—but *Invasion of the Body Snatchers* (1978) is a remake done right. Updating the 1956 sci-fi classic, it tells the chilling story of alien spores that infect San Franciscans and turn them into "a new life form" (how perfect, "a new life form" in the bohemian city that embraces all lifestyles). After an effective opening scene that shows the spores drifting through space toward Earth, the first hour presents creepy clues about what's happening: characters mention that a loved one seems "different," is "just not the same person," has become "less human." Spouses say "that's not my wife" and "he isn't my husband." Strangers stare dispassionately from behind windows, people in obvious distress are ignored, and residents run randomly down the street. With repeated viewings, many subtle details become conspicuous signs.

Sixty-two minutes into the movie, two characters guess that the strange flowers they're noticing around the city are possibly toxic and may even be extra-terrestrial. Ten minutes later we finally see the full transformation of humans into scary pod people lacking all emotions. Most of the movie's last forty minutes are devoted to exciting chases that lead to a shocking finale.

It's a smart, suspenseful, and occasionally funny movie populated with some familiar faces that modern audiences will recognize from other sci-fi hits, including Donald Sutherland (2000's *Space Cowboys*), Leonard Nimoy (TV's *Star Trek*), Veronica Cartwright (1979's *Alien*), and Jeff Goldblum (1986's *The Fly*). Kevin McCarthy, star of the original *Invasion of the Body Snatchers*, returns to again scream his "You're next!" warning (this time he meets the abrupt fate awaiting anyone who races into traffic). There are sci-fi stars behind the scenes, too. Ben Burtt, whose sound effects in *Star Wars* (1977) won an Oscar, created the hideous screeches of the pod people. Director Philip Kaufman, after the box-office success and strong critical reception of *Body Snatchers*, would soon fly high again with another excellent movie involving space, *The Right Stuff* (1983).

While it may not have the same immediacy as the original *Body Snatchers*, which set its paranoid story in the McCarthy-era 1950s, 1978's *Body Snatchers* is still terrific, thought-provoking entertainment. For many viewers the weirdest sight isn't of a transformed human, but of a dog ... with a realistic human face. A 1971 movie, *The Mephisto Waltz*, had done something similar, but it's even freakier here.

ADDED ATTRACTION: The *Phantasm* Phenomenon

Just as *Invasion of the Body Snatchers* was concluding its successful theatrical run in early 1979, a frightening new franchise was getting started. *Phantasm* took a different path to box-office success: whereas *Body Snatchers* told a familiar, linear, understandable story with a good-sized budget and established stars, *Phantasm* was thoroughly original, telling its strange story with a miniscule budget and unknown actors. Its writer/director/cinematographer/editor, Don Coscarelli, who was only in his early twenties, is probably the youngest *auteur* mentioned in either of our *Daring Decade* books. *The Cambridge English Dictionary* says a phantasm is "something that is seen or imagined but is not real," a definition that helps explain this almost incomprehensible movie. Two brothers probe "something weird" at a creepy funeral parlor, leading to ghoulish characters, chases in the dark, and a quick visit to an alien planet (weren't expecting *that*, were you?). A surprise "dream-sequence" ending reveals that a lead character we think is alive has been dead all along, and conversely some important dead characters are actually alive. Some scenes—a nighttime bedroom attack, a flying metal sphere that zooms through hallways and drills into skulls to unleash torrents of blood, chopped-off fingers that ooze yellow blood and continue to twitch—are shockingly effective, while a few elements seem derivative—the funeral parlor is the same exact mansion used in *Burnt Offerings* (1976), the snarling little minions are the evil twins of the Jawas in *Star Wars* (1977), and the music occasionally sounds just like "Tubular Bells" from *The Exorcist* (1973). *Phantasm* phans made this movie a horror hit, leading to decades of sequels.

A L I E N
In space no one can hear you scream.
TWENTIETH CENTURY FOX PRESENTS
A L I E N
TOM SKERRITT SIGOURNEY WEAVER VERONICA CARTWRIGHT HARRY DEAN STANTON
JOHN HURT IAN HOLM & YAPHET KOTTO AS PARKER
EXECUTIVE PRODUCER RONALD SHUSETT PRODUCED BY GORDON CARROLL, DAVID GILER AND WALTER HILL DIRECTED BY RIDLEY SCOTT
STORY BY DAN O'BANNON & RONALD SHUSETT SCREENPLAY BY DAN O'BANNON MUSIC JERRY GOLDSMITH PANAVISION® EASTMAN KODAK COLOR®
PRINTS BY DELUXE®
70MM DOLBY STEREO
IN SELECTED THEATRES
MOTION PICTURE SOUNDTRACK AVAILABLE ON 20TH CENTURY FOX RECORDS & TAPES.

1979

In Film

- Oscar for Best Picture: *Kramer vs. Kramer.*
- Most Oscar wins (five): *Kramer vs. Kramer.*
- Most Oscar nominations (nine): *All That Jazz, Kramer vs. Kramer.*
- At the April 9th Oscar ceremony, John Wayne makes his final public appearance and gives out the Best Picture award.
- Top-grossing movie: *Kramer vs. Kramer.*
- Top-grossing comedy: *The Jerk.*
- Top-grossing horror or sci-fi: *The Amityville Horror.*
- *Alien, The Amityville Horror, The Muppet Movie, Phantasm,* and *Star Trek: The Motion Picture* launch new movie franchises.
- Disney releases its first PG-rated movie, *The Black Hole.*
- Average price for an adult movie ticket: $2.50.
- Five memorable actors: Robert Duvall, Dustin Hoffman, Jack Lemmon, Roy Scheider, Peter Sellers.
- Five memorable actresses: Candice Bergen, Sally Field, Mariel Hemingway, Bette Midler, Meryl Streep.
- Movie debuts: Rosanna Arquette, Matt Dillon, Diane Lane, Mickey Rourke, Patrick Swayze.
- Deaths include Joan Blondell, Jack Haley, Merle Oberon, Mary Pickford, Jean Seberg, John Wayne, producer Darryl Zanuck, and director Nicholas Ray.

In America

- President Jimmy Carter gives a televised speech describing America's "crisis of confidence."
- American citizens and diplomats are taken hostage at the U.S. Embassy in Iran.
- An oil crisis causes a gallon of gas to jump in price approximately thirty percent over 1978 prices; with drivers fearing shortages, long lines form at gas stations.
- With *The China Syndrome* in theaters, an accident occurs at Pennsylvania's Three Mile Island nuclear plant.
- A riot at "Disco Demolition Night" in Chicago's Comiskey Park forces the home team, baseball's White Sox, to forfeit the game.
- New technology: the Asteroids arcade game, the Atari 400 Home Computer System ($595), Mattel's Intellivision game system, and Sony's Walkman.
- New cars: Chevrolet Citation, Volkswagen Jetta.
- New products: DustBuster, McDonald's Happy Meal, Honey Nut Cheerios, Mello Yello and Sunkist soft drinks, Tostitos.
- Sports champions: Pittsburgh Steelers at Super Bowl XIII, Montreal Canadiens in hockey, Seattle Supersonics in basketball, Pittsburgh Pirates in baseball.
- Bestselling books include V.C. Andrews' *Flowers in the Attic*, Stephen King's *The Dead Zone*, Robert Ludlum's *The Matarese Circle*, Norman Mailer's *The Executioner's Song*, William Styron's *Sophie's Choice*, Tom Wolfe's *The Right Stuff*.
- Music: Disco dominates the charts; No Nukes concerts at Madison Square Garden; eleven fans die outside a Who concert in Cincinnati; new albums include AC/DC's *Highway to Hell*, Cheap Trick's *Cheap Trick at Budokan*, the Clash's *London Calling*, Fleetwood Mac's *Tusk*, Led Zeppelin's *In Through the Out Door*, Michael Jackson's *Off the Wall*, Pink Floyd's *The Wall*, Supertramp's *Breakfast in America*, Tom Petty and the Heartbreakers' *Damn the Torpedoes*; new songs include Blondie's "Heart of Glass," the Doobie Brothers' "What a Fool Believes," the Eagles' "Heartache Tonight," Gloria Gaynor's "I Will Survive," Rupert Holmes' "Escape (The Piña Colada Song)," the Knack's "My Sharona," Peaches and Herb's "Reunited."
- TV debuts: *The Dukes of Hazzard, The Facts of Life, Hart to Hart, Knots Landing, Real People, This Old House*, and the ESPN, Nickelodeon, and TMC (The Movie Channel) networks.
- Deaths include Mamie Eisenhower, S.J. Perelman, Nelson Rockefeller, Richard Rodgers, Sid Vicious.

The Warriors

Released: February 1979
Director: Walter Hill
Stars: Michael Beck, James Remar, Deborah Van Valkenburgh
Academy Awards: None

PREVIEW: A small gang tries to get from Manhattan to Coney Island with rival gangs in pursuit.

NOW SHOWING: In the City

Imagine an entire movie expanding on the fight between Alex's droogs and Billyboy's thugs that occurs early in *A Clockwork Orange* (1971). Distinctive clothes, stylized vocabulary, brawling teens—that's *The Warriors* (1979). Essentially it's an unrelenting chase movie as one gang, the Warriors, gets targeted by other New York City gangs who mistakenly think the Warriors have killed the area's "one and only" leader just as he was peacefully uniting everyone. We follow nine Warriors through one grim night and into the next morning as they try to ride subway trains home to Coney Island with adrenalized rivals and cops in pursuit.

Director Walter Hill gives *The Warriors* a dark vibe that captures 1970s New York at its grittiest. Graffiti and trash are everywhere, and creepy adversaries might appear from the shadows at any moment. Into this war-zone setting march cartoonish characters who aren't much more realistic than the dancing gangs in *West Side Story* (1961). The Warriors themselves sport leather vests, but other gangs, with names like the Moon Runners, Rogues, Baseball Furies, and Saracens, wear glittery robes, baseball uniforms, camouflage, mime outfits (seriously, mime outfits?), even roller skates and KISS face paint. Complementing their borderline-campy costumes is a unique vocabulary: "I wish we was packed," "Nobody lip-off," "Remember, boppers, be looking good." If all this sounds vaguely silly, like something from a comic book, that's intentional, and a later "director's cut" actually added comic-book panels as interstitial transitions.

The Warriors dominate the movie, but they're not likeable heroes. They "tag" a cemetery and incinerate an anonymous car; one Warrior is arrested for roughing up a woman who's alone in the park. They can fight, certainly, and Swan (Michael Beck) has Jon Bon Jovi's swagger and looks, but these guys are still lowlife criminals who eventually decide that "it's all out there, all we gotta do is just figure out a way to go steal it."

Though many critics dismissed *The Warriors* as being too simplistic (true, we know nothing about the characters and hear no back stories), young people rallied to the nonstop action and the artistic visuals that are propelled by dynamic electronic music (culminating with Joe Walsh's "In the City"). We were impressed, but not moved, by the energetic world of *The Warriors*; others, however, took some kind of validation or inspiration from it, and legends circulated that theaters erupted into violence when rival gangs attended.

ADDED ATTRACTION: Gangway!

The Warriors was the first of *five* gang-themed movies in 1979. In March, *Boulevard Nights* took a more realistic look at East L.A.'s gang life with an emotional story about a mature brother struggling to keep his defiant, paint-sniffing younger brother from falling into gang violence. Next, a June twofer: *Sunnyside* introduced Joey Travolta

(John's older brother) as a New York gang member trying to escape the turf wars, and *Walk Proud* miscast Robby Benson as a soft-spoken Chicano who's torn between his L.A. gang and romance with a rich white girl. The Elton John ballad notwithstanding, *Walk Proud* feels more authentic and affecting of these two movies, but both were barely seen then and are faintly remembered now. July brought Philip Kaufman's nostalgic *The Wanderers*, with Ken Wahl as a handsome Italian-American gang leader in 1963. Light moments and fun early-'60s tunes a la *American Graffiti* (1973) are balanced by a startling death, pregnancy, the JFK assassination, a huge violent rumble, and a son smashing a bottle on his father's head. A symbolic coda, involving Bob Dylan's "The Times They Are A-Changin'," signals the end of an era.

Norma Rae

Released: March 1979
Director: Martin Ritt
Stars: Sally Field, Ron Leibman, Beau Bridges
Academy Awards: Two wins (Best Actress—Sally Field; Best Song), plus two more nominations (Best Picture; Best Writing)

PREVIEW: A struggling woman helps unionize the oppressive textile factory where she works.

NOW SHOWING: Making a Difference

Norma Rae (1979) is another of the decade's notable movies about labor struggles, a strong group that includes Oscar winners *Bound for Glory* (1976) and *Harlan County U.S.A.* (1976). Besides earning critical raves, *Norma Rae* became a box-office hit, a surprise considering its unglamorous subject and gritty realism at a time when the high-flying *Star Wars* (1977) and rowdy *Animal House* (1978) were redefining audience tastes. Nevertheless, the skillful craftsmanship and serious intentions of *Norma Rae*, like the tenacious title character herself, couldn't be ignored.

Martin Ritt, who had already directed *The Molly Maguires* (1970), *Sounder* (1972) and *The Front* (1976), was no stranger to movies with a social conscience. Here he tells a powerful, sometimes heartbreaking, and ultimately uplifting story of oppressed workers who are grinding their lives away inside a noisy, unhealthy textile factory in modern-day Alabama. Based on a real person, thirty-one-year-old Norma Rae (Sally Field) is one of these workers with the same depressing, low-paying job that her parents still have right alongside her. Ritt presents all sides of his heroine: she works hard, goes to church, and is a passionate single mother, but she's also a big mouth who meets men in motels and drunkenly vomits in front of friends.

This spitfire forms a platonic alliance with Reuben (Ron Liebman), an abrasive labor organizer who is recruiting members for the Textile Workers Union of America. Under his influence, Norma Rae transitions from a downtrodden nobody into a formidable unionizer who courageously champions solidarity at the risk of her job. Her most unforgettable moment comes as she's about to be dragged from the factory; she climbs onto a table, holds up a sign that reads "Union," and silently glowers at her colleagues. She's arrested and fired, but the employees vote their support. The last two minutes show this small woman standing alone in front of the imposing factory she's conquered (a potent image, though we wish epilogue text had summarized everyone's future lives).

Field, previously best-known as TV's perky Gidget and the runaway bride in *Smokey and the Bandit* (1977), gives a career-making performance. Often looking tired and sweaty, she still commands the resilient inner strength of this indomitable force of nature. Ritt, meanwhile, uses a handheld camera in an actual factory populated with real workers, giving the movie documentary-style authenticity. For him, for Field, and for the effective supporting cast, *Norma Rae* is a triumph.

ADDED ATTRACTION: ... And Pacino for All

Seven months after *Norma Rae*, another well-intentioned, socially relevant movie drew audiences and critical acclaim. Dominated by Al Pacino's power-house, Oscar-nominated performance, *... and justice for all.* (1979) is director Norman Jewison's episodic satire "about our wonderful judicial system." Like *Catch-22* (1970), the movie uses illogical absurdities to expose an institution's inconsistencies and hypocrisies: a gun-toting judge is "a suicidal maniac," another judge advocates "unjust punishment" for others but desperately wants to clear himself of the terrible crime he really has committed, and an unethical ethics committee thinks that a lawyer with a speech impediment is drunk. And also like *Catch-22*, the movie has tragic deaths. Pacino plays an honest, idealistic defense attorney who starts out calm but eventually erupts into wild-eyed fury, attacking another lawyer's car and famously screaming "You're out of order!" in the climactic over-the-top trial. Overloaded with subplots, this chaotic movie is uneven, but it's still entertaining.

Sally Field.

The China Syndrome

(One of 1979's five **FAR-OUT** movies)

Released: March 1979

Director: James Bridges

Stars: Jack Lemmon, Jane Fonda, Michael Douglas

Academy Awards: Four nominations (Best Actor—Jack Lemmon; Best Actress—Jane Fonda; Best Writing; Best Art Direction)

PREVIEW: A TV crew investigates structural flaws and conspiracies at a nuclear power plant.

FINE LINE: "The vibration I felt during the turbine trip. It bothered me. But it sure didn't bother anyone else." (Engineer Jack Godell, describing what he alone perceives is a serious issue at the nuclear plant.)

CLOSE-UP: There's no music soundtrack, and other than incidental music heard in the background the only song in the movie is Stephen Bishop's "Somewhere in Between," which plays for two minutes as the news crew drives north from Hollywood to the nuclear plant during the opening credits.

NOW SHOWING: This Is What Time It Is

After years of campy disaster movies, *The China Syndrome* (1979) emerged at decade's end as a serious disaster movie on a somber mission. This riveting thriller isn't about disaster survival, as *Airport* (1970), *Earthquake* (1974), and others had been; *The China Syndrome* advocates disaster *prevention* by dramatizing the inherent danger of nuclear power. This is one of the things that make *The China Syndrome* unique. The makers of disaster movies like *The Poseidon Adventure* (1972) and *The Hindenburg* (1975) weren't trying to bring about actual political or cultural change, but that seems to be the intent with *The China Syndrome*. The movie's tone is solemn, its anti-nuclear message real.

The China Syndrome follows some of the conventions of disaster movies: Oscar winners head the excellent cast (Jane Fonda, Jack Lemmon), there's a conflict between energetic, rebellious heroes (Michael Douglas) and corrupt villains (the power company), the effective sets and special effects make the power plant's interiors seem totally convincing, and the movie even has the pop song that the genre usually requires. However, *The China Syndrome* veers away from the template created by other disaster movies. It includes no epic musical score, for one thing, but that actually works to the movie's advantage. When total silence, not some rousing John Williams anthem, accompanies the final credits, the effect is chilling as the audience considers what has just happened in the theater, and what might happen outside at any moment. Additionally, there are no cute children in peril, no silly romantic subplots, and no dopey comedy scenes that distract our focus. Instead, *The China Syndrome* keeps the spotlight on the intense drama of the unfolding events.

Those events begin when a TV news crew happens to be on hand during a minor incident at a nuclear power plant north of Los Angeles. At first the power company explains away the event as just a routine occurrence, but details soon surface that reveal serious flaws in the plant's construction. Aiding the crew is Jack Godell (Jack Lemmon), an experienced engineer with a conscience. Godell suspects a cover-up, which he privately confirms via some industrious research. But to protect its billion-dollar investment, the conspiratorial power company will go to any length, even murder, to suppress his findings, and indeed one member of the news team is killed in a highway "accident." The presence of a sinister conspiracy echoes a familiar theme of memorable 1970s movies like *Soylent Green* (1973), *The Parallax View* (1974), *Three Days of the Condor* (1975), *Capricorn One* (1978), and many others. At the end of a long decade that had included the real-life dramas of the Pentagon Papers and Watergate, continued investigations into JFK's assassination, and alternative theories to everything from the lunar landings to the death of Elvis Presley, viewers knew from conspiracies.

Jack Lemmon, Michael Douglas, and Jane Fonda.

Desperate to deliver his crucial message about inadequate safety measures at the plant, Godell takes one member of the news crew hostage inside the control room in hopes of forcing a public broadcast of his vital information. After a long, tense confrontation, the plant's executives create a strong diversion that distracts Godell long enough for armed personnel to get into the room with their guns blazing. Fortunately these terrible events are slyly captured by one of the members of the news team with a TV camera. During the subsequent live broadcast, the previously fluffy reporter (Jane Fonda), who formerly specialized in lightweight entertainment features, matures into a tough and confrontational journalist who capably relays her report with insight and urgency.

As smart as the writing is and as good as the performances are (especially by Lemmon as the troubled whistle-blower, his best role since 1973's *Save the Tiger*), it's the Oscar-nominated art direction that really intensifies the suspense. The interiors of the power plant are as realistic as other interiors we can imagine but wouldn't normally see, like the ship's guts in *The Poseidon Adventure*, the dirigible's inner hull in *The Hindenburg* or the *Washington Post* offices in *All the President's Men* (1976). The man-made flaws in the plant are miniscule, almost undetectable, but believable, so it's not as if we're watching something truly improbable, like the incoming threat in *Meteor* (1979), turning into a catastrophe. The settings, the physical details, the technology, all of it seems real.

Viewers come away educated by all the understandable information presented in the movie, wrung out by the mounting tension, and shocked by the sudden ending that kills the hero and leaves the others hopeful that his death wasn't in vain. Viewers also leave with lots to contemplate from this cautionary tale, which was especially true in the spring of 1979 when *The China Syndrome* was opening in theaters and within weeks the disaster at Three Mile Island in Pennsylvania was focusing national attention on the very themes the movie was already presenting. In fact, the movie even points specifically to that state with a description of how the radioactive cloud would "render an area the size of Pennsylvania uninhabitable." Reel life, it seemed, was becoming real life right before everybody's eyes.

Understandably, *The China Syndrome* was a major box-office hit, and the movie would go on to be nominated for four Oscars. It would also inspire a number of other good nuclear-themed movies, including *Silkwood*, *Testament*, and *WarGames* (all 1983). Not many '70s movies were as powerful as *The China Syndrome*; even fewer felt as important.

ADDED ATTRACTION: *MAD* Magazine's Parodies of 1977-1979 Movies

The China Syndrome got its own movie parody, "The China Sin-Dome," in *MAD* magazine (the parody ran in March 1979). Below are twenty-five other 1977-1979 movies that were similarly honored, followed by the titles of the parodies. *MAD*'s parodies of 1975-1976 movies are with the entry for *One Flew Over the Cuckoo's Nest* (1975).

- 1977 movies
  Airport '77: "Airplot '77"
  Black Sunday: "Blimp Sunday"
  Close Encounters of the Third Kind: "Clod Encounters of the Absurd Kind"
  The Deep: "The Dip"
  The Spy Who Loved Me: "The Spy Who Glubbed Me"
  Saturday Night Fever: "Saturday Night Feeble"
  Star Wars: "Star Roars"
- 1978 movies
  Animal House: "Abominal House"
  Coma: "Coma-Toast"
  Eyes of Laura Mars: "The Eyes of Lurid Mess"

Grease: "Cease"
Heaven Can Wait: "Heaving Can Wait"
Invasion of the Body Snatchers: "Invasion of the Booty Snatchers"
Jaws 2: "Jaw'd, Too"
The Lord of the Rings: "The Ring and I"
Superman: "Superduperman"

- 1979 movies
Alien: "Alias"
The Amityville Horror: "The Calamityville Horror"
Apocalypse Now: "A Crock O' (Blip!) Now"
Being There: "Being Not All There"
The Concorde … Airport '79: "The Corncorde – Airplot '79"
Kramer vs. Kramer: "Crymore vs. Crymore"
Moonraker: "Moneyraker"
Rocky II: "Rockhead II"
Star Trek: The Motion Picture: "Star Blecch: The (GACCK!) Motion Picture"

Hair

Released: March 1979
Director: Milos Forman
Stars: John Savage, Treat Williams, Beverly D'Angelo
Academy Awards: None

PREVIEW: Hippies frolic in New York City and then assist a young visitor who has been drafted.

NOW SHOWING: Turn On, Tune In, Get a Job

Being a fan of '70s movies doesn't mean loving every single one. Many were mediocre, even horrible—we're looking at you, *Exorcist II: The Heretic* (1977). *Hair* isn't *Heretic* bad, but it's maddening. Not because it changes the hit Broadway musical; we'll accept the adaptation and let the show's devotees protest alterations to the original songs, to the free-flowing story, and to the ending. Nor will we criticize the movie's sincere antiwar message or the hard-working performers, especially Treat Williams, who never walks when he can run or bounce.

Seeing *Hair* again today reminds us how we felt seeing it in 1979. Even then it seemed dated and desperate. This was eleven years after the Broadway show had opened; other musicals have had similar gaps—*My Fair Lady*, the 1956 show/1964 movie—and won major Oscars, but they weren't trying to be hip and provocative. *Hair* tells the musical story of irresponsible hippies who panhandle and cavort in New York City. They decide to help a straight-laced newcomer who's visiting before going into the army. Eventually the hippies drive to the newcomer's Nevada army base and orchestrate a preposterous switcheroo that tragically backfires. Director Milos Forman fills scenes with energetic movement. There's real artistry in the presentation, which is immediately obvious in the early "Aquarius" number that blends the famous song with joyous, athletic choreography that even has the horses dancing.

But what's *Hair* glorifying? The hippies aren't adorable, funny charmers, they're selfish, sanctimonious jerks. For example, they crash a private black-tie party, arrogantly insult the elderly hosts, and destroy everyone's expensive feast. How groovy! The head hippie brags that's he's street-smart and can get bail money, but he merely sponges off his parents. The hippies steal cars and clothes, one hippie is a dead-beat dad, and the extremely pregnant girl lines up for LSD. "I happen to think you're ridiculous," the newcomer astutely declares.

We're fans of musicals, just not this one. Several songs—the powerful "Easy to Be Hard," the cast-of-thousands "Let the Sunshine In"—resonate, but others sound like random improvisations. Some lyrics try to shock with explicit sexual terms and crude racist labels, and some are children's nonsense rhymes ("Song-song-song-sing, sing-sing-sing song" sounds like Morse code for "out of ideas"). Plenty of people nostalgically celebrate this movie, the show, and the community. We get that. But to us, for everything admirable in *Hair* there's something else that's harebrained.

ADDED ATTRACTION: *More* Is Less

To show we're not picking on *Hair*, that year we were slightly underwhelmed by another '60s-inspired movie. *More American Graffiti*, the ambitious sequel to the beloved *American Graffiti* (1973), returns most the original cast (not Richard Dreyfuss, conspicuously), now under the direction of B.W.L. Norton. Intertwining stories like *American Graffiti* did, *More American Graffiti* moves the innocent 1962 characters to 1964-1967 and daringly goes dark with combat footage and death. In the two best (and longest) segments, Toad (Charles Martin Smith) is a smart-alecky soldier who goes A.W.O.L. and heads into Vietnam's menacing jungle singing and wearing a loud Hawaiian shirt, an escape that is going to keep him alive for about five minutes; meanwhile, John Milner (Paul Le Mat) is back home and struggling to win drag races and court a beautiful foreigner before eventually driving toward the sad fate foretold in *American Graffiti*'s epilogue. Harrison Ford, *American Graffiti*'s cocky and reckless hot rodder, has a nifty two-minute cameo as a tough law-enforcing motorcycle cop, and lively scene-stealer Candy Clark turns her Sandra Dee fashions from the first movie into the free-spirited hippie lifestyle in San Francisco. Great '60s music, trippy split-screens, varying film styles for the different segments, and familiar characters make *More American Graffiti* mildly entertaining, but overall the movie feels disjointed and disappointing compared to its classic predecessor.

Old Boyfriends

Released: March 1979
Director: Joan Tewkesbury
Stars: Talia Shire, Richard Jordan, John Belushi
Academy Awards: None

PREVIEW: A woman revisits her romantic past by driving cross-country to see old boyfriends.

NOW SHOWING: Into the Time Machine

Joan Tewkesbury's *Old Boyfriends* (1979) drew inordinate attention because John Belushi, fresh off *Animal House* (1978), is in it, albeit for only nineteen minutes. Belushi adds energy and even sings songs, something he'd already done as a Blues Brother on

TV's *Saturday Night Live* in 1978. But other than his appearance, *Old Boyfriends* is a sluggish melodrama that doesn't deliver on its interesting premise.

Talia Shire, an Oscar nominee for *Rocky* (1976), plays Dianne Cruise, a psychologist who's just been left by her husband. After surviving a suicide attempt, she decides to drive from L.A. to the Midwest to visit three old beaus: "If I could figure out who I was when I loved them," she narrates, "then I would know who I am now, and maybe love myself too."

Reading aloud from her old diary as she goes, Cruise visits the three in the reverse chronological order of their relationships. The first meeting in Colorado with her college love (Richard Jordan) is sweet, and she stays with him for several days. In Minnesota her meeting with Belushi's character, who plays Holiday Inns with his band, shows she's not really seeking self-discovery but merely wants silly revenge on the crude guy who scandalized her in high school. Finally, her "seventh-grade crush" in Michigan has been killed in Vietnam, so she romances his disturbed younger brother (Keith Carradine), with disastrous results. Returning home, she finds a surprise waiting for her. As the movie's tone veers from segment to segment, Shire plays her character differently with each encounter (she feigns a sexy seduction with Belushi). Regrettably *Old Boyfriends* is more boring than it sounds, and it's not helped by dramatic music that sounds like it's from another movie.

Seven months later Joan Micklin Silver's *Head Over Heels* premiered. This sensitive, talky romantic comedy has the "nice, dull" lead (John Heard) speak directly to the audience as he obsesses over his ex-lover (Mary Beth Hurt). Flashbacks show their first meeting, their "perfect" relationship, and his "weird paranoid behavior" that leads to their break-up an hour into the movie. He can't let go, however, and anxiously hopes for another chance. When this movie failed at the box office, the studio tried re-releasing it with a new title, *Chilly Scenes of Winter*, and a new ending that reverses the outcome of the original version. While it's significant that women had directed this and *Old Boyfriends*, two insightful movies with artistic ambitions, a mainstream commercial hit by a woman director wouldn't arrive until Amy Heckerling's *Fast Times at Ridgemont High* (1982).

ADDED ATTRACTION: Women Directors in the 1970s

Here at decade's end we list seventeen feature films from the 1970 that were directed by women.

- Joan Darling
  First Love (1977)
- Barbara Loden
  Wanda (1970)
- Elaine May
  A New Leaf (1971)
  The Heartbreak Kid (1972)
  Mikey and Nicky (1976)
- Joan Micklin Silver
  Hester Street (1975)
  Between the Lines (1977)
  Head Over Heels (1979)
- Joan Rivers
  Rabbit Test (1978)

- Stephanie Rothman
  The Student Nurses (1970)
  The Velvet Vampire, aka *Cemetery Girls* (1971)
  Group Marriage (1973)
  Terminal Island (1973)
  The Working Girls (1974)
- Joan Tewkesbury
  Old Boyfriends (1979)
- Jane Wagner
  Moment by Moment (1978)
- Claudia Weill
  Girlfriends (1978)

Manhattan

Released: April 1979
Director: Woody Allen
Stars: Woody Allen, Mariel Hemingway, Diane Keaton
Academy Awards: Two nominations (Best Supporting Actress—Mariel Hemingway; Best Writing)

PREVIEW: Couples break up, reconcile, and experience life and culture in modern Manhattan.

NOW SHOWING: Rhapsody in Black and White

Some Woody Allen fans rank *Manhattan* (1979) above *Annie Hall* (1977), his Oscar-winning breakthrough. We'll call it a tie, noting strong distinctions that are like the differences between magnificent, perfectly controlled symphonies and wildly riffing jazz. *Manhattan*, telling a straightforward, if complicated story in gloriously old-fashioned black and white against a soundtrack of gorgeous instrumentals, is more traditional, whereas *Annie*, zig-zagging chronologically and incorporating creative flourishes (animation, split-screen, subtitles, etc.), is boldly innovative. Both movies are cerebral, both intermingle drama with comedy, and both end with Allen's character wistful and alone. And both are among the decade's towering artistic achievements.

Possibly audiences were squirming in 1979 (even more now) because *Manhattan*'s central romantic relationship matches Isaac, a forty-two-year-old writer (Allen) and Tracy, a seventeen-year-old high-schooler (Mariel Hemingway). Note, however, that nobody else in the movie raises objections; Isaac and Tracy openly date and hold hands, her parents let her sleep over, and all his friends, including a married woman, encourage him to pursue this dazzling wise-beyond-her-years girl.

But the movie isn't about her. It's about the grown-ups around her who sabotage their own lives because, as Isaac says, that "keeps them from dealing with more unsolvable, terrifying problems about the universe." Isaac abruptly quits his job, changes apartments, leaves Tracy for neurotic Mary (Diane Keaton), and tries to win Tracy back. Mary and Isaac's best friend both induce similar turmoil. These aren't stupid people: they work in the arts, visit museums, and together mention Ingmar Bergman seven times. Life isn't randomly shifting these characters; they're intentionally shifting life, and suffering for their ill-considered choices.

Diane Keaton and Woody Allen.

Manhattan's unimpeachable elements are its poster-worthy images and graceful music. New York has never looked more ravishing than it does in this majestic widescreen spectacle filmed by master cinematographer Gordon Willis. Throughout, George Gershwin's lush melodies complement the actions: the cheery "Love Is Sweeping the Country" accompanies a lively father-son escapade; the sumptuous "He Loves and She Loves" backs a passionate kiss in a hansom cab; "I've Got a Crush on You," "S'Wonderful," and "Embraceable You" play as an affair progresses; "But Not for Me" softly leads into the last scene when Isaac sadly realizes that "the nicest times" and "Tracy's face" really are flying out of his life, probably forever. It's a quiet, poignant, beautiful moment. You might find a '70s movie you prefer over *Manhattan*, but you might not find one that's more poetic.

ADDED ATTRACTION: May/December Relationships

Any controversy over the age differences in *Manhattan* didn't keep the movie from being one of Woody Allen's biggest box-office hits. Born in 1935, Allen is eleven years older than Diane Keaton, and he's fourteen years older than Meryl Streep, who plays Isaac's ex-wife in the movie. Then there's the twenty-six-year chasm between him and Mariel Hemingway. It's not the widest age gap of the late 1970s, and Hemingway isn't the youngest actress playing a character in a May/December relationship during these years (Hemingway was seventeen when *Manhattan* premiered; *Pretty* Baby pairs Brooke Shields, twelve when the movie opened in 1978, with twenty-eight-year-old Keith Carradine). In the following list, all eight late-'70s movies show actresses getting romantically involved with actors who are at least twenty years older; the real-life age differences in the first six films are greater than the Allen/Hemingway pairing in *Manhattan* (actual ages follow the names).

- *The Betsy* (1978): Katharine Ross, 38; Laurence Olivier, 71
- *Farewell, My Lovely* (1975): Charlotte Rampling, 29; Robert Mitchum, 58
- *Girlfriends* (1978): Melanie Mayron, 26; Eli Wallach, 63
- *The Greek Tycoon* (1978): Jacqueline Bisset, 34; Anthony Quinn, 63
- *Network* (1976): Faye Dunaway, 25; William Holden, 58
- *The Other Side of Midnight* (1977): Marie-France Pisier, 33; Raf Vallone, 61
- *Taxi Driver* (1976): Jodie Foster, 14; Harvey Keitel, 37
- *10* (1979): Bo Derek, 23; Dudley Moore, 44

A Little Romance

Released: April 1979
Director: George Roy Hill
Stars: Diane Lane, Thelonious Bernard, Laurence Olivier
Academy Awards: One win (Best Music), plus one more nomination (Best Writing)

PREVIEW: Two smitten teens in France run off together so they can share a first kiss in Venice.

NOW SHOWING: Here's Looking at You, Kids

In spring 1979, filmmakers' fancies turned to love. Three romantic movies premiered within a four-week span—chronologically, and also in order of excellence, they were *Manhattan*, *A Little Romance*, and *Hanover Street*. Interestingly, all three ended with their lovers separated. As Minnie Riperton and Suzi Quatro both sang on new albums that year, "Love Hurts."

A Little Romance is a warm, graceful charmer about two thirteen-year-olds who meet in Paris and believe they'll "love each other forever" if they kiss in a gondola under Venice's Bridge of Sighs. Diane Lane, in her movie debut, plays the American girl who's got a 167 IQ, reads Heidegger "for fun," and uses words like "etymological." Thelonious Bernard is her equally brainy French beau; he loves American movies, so he asks her to "mosey on down here a piece," calls himself "Bogie," and toasts her with "Here's looking at you, kid." Their conversation topics include existentialism and German poetry.

Accompanied by Julius (Laurence Olivier), a sympathetic old man they befriend, the trio flees Paris midway through the movie and heads for Italy by train. Later they all get on bikes to blend in alongside Italian cyclists, with even the seventy-two-year-old Olivier wobbling through Verona on two wheels. Bikes were certainly abundant in 1979 movies: they're here for five minutes, they dominate *Breaking Away*, a cycling race concludes *Old Boyfriends*, dad teaches his son to ride in *Kramer vs. Kramer*, and Kermit is a pedaling fool

Diane Lane and Thelonius Bernard.

in *The Muppet Movie*. When even amphibians are cycling, bikes must've really been a thing that year.

Miraculously the trio reaches Venice despite making dumb mistakes, like losing all their money, attracting police attention, and counting on their creaky senior citizen to flee on a bicycle. But there's so much sincerity in their innocent pursuit that we overlook the implausible and instead cheer on the imaginable, that golden smooch before childhood is gondola with the wind. The teary coda finishes with a poignant freeze frame that recalls the ending of *Butch Cassidy and the Sundance Kid* (1969), which makes sense since George Roy Hill directed both movies. While Olivier is occasionally so hammy that he should have honey-glazed carrots beside him, the kids are sweet without being saccharine, the scenery and locations are lovely, and Georges Delerue's spritely, elegant music is so enchanting it won an Oscar. Approached with an open heart, *A Little Romance* makes a big impression.

ADDED ATTRACTION: Movie Marquees, 1978-1979

In its first two minutes *A Little Romance* shows clips from *The Big Sleep* (1946), *True Grit* (1969), *Butch Cassidy and the Sundance Kid* (1969), and *Hustle* (1975). Here are other 1978-1979 movies where a marquee, or an actual clip, announces another real movie. For more movie marquees, see the entry for *Slap Shot* (1977).

- *The Black Stallion* (1979): A theater marquee displays *The Spiral Staircase* (1945) and *The Jungle Princess* (1936).
- *Days of Heaven* (1978): The main characters watch ten seconds of Charlie Chaplin's *The Immigrant* (1917).
- *Foul Play* (1978): Scenes from *This Gun for Hire* (1942) are shown inside a theater.
- *Gray Lady Down* (1978): Survivors in the sunken sub watch *Jaws* (1975).
- *Grease* (1978): Previews for *The Blob* (1958) and *Hollywood or Bust* (1956) at the drive-in.
- *The Great Santini* (1979): *Rome Adventure* (1962) is on a marquee in Beaufort, South Carolina.
- *Hooper* (1978): Hooper (Burt Reynolds) watches a ten-second clip of the river disaster in another Reynolds movie, *Deliverance* (1972).
- *Manhattan* (1979): Midway through the movie, the Cinema Studio displays *Chûshingura* (1962) and *Earth* (1930) on its marquee.
- *1941* (1979): With a battle outside, General Stilwell sits in a Hollywood theater and watches *Dumbo* (1941).
- *Old Boyfriends* (1979): *Star Wars* (1977) is displayed on the marquee at Grauman's Chinese Theater.
- *Same Time, Next Year* (1978): Elvis Presley's *Love Me Tender* (1956) is playing at New York's Paramount Theater.
- *Up in Smoke* (1978): Cheech and Chong stop near Grauman's Chinese Theater, where *Star Wars* (1977) is playing.
- *The Wanderers* (1979): In the first two minutes a Bronx theater advertises *Battle Cry* (1955) and *War Is Hell* (1961); a later marquee shows *The Man with the X Ray Eyes* (1963) and *Palm Springs Weekend* (1963).
- *Yanks* (1979): A fight erupts inside a theater lobby where *Song of the Islands* (1942) is playing.

1979

Saint Jack

Released: April 1979
Director: Peter Bogdanovich
Stars: Ben Gazzara, Denholm Elliott, James Villiers
Academy Awards: None

PREVIEW: An affable Singapore pimp has trouble with rivals and later makes an unsavory deal.

NOW SHOWING: We'll Always Have Singapore

What a roller-coaster decade the '70s were for director Peter Bogdanovich. After three 1971-1973 hits (*The Last Picture Show*, *What's Up, Doc?*, *Paper Moon*), he plummeted with three mid-decade box-offices failures (*Daisy Miller*, *At Long Last Love*, *Nickelodeon*), and then soared back with an excellent low-budget drama, *Saint Jack* (1979). It's one of Bogdanovich's best movies.

It's one of Ben Gazzara's best, too. This consistently convincing actor is totally engrossing as Jack Flowers, an amiable, well-connected pimp who seems to like—and be liked by—everyone he runs into. Charming, smart, and fearless, he ambles through Singapore's big hotels and back alleys with equal ease, wearing casual tropical shirts, smoking stogies, and providing girls and assistance to friends and strangers. Flowers is a decent, unflappable loner, like another resilient New Yorker succeeding on his own terms in an exotic land, Rick in *Casablanca* (1942). Like Rick, Flowers is no romantic idealist ("People make love for so many crazy reasons, why shouldn't money be one of them?"), and he bids adieu to his favorite girl with a casual *Casablanca*-ish "so long, kid." And like Rick, Flowers is in a moral quandary.

While interesting locals and colorful ex-patriots drift in and out, Singapore itself is the movie's other main character. Bogdanovich roams the island to capture modern street life and shadowy subcultures (he makes a minor James Bond connection with Shirley Bassey's "Goldfinger" accompanying a seduction and George Lazenby, the first post-Connery 007, playing a senator). The slow-developing first half of the movie sets up the fascinating world that Flowers confidently navigates. The first real action starts fifty-six minutes in when knife-wielding rivals surround Flowers; typically, he keeps his cool, even after they tattoo curses up and down both his arms (he simply gets redecorated with more tattoos).

But after a friend dies suddenly, Flowers reconsiders his direction and sees a way back to the states via a lucrative blackmail scheme offered by a mysterious American (Bogdanovich himself). Flowers knows the sordid deal involving a senator and unsavory photos "stinks," yet he fulfills his side of the bargain in suspenseful scenes that Bogdanovich presents in near-total silence. Eventually Flowers has to decide if this is really who he is. There's no heartbreaking *Casablanca*-style romance, and Flowers' soul-searching dilemma doesn't have the profundity of a war-changing event, but *Saint Jack*'s last act is still riveting and satisfying as it aims to its jaunty conclusion.

ADDED ATTRACTION: Go Direct Yourself, Part Two

Director Peter Bogdanovich appears for about eight minutes as the man who presents the blackmail scheme. Here are additional 1978-1979 movies in which the directors gave themselves small roles. We're not including leading roles, like when John

Cassavetes starred in his own movies. For a similar list of 1975-1977 movies, see the entry for *Burnt Offerings* (1976).

- *Apocalypse Now* (1979): Twenty-seven minutes in, Francis Ford Coppola is on the riverbank with a film crew, exhorting the arriving soldiers to not look at the camera and to "go on! Keep going!"
- *Being There* (1979): Seventy-six minutes in, Hal Ashby, with a beard and glasses, works quietly in the background of a *Washington Post* office.
- *Big Wednesday* (1978): During the opening credits, an old black-and-white photo shows director John Milius at the beach. Twenty-eight minutes later, he steps from the shadows and offers "reefers, mari-huana."
- *The Black Hole* (1979): Sixty-four minutes in, Alex rips a metallic mask off a humanoid, revealing the face of director Gary Nelson.
- *Coming Home* (1978): Near the end, the passenger flashing the peace sign from inside a Porsche is director Hal Ashby.
- *Convoy* (1978): Sixty-eight minutes in, Sam Peckinpah is the sound engineer standing in the back of a pickup truck.
- *The Electric Horseman* (1979): Twenty minutes in, Sydney Pollack gets brushed off by Jane Fonda's character inside a Vegas casino.
- *Invasion of the Body Snatchers* (1978): Philip Kaufman knocks on the phone booth sixty-five minutes into the movie.
- *Martin* (1978): Sixty-three minutes in, George Romero comes to dinner as Father Howard.
- *The Muppet Movie* (1979): Twelve minutes in, James Frawley is the waiter serving frog legs inside the El Sleezo Café.
- *Rabbit Test* (1978): Forty-seven minutes in, director Joan Rivers runs down a hallway as a nurse and drops a tray with a "hot colon." "Please don't say anything," she says, "he'll just wear a bag."
- *Superman* (1978): In the 2000 extended version, Richard Donner talks to Clark Kent eighty-eight minutes into the movie.
- *An Unmarried Woman* (1978): For two minutes Paul Mazursky is one of the diners at the table during Erica's blind-date lunch.

Hanover Street

Released: May 1979
Director: Peter Hyams
Stars: Harrison Ford, Lesley-Anne Down, Christopher Plummer
Academy Awards: None

PREVIEW: An American pilot in love with an English nurse flies a war mission with her husband.

NOW SHOWING: Han Solo Street

With the Vietnam War concluding in 1973, the number of American war movies made during the 1970s quickly dwindled from a high of ten in 1970 (counting comedies like

M*A*S*H and *Catch-22*) to just one—*Midway* (1976)—from 1973 to 1976; by comparison, *eleven* war-related movies were released in a single month, May, of 1943. War movies began reappearing late in the 1970s, and one, *The Deer Hunter* (1978), was even named Best Picture. Movie-wise, America was ready to go back to the front.

Highlighted by *Apocalypse Now*, 1979 produced four war features, one of them a comedy—*1941*—plus two romances—*Yanks* (see "Added Attraction") and *Hanover Street*. While much of the attention paid to *Hanover Street* focused on Harrison Ford, starring in one of his first movies after *Star Wars* (1977), much of the criticism noted the clichéd, melodramatic plot. That's what's daring about *Hanover Street*: in the same year when *Apocalypse Now* pushed every war-movie boundary, *Hanover Street* jumped backwards to the 1940s. Echoing *A Yank in the R.A.F.* (1941), *Eagle Squadron* (1942), and other American-officer-in-England-meets-a-girl movies, *Hanover Street* blends World War Two with an old-fashioned love story.

Set in the aforementioned 1943, the movie casts Ford as an American pilot who falls for lovely Lesley-Anne Down, a married London nurse who won't reveal her name, even after they sleep together and he declares his love. In the last forty-five minutes Ford's character escorts Down's husband on a dangerous mission, with both men disguised in enemy uniforms (just like when Han and Luke infiltrated *Star Wars*' Death Star). Good action scenes lead to an emotional parting speech reminiscent of Rick's noble farewell to Ilsa in *Casablanca* (1942). Ford is a handsome, wise-cracking hero, and after flirting with Leia in *Star Wars* he finally gets some real bedroom action (in *Hanover Street*'s first half he's in bed almost as often as he's in the air). The movie is watchable, but corny dialogue—"If you die on me, I'll kill you"—grounds what might've been high-flying drama.

Harrison Ford and Lesley-Anne Down.

Hanover Street wasn't a hit, and neither was Ford's next movie, *The Frisco Kid*, premiering two months later. This mildly amusing western comedy pairs Ford (a serious bank robber) with Gene Wilder (a naïve, thoroughly likeable Polish rabbi) on a dangerous cross-country journey in the 1850s. Some gunfights, a little slapstick, and a few sweet moments are spread over two long hours.

ADDED ATTRACTION: *Yanks* a Lot

Yanks (1979) goes beyond soap opera to industrial-strength-detergent opera. Again it's 1943, and American soldiers are filling small English towns to prepare for 1944's D-Day invasion. As two American/British love affairs (a low-key Richard Gere and Lisa Eichhorn, and also William Devane and Vanessa Redgrave) slowly develop, all the Yanks learn that "it's their country and you gotta play by their rules, even if you don't understand 'em sometimes." England looks green and beautiful, the historical details seem authentic, and everyone emotes admirably in the final train-station sendoffs, but this plodding 139-minute talkfest has no battle scenes and barely any action at all besides those damn Yankees getting into some quick fights and one three-minute

246 THE DARING DECADE: VOLUME TWO

joyride on a B-25 (the same bomber that Harrison Ford's character flies in *Hanover Street*). Director John Schlesinger indulges in screen-filling close-ups and let's Eichhorn whisper for nearly the entire movie. Modern audiences will have to suppress a smile when Gere somberly says "that's what she said" while exiting a room.

Alien

(One of 1979's five **FAR-OUT** movies)
Released: May 1979
Director: Ridley Scott
Stars: Sigourney Weaver, Tom Skerritt, Ian Holm
Academy Awards: One win (Best Visual Effects), plus one more nomination (Best Art Direction)

PREVIEW: Astronauts must kill the monstrous alien hiding in their ship before it kills them.

FINE LINE: "You still don't understand what you're dealing with, do you? A perfect organism; its structural perfection is matched only by its hostility." (Science Officer Ash, describing the alien's capabilities to the crew.)

CLOSE-UP: Mother, the computer on board the *Nostromo*, needs to use spell-check.

- 4 minutes into the movie: the first computer screen misspells the Weyland-Yutani Corporation (the owners of the ship) as "Keylan Yutani" (eleven minutes later another screen spells the first name as "Weylan").
- 9 minutes: the "Overmonitoring Address Matrix" screen spells alignment as "allignment."
- 79 minutes: Ripley reads "Emergency Command Overide" (not "override") on a computer screen.
- 80 minutes: "Priority One" says to "insure return of organism." So, Mother is telling Ripley to buy an insurance policy? No, actually Ripley is supposed to "ensure" the alien's return.

NOW SHOWING: The Perfect Organism

We've still got scratch marks in our arm dating back to 1979 when the girl sitting to our right in a theater (a girl we didn't even know) clamped onto us during the heart-stopping climax to *Alien* (1979). That's what this movie does—it turns strangers into allies who are trying to survive one of the scariest movies ever made. (The girl we *did* know, by the way, was slumped to our left with her hands over her face.)

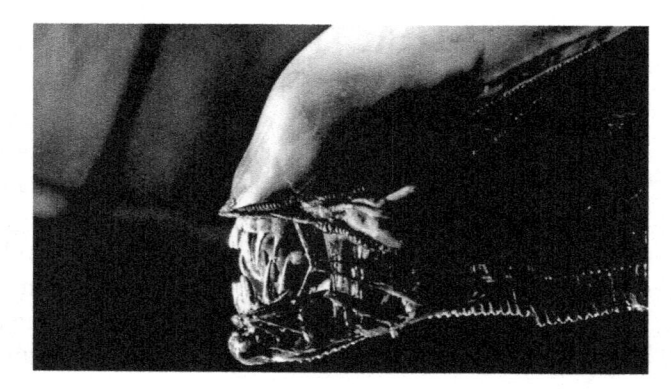

Director Ridley Scott would go on to Oscar-winning glory with *Gladiator* (2000), but *Alien* still feels like his most flawless film. Updating a creature-loose-inside-the-ship idea first presented in *It! The Terror From Beyond Space* (1958), and delaying the monster's full appearance the way *Jaws* (1975) had withheld the shark's first close-up, Scott mercilessly builds *Alien*'s terrors. They start with the exploration of a derelict vessel on a stormy planetoid, accelerate quickly as an infected crewmember dies in a famously shocking chest-bursting scene, and intensify when the fully grown beast stands for the first time and drags its first helpless victim into the darkness. Audiences screamed out loud when a suspenseful pursuit in a claustrophobic air shaft ends with the hidden creature suddenly lunging from the darkness to grab its prey. And the last sequence with the lone remaining crewmember running down hallways with the ship counting down to nuclear detonation is so relentlessly terrifying it's ridiculous.

It's all done so stylishly, so realistically, that only *2001: A Space Odyssey* (1968), *Star Wars* (1977), and *Close Encounters of the Third Kind* (1977) were in *Alien*'s science-fiction league, and none of those stellar epics marshaled its effects to petrify viewers. Those other three movies surprised, mystified, and entertained their audiences; *Alien* terrifies them with perfectly realized, perfectly terrifying environments, iconic new creatures, and shocking scenes. What's more, the twisting story keeps viewers off balance so they never know what to expect. For instance, the distress signal the crew picks up turns out to be, not a plea for help, but a warning. The inhabitants of the derelict vessel that the crew investigates aren't helpless, injured passengers, they're enormous, long-dead monsters. The curious eggs inside the derelict ship aren't sources of benign, exciting new life, they're actually booby traps that launch disgusting killers. The alien's frightening mouth hides another fearsome mouth inside. The computer named Mother doesn't soothe, it coldly calculates and reports. Perhaps the most disorienting developments is the side story with Ash (see "Added Attraction"), which completely amplifies the freak factor: we'd already seen the stoic captain, seemingly the reasonable, brave hero, get killed, so if Ash, seemingly a logical human, could turn out to be a duplicitous robot, then who knew where this movie was going to go.

Where it was going was toward female empowerment. Before *Alien*, had there ever been such a kick-ass movie heroine as Ellen Ripley? Not merely a courageous female protagonist who endures, like young Dorothy in *The Wizard of Oz* (1939), or tough cookies like Hildy Johnson in *His Girl Friday* (1940) and Constance Miller in *McCabe & Mrs. Miller* (1971), or even Laurie Strode, who resourcefully fends for herself until a gun-toting male rescuer arrives in *Halloween* (1978). We mean ferocious villain-slaying women who do their own rescuing, thank you. The title character in *Coffy* (1973) did raise the bar for strong-willed movie heroines, but she was fighting flesh-and-blood gangsters, not an unkillable creature.

Not only was Ripley (Sigourney Weaver) a new kind of movie heroine, so too was her opponent a new kind of movie monster. Pre-*Alien*, most women who triumphed in movies were usually battling deceitful husbands, devious businessmen, local hoodlums, and other small-scale antagonists. What makes Ripley's victory so emphatic is that she defeats

Sigourney Weaver.

the universe's ultimate predator in a one-on-one battle inside a confined space where no outside help is possible. *Alien*'s alien is a living organism, but it's such an unassailable hunter with such extraordinary abilities and defenses that it might as well be a machine permanently switched to Attack mode (no wonder the amoral Weyland-Yutani company is willing to sacrifice the entire crew to bring one back for its weapons division). As if silent guile, relentless aggression, acid blood, and extendable skull-piercing teeth aren't enough advantages, the creature can also camouflage itself inside the ship. Victims don't even know it's there until the alien already has them in its clutches, a lesson Ripley learns for herself in the last sequence inside the escape shuttle. And so resilient is this beast, even after it's jettisoned into space we still wonder if it is somehow going to get back, or if it has left eggs somewhere in the ship.

To appreciate *Alien* now, you have to forget Linda Hamilton's buff character in the later *Terminator* movies, Uma Thurman's determined Beatrix Kiddo in the *Kill Bill* slaughterfests of the twenty-first century, and other memorable screen queens who followed in Ripley's footsteps (even Ripley herself in the subsequent *Alien* sequels). You also have to ignore the later Predator and other highly evolved sci-fi killers who came afterwards. *Alien* preceded all of them. And unlike other monster movies that have lost their effectiveness over time (is anyone still frightened by *Frankenstein*?), *Alien* has aged well because the fears it taps into so effectively are primordial and universal. Even when you know the shocks are coming, *Alien* still resonates like your most vivid nightmare.

ADDED ATTRACTION: Ash the Robot

One of *Alien*'s biggest surprises comes two-thirds of the way through the movie when Ash (Ian Holm) is revealed to be a machine. Before this shocking moment, small pieces of evidence have suggested Ash's true nature as both a robot and a company lackey. The following clues (and times in parentheses) are from the 1979 theatrical release.

- 7 minutes into the movie:
  Ash always seems slightly different from the rest of the crew. At the first meal, everyone else is in casual robes and tee-shirts; Ash arrives late, in full uniform. Everyone else interacts amiably, but Ash is consistently humorless and officious.

- 11 minutes:
  Captain Dallas delivers the startling news about their unexpected location; everyone but Ash is surprised.

- 12 minutes:
  Upon receiving the alien signal, some crewmembers want to continue homeward, but Ash quotes from the contract to remind them they are obligated to investigate.

- 30 minutes:
  Ripley deciphers the signal as a warning; Ash coolly talks her out of alerting the rescue party.

- 36 minutes:
  Ash, prioritizing the company over crew safety, disobeys the quarantine order and admits the search party back into the ship.

- 50 minutes:
  Dallas tells Ripley that on five previous occasions he had shipped out with a different Science Officer; two days before this current trip departed, the company replaced that person with Ash. Ripley says she doesn't trust Ash, and Dallas agrees.

- 52 minutes:
  Before returning to their sleep chambers, everyone forms a semi-circle around the dining table, except Ash, who sits alone, facing the others.
- 56 minutes:
  As Kane retches and struggles to breathe, Ash sits still and watches. Once the infant alien bursts free, Ash insists that nobody touch it.
- 57 minutes:
  As the others solemnly watch Kane's body being shot into space, Ash walks away.
- 75 minutes:
  The others are visibly upset when Dallas is killed; Ash has no reaction.
- 77 minutes:
  For the second time Ripley asks Ash about defeating the creature, and again he calmly tells her he's "still collating" (what he means is "still protecting the alien").
- 80 minutes:
  As Ash and Ripley begin their final confrontation in the sealed room, some kind of white fluid—synthetic blood? lubricant?—seeps from Ash's forehead.
- 82 minutes:
  Ash unplugged—clubbed in the head, Ash whirls around the room, emitting strange, high-pitched noises and spraying white liquid. Hit again, Ash's head bends completely backwards to reveal a cluster of leaking tubes in his neck. "It's a robot!" a horrified crewmember finally declares.

Ian Holm.

Escape from Alcatraz

Released: June 1979
Director: Don Siegel
Stars: Clint Eastwood, Patrick McGoohan, Roberts Blossom
Academy Awards: None

PREVIEW: Three convicts carry out a daring plan to escape from the prison on Alcatraz Island.

NOW SHOWING: Devil's Island

Escape from Alcatraz (1979) is the final collaboration between director Don Siegel and actor Clint Eastwood, and it's a good one. Their five-movie pairing included *Dirty Harry* (1971), the violent, polarizing movie with Eastwood as a controversial vigilante cop. In *Escape* he switches sides to play a real-life convict who in 1960 was locked up in Alcatraz, the notorious citadel in San Francisco Bay. His character, Frank Morris, is there for "burglary, armed robbery, grand larceny" and previous escapes "from quite a few prisons." He's the baddest mother in the yard, a tough loner who can pummel a menacing knife-wielding behemoth (Morris foreshadows Jon Voight's brutal, resolute character in 1985's *Runaway Train*).

Morris, who's unemotional and racist, isn't someone the audience would normally be rooting for, but we do, for the same reason we cheered on the prisoners in *Papillon* (1973). Like that movie's Devil's Island, Alcatraz is so harsh that you're hoping the prisoners will bust out and expose the system. Patrick McGoohan plays the cruel, petty warden who has no name (he's just "Warden" in the credits) and takes sadistic satisfaction from denying basic privileges.

The movie divides into thirds, starting with forty-three minutes that establish the hostile world on the Rock. In the next section Morris uses his "superior" I.Q. to devise an ingenious, detailed prison break, even though everyone tells him escape is impossible. He welds together a new tunneling tool, makes a crude power drill out of an electric fan, fashions a realistic "dummy head" for his cell, and reads about makeshift rafts and life preservers in *Popular Mechanics*. The last nineteen minutes present the tense escape he attempts with two accomplices. The warden later insists the men drowned, but closing text notes that the "massive search" for bodies was unsuccessful, so possibly the three prisoners did indeed survive. Alcatraz, we learn, closed the next year.

Using actual locations, director Siegel makes everything so authentic that the movie plays almost like a procedural documentary. The grim vibe is totally different from jokey prison movies like *The Longest Yard* (1974): many scenes are dark and claustrophobic, there's minimal dialogue and camaraderie, and the laconic, business-like Morris gets almost no back story ("What kind of childhood did you have," he's asked; "Short," he curtly replies). Atmospheric and stylish in an efficient, gritty way, *Escape from Alcatraz* takes the successful Siegel/Eastwood partnership out on a strong, well-played note.

ADDED ATTRACTION: Prison Sells

Before the 1970s, Hollywood had already made scores of movies about prison escapes; one great example was literally called *The Great Escape* (1963). The following '70s movies, listed chronologically with their stars, all include jailbreaks (some of these escapes, like the one in *Dillinger*, are memorable without being especially long).

- *There Was a Crooked Man* (1970): Kirk Douglas
- *The Pursuit of Happiness* (1971): Michael Sarrazin
- *The Big Doll House* (1971): Judy Brown
- *Women in Cages* (1971): Jennifer Gan
- *The Big Bird Cage* (1972): Anitra Ford
- *Black Mama White Mama* (1973): Pam Grier

- *Dillinger* (1973): Warren Oates
- *I Escaped from Devil's Island* (1973): Jim Brown
- *The Slams* (1973): Jim Brown
- *Papillon* (1973): Steve McQueen
- *Breakout* (1975): Charles Bronson
- *Mean Dog Blues* (1978): Gregg Henry
- *On the Yard* (1978): John Heard
- *Seabo*, aka *Buckstone County Prison* (1978): Earl Owensby
- *Midnight Express* (1978): Brad Davis

The Muppet Movie

Released: June 1979
Director: James Frawley
Stars: Jim Henson, Frank Oz, Jerry Nelson
Academy Awards: Two nominations (Best Song; Best Music)

PREVIEW: Kermit and his new pals take a musical road trip to follow their dreams in Hollywood.

NOW SHOWING: Green Is Gold

With *Escape from Alcatraz* and *The Muppet Movie* opening simultaneously in 1979, audiences had a careful choice to make. Dark prison drama, or sunny musical comedy? Clint Eastwood, or Kermit the Frog? One was a disastrous option for children, but adults couldn't go wrong.

Like another 1979 movie, *Star Trek: The Motion Picture*, *The Muppet Movie* was based on a popular TV show, here *The Muppet Show*, which had debuted in 1976 and was still winning Emmy Awards. A Muppet-based *movie*, however, was a daring project asking a big question: would anyone besides the show's fans pay to watch ninety-five minutes of puppets when they could already see the half-hour show for free?

The answer was an enthusiastic yes, and *The Muppet Movie* became one of 1979's top-ten box-office hits. This audience-pleasing charmer has such universal appeal that even if you don't know Gonzo from Fozzie you'll quickly understand the characters: Kermit the sweet amphibian, Missy Piggy the impulsive diva, Animal the ravenous whatever-he-is, and dozens more. The simple plot has Kermit heading to Hollywood and making new friends as he goes. They sing,

Miss Piggy.

have adventures, and overcome a persistent villain. At one point characters read the screenplay aloud before inventing "a clever plot device," and midway through the movie the rolling film literally breaks. A climactic cast-of-hundreds production number adds a "keep believing!" exclamation point.

Viewers may be so enchanted they'll forget they're watching felt puppets. TV's Muppets stayed indoors, but now they're outside doing new things: Kermit, for instance, plays a banjo, rows a boat, and rides a bike (not just in long-distance shots, but with close-ups of his pedaling feet). Adding to the fun are many celebrity cameos, including Mel Brooks, Bob Hope, Steve Martin, Richard Pryor, and *Sesame Street*'s Big Bird, though these stars usually exit in under a minute—Carol Kane's two appearances total all of four seconds.

Not everyone will get the Hare Krishna, Jascha Heifetz, and Fats Waller references, and the comedy offers more quiet chuckles than laugh-out-loud hysterics, but everyone should delight in the catchy, sometimes profound songs. For kids, *The Muppet Movie* is mandatory viewing; for adults who saw it long ago, indulge in the nostalgic memories; for newcomers, just surrender, smile, and be inspired by the finale that reminds us, "What was once juvenile-ish is grown-up and stylish." As clichéd as it sounds, this movie really is for all ages.

ADDED ATTRACTION: Ladies' Day

The North Avenue Irregulars (1979) was another movie parents and kids could share. During the '70s Disney released almost fifty movies, many of them inoffensive, formulaic live-action comedies that presented various combinations of animals, kids, nutty elders, missing loot, inept cops, bungling criminals, wacky chases and familiar screen veterans. *The North Avenue Irregulars* stylishly checks all those boxes. When the police can't stop the illegal gambling that's overtaking a nice town, five local church ladies go undercover to bust up the bookies. For much of this fast-paced movie the ladies attempt stealthy pursuits that put them in amusing situations, culminating in a wild demolition-derby style finale that crashes lots of nostalgia-inducing '70s cars together. The real fun comes from watching the spirited irregulars—among them screen stars Cloris Leachman and Barbara Harris—who look like they're having some giggles, with TV friends Ruth Buzzi, Alan Hale Jr., and more for lively support. Boyish Edward Herrmann is a hip motorcycle-riding pastor/single dad who recruits the ladies and wins Susan Clark at the end. The shaggy rock band, the jokes about *Serpico*, Batman, and CB-radio "smokies," and the funny bit with Karen Valentine in full-floozy disguise all suggest that Disney was pushing its conservative envelope a bit. Compared to the early-decade silliness of *The Boatniks* (1970), *The North Avenue Irregulars* helped Disney end the '70s with something slightly more than the regular routine.

Moonraker

Released: June 1979
Director: Lewis Gilbert
Stars: Roger Moore, Lois Chiles, Michael Lonsdale
Academy Awards: One nomination (Best Visual Effects)

PREVIEW: 007's search for a hijacked space shuttle leads him to outer space and global peril.

NOW SHOWING: ♫ You're a Heartbreaker, Dream Maker, *Moonraker* ... ♫

As the end credits for *Moonraker* (1979) boast, this lavish movie was filmed "on location in ITALY, BRAZIL, GUATEMALA, U.S.A. and OUTER SPACE!" James Bond movies, especially *You Only Live Twice* (1967), had flown into space before, but 007 himself didn't become an astronaut until *Moonraker*. After the massive success of *Star Wars* (1977), producers juggled the order of subsequent Bond movies so that the Earth-bound *For Your Eyes Only* (1981), which had been announced at the end of *The Spy Who Loved Me* (1977) as the next Bond movie, was postponed in favor of the space-themed *Moonraker*, which happens to feature lots of *Star Wars*-like laser blasters.

The Bond movie with the biggest budget up to that time, *Moonraker* became the biggest moneymaker on the Bond market until *GoldenEye* (1995). The visual effects and spectacular settings, including French chateaux, Venice landmarks, and Brazilian jungles, impressed everyone, and Shirley Bassey returned for another Bond song after singing the themes to *Goldfinger* (1964) and *Diamonds Are Forever* (1971). However, hardcore fans and some critics assailed *Moonraker* for its silliness and ludicrous plot developments, as when the monstrous assassin Jaws (Richard Kiel), returning from *The Spy Who Loved Me*, gets a girlfriend, becomes Bond's *ally*, and even speaks. Also, the villain, Drax, is rarely in the movie, is easily killed off, and is severely underplayed by a languid Michael Lonsdale. As *Goldfinger* proved, the best Bond movies have resilient, deliciously wicked villains.

Moonraker veers dramatically from Ian Fleming's 1955 novel. The book's first third is devoted to a bridge game where Bond out-cheats Drax (the movie gives bridge a one-line mention). *Moonraker* on the page is a single nuclear-armed rocket that Drax, a Nazi, aims at London. Bond saves the city but surprisingly doesn't get the girl, Gala Brand. Bond is thirty-seven in the book; Roger Moore is fifty-two when he plays him.

In the movie, Drax commands a fleet of *Moonraker* space shuttles from his orbiting space station. He intends to release a lethal nerve gas that will destroy Earth's population and replace it with a "super race" of "perfect physical specimens." Teamed with a smart, beautiful CIA agent (Lois Chiles), Bond survives a deadly centrifuge spin, a giant-snake wrestling match, two boat chases, and an aerial-cable-car battle. He also says, "My name is Bond, James Bond," sleeps with three different women, and gets the girl. Thankfully, some traditions don't change.

Lois Chiles and Roger Moore.

ADDED ATTRACTION: The Iceman Cometh

With its big budget and audience-wowing action, *Moonraker* represents one end of the science-fiction spectrum. Light-years away is *Quintet*, a slow, lugubrious sci-fi snoozer that drew big yawns and sparse attendance earlier that year. Any interest incited by the principals—director Robert Altman and leading man Paul Newman—is overwhelmed by the sheer boredom generated by an incoherent plot involving a never-explained board game called Quintet. Future Earth has become a frozen wasteland, its raggedy inhabitants huddle in a ruined city, and Quintet is "the only thing of value." Newman's character wanders in from the ice and soon realizes that all the Quintet players are being killed off. Figuring his days are numbered, he tries to understand the game's meaning, but "searching," he's ultimately told (and we finally concede), "is pointless." Impenetrable discussions about "the unknown" and how the game "is life itself" clarify nothing, and one exasperated character bravely admits, "I don't know what you're talking about." Bizarrely, Altman shot most scenes through a gel-smeared lens that blurs the screen's edges, either to replicate the frosty atmosphere or to soothe the viewer's sleepy eyes. Altman's adamantine fans passionately defend *Quintet* as a bold existential experiment, but we were baffled in 1979 and still are. Two months later Altman's *A Perfect Couple* was another disappointment. Altman had kicked off 1970 with the January release of *M*A*S*H*, his best movie, and he had filled his busy decade with notables like *McCabe & Mrs. Miller* (1971), *Nashville* (1975) and others, but he left the '70s with two of his worst movies, taking him from *M*A*S*H* to *C*R*A*S*H*.

Breaking Away

Released: July 1979
Director: Peter Yates
Stars: Dennis Christopher, Dennis Quaid, Daniel Stern
Academy Awards: One win (Best Writing), plus four more nominations (Best Picture; Best Supporting Actress—Barbara Barrie; Best Director; Best Music)

PREVIEW: Four friends decide to compete in a long-distance bike race against snobby rivals.

NOW SHOWING: *Tutto Bene, un Film Fantastico*!

Without going all kumbaya on you, we clearly recall that in 1979 the ending of *Breaking Away* inspired the theater audience around us to stand and cheer in unison. Even the movie's villain smiles and applauds the outcome, it's that joyous.

The very definition of a feel-good hit, this warm, witty, intelligent movie is one of the decade's highlights and is a top candidate for the Best Sports Movie award. Like another great coming-of-age movie, *American Graffiti* (1973), it presents four young guys who are on the brink of big decisions in a rural town that is vividly rendered. Both movies culminate with a dramatic race (*Graffiti*'s quarter-mile sprint lasts only twenty seconds, while *Breaking Away*'s marathon spans a hundred miles and twelve minutes). And both movies put a mostly no-name cast into wonderfully written scenes that are thrilling, or hilarious, or poignant.

Breaking Away's working-class guys contend with the rich frat boys from nearby Indiana University. Early conflicts finally play out at the annual Little 500 bike race.

Memorable moments lead up to the exciting finish-line duel: the "townie" Dave (Dennis Christopher) chasing the elite girl to deliver her notebook, for instance, and later serenading her in Italian as she watches from her sorority-house window. Or his attempt to "draft" the Cinzano truck on Interstate-69 so he can hit sixty mph on his bike, a beautifully paced four minutes with no dialogue, just suspense and satisfaction when he catches his dream. There's heartbreak, too, like the hard "everybody cheats" lesson Dave learns when he finally meets his Italian heroes. Plus there are wise, entertaining parents, something *Graffiti* doesn't have; one parent (Barbara Barrie) got an Oscar nomination, and the other (Paul Dooley) got robbed.

Dennis Christopher.

After countless viewings we're still struggling to find flaws. Dave's training session inside the car wash? A little far-fetched. Maybe the race results aren't very surprising, what with the lovable underdogs dressed in white, but other Davids had lost to Goliaths in *The Bad News Bears* (1976) and *Rocky* (1976), so perhaps we're too quick to predict. Also, after the race half the guys remain stuck in their routine lives (two really do break away: Dave starts college, and one guy gets married, though he's broke and seems unemployable). Resolutions for all four would've been nice. That's all we've got. Any movie that's seriously comparable to *American Graffiti* must be a winner, and *Breaking Away* is, in every way.

ADDED ATTRACTION: Surf's Up

Three months before *Breaking Away*, Dennis Christopher starred in an unsuccessful coming-of-age movie called *California Dreaming* (1979). A geek from Chicago who can "always manage to say something ridiculous," he comes to a cool little California beach town to pick up the surfin' vibe. He clumsily tries to use words like "copacetic" and wears black shoes and socks at the beach until the locals help him fit in. The movie awkwardly mixes tones: the first half weakly emulates the 1960s Frankie-and-Annette beach comedies (though it shows more skin and doesn't have as much spirited fun), while the second half steers toward melodrama and even kills off a key character. Bummers: an embarrassing bathroom encounter and a slobbery make-out scene are simply awful. Bitchen: the surfing footage and the town's nostalgic surf culture had us totally stoked. Where *California Dreaming* really excels is with its BPM's: the movie's blondes-per-minute ratio is amazing, both from the guys and girls.

The Amityville Horror

Released: July 1979
Director: Stuart Rosenberg
Stars: James Brolin, Margot Kidder, Rod Steiger
Academy Awards: One nomination (Best Music)

PREVIEW: A family moves to a house with a murderous history and has frightening experiences.

NOW SHOWING: Amity Calamity

The Amityville Horror (1979) is a perplexing movie. On the one hand, it was an enormous blockbuster, spawning numerous sequels and attracting legions of devoted fans who nostalgically recall its scariest moments. On the other hand, *The Amityville Horror* is filled with routine horror clichés and unanswered questions.

Based on Jay Anson's novel (itself based on allegedly true events), the movie starts with a motiveless murder spree inside a magnificent house in Amityville, Long Island. A year later (1975), a nice family buys the house, unconcerned about the past: "Houses don't have memories," says George (James Brolin). When the family moves in, they quickly notice eerie little moments, like a room that feels too cold, a bad smell that mom (Margot Kidder) can't identify, and a toilet that overflows with black goo (all things that are fairly explainable). A visiting priest (Rod Steiger) gets the worst of it when he enters the house and houseflies fill the room, followed by a demonic command to "get out!"

Soon the terrors escalate. Doors burst off hinges, windows shatter, a crucifix turns upside-down, a hidden basement room reveals an apparition, and more. On the surreal last night, a red-eyed pig monster glares from an upstairs window, George falls into a slimy pit, and mom briefly looks like a wrinkled hag. Enough's enough: final text tells us the family instantly abandons the house and moves away. Unfortunately, the anti-climactic conclusion leaves the frustrated audience hanging. The bizarre things we've seen for ourselves—the laughable pig beast, the bleeding walls, the basement apparition, etc.—was any of that real, or just imagined? And how is a haunted house able to wreak havoc in other parts of town, as when a priest's car suddenly lurches out of control and a church statue is damaged? There's a brief attempt to suggest that witchcraft was once practiced on the site, but that theory only leads to more questions, like why there haven't been any subsequent supernatural episodes.

James Brolin and Margot Kidder.

All the leads emote strenuously (especially Rod Steiger, the biggest ham outside of a Hormel factory). The best character is the first and last one we see: the expressive house itself, which glows with creepy malevolence. However, the whole enterprise seems too desperate, has too many cheesy red herrings, and is too nonsensical to rank anywhere near the decade's horror classics, especially *The Exorcist* (1973), *The Omen* (1976), and *Carrie* (1976).

ADDED ATTRACTION: Movies Based on Bestsellers

The Amityville Horror was based on Jay Anson's bestselling book from 1977. Dozens of other late-'70s movies were also based on bestselling or classic novels. Here are thirty alphabetically listed American movies from 1975-1979 and the source novels that preceded them. Novels with titles that are different from their later movies are noted.

Movie (Year)	Book's Author (Publication Year)
Barry Lyndon (1975)	*The Luck of Barry Lyndon*, William Makepeace Thackeray (1844)
Being There (1979)	Jerzy Kosinski (1971)
The Betsy (1978)	Harold Robbins (1971)
The Big Sleep (1978)	Raymond Chandler (1939)
Black Sunday (1977)	Thomas Harris (1975)
Breakheart Pass (1976)	Alistair MacLean (1974)
Carrie (1976)	Stephen King (1974)
The Choirboys (1977)	Joseph Wambaugh (1975)
Coma (1978)	Robin Cook (1977)
The Day of the Locust (1975)	Nathanael West (1939)
Demon Seed (1977)	Dean Koontz (1973)
Dracula (1979)	Bram Stoker (1897)
The Fury (1978)	John Farris (1976)
Go Tell the Spartans (1978)	*Incident at Muc Wa*, Daniel Ford (1967)
The Great Santini (1979)	Pat Conroy (1976)
The Island of Doctor Moreau (1977)	H.G. Wells (1896)
Jaws (1975)	Peter Benchley (1974)
The Last Remake of Beau Geste (1977)	*Beau Geste*, P.C. Wren (1924)
Looking for Mr. Goodbar (1977)	Judith Rossner (1975)
Marathon Man (1976)	William Goldman (1974)
92 in the Shade (1975)	Thomas McGuane (1973)
Once Is Not Enough (1975)	Jacqueline Susann (1973)
One Flew Over the Cuckoo's Nest (1975)	Ken Kesey (1962)
The Other Side of Midnight (1977)	Sidney Sheldon (1973)
Saint Jack (1979)	Paul Theroux (1973)
Semi-Tough (1977)	Dan Jenkins (1972)
The Seven-Per-Cent Solution (1976)	Nicholas Meyer (1974)
The Stepford Wives (1975)	Ira Levin (1972)
Winter Kills (1979)	Richard Condon (1974)
Wise Blood (1979)	Flannery O'Connery (1952)

Rock 'n' Roll High School

Released: August 1979
Director: Allan Arkush
Stars: P.J. Soles, Vincent Van Patten, the Ramones
Academy Awards: None

PREVIEW: A young fan of the Ramones will do anything to get the songs she's written to the band.

NOW SHOWING: "Detention for Life"

It wasn't the midnight-movie landmark that *The Rocky Horror Picture Show* (1975) was, but *Rock 'n' Roll High School* (1979) was still a box-office success, and it remains a fan favorite. This Roger Corman-produced cheapie has a lightweight story (a Vince Lombardi High School student will do whatever it takes to get her songs into the hands of her favorite rock group), juvenile comedy (fast-motion, a blow-up doll), and only a couple of witty lines (a highlight: "Do your parents know that you're Ramones," asks the tyrannical principal). It also has some of the elements typical of Corman's productions, such as anti-establishment attitudes, cool cars, and big gratuitous explosions. There's not much you would call "subtle," so we appreciate some of the small, hilarious details, as in the scene twenty-three minutes into the movie when a "Rock-o-meter" machine is used to test decibel levels. The levels are marked with famous '70s names, going from the softest (Debby Boone, Donny & Marie, Kansas) up through the loudest (Led Zeppelin, Ted Nugent, the Stones, etc.). Good times.

The lead girls, energetic super-fan Riff and her smart sidekick Kate, are played by P.J. Soles and Dey Young, two appealing actresses who energize the movie (especially Soles, always in motion and always in wild clothes). And then there are the legendary Ramones, more a force of nature than a punk-rock group. They're all over the soundtrack (along with classics by Alice Cooper, Chuck Berry, and others), and, even better, they perform

The Ramones and P.J. Soles.

live (by playing themselves and performing live, they join other big-name '70s bands who appeared as themselves in late-'70s movies, including the Who in 1975's *Tommy*, Tom Petty and the Heartbreakers in 1978's *FM*, and Aerosmith in 1978's *Sgt. Pepper's Lonely Hearts Club Band*). Here the Ramones play "I Just Wanna Have Something To Do" to a sidewalk crowd and "I Want You Around" in Riff's bedroom. In a rowdy eleven-minute concert they rip through "Blitzkrieg Bop," "Teenage Lobotomy," "California Sun," "Pinhead," and "She's the One." They end up playing "Do You Wanna Dance?" inside the school as motorcycles, soap suds, food fights, football players, and cheerleaders cavort through the halls. The "classic confrontation between mindless authority and the rebellious nature of youth" climaxes with, what else, the Ramones belting out "Rock 'n' Roll High School" as the school explodes. So it doesn't make sense; dumb fun never does. Gabba gabba hey.

ADDED ATTRACTION: How Old Are Those Teenagers?

Born in 1950, P.J. Soles is a twenty-nine-year-old playing a teen who's still in high school in this movie. Here are some other 1975-1979 movies with teenage roles played by grown-up stars (the stars' real ages in the years when their movies came out are in parentheses).

- *Almost Summer* (1978)
  High-schoolers Christine, Kevin, Bobby, and Donna: Lee Purcell (31); Tim Matheson (31); Bruno Kirby (29); Didi Conn (27)
- *American Hot Wax* (1978)
  Teenage Louise: Laraine Newman (26)
- *Annie Hall* (1977)
  High-schooler Annie (in a Chippewa Falls flashback): Diane Keaton (31)
- *The Buddy Holly Story* (1978)
  Buddy Holly (19 at the start of the movie): Gary Busey (34)
- *Capone* (1975)
  Al Capone (19 in early scenes): Ben Gazzara (45)
- *Carrie* (1976)
  High-schooler Carrie: Sissy Spacek (27)
- *Cooley High* (1975)
  Preacher (17): Glynn Turman (28)
- *Corvette Summer* (1978)
  High-schooler Kenneth: Mark Hamill (27)
- *Grease* (1978)
  High-schoolers Rizzo, Sonny, and Sandy: Stockard Channing (34); Michael Tucci (32); Olivia Newton-John (30)
- *Halloween* (1978)
  High-schooler Annie: Nancy Loomis (29)
- *I Wanna Hold Your Hand* (1978)
  High-schooler Pam: Nancy Allen (28)
- *Star Wars* (1977)
  Farm-boy Luke, eager to "transmit" his "application to the academy": Mark Hamill (26)
- *Tommy* (1975)
  Tommy, British schoolboy: Roger Daltrey (31)

Apocalypse Now

(One of 1979's five **FAR-OUT** movies)

Released: August 1979

Director: Francis Ford Coppola

Stars: Martin Sheen, Marlon Brando, Robert Duvall

Academy Awards: Two wins (Best Cinematography; Best Sound), plus six more nominations (Best Picture; Best Supporting Actor—Robert Duvall; Best Director; Best Writing; Best Editing; Best Art Direction)

PREVIEW: In the Vietnam War, an Army captain makes a perilous journey to kill a rogue officer.

FINE LINE: "I was going to the worst place in the world, and I didn't even know it yet. Weeks away and hundreds of miles up a river that snaked through the war like a main circuit cable plugged straight into Kurtz." (Willard's narration nine minutes into the movie; his metaphoric language adds eloquence to this brutal war movie, as do the lines characters quote from Rudyard Kipling's "If" and two T.S. Eliot poems)

CLOSE-UP: There are early clues that what seems like a dark, ominous movie might get crazy and could have some black humor in it. For instance, the song playing at the beginning is literally "The End." Then, in the ten-minute meeting when Willard first hears about Kurtz, two officers played by G.D. Spradlin and Harrison Ford wear nametags identifying two movie directors, Roger Corman and George Lucas. A few minutes later a really offbeat moment arrives when one sailor water skis behind the patrol boat while another sailor dances to the Stones' "(I Can't Get No) Satisfaction."

NOW SHOWING: "Obviously Insane"

Whenever film fans talk about great movies of the 1970s, *Apocalypse Now* (1979) inevitably comes up. A mammoth achievement that routinely appears on "best ever" lists, it's unquestionably one of the decade's monuments of cinematic artistry.

But whenever film fans talk about the most indulgent and excessive movies of the '70s, *Apocalypse Now* again comes up. An audacious spectacle that's both astonishing and at times incoherent, *Apocalypse Now* plays like a fever dream and is the very definition of "daring."

That the movie exists at all is a minor miracle, considering Francis Ford's Coppola's long struggle to overcome set-destroying typhoons, his star's heart attack, and out-of-control costs as he shot over a *million* feet of footage. Echoing *Heart of Darkness*, Joseph Conrad's 1898 masterpiece, Coppola presents a trip up a dark river to expose, as Conrad did, the chaotic results when a civilized nation attempts to impose its will on a remote jungle. Among the many book/movie parallels, Conrad's and Coppola's boat helmsman dies from a spear flung from the riverbank. Both journeys lead to Kurtz, an isolated leader who's gone rogue deep in the jungle (Conrad's Kurtz is a nineteenth-century ivory trader in Africa, Coppola's is a modern U.S. Army colonel in Cambodia). Both stories make Kurtz a madman who's worshipped by natives in a compound decorated with skulls on pikes. Both narrators are greeted by a voluble character who says Kurtz has "enlarged my mind." Both Kurtzes scrawl a message to "exterminate" the natives; both men die whispering "the horror!" Coppola does change Conrad's story, besides updating the setting to the Vietnam War. Conrad's Marlow retrieves Kurtz, though Kurtz dies of sickness on the way back; Coppola's Captain Willard (Martin Sheen) is on a secret mission to "terminate with extreme prejudice," and he kills Kurtz with a machete.

Whether or not movie viewers are even aware of *Heart of Darkness* is immaterial, since most come to see what Coppola's done, not to see what Coppola's done to Conrad's book. It's Coppola's individual scenes, not the overall plot, that make *Apocalypse Now* so memorable.

Martin Sheen.

For example, the movie opens with a dramatic jungle/hotel montage backed by the Doors' haunting "The End." The first person we see, Willard, is shown upside-down, suggesting a skewed view of events to come. It's a startling, tone-setting beginning.

After a meeting to discuss Kurtz's "unsound" methods and Willard's orders, nineteen minutes into the movie we're on the river. Quickly the mission spins into a series of bizarre episodes that illustrate the absurdity of America's involvement in Vietnam. An old-fashioned cavalry bugler initiates a charge, "Ride of the Valkyries" blasts through the skies, and helicopters attack a village, all so soldiers can surf in a combat zone. A wild tiger reminds two modern men how much they don't belong in the jungle. A USO tour presents phallic light towers and three dancing *Playboy* Playmates, not an old-fashioned Bob Hope show. A young sailor under attack crafts the arrow-through-the-head trick, carries a puppy into battle, and declares, "This is better than Disneyland!"

The craziness and bloodshed prepare us for the final forty minutes when Willard at last meets Kurtz. Conrad's Kurtz was skeletal, but Coppola's is immense. Marlon Brando (who gets top billing) is in the movie for only seventeen minutes, but he completely dominates his scenes, which are filmed in deep shadows to illustrate the darkness in his soul. Unfortunately, viewers who've been thinking the movie is a Trojan Horse of impressive entertainment that's holding a profound revelation inside will be disappointed, because the horse is hollow. Kurtz, we've heard, is a powerful warrior, but he surrenders without a fight. Some of his ponderous statements are ambiguous pseudo-philosophical nonsense, proving he's "obviously insane." Accept that, and Kurtz's murky scenes are explicable; expect a clear, powerful lesson to leave with, and you'll be frustrated. We recall a line from *Heart of Darkness*: by including Kurtz's occasional gibberish, Coppola becomes one of those "tellers of tales" who are "unaware of what their audience would best like to hear."

Marlon Brando.

Groping for an ending, Coppola settled on a bad match between the slaying of Kurtz and actual footage of natives slaughtering a water buffalo. Intercut the way the last assassinations in *The Godfather* (1972) were brilliantly paired with a baptism, this gruesome sequence isn't edifying, it's appalling. The final presentation of end credits will depend on which version of the movie you're watching. In the much-hyped initial release, which sold advance tickets like a concert and issued printed programs, there were no end credits beyond a single copyright notice. Later releases added six minutes of traditional credits accompanied by fiery jungle explosions (Coppola's 2001 revision, *Apocalypse Now Redux*, ends without explosions).

Viewers and critics (including Gene Siskel and Roger Ebert, who vigorously argued opposite sides on TV) have been debating *Apocalypse Now* since its premiere. We've come away from our many viewings with the sense that the movie, for all its fascinating scenes and quotable lines, loses its way in its last third. Yet we're still mesmerized, because Coppola understands that movies are an experiential medium. *Apocalypse Now* isn't the decade's best film—it isn't even the decade's best Francis Ford Coppola film—but it is an essential experience. Conrad and Coppola both include the statement that Kurtz can't be judged like "an ordinary man." Likewise, *Apocalypse Now*, bold, riveting, and flawed, can't be judged like an ordinary movie.

ADDED ATTRACTION: Apocalypse Then

Nominated for 1979's Best Documentary Oscar, *The War at Home* (1979) shows the anti-war protests in America from 1963 to 1973. The focus is on Madison, Wisconsin, a sleepy "all-American town" known as a "hotbed of lethargy" that gets turned into "a war zone" by "an outright revolution." A 1966 take-over of the University of Wisconsin's Administration Building is relatively peaceful, but a year later a Dow Chemical protest escalates to violence and tear gas. A 1969 war protest includes fire bombings, and then, most tragically, a 1970 detonation inside an on-campus research building kills an innocent victim. Blending interviews with the participants, Vietnam combat scenes, archival footage from the '60s, and music by Bob Dylan and "The Ballad of the Green Beret," *The War at Home* is an informative and important movie.

Starting Over

Released: October 1979
Director: Alan J. Pakula
Stars: Burt Reynolds, Jill Clayburgh, Candice Bergen
Academy Awards: Two nominations (Best Actress—Jill Clayburgh; Best Supporting Actress—Candice Bergen)

PREVIEW: A divorced man begins a new relationship, but then his ex-wife decides to come back.

NOW SHOWING: Fresh Start

Starting Over (1979) isn't just this movie's title; it's also a description of career moves. This was screenwriter James L. Brooks's first movie after a successful decade in television (he co-created *The Mary Tyler Moore Show*, among others), and it put him on the path to the first movie he'd direct, the Oscar-winning *Terms of Endearment* (1983). Similarly, *Starting Over* was a major digression for Burt Reynolds. Ditching the macho strutting (and

Candice Bergen, Burt Reynolds, and Jill Clayburgh.

occasional moustache) of *Deliverance* (1972), *The Longest Yard* (1974), and *Smokey and the Bandit* (1977), Reynolds goes calm and sensitive as Phil Potter, a writer going through a divorce and tentatively starting to date again, which means awkward fix-ups, membership in a support group, and lots of '70s phrases about growth, self-awareness and "getting to know yourself."

Reynolds is thoroughly appealing as an easy-going, vulnerable man who gets so stressed he hyperventilates and collapses in public. The only time Reynolds breaks character comes forty-six minutes into the movie when he uncharacteristically plays a prank, resorts to his signature cackle, and cockily says this rascally behavior shows his "best side." The cackle is jarring and wrong, the statement is false, and for a moment Reynolds seems to be serving his typical good-ol'-boy audience, not the thoughtful, mature character he's created so far.

Most of the time, though, Reynolds smartly underplays, which puts the spotlight on the two women in his life. Candice Bergen is the dazzling, self-assured ex-wife who announces she wants to reunite via a strident love song she's written. Unfortunately, she's a jaw-droppingly awful singer, so it's hilarious watching this caterwauling character give it her all. Jill Clayburgh, meanwhile, plays Potter's nervous plain-Jane girlfriend. Completely de-glamorized, she's dunked repeatedly in a pool and in one emotional scene has a runny nose worthy of Regan in *The Exorcist* (1973). When she and Potter break up, she gets into an inauthentic chemistry-deficient relationship with a dufus basketball player, but she returns for the happy-ever-after ending the audience has been rooting for. Both actresses are terrific, and both got well-deserved Oscar nominations.

That Potter ultimately rejects the stunning ex- for the quirky newcomer reminds us of another movie about a low-key writer facing a similar choice, *The Accidental Tourist* (1988). Both of these intelligent, well-written movies were made for adults and represent the kind of graceful, sophisticated romantic comedies and dramas that now seem to be on the endangered-species list.

ADDED ATTRACTION: "Super-duper Hooper"

A year before *Starting Over*, Reynolds starred in two vastly different comedies. Critics and audiences weren't really ready for *The End* (1978), a satirical black comedy that Reynolds directed and starred in as a man with a fatal disease who repeatedly tries to kill himself. The starry cast includes Sally Field, Joanne Woodward, and Carl Reiner, but they couldn't pull this unusual movie up to the blockbuster levels of Reynolds' biggest hits. Two months later Reynolds played a more familiar character in *Hooper*, a simple-but-good action movie that became one of 1978's top box-office successes. Teamed once again with Sally Field, and unleashing his high-pitched cackle every few minutes, Reynolds plays "Super-duper Hooper," a swaggering Hollywood stuntman who's confronting pain, age, and younger competition represented by studly Jan-Michael Vincent. Directed by Hal Needham, the legendary stuntman who directed Reynolds in *Smokey and the Bandit* (1977), *Hooper* is filled with awesome "gags" (stunts), especially in an explosive four-minute climax that culminates with a rocket-powered Trans-Am soaring over a river.

10

Released: October 1979
Director: Blake Edwards
Stars: Dudley Moore, Bo Derek, Julie Andrews
Academy Awards: Two nominations (Best Song, Best Music)

PREVIEW: A successful middle-aged man obsesses over a younger woman who is on her honeymoon.

NOW SHOWING: The Heartbreak Man

In *The Heartbreak Kid* (1972), a young newlywed on his seaside honeymoon falls for a beautiful single woman and finds contentment. In *10* (1979), an older single man pursues a beautiful newlywed who's on her seaside honeymoon and finds disappointment. What's the lesson, that romantic comedies had soured by decade's end? Seems plausible. Years of war, political scandal, social upheavals and drugs can knock the exuberance right out of adults who are chasing their romantic fantasies.

Culturally speaking, there's no contest between the two movies, because *10* was by far the bigger hit (one of 1979's biggest), and it made a much stronger impression. Dudley Moore and Bo Derek became stars, Ravel's *Boléro* aroused whole new audiences, and everyone started ranking everything, especially potential mates, on a one-to-ten scale. Impact-wise, *10* was an 11.

Director Blake Edwards had already made a terrific movie with a serious theme, *Days of Wine and Roses* (1962), followed by a long streak of lightweight comedies, including three 1975-1978 *Pink Panther* movies. Edwards goes semi-serious in *10* with a story about forty-two-year-old George Webber (Moore), a rich composer with a lovely, caring girlfriend, a Malibu beach house, a Rolls-Royce, and a midlife crisis. Feeling "betrayed" because his successful life somehow isn't *better*, he pursues "a vision" who's on her Mexican honeymoon (the vision, Bo Derek, is in the movie for about twenty-six minutes and isn't given much to do besides looking like a bronze goddess and jogging in slow-motion). One heroic act lands George in the bride's bed, where he's turned off by the casual sex she invites, so back he goes to Malibu and true love.

Webber's struggle to find middle-age meaning would be more endearing if he were more admirable. While he's talented and witty, he's also a heavy drinker and a peeping Tom, he uses degrading terms for women and gays, he has multiple affairs and joins an orgy, and he's described as "unnaturally belligerent, exhaustingly childish." That he emerges much better off at the end than he was at the beginning seems wrong. Audiences, though, surrendered to the abundant slapstick humor (the scenes with a

Bo Derek.

Novocaine-numbed Webber, and his awkward stumbles across scorching sand, are hilarious). *10* gets points for style and smiles, but it loses them with its two-hour length and its heavy-handed attempts to be socially meaningful. To fans who claim *10*'s a ten, we ask, "Out of what?"

ADDED ATTRACTION: Iconic Movie Hairstyles of the 1970s

Bo Derek's cornrows in *10* were instantly recognized as one of the decade's most distinctive and influential hairstyles. The next ten chronologically listed movies from the 1970s also presented actresses with a flair for hair.

- *Love Story* (1970): Ali MacGraw's straight, flat, lustrous hair.
- *Klute* (1971): Jane Fonda's revolutionary shag.
- *The Omega Man* (1971): Rosalind Cash's awesome Afro.
- *Cabaret* (1972): Liza Minnelli's short, sharp haircut.
- *The Great Gatsby* (1974): Mia Farrow's wavy bob (that's what she wore when she landed on *People* magazine's first cover March 4, 1974).
- *Shampoo* (1975): Julie Christie's dramatic shoulder-length cut.
- *Logan's Run* (1976): Farrah Fawcett's famous feathered hairstyle, debuted three months earlier on TV's *Charlie's Angels*.
- *Star Wars* (1977): Carrie Fisher's coiled "headphones," one of the most famous (and most parodied) hairstyles in movie history.
- *Grease* (1978): Olivia Newton-John's bad-girl makeover replaced her bangs and ponytail with big wrangly curls.
- *Manhattan* (1979): Meryl Streep's thick side-swept hair, cascading over one shoulder.

The Black Stallion

Released: October 1979
Director: Carroll Ballard
Stars: Kelly Reno, Mickey Rooney, Teri Garr
Academy Awards: One win (Special Achievement Award for Sound Editing), plus two more nominations (Best Supporting Actor—Mickey Rooney; Best Editing)

PREVIEW: A boy and a wild stallion survive a sea disaster and then train for an important race.

NOW SHOWING: Black, the Stallion

Joining the long list of egregious Oscar oversights during the 1970s—the non-nominations for performances by Dustin Hoffman in *Little Big Man* (1970), by Ruth Gordon in *Harold and Maude* (1971), and by Robert Shaw in *Jaws* (1975), plus the omissions of *Badlands* (1973), *Close Encounters of the Third Kind* (1977), and *Alien* (1979) as Best Picture nominees—was one of 1979's most gorgeous visual experiences, *The Black Stallion*. We first watched this dazzling movie in a theater alongside a spellbound audience that sat with mouths half-open. Cinematographer Caleb Deschanel's non-nomination for an Oscar suggests a ballot-counting malfunction, or something equally ridiculous.

Based on Walter Farley's classic children's book, *The Black Stallion* DVD is typically found in the children's section of libraries. Adults, however, will fully appreciate its wonders, though they'll see the clichéd David-vs.-Goliath ending coming way before the homestretch. In the movie's magical first half, a 1946 shipwreck lands two survivors, young Alec (Kelly Reno) and an unruly stallion, on a deserted Mediterranean island. This section is almost dreamlike, with Alec and the horse (called Black) saving each other's lives and gradually forming an unbreakable bond ("gradually" is the operative word here—the horse is fast, but this two-hour movie isn't). The first-half highlight is a seven-minute sequence of the two strangers parrying gingerly, finally becoming friends, and galloping joyously through shallow surf. We clocked twenty-eight minutes with no words, just subtle sounds and stunning poster-worthy images of sunsets, silhouettes, mesmerizing underwater movements, and panoramic vistas. This movie also features the best acting by an animal since Ben the rat turned evil in *Willard* (1971).

Once Italian fishermen discover the pair and return them to civilization, events become more predictable, especially for anyone who's seen *National Velvet* (1944). Mickey Rooney, who had a similar role in *Velvet* (a wall photo even shows Rooney in that movie), trains Alec and Black for a prestigious match race. Long-distance shots of the tiny boy and lone horse training on the vast racetrack emphasize the epic scale of their challenge. The climactic four-minute sprint presents the best horseracing footage since *The Reivers* (1969), and the thrilling finish equals the bike-race finale in *Breaking Away* (1979). Everything's done with so much grace and beauty—the end credits include a lingering shot of the decade's best rainbow, a rare double—that critics and audiences haven't just praised *The Black Stallion*, they've treasured it.

ADDED ATTRACTION: The NFPB's NFR

Since 1989, the National Film Preservation Board has added movies to its National Film Registry. Up to twenty-five "culturally, historically, or aesthetically significant films" join the list each year. *The Black Stallion* was added in 2002; here are other 1975-1979 feature films included in the NFPB's NFR, grouped by the years when the movies were released.

- **1975:** *Dog Day Afternoon, Hester Street, Jaws, Nashville, One Flew Over the Cuckoo's Nest, The Rocky Horror Picture Show*
- **1976:** *All the President's Men, Network, The Outlaw Josey Wales, Please, Don't Bury Me Alive!, Rocky, Taxi Driver*
- **1977:** *Annie Hall, Close Encounters of the Third Kind, Eraserhead, Saturday Night Fever, Star Wars*
- **1978:** *Animal House, Days of Heaven, The Deer Hunter, Girlfriends, Halloween, Killer of Sheep, Superman*
- **1979:** *Alien, All That Jazz, Apocalypse Now, Being There, Boulevard Nights, Manhattan, The Muppet Movie, Norma Rae*

Meteor

Released: October 1979
Director: Ronald Neame
Stars: Sean Connery, Natalie Wood, Karl Malden
Academy Awards: One nomination (Best Sound)

PREVIEW: America and Russia fire nuclear missiles at a huge meteor due to collide with Earth.

NOW SHOWING: Meteocre

By 1979 the disaster-movie genre was on life-support. The late entries trying to revive it included *Avalanche* (1978), producer Roger Corman's failed attempt to relocate the usual disaster elements—an arrogant executive (here a ski-resort owner who ignores "unstable snow" warnings), couples in turbulent relationships, cute kids, etc.—to a scenic Colorado setting that gets buried under snow, rocks, and Styrofoam. The last half-hour adds additional dangers (including an ambulance-over-a-bridge explosion) before sorting out the survivors, among them Rock Hudson and Mia Farrow. Unlike previous disaster movies, *Avalanche* is short and has some nudity. Critics and audiences were unimpressed. Next, in mid-1979 *City on Fire* reunited Shelley Winters and Leslie Nielsen from *The Poseidon Adventure* (1972) for another go at the disaster genre. Henry Fonda and Ava Gardner also punch the clock in this cliché-filled story about a disgruntled ex-employee who ignites a refinery that's in the *center* of an unnamed city. The fast-spreading fire threatens a hospital near the refinery (what genius planned this burg?) and turns the sky orange. A baby is delivered, kids are rescued, troubled relationships are mended—you know the disaster drill. Though *City on Fire* might have the most pyrotechnics of any '70s movie, anyone who's seen *The Towering Inferno* (1974) probably leaves with a been-there-burned-that feeling.

The genre's last gasp of the decade really put the "disaster" in "disaster movie." Instead of a mere ski resort or a single city, *Meteor* ambitiously imperils the entire planet with an incoming five-mile-wide meteor. Unlike the fast-moving spacecraft and state-of-the-art effects in *Star Wars* (1977), *Meteor* crawls along at a sluggish pace and offers bargain-basement effects, including avalanche scenes snipped directly from *Avalanche*. On the ground, there's too much talk and too many shots of people watching screens; up in space, the big rock tumbles in slow-motion, and the missiles launched to intercept it move like they're stuck in first gear. Mid-movie some meteor "splinters" push a tidal wave onto Hong Kong and blast through Manhattan, leading to stock footage of collapsing skyscrapers. The movie's budget, evidently, went to salaries for Sean Connery (under an obvious toupee), Natalie Wood (a Russian astrophysicist who's actually speaking Russian), and Henry Fonda (the president, as in 1964's *Fail-Safe*). The budding Connery/Wood romance? That's a disappointing *nyet*. Ironically, director Ronald Neame, whose *The Poseidon Adventure* helped bring the genre to life in 1972, helps make it flatline as the decade ends.

ADDED ATTRACTION: More 1975-1979 Movies with All-Star Casts

The "all-star cast" wasn't a new marketing technique, of course. *Airport* (1970) and *That's Entertainment!* (1974) are examples of 1970-1974 movies packed with movie stars. The tradition continued in the late 1970s with *Meteor* and nine other movies.

- *Airport '77* (1977): Joseph Cotton, Olivia de Havilland, Lee Grant, George Kennedy, Christopher Lee, Jack Lemmon, James Stewart
- *Apocalypse Now* (1979): Marlon Brando, Robert Duvall, Harrison Ford, Frederic Forrest, Dennis Hopper, Martin Sheen
- *A Bridge Too Far* (1977): Dirk Bogarde, James Caan, Michael Caine, Sean Connery, Elliott Gould, Gene Hackman, Anthony Hopkins, Laurence Olivier, Ryan O'Neal, Robert Redford, Maximilian Schell, Liv Ullmann
- *Death on the Nile* (1978): Bette Davis, Mia Farrow, George Kennedy, Angela Lansbury, David Niven, Maggie Smith, Peter Ustinov
- *Meteor* (1979): Sean Connery, Henry Fonda, Trevor Howard, Martin Landau, Karl Malden, Natalie Wood
- *Midway* (1976): James Coburn, Henry Fonda, Glenn Ford, Charlton Heston, Robert Mitchum, Cliff Robertson, Robert Wagner
- *Network* (1976): Ned Beatty, Faye Dunaway, Robert Duvall, Peter Finch, William Holden
- *1941* (1979): Dan Aykroyd, John Belushi, James Caan, John Candy, Christopher Lee, Tim Matheson, Toshirô Mifune, Robert Stack
- *Silent Movie* (1976): Anne Bancroft, Mel Brooks, James Caan, Sid Caesar, Marty Feldman, Liza Minnelli, Paul Newman, Bernadette Peters
- *The Swarm* (1978): Michael Caine, Richard Chamberlain, Olivia de Havilland, José Ferrer, Henry Fonda, Lee Grant, Ben Johnson, Fred MacMurray, Katharine Ross, Richard Widmark

The Great Santini

Released: October 1979

Director: Lewis John Carlino

Stars: Robert Duvall, Blythe Danner, Michael O'Keefe

Academy Awards: Two nominations (Best Actor—Robert Duvall; Best Supporting Actor—Michael O'Keefe)

PREVIEW: A tough Marine exerts rigid discipline on his family, especially on his oldest son.

NOW SHOWING: Father Knows Best

After audiences had gotten used to wise, caring fathers on TV shows—*Father Knows Best*, *The Brady Bunch*, etc.—and in movies—*To Kill a Mockingbird* (1962), even *The Godfather* (1972)—*The Great Santini* (1979) unleashed a domineering father whose discipline is so strict his children call him "Godzilla" and "King Kong." At work, Bull Meechum is The Great Santini (his *"nom de guerre"*), a top fighter pilot who brags that he's "the meanest toughest screamingest squadron commander in the Marine Corps" (there's no combat, though there are eight minutes aloft in F-4 Phantoms). At home, Meechum enforces his fierce take-no-prisoners, win-at-all-costs attitude on his pretty wife and four capable kids. He makes them all address him as colonel or sir, he orders morning "inspections," he's so competitive he cheats in family games, and he announces he wants to give his sons "the gift of fury." It's as if *The Great Santini* is revealing the home life of the gruff general in *Patton* (1970) or the caustic drill sergeant in *Full Metal Jacket* (1987), other men better at war than at peace. We won't see tougher parenting until axe-wielding Jack Torrance hunts young Danny in *The Shining* (1980).

The cast makes *The Great Santini* truly great. Robert Duvall, already well-known for playing vital supporting characters in landmarks like *M*A*S*H* (1970), *The Godfather*, *Network* (1976), and *Apocalypse Now* (1979), expands a potentially one-note monster into a multi-dimensional human being. The ugliest moments—flinging a basketball seventeen times at his eighteen-year-old son's head and mercilessly taunting him, embarrassingly storming onto a basketball court during a game and bullying his son into violence, and drunkenly brawling with his entire family—are balanced by laughing frat-boy antics with his brother officers, boisterous sing-alongs on family trips, and an intense five-minute scene when Meechum finally breaks down and cries. We don't *admire* this tempestuous, hard-charging man who's more commanding officer than father, but Duvall makes us *know* him. Equally stellar are Blythe Danner, who delicately balances support for her husband with her commitment to hold the family together, and Oscar-nominated Michael O'Keefe, who's outstanding in his star-making role as the sensitive son frequently targeted by Meechum (O'Keefe's also a convincing basketball player, just as he'll be a convincing golfer in 1980's *Caddyshack*).

The Great Santini is a tough, honest, well-made movie that ranks with *Norma Rae*, *Kramer vs. Kramer*, and just a few others as the elite dramas of 1979.

ADDED ATTRACTION: Playoff Contender

North Dallas Forty was another strong drama in theaters in the fall of 1979. Like *The Great Santini*, it's dominated by an actor giving a career-highlight performance in a macho role, here Nick Nolte as an aging pro-football star. His body "twisted and scarred," Nolte's character lives with so much pain that he constantly drinks, gulps pain pills, and takes numbing injections. Despite some wild party scenes and occasional humor, there's more bitterness than celebration as all the players deal with injuries and callous, manipulative owners. *North Dallas Forty* bucks traditional sports-movie clichés: the focus is on behind-the-scenes team meetings, practices, and locker-room preparation, not the actual games; the team is a front-runner, not an underdog; there's no thrilling come-from-behind championship victory; and the hero's career ends in humiliation. Disappointingly, the big final game is played in a darkened, virtually empty stadium instead of a celebratory Super Bowl-like setting, and the game is shorter (and only slightly more violent) than the one the doctors played at the end of *M*A*S*H* (1970). Still, the rest of this entertaining movie feels totally authentic, and it effectively conveys the passion and power of the most ferocious players, especially the two outrageous brutes played by Bo Svenson and real-life NFL star John Matuszak.

The Rose

Released: November 1979

Director: Mark Rydell

Stars: Bette Midler, Alan Bates, Frederic Forrest

Academy Awards: Four nominations (Best Actress—Bette Midler; Best Supporting Actor—Frederic Forrest; Best Editing; Best Sound)

PREVIEW: The excessive demands made on an exhausted rock star push her to total destruction.

NOW SHOWING: Bette Blossoms

When we meet Rose, she's already starting to wither. In the first six minutes of *The Rose* (1979), Mary Rose Foster, an overworked rock star played with unrestrained passion by Bette Midler, quickly goes from drunkenly stumbling out of a jet to commanding a concert stage to begging her manager for the long vacation that never comes, thanks to tour commitments and the outrageous money to be made. Her movie-long descent to complete destruction is marked by reckless behavior, liquor, drugs, and other decadent excesses already seen in two other '70s dramas showcasing talented divas, 1972's *Lady Sings the Blues* and 1976's *A Star Is Born* (*The Rose* nods to both movies in a scene when drag queens briefly perform as Diana Ross and Barbra Streisand). Compared to those other movies, *The Rose* is closer in spirit to the first because Midler's warts-and-all character, like Ross's Billie Holiday, is far rougher than Streisand's dignified Esther.

The Rose is about a train wreck, and Midler is utterly convincing as the hurtling train. It's not Midler's first movie, but it's the one that established her as a major star after she'd conquered popular music, television, and the stage (by 1979 she'd already won a Grammy, an Emmy, and a Special Tony Award). Rose, very loosely modeled after Janis Joplin, is a profane, volatile force of nature who instantly shifts from tearful vulnerability to uncensored fury. Fired ninety-two

Bette Midler.

minutes into the movie, she careens through hurt/helpless/crying/angry/romantic/happy/intimate emotions, all as the same complex person in one impressive four-minute scene. And like Ross in *Lady*, Midler is willing to look bad—makeup running, hair untamed—when her anguished character crashes.

Some viewers criticize the clichéd melodrama (naturally Rose has to die onstage during her final concert), our superficial understanding of the root causes of her dissipation (her hometown and parents seem pretty normal), and the 134-minute length. But *The Rose*'s music overwhelms these thorny issues. Midler sings for almost a third of the movie, and she's riveting. She revs up hard-driving songs like a whirling Tasmanian devil and aches with raw pain in the slow, heartfelt numbers. Using an all-star team of Oscar-winning/Oscar-nominated cinematographers, director Mark Rydell has fashioned an entertaining movie about "one of the best singer-ladies in the history of the world, pure and simple," as Rose is called. Operating at the height of her magnificent powers in 1979, that might've been Midler, too.

ADDED ATTRACTION: The Minor Event

Diana Ross didn't make a movie in 1979, but Barbra Streisand sure did, in fact she even co-produced it. *The Main Event* is an amusing romantic comedy that reteams her with Ryan O'Neal seven years after their zany *What's Up, Doc?* (1972). Like *Doc*, *Event* was a box-office smash, but unlike *Doc*, *Event* underwhelmed many reviewers. Streisand plays an energetic businesswoman who holds the contract on an out-of-shape boxer (O'Neal). She orchestrates a big fight, he trains diligently, they bicker before falling in love—everything's pretty predictable, except for the preposterous ending (imagine if Streisand's character had ripped up O'Neal's hard-won check at the end of *What's Up, Doc?*) and the many playful "nose" references (for example, Streisand's company makes Le Nez perfume, and someone tells her, "They don't call you The Nose for nothing!"). The exercise class, Streisand's short-shorts and gravity-defying perm, the big Ford station wagons with wood-panel sides, and the disco theme song all help make *The Main Event* a movie of its time, but it's too long and has too many arguments and punchless jokes to be a knockout comedy for *all* time.

Star Trek: The Motion Picture

Released: December 1979
Director: Robert Wise
Stars: William Shatner, Leonard Nimoy, DeForest Kelley
Academy Awards: Three nominations (Best Art Direction; Best Visual Effects; Best Music)

PREVIEW: The *Enterprise* is sent to oppose a menacing energy cloud that is approaching Earth.

NOW SHOWING: Slow-Motion

To the delight of fans across the galaxy, *Star Trek*, the 1960s TV show, finally became *Star Trek*, the 1979 big-budget movie. Perhaps the primary lure of *Star Trek: The Motion Picture* was its familiar cast, but the real reward was the spectacular Oscar-nominated imagery, which dazzles like an updated version of the magnificent *2001: A Space Odyssey* (1968). Both epics showcase stately, gleaming vessels and metaphysical wonders of the universe; both should be seen on the largest screen possible.

Unfortunately, *Star Trek*'s vessels and visuals serve a sluggish plot. After a dramatic opening sequence that shows a new alien adversary (a menacing energy cloud) destroying the old alien adversary (the Klingons), everything downshifts into slow-motion: thirty-six minutes for the new-and-improved *Enterprise* to depart; thirteen more for Spock to beam aboard; a total of eighty-two minutes to name the main opponent, V'Ger, with fifty minutes still to go. Only die-hards can contentedly trek that long.

Director Robert Wise was a sci-fi veteran (1971's *The Andromeda Strain*), but he was also a long-movie veteran (1966's *The Sand Pebbles*, a whopping 182 minutes). In *Star Trek*, Wise indulges in a four-minute appreciation of the *Enterprise*'s exterior and a ten-minute drift through the alien cloud's interior. This leisurely approach could've worked had the story been riveting, but it's not. It's certainly ambitious, involving a protracted search for the ultimate "Creator" with evolutionary implications, but it becomes nonsensical once the helmetless team walks out of the *Enterprise* in deep space and hotwires a "living machine" so it can "physically join with a human." Even Captain Kirk (William Shatner) calls the plot developments "absolutely incredible." Exactly, as in "absolutely not credible."

Leonard Nimoy, William Shatner, and DeForest Kelley.

Happily, all the TV characters return, like old friends after a long vacation. Kirk looks fit and well-touped, Spock (Leonard Nimoy) initially has shaggy hair, and McCoy (DeForest Kelley) arrives fully bearded. They're as forceful/odd/cranky as ever, though now everybody sports twenty-third-century unisex uniforms. Especially notable is the movie's powerhouse music, courtesy of the prolific Jerry Goldsmith (he also scored that year's *Alien* and *twenty-two* additional 1975-1979 movies). So there are enjoyable elements in *Star Trek: The Motion Picture*, as there would be in anything this massive and expensive. That point was proved exactly one week later with the release of *1941* (1979), another labored, intermittently entertaining movie that was probably more exciting in the studio pitch meeting than it was in the theater.

ADDED ATTRACTION: Time for *Time After Time*

After the rocketing success of *Star Wars* (1977) and *Close Encounters of the Third Kind* (1977), studios launched a fleet of science-fiction movies. In 1979 *Star Trek*, *Alien*, *The Black Hole*, and *Meteor* followed in the *Star Wars*/*Close Encounters* slipstream. Dwarfed by those mega-movies is *Time After Time* (1979), a smaller but thoroughly engaging sci-fi thriller that's the anti-*Star Wars*: there are no space battles or alien creatures, just a brisk story told with wit and inventiveness by writer/director Nicholas Meyer. The movie matches the notorious Jack the Ripper (David Warner) against the sci-fi writer H.G. Wells (Malcolm McDowell) after the Ripper uses a nineteenth-century time machine, the one Wells had written about in his 1895 novel, to hide in twentieth-century San Francisco, where he's no longer a "freak," just an "amateur." The Victorian Wells follows the Ripper into the future and gives chase through the modern city. He's amusingly befuddled by the world of 1979, and even finds love, before confronting his quarry in a final showdown.

1941

Released: December 1979
Director: Steven Spielberg
Stars: John Belushi, Dan Aykroyd, Tim Matheson
Academy Awards: Three nominations (Best Cinematography; Best Sound; Best Visual Effects)

PREVIEW: Soon after Pearl Harbor, people in L.A. panic when they think they're under attack.

NOW SHOWING: Bombs Away

Having conquered the thriller with *Duel* (1971), the adventure movie with *Jaws* (1975), and the sci-fi epic with *Close Encounters of the Third Kind* (1977), boy-wonder director Steven Spielberg decided to tackle another genre, the sprawling big-cast slapstick comedy, with *1941* (1979). Unfortunately, like acclaimed director Stanley Kramer with his bloated *It's a Mad, Mad, Mad, Mad World* (1963), Spielberg delivered on the sprawl, the cast, and the slapstick, just not the comedy. For all its big-name stars and spectacular Oscar-nominated effects, *1941* musters only modest, intermittent amusement.

The movie begins with a 141-word crawl about the 1941 Pearl Harbor attack and Southern California's anxious preparations for a follow-up offensive that is supposedly imminent. Then comes one of the few good scenes, a six-minute *Jaws* spoof with that movie's first victim, Susan Backlinie, again getting surprised in the water, this time by a submarine instead of a shark. It's downhill from there. Tim Matheson, playing the same kind of aggressive Casanova who romped through *Animal House* (1978), lamely woos Nancy Allen with what she calls "immature sexual innuendos." "Immature" could be the operative adjective for the entire movie, thanks to its crude bathroom jokes, juvenile blackface gags, and wanton destruction of streets and structures. There are chaotic musical numbers, a few minor cameos (John

Dan Aykroyd.

Landis, Penny Marshall, James Caan, among others), and some familiar faces from *Jaws* (Lorraine Gary and Murray Hamilton, in addition to Backlinie). After scoring Spielberg's *The Sugarland Express* (1974), *Jaws* (1975), and *Close Encounters of the Third Kind* (1977), superstar composer John Williams returns too. None of the people mentioned so far, however, would put *1941* on their highlight reels.

"It's gonna be a long war," says Robert Stack's character, but he could be describing this tedious movie that is hampered by too many subplots and too few legitimate laughs. Admittedly, a bit about lost submariners relying on the tiny compass from a Cracker Jack box is kind of funny, and there's a cute nod to a classic comedy, *It Happened One Night* (1934), when Wendy Jo Sperber flags down a ride by lifting her skirt above her ankle. But more typical is the noisy ending, when for no apparent reason ten screen-filling explosions continue randomly through the closing credits. Spielberg's remarkable career momentum was temporarily slowed by this embarrassing failure, but thankfully the awesome *Raiders of the Lost Ark* (1981) was right around the corner.

ADDED ATTRACTION: Singing Actors, Part Two

Slim Pickens croaks out snippets of two songs in *1941*, a short cowboy ditty and then "Over There." Besides Pickens, these other non-singing actors were not afraid to croon a tune in 1978-1979 movies. For non-singing actors who sang in 1975-1977 movies, see the entry for *At Long Last Love* (1975).

- Dennis Christopher, *Breaking Away* (1979): Riding his bike early in the movie, he sings a minute of a song in Italian, and later he stands in the garden and serenades his beloved as she sits at her window.
- Timothy Dalton, *Sextette* (1978): Mae West joins him for an excruciating rendition of "Love Will Keep Us Together"; later, Dom DeLuise belts out the Beatles' "Honey Pie."
- Richard Dreyfuss, *The Goodbye Girl* (1977): Thirty seconds of "How About You"; also, twice in *The Big Fix* (1978) he sings the children's song "Animal Fair."
- Steve Martin, *The Jerk* (1979): Bernadette Peters teams up with Martin for "You Belong to Me."
- Dudley Moore, *10* (1979): Two minutes of "It's Easy to Say," some of it sung with Julie Andrews.
- Robert Redford, *The Electric Horseman* (1979): He and Jane Fonda sing thirty seconds of "America the Beautiful."
- Nipsey Russell, *The Wiz* (1978): The comedian sings two numbers as the Tinman, including "Slide Some Oil to Me."
- Sylvester Stallone, *Paradise Alley* (1978): Sly growls the movie's opening and closing theme song, "Too Close to Paradise."
- Henry Winkler, *The One and Only* (1978): He playfully sings a comically bad "Getting to Know You."

The Jerk

Released: December 1979
Director: Carl Reiner
Stars: Steve Martin, Bernadette Peters, Catlin Adams
Academy Awards: None

PREVIEW: A naïve simpleton becomes rich and lives extravagantly until he loses everything.

NOW SHOWING: A Wild and Crazy Guy

Released the same weekend as *1941*, *The Jerk* (1979) is a low-budget, generally hilarious comedy that became one of the year's biggest box office hits, making it the opposite of Spielberg's laughless extravaganza. *The Jerk* had a comic genius, Carl Reiner, at the helm (he also appears briefly), and America's hottest comedian, Steve Martin, in his first starring role after he'd been filling arenas with wild-and-crazy antics that included an arrow-through-the-head prop.

The Jerk springboards from Martin's stand-up routine about being "born a poor black child." Martin plays Navin, a white bum in the opening scene who starts recalling the crazy adventures that brought him "wealth, power, and the love of a beautiful woman," which are now all lost. Midway through the movie he suddenly becomes wealthy after inventing a successful gadget. He marries his devoted girlfriend, Marie (Bernadette Peters), splurges on black-velvet paintings and a gaudy mansion, and is enjoying a ridiculously wealthy lifestyle when catastrophic lawsuits leave him bankrupt and alone. A happy ending reunites Navin with Marie, his black family, and his money. It's the classic rags-to-riches-to-rags-to-riches saga.

The movie presents a stream of verbal and physical absurdity without ever bogging down or getting topical. Not everything works, and Martin mugs too much, but there's plenty to enjoy. Fun sight gags (Navin pulling an inflated balloon from his jacket) and nifty jokes pop up continuously (we confess to saying "Ahhh, it's a *profit* deal" for decades). Since Martin is a gifted physical comedian, it's a treat watching him perform various dance numbers. A few jokes are bawdy, a few others—the dog's profane name, a kung fu fight, Navin shambling along with dropped pants—are juvenile. So there's something for every taste. The best scenes are the quiet ones where Reiner reins Martin in, as when Navin and Marie sing a gentle fireside song and Marie finishes on a cornet, or when Navin whispers to Marie as she sleeps. The title's wrong, though. All energy and optimism, Navin is a guileless, simple-minded innocent, not a selfish, obnoxious jerk. A more apt title would've been *The Idiot*, but Dostoyevsky already took it.

Bernadette Peters and Steve Martin.

Martin's first movie is like Woody Allen's early *Bananas* (1971): they're both spirited and uneven, silly and surreal, with clever highlights and a romantic sweetness that point to more sophisticated masterpieces ahead. *The Jerk* successfully puts Martin on the path to his *Annie Hall*, *Roxanne* (1987).

ADDED ATTRACTION:
The One and Only Henry Winkler

There's an actual jerk in the comedy that Carl Reiner directed just before *The Jerk*. Set in the 1950s, *The One and Only* (1978) stars Henry Winkler as a self-absorbed drama student who introduces himself as "the one and only Andy Schmidt" and on a first date announces, "Let's talk about ME!" At inappropriate times he bursts into song, does impressions, and improvises bits. After marrying a sweet girl (Kim Darby), Andy starts scuttling for acting jobs. He ends up as a pro wrestler trying out different personas (including a swastika-wearing Nazi) before settling on "The Lover" in a long blond wig. Winkler, super-cool Fonzie on TV's *Happy Days*, has irrepressible exuberance, but the character is less hilarious than he is obnoxious. This offbeat movie is more notable as the first from screenwriter Steve Gordon; his next (and his directorial debut) would be a little something called *Arthur* (1981), the Oscar-nominated smash hit starring Dudley Moore.

All That Jazz

(One of 1979's five **FAR-OUT** movies)

Released: December 1979

Director: Bob Fosse

Stars: Roy Scheider, Leland Palmer, Ann Reinking

Academy Awards: Four wins (Best Editing; Best Art Direction; Best Costume Design; Best Music), plus five more nominations (Best Picture; Best Actor—Roy Scheider; Best Director; Best Writing; Best Cinematography)

PREVIEW: An overworked director tries to keep up with the stresses intensifying around him.

FINE LINE: "If I die, I'm sorry for all the bad things I did to you. And if I live, I'm sorry for all the bad things I'm gonna do to *you*." (Joe Gideon, apologizing first to his ex-wife, then to his girlfriend, as he heads into surgery.)

CLOSE-UP: Forty-five minutes into the movie, Joe Gideon invites the producers in to see the "Take Off With Us" number he's working on. Next to the group is a blonde dancer, stretching against a vending machine; when one of the producers asks if she would "mind doing that somewhere else," she whispers "sorry" and leaves. That dancer is Nicole Fosse, the sixteen-year-old daughter of Bob Fosse and Gwen Verdon.

NOW SHOWING: "It's Showtime, Folks!"

Had director Bob Fosse not made *Cabaret* (1972), we'd be applauding *All That Jazz* (1979) as the decade's best musical. It's certainly the most radical. Instead of using a traditional storyline with sympathetic characters and the inevitable happy ending, *All That Jazz* subverts all expectations. Some quick examples: the star of this big musical can't really sing or dance (he barely does either), and his character dies in the last scene. *All That Jazz* is a revolutionary, fascinating, sometimes breathtaking work that dazzled audiences (especially those interested in the world of Broadway) and earned nine Oscar nominations. It's the decade's last must-see musical.

Significantly, even though there's much beauty and spectacle to come, the first sound in the movie comes with the screen still dark: coughing. Soon we see Joe Gideon (Roy Scheider) in a morning routine that incorporates Vivaldi, Alka-Seltzer, eye drops, Dexedrine, and a shower (which he takes while he's still smoking), all culminating in a self-starting declaration of "it's showtime, folks!" into the mirror. This ritual occurs only in the first half of the movie, and it comes with more frequency—the second one is twenty-one minutes later, then thirteen, then ten—as the pressures mount up. Joe is trying to stage a major Broadway musical while simultaneously editing a movie that is over budget and behind schedule. In addition, he's got a daughter he's trying to find time for, a steady girlfriend, one-night flirtations he can't resist, and an ex-wife who explicates all his past infidelities to him. This stressful imbalance is summarized in the final number when the emcee says, "His success in show business was matched by failure in his personal relationship bag. Now *that's* where he really bombed."

Roy Scheider and Erzsebet Foldi.

Ironically, this warts-and-all presentation of Joe's life is given by the man who actually lived it, director and co-writer Bob Fosse. *All That Jazz* is filled with touchstones from Fosse's life (see "Added Attraction"), which he fearlessly examines to juxtapose his professional ambitions alongside his personal flaws. For instance, we see Fosse's creative process when he labors to conceive a daring "Air-rotica" celebration of beautiful bodies for a mediocre song he doesn't like ("Take Off With Us"). Later we see dance at its most joyous when his girlfriend and his daughter skillfully perform a playful "unrehearsed tribute" they've put together. But interspersed with these great moments are unflinching scenes that reveal Joe (and Fosse) to be an unabashed hedonist who admittedly lies whenever he needs to, cheats whenever he can, and says "I love you" whenever it works. "Sex sex sex, can't he ever think of anything but sex," laments the frustrated songwriter

Sandahl Bergman and dancers.

in the movie; "you son of a bitch," says his ex-wife to his face; "this cat was never nobody's friend," announces the emcee. No wonder Joe/Fosse always wore black. He's doomed.

His destiny takes the shape of Angelique (Jessica Lange), the seductive fantasy woman Joe talks with throughout the movie. Near the end we realize she's the Angel of Death come to claim him. Sixty-six minutes into this 123-minute movie, the story darkens when Joe has chest pains and is rushed to the hospital. But even as he confronts angina and "total blockage in two arteries," he continues to drink, smoke, and carouse. We squeamishly witness Joe's gory chest surgery, yet he parties relentlessly and is warned by the cardiologist that he's "foolishly and childishly flirting with disaster." We could lose sympathy for someone so intent on destroying himself, but he pleads with Angelique for more time and delivers two redemptive hallucinations in the final half-hour. The first "Hospital Hallucination" lasts nine minutes and has the women in his life performing their sad goodbyes; the movie's grand finale lasts two minutes longer as Joe makes "his final appearance on the great stage of life" and sings his own farewells. Some viewers may denounce these surreal scenes as being pretentious and self-indulgent, but we think they show Fosse at his artistic best. His story concludes with a dazzling mini-concert that blends all the people in his life, familiar songs, inventive costumes, and brilliant staging.

Fosse populates his movie with memorable casting choices. To play his fictionalized self, Fosse cast a dramatic actor, Roy Scheider, previously known for *The French Connection* (1971) and *Jaws* (1975). A former boxer, Scheider brings a gritty toughness to the role of the driven, perfectionistic showman. The long-limbed gravity-defying Ann Reinking, who's basically playing herself, puts on an athletic display of power and grace anytime she starts dancing. Blonde Amazon Sandahl Bergman is sexuality incarnate in the "Take Off With Us" show-stopper. In addition, amazing dancers are everywhere, from the open audition early in the movie (a long sequence that includes twelve pirouetting dancers edited smoothly together as one performer) to the group that is endlessly rehearsing in the studio. Subtract all the dialogue, just run the musical numbers, and you'd still have a mesmerizing movie.

The train-wreck of Joe's life finally crashes after his last hallucinated goodbye to a standing ovation. Angelique, with a knowing smile, waits for him. Just as they're about to embrace, we get the movie's last sound and last shot—a zipper closing the bag around Joe's dead body on the hospital table. For the closing credits, the showman goes out the only way he knows how: with Broadway legend Ethel Merman belting out Irving Berlin's iconic "There's No Business Like Show Business." Bravo.

ADDED ATTRACTION: All That Reality

A dozen connections between *All That Jazz* and Bob Fosse's actual life.

- The movie's title is also the title of the most famous song in *Chicago*, Fosse's 1975 Broadway musical.
- Joe remembers scenes from his teenage years when he was an aspiring dancer in a burlesque show; as a teenager, Fosse danced professionally in small nightclubs and burlesque theaters.
- The movie Joe is struggling to finish—*The Standup*, about an edgy comedian played by Cliff Gorman—echoes Fosse's 1974 movie *Lenny*, about an edgy comedian played by Dustin Hoffman.

- Eddie, the editor Joe works with in the editing room, is played by Alan Heim, the actual editor of *Lenny* and *All That Jazz*.
- Leland Palmer plays Audrey Paris, Joe's ex-wife and consistent ally seemingly based on Fosse's wife Gwen Verdon.
- Joe's daughter, Michelle, seems to be based on Fosse's actual daughter, Nicole, who briefly appears in *All That Jazz*.
- Joe's girlfriend, Kate Jagger, is played by Ann Reinking, Fosse's real-life girlfriend for most of the 1970s. During the decade Reinking appeared in three of Fosse's Broadway musicals.
- One of the main dancers from *Cabaret* (1972), Kathryn Doby, plays Joe's dance assistant in *All That Jazz*.
- Ben Vereen, a dancer in Fosse's *Sweet Charity* (1969) and one of the leads in Fosse's hit Broadway musical *Pippin* (1972), plays O'Connor Flood, the emcee at the end of *All That Jazz*.
- Frankie Man, who plays a comic in *Lenny* (1974), also plays a comic in *All That Jazz*.
- In *All That Jazz*, John Lithgow plays a rival Broadway director who is apparently based on one of Fosse's peers, Harold Prince (the glasses atop his head are a tip-off).
- At the end of *All That Jazz*, Joe dies of a heart attack; in 1987, Bob Fosse died of a heart attack.

Kramer vs. Kramer

(One of 1979's five **FAR-OUT** movies)

Released: December 1979

Director: Robert Benton

Stars: Dustin Hoffman, Meryl Streep, Justin Henry

Academy Awards: Five wins (Best Picture; Best Actor—Dustin Hoffman; Best Supporting Actress—Meryl Streep; Best Director; Best Writing), plus four more nominations (Best Supporting Actor—Justin Henry; Best Supporting Actress—Jane Alexander; Best Editing; Best Cinematography)

PREVIEW: Divorced parents square off in court, each hoping to get custody of their young son.

FINE LINE: "What law is it that says a woman is a better parent simply by virtue of her sex?" (Ted in court, arguing for child custody.)

CLOSE-UP: Six minutes into the movie, Joanna explains to Ted why she's leaving: "It's not you, it's me, it's my fault." Many dictionaries attribute "it's not you, it's me" to different 1980s articles and movies; in a 1993 *Seinfeld* episode George Costanza angrily claims that *he* "invented" this line. Clearly *Kramer vs. Kramer*'s precedes them all. Actually, we believe the line was first spoken in the Jack Lemmon/Judy Holliday comedy *Phffft* (1954): "It's not you, it's me. The whole thing is my fault."

NOW SHOWING: "I Want My Son"

After surging throughout the 1970s, America's divorce rate finally hit its all-time high in 1979 when divorce ended 53% of all marriages, a number that effectively doubled the 1969 percentage (the divorce rate then leveled off and started to decline in 1982). In addition, a decade of feminism had brought more women than ever into the workplace by 1979, and "self-actualization" had become a familiar goal thanks to everything from the Human Potential Movement and Transcendental Meditation to movies like *Up the Sandbox* (1972) and *Annie Hall* (1977).

Kramer vs. Kramer (1979) weaves all three of these threads—divorce, women's increasing independence ("women's lib" is actually mentioned in the movie), and self-actualization—into a richly textured story of one couple's break-up. Other '70s movies had dealt with divorce—comedies like *Play It Again, Sam* (1972) and *Starting Over* (1979), dramas like *An Unmarried Woman* (1978) and *Interiors* (1978)—but *Kramer vs. Kramer* seemed like the timeliest, most eloquent expression of divorce's hurtful effects. Audiences responded and made *Kramer vs. Kramer*—a quiet, meticulous, beautifully photographed movie without spaceships, disasters, sharks, or guns—1979's top box-office success, placing it above action-packed heavyweights like *Star Trek: The Motion Picture*, *Alien*, and *Apocalypse Now*.

The divorce that precipitates the main story happens without hysterics or flung dishes (in fact, we never see any divorce proceedings, we just become aware that they're over). In the movie's first eight minutes Joanna (Meryl Streep) leaves her workaholic husband of eight years, Ted (Dustin Hoffman), and young son, Billy (Justin Henry), in their upscale New York apartment and heads out, as she explains later, to "find something interesting to do for myself in the world." Joanna, a mother abandoning her only child, initially seems like the movie's villain, but as the story turns to Ted and Billy for the next thirty-eight minutes we see how oblivious Ted has been in the past. He can't make a basic breakfast, he awkwardly shops for groceries, and he doesn't even know what grade Billy is in. Near the end of the movie, when Joanna describes her resentment toward Ted and his career obsession in court, we'll already know what she's talking about.

The joy of the movie is seeing Ted bonding with Billy and working to improve their lives. Their first breakfast together ends up with messes, burns, and shouting, and soon they're subsisting on donuts and TV dinners; however, by the end of the movie Ted and Billy are working silently and quickly like a well-choreographed team to crank out perfect French toast. Nurturing Billy and helping him through difficult times, Ted evolves into a sensitive, caring father.

Thus is the stage set for the child-custody battle that dominates the movie's second half. Child custody is another current social thread woven into *Kramer vs. Kramer* (1979, in fact, was the year that California passed America's first joint-custody law). After eighteen months away Joanna returns

Dustin Hoffman, Meryl Streep, and Justin Henry.

with a new job, a lover, and the announcements "I think I found myself" and "I want my son." Ted refuses, but his efforts to hold onto Billy are frustrated when he's fired because he's been neglecting his work (he's also neglected the big warning in the boss's office—a highly visible poster for the 1937 movie *You Can't Have Everything*). Ted scrambles successfully to land a job and eventually makes an eloquent plea in court, but all his recent experiences are manipulated against him: Joanna's lawyer makes it look like Ted can't hold a job, Billy's playground accident gets magnified into a life-threatening emergency, etc. Joanna, meanwhile, delivers long, passionate courtroom testimony about their frustrating lives together and her need to become "a whole human being." Their nineteen minutes in court are fascinating and powerful.

Elevating this movie beyond overwrought domestic melodrama are the sublime cast and the smooth, polished direction. Hoffman, Streep, and Henry are so convincing that their fictional characters seem like actual people with real feelings and flaws. Earlier in the '70s Hoffman had played some idiosyncratic roles—*Little Big Man* (1970), *Lenny* (1974)—but here he becomes a totally credible "normal" guy struggling through a crisis. Streep appears for only thirty-one minutes (though it seems longer), and she skillfully keeps her character from being completely unsympathetic. Henry, unforced and instinctive, gives one of the best child performances in a decade rich with young stars like Quinn Cummings, Jodie Foster, and Tatum O'Neal. Academy Award voters gave Hoffman and Streep their first Oscars and a nomination to Henry, making him still the youngest Oscar nominee. Writer/director Robert Benton, a nominee for co-writing *Bonnie and Clyde* (1967), also won his first two Oscars here. While there's plenty of conversation in the movie, some of Benton's most memorable scenes—donuts for breakfast, Ted anxiously waiting at the Christmas party to find out about his job interview, the final French toast—have virtually no dialogue at all. Throughout Benton maintains a delicate balance so that we don't end up favoring one parent over the other but instead see all sides of their complicated issues. By the mid-1980s Benton, Hoffman and Streep would all have won additional Oscars.

Kramer vs. Kramer may not seem like a groundbreaker today, but it did in 1979. What still works is the heartfelt emotion at the movie's core. The love and pain continue to resonate, and this well-made movie feels as compelling and authentic now as it did then.

ADDED ATTRACTION: Young Stars

These performers, all fourteen or under, join eight-year-old Justin Henry on the list of prominent child stars of the 1970s.

- Linda Blair: *The Exorcist* (1973)
- Quinn Cummings: *The Goodbye Girl* (1977)
- Ike Eisenmann: *Escape to Witch Mountain* (1975)
- Jodie Foster: *Taxi Driver* (1976)
- Cary Guffey: *Close Encounters of the Third Kind* (1977)
- Alfred Lutter: *Alice Doesn't Live Here Anymore* (1974)
- Sean Marshall: *Pete's Dragon* (1977)
- Tatum O'Neal: *Paper Moon* (1973)
- Peter Ostrum: *Willy Wonka & the Chocolate Factory* (1971)
- Kelly Reno: *The Black Stallion* (1979)

- Kim Richards: *No Deposit No Return* (1976)
- Ricky Schroder: *The Champ* (1979)
- Brooke Shields: *Pretty Baby* (1978)
- Susan Swift: *Audrey Rose* (1977)

The Black Hole

Released: December 1979
Director: Gary Nelson
Stars: Maximilian Schell, Anthony Perkins, Yvette Mimieux
Academy Awards: Two nominations (Best Cinematography; Best Visual Effects)

PREVIEW: Astronauts encounter a mad genius on a huge spaceship that is orbiting a black hole.

NOW SHOWING: Lost in *The Black Hole*

How could *The Black Hole* (1979) disappoint? Disney ambitiously spent $20 million, a huge sum back then, in a bold effort to reach new audiences with the studio's first PG movie. Two Best Actor Oscar winners (Maximilian Schell, Ernest Borgnine) star, and Oscar winners created the special effects, costumes, and music. Just the idea of a futuristic voyage into a black hole should've been enough to jump-start an exciting movie. Unfortunately, anyone who had enjoyed the awe-inspiring *2001: A Space Odyssey* (1968) and the epic *Star Wars* (1977) probably viewed *The Black Hole* as a missed opportunity.

At the time the movie's Oscar-nominated visuals drew raves from *Time*, *Newsweek*, and other major magazines. Instead of an inky black universe, here the cosmic star fields are beautiful shades of blue. The black hole itself is a swirl of light and color. The impossibly elegant *Cygnus* has immense open atria and exquisite crystal chandeliers. The ominous robot Maximilian is an effective villain, and everyone fires cool double-barreled pistols. But didn't those same praising magazines notice Yvette Mimieux's character wearing a simplistic hat made out of crushed aluminum foil during her rescue? Or the wires that are visible everywhere? Wires to lift the weightless crew, wires to hoist the flying robot, so many conspicuous wires. Two years after *Star Wars*, it isn't a good look.

Disney's lofty ambitions for *The Black Hole* are obvious immediately, because the movie opens with John Barry's stately two-minute overture; MGM had begun *2001* this way, immediately signaling the movie's serious intentions and departure from typical low-budget science-fiction. The pretentious screenplay then refers to Dante's *Inferno*, quotes *Genesis*, and turns totally incomprehensible in the trippy finale, which has echoes of *2001*'s famous Star Gate sequence and *Star Wars*' jump into hyperspace as everyone plunges into the black hole, where they experience ... something we still can't explain. An *unhelmeted* character floats in the vacuum of space, merges with a robot, and stands on a rocky promontory surveying a Miltonian hell. Other characters stretch and spin in slow-motion. An angel soars through a cathedral of light. The survivors fly into an eclipse. We think.

Maybe only kids will get it, or will be willing to overlook the bad science of a huge meteor slowly rolling through the ship's interior like the boulder in *Raiders of the Lost Ark* (1981). *The Black Hole* isn't awful, but it is a confusing let-down.

ADDED ATTRACTION: That Darn Alien

A year before *The Black Hole*, Disney explored the sci-fi territory claimed by *Close Encounters of the Third Kind* (1977). Science-fiction's appeal is that anything is theoretically possible—ergo, Disney's *The Cat from Outer Space* (1978), a close encounter of the furred kind in which the alien looks like an ordinary housecat. This overlong live-action comedy slightly foreshadows *E.T.* (1982): both movies present an alien alone on Earth who applies other-worldly powers, who tries to return home, and who sends a two-wheeled vehicle flying to escape pursuers. Thanks to a special collar that "amplifies brain power," that cat from outer space communicates via "thought transference" (heard as the voice of Ronnie Schell, who also appears as a soldier). Since the far-out feline can levitate objects, open any door, and stop things that are in motion, naturally a James Bond-style villain wants it, leading to—what else in a Disney movie?—a ludicrous final chase. The likeable cast includes Ken Berry, Sandy Duncan, and the two colonels from TV's *M*A*S*H*, McLean Stevenson and Harry Morgan. Disney then launched more sci-fi/comedy with *Unidentified Flying Oddball* (1979), which has a time-traveling astronaut visiting Camelot, a la Twain's *A Connecticut Yankee in King Arthur's Court*. The routine shenanigans might please nostalgic adults and undemanding kids—after all, in sci-fi anything is theoretically possible.

Being There

Released: December 1979

Director: Hal Ashby

Stars: Peter Sellers, Shirley MacLaine, Melvyn Douglas

Academy Awards: One win (Best Supporting Actor—Melvyn Douglas), plus one more nomination (Best Actor—Peter Sellers)

PREVIEW: Powerful people assign profound meaning to the innocent words of a child-like man.

NOW SHOWING: Being Nowhere

Being There generated such rapturous reviews that we approached it in 1979 like we were entering a hallowed cathedral. Many people still revere this movie as a spiritual experience, that or a hilarious comedy. We'll concede that it's visually beautiful, has a well-intentioned satirical message, and offers some amusing moments, but we didn't feel life being changed by *Being There*. Actually, we felt life being slowly drained away by a movie that stretches one joke across 130 minutes.

As fans of director Hal Ashby's movies, we'd eagerly accepted the quirky May/December romance in *Harold and Maude* (1971). *Being There* asks too much. We're supposed to believe that Chance (Peter Sellers), an illiterate, mild-mannered simpleton who's "never been allowed outside of the house" and who's absorbed all he knows from watching random TV shows, becomes a presidential advisor and candidate simply by being polite and making rudimentary statements about gardening. Chance giggles out of context and is "always going to be a little boy," yet somehow experts and elders consider him "insightful," "direct," "intuitive," and "brilliant." Chance doesn't intentionally dupe them, they dupe themselves: he mentions seasonal "growth in the spring," and the president hears a "refreshing and optimistic" political strategy. The ironic

Peter Sellers.

profundity projected onto his blank expression and naïve utterances constitutes the movie's one redundant joke. Only the black maid realizes he's "dumb as a jackass" and spouts "gobbledygook."

Sellers, the zany *farceur*, maintains a pitch-perfect less-is-more delivery for this one-note character. But elsewhere the movie falls as flat as Chance's intonations. A lame running gag involves the president's impotence, and Shirley MacLaine's character, misinterpreting Chance's I-like-to-watch declaration, embarrassingly pleasures herself while he channel-surfs beside her. Much is made of the last shot when Chance literally walks on water, though nothing else in the movie suggests he's Christ-like (other than the inadvertent "miracle" of ingenuous comments turning into meaningful advice). To us this ending, which wasn't in Jerzy Kosinski's original novel, is a cheat, like we've watched Maude come back to life in *Harold and Maude* or Chief Brody awake from a nightmare at the end of *Jaws* (1975). Also controversial are the three minutes of tone-changing outtakes that accompany the final credits. Commonplace now, this idea was a novelty then, though it was more appropriate when comical outtakes concluded Burt Reynolds' goofy *Hooper* (1978). We weren't deflated by this last silliness; the walking-on-water scene had already done that.

ADDED ATTRACTION: Preacher Man

Being There shares some traits with John Huston's *Wise Blood*, another unusual 1979 movie that mixes humor, drama and religious themes. Both are based on books (*Wise Blood* on Flannery O'Connor's 1952 novel) and both were made by great directors who use uneducated characters for satirical purposes. Brad Dourif is excellent as an army vet who comes to a Southern town, announces "I don't believe in anything," preaches "nothin' matters but that Jesus don't exist," and makes himself the fierce head of the Church Without Christ. Around him are religious con artists, an uninhibited preacher's daughter, and a "shiftless crazy boy" who talks to monkeys and claims he "can see signs" because he has "the gift" of "wise blood." It's a thoroughly original, hard-to-categorize movie that veers from comic episodes (a stolen gorilla costume, a car plunging into a lake) to angry confrontations and a disturbing last act where Dourif's conflicted character seeks redemption by physically destroying himself.

AFTERWORD

Michael O'Keefe was still a New York teenager when he landed a key role on the hit TV show *M*A*S*H* in 1974. More TV appearances, including another *M*A*S*H* episode, *Maude*, two episodes of *The Waltons*, and several TV movies led to his big-screen debut as a sailor in the submarine-disaster movie *Gray Lady Down* (1978). His very next movie role, as the smart, sensitive, basketball-playing son in the riveting drama *The Great Santini* (1979), brought him an Oscar nomination as Best Supporting Actor. A year later he starred in *Caddyshack* (1980), the golf-themed classic in which he played the lead caddy alongside Chevy Chase, Bill Murray, Rodney Dangerfield, and other comedy legends. In the '80s he starred in some more sports-related movies, playing an Olympics-bound gymnast in the psychological drama *Split Image* (1982) and a star baseball player in Neil Simon's *The Slugger's Wife* (1985). Since then his many television, movie, and Broadway appearances include important roles on TV's *Roseanne*, *Law & Order: Criminal Intent*, *Homeland*, *Masters of Sex*, and *Sneaky Pete*; two movies with Jack Nicholson, *Ironweed* (1987) and *The Pledge* (2001); and the George Clooney movie *Michael Clayton* (2007). He has also directed a documentary, written lyrics for songs recorded by Bonnie Raitt, and penned a book of poems called *Swimming From Under My Father* (2009). Michael was on the set of *City on a Hill*, Kevin Bacon's show on Showtime, when he graciously answered our questions in early 2020. Our thanks to Michael O'Keefe for contributing to our book.

Not including your own movies, do you have a favorite from the 1970s?

My favorite '70s movies include *Harold and Maude*, *The Last Detail*, *Five Easy Pieces*, *Mean Streets*, *The Godfather*, and *The Godfather: Part II*.

Many fans and movie critics have called the 1970s a "golden age" for movies. Did you have a sense at the time that you were part of a golden age?

At absolutely no time did I have any sense that I was part of any golden age, or anything like that. I was struggling to make a living as a young actor, and was happy and grateful to have opportunities. It was only in retrospect that I was able to look back and see that era as a special one in the annals of movie history.

What was your favorite movie-going experience of the 1970s?

Going to see the movie *Hair* at the Zeigfeld Theatre on 55th Street in Manhattan under the influence of LSD was probably my favorite movie experience of the '70s. I could also say that it was the most harrowing, uncomfortable experience I ever had at the movies in my life. For the record, I do not advocate the use of any kind of drugs at all. However, I was a child of the '60s and '70s, and that's just one of the things we did back then.

What was it like making *The Great Santini* in 1979? In particular, you were working with a heavyweight actor, Robert Duvall, who had been in both *Godfather* movies and had been nominated for an Oscar. What important lessons did you learn from that experience?

Working with Robert Duvall on *Santini* was one of the most singular experiences I ever had as a person, and as an actor. Duvall has a capacity to gather you into his force field as an actor and carry you along with him. Without that performance, without Pat Conroy's novel, without Lewis Carlino (the director and writer of the film), I don't think I would've had the career I had. Nor would I have become the person I became. I owe them all debts of gratitude I can never fully repay.

You look like a skilled basketball player in *The Great Santini*. Later you have a smooth, effortless golf swing in *Caddyshack*. Have you continued playing basketball and golf since these movies?

Thanks for the compliments about my athletic capacities as a young man. These days, I mainly work on Taiji and Qi Gong.

With Blythe Danner in The Great Santini.

You earned an Oscar nomination for *The Great Santini* when you were still in your early twenties and just starting your movie career. Do you remember the moment when you got the news of your nomination?

I heard about my nomination while I was on the train platform at 125th Street and Park Avenue in Manhattan waiting to take the train to the suburbs to see my parents for dinner. In those days, we used pay phones. And I was talking to my agent on the pay phone from there when he told me. That was pretty cool.

With Chevy Chase in Caddyshack.

Late in 1979 you started filming *Caddyshack* with comedy legends like Chevy Chase, Bill Murray, and Rodney Dangerfield. As you were making it, did you sense that it would become a classic?

Making *Caddyshack*, I had no idea it was going to become a classic. Actually, we all barely survived the entire experience. There was a lot of fun and craziness. More to follow about that.

What was the silliest thing about the 1970s?

The silliest, stupidest thing about making movies in the 1970s was that everybody was under the impression that using drugs and alcohol was somehow a good idea, and was even necessary to creating film and television. This was, of course, the greatest delusion of the era. And there are a number of casualties that we left behind because of that. Doug Kenney, producer and co-writer of *Caddyshack*, comes to mind. He was one of the most talented, intelligent, and affable people I ever met. But he was addicted to cocaine, and he ended up committing suicide after we completed *Caddyshack* because of it. That was a profound lesson for me.

Michael in 2020. Photo courtesy Michael O'Keefe.

How was it different working on 1970s movies as compared to working on movies in later decades?

While filmmaking techniques have changed enormously over the years, the experience is basically the same. We tell stories about people experiencing peaks and valleys, and hopefully we shed a little light on ourselves. It's kind of what I like about being an actor. There's a sense of consistency, routine, and even ritual about what we do.

Can you compare the mood of the '70s with the mood of 2020?

The people I admire, and am inspired to work with, have the same values now that we had back then. They want to make stories about human endeavors, with historical accuracy, and a bit of poetry to them. I still want to do the things now that I wanted to do when I was a young actor. Even after all these years I still have a kind of awe and wonder about what we do and how we do it.

—Michael O'Keefe

APPENDIX

Movies by Genre: 1975–1979

The book's main entries, divided into genres and then listed alphabetically.

Animation
The Many Adventures of Winnie the Pooh
Pete's Dragon
The Rescuers

Comedy
Animal House
Annie Hall
Being There
California Suite
Car Wash
Cooley High
Freaky Friday
The Goodbye Girl
High Anxiety
The Jerk
The Kentucky Fried Movie
The Last Remake of Beau Geste
Love and Death
The Muppet Movie
Oh, God!
Rabbit Test
Silent Movie
Smile
Smokey and the Bandit
The Strongest Man in the World
10

Crime/Crime Comedy
Black Sunday
The Boys from Brazil
Breakheart Pass
Candleshoe
Coma
The Deep
Dog Day Afternoon
The Eiger Sanction
Escape from Alcatraz
Eyes of Laura Mars
Foul Play
French Connection II
Fun with Dick and Jane
Lucky Lady
Marathon Man
Midnight Express
Moonraker
Murder by Death
Night Moves
Silver Streak
The Spy Who Loved Me
Three Days of the Condor

Disaster
Airport '77
The Big Bus
The China Syndrome
Gray Lady Down
The Hindenburg
Meteor

Documentary
The Last Waltz
The Song Remains the Same

Drama
The Adventures of the Wilderness Family
All the President's Men
Aloha, Bobby and Rose
Barry Lyndon
The Betsy
Bite the Bullet
The Black Stallion
Bound for Glory
Capricorn One
Coming Home
Days of Heaven
The Driver

Eraserhead
Every Which Way But Loose
The Front
The Great Santini
The Great Waldo Pepper
Hester Street
Interiors
Julia
Kramer vs. Kramer
The Last Tycoon
Mandingo
The Man Who Would Be King
Nashville
Network
Norma Rae
One Flew Over the Cuckoo's Nest
Pretty Baby
Saint Jack
Sorcerer
Taxi Driver
3 Women
Treasure of Matecumbe
The Turning Point
An Unmarried Woman
The Warriors

Horror
The Amityville Horror
Burnt Offerings
Carrie
Empire of the Ants
The Fury
Halloween
The Hills Have Eyes
Jaws
Jaws 2
King Kong
The Omen
Orca
The Stepford Wives

Musical
All That Jazz
At Long Last Love
The Buddy Holly Story
Grease
Hair
New York, New York
Rock 'n' Roll High School
The Rocky Horror Picture Show
The Rose
Saturday Night Fever
Sgt. Pepper's Lonely Hearts Club Band
A Star Is Born
Tommy

Romance
Gable and Lombard
Heaven Can Wait
A Little Romance
Manhattan
Old Boyfriends
Robin and Marian
Shampoo
Starting Over

Science-Fiction / Fantasy
Alien
At the Earth's Core
The Black Hole
Close Encounters of the Third Kind
Death Race 2000
Escape to Witch Mountain
Invasion of the Body Snatchers
Logan's Run
Star Trek: The Motion Picture
Star Wars
Superman

Sports
The Bad News Bears
Big Wednesday
Breaking Away
Rocky
Slap Shot

War/War Comedy
Apocalypse Now
The Deer Hunter
Hanover Street
MacArthur
1941

Western/Western Comedy
The Apple Dumpling Gang
Buffalo Bill and the Indians, or Sitting Bull's History Lesson
The Outlaw Josey Wales
The Shootist

Most Popular Movies: 1975–1979

According to the rankings at boxofficemadness.wordpress.com, these thirty-five titles are the biggest box-office hits of the late 1970s, separated into the years of release and then listed in order (highest earnings first).

1975
Jaws
One Flew Over the Cuckoo's Nest
Shampoo
Dog Day Afternoon
The Return of the Pink Panther
Three Days of the Condor
Funny Lady

1976
Rocky
A Star Is Born
King Kong
Silver Streak
All the President's Men
The Omen
The Bad News Bears

1977
Star Wars
Close Encounters of the Third Kind
Saturday Night Fever
Smokey and the Bandit
The Goodbye Girl
The Deep
The Spy Who Loved Me

1978
Grease
Superman
Animal House
Jaws 2
Heaven Can Wait
Every Which Way But Loose
Hooper

1979
Kramer vs. Kramer
Star Trek: The Motion Picture
The Jerk
Rocky II
Alien
Apocalypse Now
10

Daring Movies: 1975–1979

There are others, of course, but these thirty-five movies from 1975–1979 all pushed the boundaries of violence, sex, or profanity, or they introduced special-effects technology, radical themes, or a unique cinematic artistry (sometimes combining several of these simultaneously). These aren't the thirty-five *best* movies of the late '70s, but they are some of the most distinctive. Listed chronologically.

1975
Barry Lyndon
Death Race 2000
Dog Day Afternoon
Jaws
Mandingo
Nashville
The Rocky Horror Picture Show
Shampoo
Tommy

1976
Carrie
Car Wash
Network
Silent Movie
Taxi Driver

1977
Annie Hall
Close Encounters of the Third Kind
Eraserhead
New York, New York
Saturday Night Fever
Slap Shot
Star Wars
3 Women

1978
Animal House
Coming Home
Days of Heaven
The Driver
Halloween
Pretty Baby
Superman
An Unmarried Woman

1979
Alien
All That Jazz
Apocalypse Now
Being There
The Warriors

Top Oscar Winners: 1975–1979

Major categories, year by year.

1975

Most Oscar Wins: *One Flew Over the Cuckoo's Nest* (five)

Best Picture (in bold): *Barry Lyndon, Dog Day Afternoon, Jaws, Nashville,* **One Flew Over the Cuckoo's Nest**

Best Actor, Actress: Jack Nicholson (*One Flew Over the Cuckoo's Nest*), Louise Fletcher (*One Flew Over the Cuckoo's Nest*)

Best Director: Milos Forman (*One Flew Over the Cuckoo's Nest*)

1976

Most Oscar Wins: *All the President's Men, Network* (four)

Best Picture: *All the President's Men, Bound for Glory, Network,* **Rocky**, *Taxi Driver*

Best Actor, Actress: Peter Finch (*Network*), Faye Dunaway (*Network*)

Best Director: John G. Avildsen (*Rocky*)

1977

Most Oscar Wins: *Star Wars* (seven)

Best Picture: **Annie Hall**, *The Goodbye Girl, Julia, Star Wars, The Turning Point*

Best Actor, Actress: Richard Dreyfuss (*The Goodbye Girl*), Diane Keaton (*Annie Hall*)

Best Director: Woody Allen (*Annie Hall*)

1978

Most Oscar Wins: *The Deer Hunter* (five)

Best Picture: *Coming Home,* **The Deer Hunter**, *Heaven Can Wait, Midnight Express, An Unmarried Woman*

Best Actor, Actress: Jon Voight (*Coming Home*), Jane Fonda (*Coming Home*)

Best Director: Michael Cimino (*The Deer Hunter*)

1979

Most Oscar Wins: *Kramer vs. Kramer* (five)

Best Picture: *All That Jazz, Apocalypse Now, Breaking Away,* **Kramer vs. Kramer**, *Norma Rae*

Best Actor, Actress: Dustin Hoffman (*Kramer vs. Kramer*), Sally Field (*Norma Rae*)

Best Director: Robert Benton (*Kramer vs. Kramer*)

Top Oscar Nominees: 1975–1979

Movies released in the second half of the decade that earned three or more Oscar nominations.

Eleven nominations
Julia (1977)
The Turning Point (1977)

Ten
Network (1976)
Rocky (1976)
Star Wars (1977)

Eight
All That Jazz (1979)
The Deer Hunter (1978)
Heaven Can Wait (1978)
Kramer vs. Kramer (1979)
One Flew Over the Cuckoo's Nest (1975)

Nine
All the President's Men (1976)
Apocalypse Now (1979)
Close Encounters of the Third Kind (1977)
Coming Home (1978)

Seven
Barry Lyndon (1975)

Six
Bound for Glory (1976)
Dog Day Afternoon (1975)
Midnight Express (1978)

Five
Annie Hall (1977)
Breaking Away (1979)
Funny Lady (1975)
The Goodbye Girl (1977)
Interiors (1978)
Nashville (1975)

Four
The China Syndrome (1979)
Days of Heaven (1978)
Jaws (1975)
The Man Who Would Be King (1975)
Norma Rae (1979)
The Rose (1979)
Same Time, Next Year (1978)
Seven Beauties (1976)
Shampoo (1975)
A Star Is Born (1976)
The Sunshine Boys (1975)
Taxi Driver (1976)
The Wiz (1978)

Three
The Boys from Brazil (1978)
The Buddy Holly Story (1978)
California Suite (1978)
Cousin Cousine (1975)
Equus (1977)
The Hindenburg (1975)
La Cage aux Folles (1978)
1941 (1979)
The Spy Who Loved Me (1977)
Star Trek: The Motion Picture (1979)
Superman (1978)
An Unmarried Woman (1978)
Voyage of the Damned (1976)

The 1975-1979 Movies on the American Film Institute's "Greatest-Hits" List

The American Film Institute, established in 1967 with Gregory Peck as its first chairperson, is an esteemed body of critics and filmmakers that works to preserve America's film heritage, to celebrate achievements in film, and also to educate with advanced film-studies programs. In 1998 and 2007 the AFI created "greatest-hits" lists called "100 Years … 100 Movies." As mentioned in our Introduction, both lists included more movies from the 1970s than from any other decade. Here are the 1975–1979 movies that the AFI recognized (numbers indicate the movies' positions on the lists). The number-one movie on both lists, by the way, was *Citizen Kane* (1941).

1998

15. *Star Wars* (1977)
20. *One Flew Over the Cuckoo's Nest* (1975)
28. *Apocalypse Now* (1979)
31. *Annie Hall* (1977)
47. *Taxi Driver* (1976)
48. *Jaws* (1975)
64. *Close Encounters of the Third Kind* (1977)
66. *Network* (1976)
78. *Rocky* (1976)
79. *The Deer Hunter* (1978)

2007

13. *Star Wars* (1977)
30. *Apocalypse Now* (1979)
33. *One Flew Over the Cuckoo's Nest* (1975)
35. *Annie Hall* (1977)
52. *Taxi Driver* (1976)
53. *The Deer Hunter* (1978)
56. *Jaws* (1975)
57. *Rocky* (1976)
59. *Nashville* (1975)
64. *Network* (1976)
77. *All the President's Men* (1976)

The Best of the '70s: 1975–1979

Our top thirty-five titles, in alphabetical order.

Alien (1979)
All That Jazz (1979)
All the President's Men (1976)
Animal House (1978)
Annie Hall (1977)
Apocalypse Now (1979)
Barry Lyndon (1975)
Breaking Away (1979)
The China Syndrome (1979)
Carrie (1976)
Close Encounters of the Third Kind (1977)
Coming Home (1978)
Days of Heaven (1978)
The Deer Hunter (1978)
Dog Day Afternoon (1975)
The Front (1976)
The Goodbye Girl (1977)
Jaws (1975)

Kramer vs. Kramer (1979)
Love and Death (1975)
Manhattan (1979)
The Man Who Would Be King (1975)
Midnight Express (1978)
Nashville (1975)
Network (1976)
Norma Rae (1979)
One Flew Over the Cuckoo's Nest (1975)
The Outlaw Josey Wales (1976)
Rocky (1976)
Saturday Night Fever (1977)
Shampoo (1975)
Slap Shot (1977)
Sorcerer (1977)
Star Wars (1977)
Taxi Driver (1976)

Best Movie: *Star Wars* (1977)

Top-Ten Money-Making Stars: 1970-1979

From 1915 to 2013, Martin Quigley's Quigley Publishing Company polled America's movie-theater owners to find out which movie stars were generating the most ticket sales. Over the decades the poll results were printed in various trade papers, including Quigley's own *Motion Picture Herald*. Here are the stars who were identified as the top money-makers of the 1970s, ranked in order with the most-popular stars first. Robert Redford is the top-ranked star the most times (three); only one star—Clint Eastwood—appears every year; and only seven women—Barbra Streisand (eight appearances), Jane Fonda (two appearances), Diane Keaton (two appearances), Jill Clayburgh (one appearance), Goldie Hawn (one appearance), Ali MacGraw (one appearance), and Tatum O'Neal (one appearance)—make the lists.

1970
1. Paul Newman
2. Clint Eastwood
3. Steve McQueen
4. John Wayne
5. Elliott Gould
6. Dustin Hoffman
7. Lee Marvin
8. Jack Lemmon
9. Barbra Streisand
10. Walter Matthau

1971
1. John Wayne
2. Clint Eastwood
3. Paul Newman
4. Steve McQueen
5. George C. Scott
6. Dustin Hoffman
7. Walter Matthau
8. Ali MacGraw
9. Sean Connery
10. Lee Marvin

1972
1. Clint Eastwood
2. George C. Scott
3. Gene Hackman
4. John Wayne
5. Barbra Streisand
6. Marlon Brando
7. Paul Newman
8. Steve McQueen
9. Dustin Hoffman
10. Goldie Hawn

1973
1. Clint Eastwood
2. Ryan O'Neal
3. Steve McQueen
4. Burt Reynolds
5. Robert Redford
6. Barbra Streisand
7. Paul Newman
8. Charles Bronson
9. John Wayne
10. Marlon Brando

1974
1. Robert Redford
2. Clint Eastwood
3. Paul Newman
4. Barbra Streisand
5. Steve McQueen
6. Burt Reynolds
7. Charles Bronson
8. Jack Nicholson
9. Al Pacino
10. John Wayne

1975
1. Robert Redford
2. Barbra Streisand
3. Al Pacino
4. Charles Bronson
5. Paul Newman
6. Clint Eastwood
7. Burt Reynolds
8. Woody Allen
9. Steve McQueen
10. Gene Hackman

1976
1. Robert Redford
2. Jack Nicholson
3. Dustin Hoffman
4. Clint Eastwood
5. Mel Brooks
6. Burt Reynolds
7. Al Pacino
8. Tatum O'Neal
9. Woody Allen
10. Charles Bronson

1977
1. Sylvester Stallone
2. Barbra Streisand
3. Clint Eastwood
4. Burt Reynolds
5. Robert Redford
6. Woody Allen
7. Mel Brooks
8. Al Pacino
9. Diane Keaton
10. Robert De Niro

1978
1. Burt Reynolds
2. John Travolta
3. Richard Dreyfuss
4. Warren Beatty
5. Clint Eastwood
6. Woody Allen
7. Diane Keaton
8. Jane Fonda
9. Peter Sellers
10. Barbra Streisand

1979
1. Burt Reynolds
2. Clint Eastwood
3. Jane Fonda
4. Woody Allen
5. Barbra Streisand
6. Sylvester Stallone
7. John Travolta
8. Jill Clayburgh
9. Roger Moore
10. Mel Brooks

Past Attractions: 1970–1974

Movies covered in *The Daring Decade: Volume One, 1970-1974*:

Airport
Airport 1975
Alice Doesn't Live Here Anymore
American Graffiti
The Andromeda Strain
The Aristocats
Badlands
The Ballad of Cable Hogue
Bananas
Bank Shot
The Barefoot Executive
Battle for the Planet of the Apes
Bedknobs and Broomsticks
The Beguiled
Ben
Beneath the Planet of the Apes
The Biscuit Eater
Black Caesar
Black Christmas
Black Girl
Blazing Saddles
Bless the Beasts & Children
Bloody Mama
Boxcar Bertha
Breezy
Brewster McCloud
Bring Me the Head of Alfredo Garcia
Butterflies Are Free
Cabaret
California Split
The Candidate
Carnal Knowledge
Catch-22
C.C. & Company
Charley Varrick
Charlotte's Web
The Cheyenne Social Club
Chinatown
Claudine
A Clockwork Orange
Coffy
Conquest of the Planet of the Apes
The Conversation
The Cowboys
Daisy Miller
The Day of the Dolphin
The Day of the Jackal
Death Wish
Deliverance
Demon Seed
Diamonds Are Forever
Diary of a Mad Housewife
Dillinger
Dirty Dingus Magee
Dirty Harry
Dirty Little Billy
Don't Go in the House
Don't Look in the Basement
Don't Open the Door
Don't Play Us Cheap
Earthquake
Emperor of the North
Enter the Dragon
Escape from the Planet of the Apes
Everything You Always Wanted to Know About Sex * But Were Afraid to Ask
The Exorcist
Fat City
Fiddler on the Roof
Five Easy Pieces
The Four Musketeers
Foxy Brown
The French Connection
Frenzy
The Friends of Eddie Coyle
The Front Page
'Gator Bait
The Getaway
Gimme Shelter
The Godfather
The Godfather: Part II
The Golden Voyage of Sinbad
Greased Lightning
The Great Gatsby
The Great White Hope
The Groove Tube
Harold and Maude
Harry and Tonto
Harry in Your Pocket
The Heartbreak Kid

Hearts and Minds
The Hellstrom Chronicle
Hell Up in Harlem
Herbie Rides Again
High Plains Drifter
The Hot Rock
Husbands
Images
The Island at the Top of the World
Jeremiah Johnson
Joe
Joe Kidd
Juggernaut
Junior Bonner
Kelly's Heroes
Klute
Kotch
Ladies and Gentlemen: The Rolling Stones
Lady Sings the Blues
The Last Detail
The Last House on the Left
The Last Picture Show
Le Mans
Lenny
The Life and Times of Judge Roy Bean
Little Big Man
Little Fauss and Big Halsy
Live and Let Die
The Longest Yard
The Long Goodbye
Lost Horizon
Love Story
Loving
Macon County Line
Magnum Force
Mame
A Man Called Horse
Man of La Mancha
The Man with the Golden Gun
M*A*S*H
McCabe & Mrs. Miller
Mean Streets
The Million Dollar Duck
Minnie and Moskowitz
The Molly Maguires
Murder on the Orient Express
Napoleon and Samantha
Ned Kelly

Norwood
Now You See Him, Now You Don't
The Omega Man
On a Clear Day You Can See Forever
On Any Sunday
The Owl and the Pussycat
The Panic in Needle Park
The Paper Chase
Paper Moon
Papillon
The Parallax View
Pat Garrett & Billy the Kid
Patton
Performance
Pete 'n' Tillie
Phantom of the Paradise
Play It Again, Sam
Play Misty for Me
Plaza Suite
The Poseidon Adventure
The Private Life of Sherlock Holmes
Return to Macon County
Robin Hood
Save the Tiger
Scandalous John
Scarecrow
Serpico
The Seven-Ups
Shaft
Shaft in Africa
Shaft's Big Score!
Silent Running
Sinbad and the Eye of the Tiger
Sisters
Skin Game
Skyjacked
Slaughterhouse-Five
Sleeper
Sleuth
Snowball Express
Sounder
Soylent Green
Start the Revolution Without Me
The Sting
Straw Dogs
The Sugarland Express
Summer of '42
Super Fly

Super Fly T.N.T.
Support Your Local Gunfighter
Sweet Sweetback's Baadasssss Song
The Taking of Pelham One Two Three
The Texas Chain Saw Massacre
That's Entertainment!
Thieves Like Us
The Three Musketeers
THX 1138
Tora! Tora! Tora!
The Towering Inferno
Truck Stop Women
Two-Lane Blacktop
Two Mules for Sister Sara
The Unholy Rollers
Up the Sandbox

Uptown Saturday Night
Vanishing Point
Von Richthofen and Brown
The War Between Men and Women
The Way We Were
Westworld
What's Up, Doc?
Where's Poppa?
Willard
Willy Wonka & the Chocolate Factory
A Woman Under the Influence
Woodstock
The Yakuza
Young Frankenstein
Zabriskie Point

BIBLIOGRAPHY

Books

Biskind, Peter. *Easy Riders, Raging Bulls: How the Sex-Drugs-and-Rock 'n' Roll Generation Saved Hollywood.* New York: Simon & Schuster, 1998.

Bordwell, David. *The Way Hollywood Tells It: Story and Style in Modern Movies.* Berkeley, CA: University of California Press, 2006.

Ebert, Roger. *Awake in the Dark: The Best of Roger Ebert.* Chicago, IL: The University of Chicago Press, 2006.

———. *Scorsese by Ebert.* Chicago, IL: The University of Chicago Press, 2008.

Friedman, Lester D., and Brent Notbohm, eds. *Steven Spielberg: Interviews.* Jackson, MS: The University Press of Mississippi, 2000.

Geissman, Grant, ed. *MAD About the Seventies: The Best of the Decade.* Boston, MA: Little, Brown and Company, 1996.

Hanson, Steve. *Lights, Camera, Action! A History of the Movies in the Twentieth Century.* Los Angeles, CA: The Los Angeles Times, a Times Mirror Company, 1990.

Hogan, Ron. *The Stewardess Is Flying the Plane! American Films of the 1970s.* New York: Bulfinch Press, 2005.

Kael, Pauline. *For Keeps.* New York: Dutton, 1994.

Kirshon, John W., ed. *Chronicle of America.* New York: DK Publishing, Inc., 1997.

Kline, Sally, ed. *George Lucas: Interviews.* Jackson, MS: The University Press of Mississippi, 1999.

Maltin, Leonard. *The Disney Films.* New York: Popular Library, 1978.

———. *Leonard Maltin's 2015 Movie Guide: The Modern Era.* New York: Plume, 2014.

O'Neill, Tom. *Movie Awards: The Ultimate, Unofficial Guide to the Oscars, Golden Globes, Critics, Guild & Indie Honors.* New York: Perigee, 2001.

Osborne, Robert. *85 Years of the Oscar: The Official History of the Academy Awards.* New York: Abbeville Press Publishers, 2013.

Peary, Danny. *Guide for the Film Fanatic.* New York: Simon & Schuster, 1986.

Pfeiffer, Lee and Dave Worrall. *The Essential Bond: The Authorized Guide to the World of 007.* New York: HarperCollins Publishers, 2000.

Phillips, Gene D., ed. *Stanley Kubrick: Interviews.* Jackson, MS: The University Press of Mississippi, 2001.

Roberts, Jerry. *The Complete History of American Film Criticism.* Santa Monica, CA: Santa Monica Press, 2010.

Schickel, Richard. *Keepers: The Greatest Films—and Personal Favorites—of a Moviegoing Lifetime.* New York: Alfred A. Knopf, 2015.

Stern, Jane and Michael Stern. *Jane & Michael Stern's Encyclopedia of Pop Culture*. New York: HarperPerennial, 1992.

Thomson, David. *The New Biographical Dictionary of Film*, 6th edition. New York: Alfred A. Knopf, 2014.

DVDs

Years indicate when the DVDs were released, not the years of the original movies.

American Grindhouse. Kino Lorber, Inc., 2010.

BaadAsssss Cinema: A Bold Look at 70's Blaxploitation Films. IFC Entertainment, 2002.

Boffo! Tinseltown's Bombs and Blockbusters. Home Box Office, Inc., 2006.

Close Encounters of the Third Kind: The Collector's Edition (DVD special features). Columbia TriStar Home Entertainment, 2001.

Corman's World: Exploits of a Hollywood Rebel. Anchor Bay Entertainment, 2012.

A Decade Under the Influence. IFC Entertainment, 2003.

Going Attractions: The Definitive Story of the American Drive-in Movie. Drive-In Doc LLC., 2014.

Going to Pieces: The Rise and Fall of the Slasher Film. Thinkfilm, 2007.

Grand Theft Auto (DVD special features). New Concorde Home Video, 2002.

The Man Who Would Be King (DVD special features). Warner Home Video, 1997.

Midnight Movies: From the Margin to the Mainstream. Starz Home Entertainment, 2007.

One Flew Over the Cuckoo's Nest (DVD special features). Warner Home Video, 2002.

The Outlaw Josey Wales (DVD special features). Warner Home Video, 2001.

Rocky (DVD special features). MGM Home Entertainment, 2006.

INDEX

People and Movies in the Book

A

Aaberg, Dennis 42, 192
ABBA 60
Abbott, Diahnne 145
Abrahams, Jim 155
Accidental Tourist, The 263
AC/DC 230
Ace Eli and Rodger of the Skies 10
Ackerman, Forrest J. 155
Across the Great Divide 47
Adams, Brooke 210-211, 226
Adams, Catlin 275
Adjani, Isabelle 206
Adventure of Sherlock Holmes' Smarter Brother, The 74, 108, 151
Adventures of the Black Stallion, The 205
Adventures of the Wilderness Family, The v, 1, 46-47, 289
Aerosmith 201, 259
Agatha 208-209
Agutter, Jenny 75-76
Airplane! 75, 123, 155, 185
Airport xv, 75, 115, 123-124, 234, 268, 296
Airport 1975 123, 184, 296
Airport '77 55, 123, 184, 235, 268, 289
Ajaye, Franklyn 94
Albert, Eddie 12-13, 57
Alcott, John 52
Alda, Alan 223-224
Alda, Rutanya 217
Aldrich, Robert 57
Alexander, Jane 68, 70, 279
Alice Doesn't Live Here Anymore 188, 281, 296
Alice, Sweet Alice, aka Communion 100, 122
Alien ix, xvii, 27, 138, 226, 229, 236, 246-249, 266-267, 272, 280, 290-292, 294
Alighieri, Dante 282
Ali, Muhammad 2
All-American Boy, The 188
Allen, Irwin 184
Allen, Karen 173, 203-204

Allen, Nancy 98, 259, 273
Allen, Paul 2
Allen, Woody xv-xvi, 20-22, 90-92, 117, 131-133, 209-210, 239-240, 276, 292, 295
All That Jazz ix, 53, 229, 267, 276-279, 290, 292-294
All the President's Men vi, xix, 50, 59, 68-71, 101, 105, 115, 175, 235, 267, 289, 291-294
Almost Summer 259
Aloha, Bobby and Rose v, 16, 135, 289
Altered States 102
Altman, Robert xv-xvi, 22-24, 34, 78-80, 95, 100, 130-131, 254
American Boy: A Profile of Steven Prince 189
American Gigolo 208
American Graffiti xi-xiii, xv, 16-17, 30-31, 56, 85, 191-192, 195, 204, 232, 237, 254-255, 296
American Hot Wax 16-17, 259
Americathon 95
Amityville Horror, The ix, 118, 229, 236, 255-257, 290
Amplas, John 216
Anderson, Jr., Michael 53
Anderson, Michael 53, 75, 152
...and justice for all. 233
Andrews, Dana 103
Andrews, Julie 264, 274
Andrews, V.C. 230
Andromeda Strain, The 175, 272, 296
Animal House, aka National Lampoon's Animal House viii, xviii, 34, 94, 103, 155, 173, 203-205, 213, 232, 235, 237, 267, 273, 289, 291-292, 294
Annie Hall vii, xvi, 21, 24, 40, 90, 92, 103, 117, 122, 131-133, 157, 166, 209-210, 219, 239, 259, 267, 276, 280, 289, 291-294
Annie Oakley 64
Ann-Margret 1, 11-12, 151
Another Nice Mess 188
Anson, Jay 118, 256-257

Apocalypse Now ix, xvii, xix, 103, 236, 244-245, 260-262, 267-269, 280, 290-294
Apocalypse Now Redux 262
Apple Dumpling Gang, The v, 32-34, 84, 290
Apple Dumpling Gang Rides Again, The 33
Arden, Eve 3
Aristocats, The 143-144, 296
Arkush, Allan 258
Arnaz Jr., Desi 130
Arquette, Rosanna 229
Arthur 276
Ashby, Hal 4-5, 108-109, 178-180, 244, 283
Ashley, Elizabeth 176
Astaire, Fred 8, 97
Astin, John 110-111
Atherton, William 53
Atkins, Doug 65
Attack of the Killer Tomatoes! 173, 185
Attenborough, Richard 88
At Long Last Love v, 8, 24, 53, 243, 274, 290
At the Earth's Core vi, 88-90, 290
Auberjonois, Rene 80
Audrey Rose 282
Avalanche 55, 267-268
Avalon, Frankie 225
Avildsen, John G. 104, 106, 292
Aykroyd, Dan 117, 268, 273

B

B-52s, The 174
Bacall, Lauren 85-86, 166
Bach, Barbara 149-150
Bach, Johann Sebastian 52
Backlinie, Susan 273-274
Bacon, Kevin 173, 204
Badham, John xi, 167-168
Badlands 211, 266, 296
Bad News Bears, The vi, 34, 50, 59, 71-72, 94, 106, 121, 205, 255, 290-291

Bad News Bears Go to Japan, The 72
Bad News Bears in Breaking Training, The 72
Bad Seed, The 100, 154
Bakshi, Ralph 160
Ballad of Cable Hogue, The 63, 296
Ballard, Carroll 266
Bananas 21, 276, 296
Bancroft, Anne 49, 53, 117, 161, 268
Band, The 39, 60, 188-189
Bank Shot 296
Barefoot Executive, The 4, 296
Barnett, Jonnie 22
Barnum, P.T. 125
Barracuda 198
Barrie, Barbara 254-255
Barry, John 282
Barry Lyndon vi, xvi, 49, 52-53, 210-211, 219, 257, 289, 291-294
Bartel, Paul 14
Baryshnikov, Mikhail 161
Bassey, Shirley 243, 253
Bass, Saul 188
Bates, Alan 181, 270
Battle Cry 242
Battle for the Planet of the Apes 296
Battleship Potemkin 21
Beach Boys, The 5, 63
Beast from 20,000 Fathoms, The 113
Beast Must Die, The 42
Beatles, The 96, 136, 180, 186, 188, 200-201, 276
Beatty, Ned 75, 100, 102, 222, 268
Beatty, Warren 1, 4-6, 70, 173, 198-199, 295
Beauty and the Beast 195
Beck, John 74, 150
Beck, Michael 231
Bedknobs and Broomsticks 84, 126, 159, 169, 296
Bee Gees, The 2, 60, 200
Begin, Menachem 174
Beguiled, The 296
Being There ix, xi, 236, 244, 257, 267, 283-284, 289, 292
Beller, Kathleen 177
Belson, Jerry 34
Belushi, John 203-205, 213, 237-238, 268, 273
Benchley, Peter 139, 257
Beneath the Planet of the Apes 76, 296
Ben 296
Benjamin, Richard 78
Benny, Jack 86
Benson, Robby 57, 232
Benton, Robert 279, 281, 292

Benton, Thomas Hart 2
Berenger, Tom 117
Berenson, Marisa 52
Bergen, Candice 24, 29, 51, 207, 229, 262-263
Bergen, Edgar 174
Bergman, Ingmar 22, 209, 239
Bergman, Sandahl 277-278
Berkeley, Busby 59
Berkowitz, David 118
Berlin, Irving 278
Berlitz, Charles 2, 124
Bermuda Triangle, The 2, 124
Bernard, Thelonius 241
Bernstein, Carl 70, 193
Bernstein, Elmer 204
Bernstein, Walter 92
Berry, Chuck 17, 258
Berry, Ken 283
Berryman, Michael 141
Best Years of Our Lives, The 178
Betsy, The vii, 53, 176-177, 241, 257, 289
Between the Lines 45, 70, 238
Beware the Blob 188
Beyond the Valley of the Dolls 206
Big Bad Mama 15
Big Bird Cage, The 250
Big Bus, The vi, 74-75, 184, 289
Big Doll House, The 250
Big Fix, The 166, 274
Big Sleep, The (1946) 166, 242
Big Sleep, The (1978) xi, xiv, 166, 182, 257
Big Wednesday viii, 42, 191-192, 244, 290
Binns, Edward 24
Birds, The 171
Birth of a Nation, The 123
Biscuit Eater, The 296
Bishop, Jennifer 210
Bishop, Stephen 155, 205
Bisset, Jacqueline 139-140, 177, 210, 241
Bite the Bullet v, 29-30, 289
Bixby, Bill 32, 34, 155
Black Bird, The 26
Black Caesar 296
Black Christmas 296
Black Girl 296
Black Hole, The ix, 138, 202, 229, 244, 272, 282-283, 290
Black, Karen 87-88
Black Mama White Mama 250
Black Stallion, The ix, 127, 205, 242, 266-267, 281, 289
Black Sunday vii, 75, 128-129, 235, 257, 289

Blair, Linda 81, 281
Blakely, Ronee 22-23
Blakely, Susan 15
Blank Generation, The 97
Blazing Saddles xv, 21, 72-74, 151, 169-170, 203, 296
Bless the Beasts & Children 296
Blish, James 42
Blob, The 188, 242
Blondell, Joan 86, 229
Blondie 97, 230
Bloodline 67
Bloody Mama 296
Blossom, Roberts 249
Blow-Up 208, 258
Blue Collar 95
Blues Brothers, The (band) 174, 237
Blues Brothers, The (movie) 155, 204
Blue Velvet 127
Boatniks, The 252
Bogarde, Dirk 268
Bogart, Humphrey 26, 51, 78, 166, 241
Bogdanovich, Alexandra 53
Bogdanovich, Antonia 53
Bogdanovich, Peter 8, 53, 104, 243
Bolling, Claude 223
Bologna, Joseph 74-75
Bonaparte, Napoleon 20-21
Bonham, John 96
Bon Jovi, Jon 231
Bonnie and Clyde 5, 25, 199, 281
Boone, Debby 118, 159, 258
Boorman, John 81
Borgnine, Ernest 57, 282
Boston 60
Bostwick, Barry 37, 205
Bottoms, Timothy 20, 120
Boulevard Nights 231, 267
Boulting, Ingrid 103
Bound for Glory vi, 108-109, 178, 189, 232, 289, 292-293
Bowie, David xi, xiii, 118, 168
Boxcar Bertha 10, 296
Boy and His Dog, A 13-14, 42, 76
Boyd, Stephen 117
Boyer, Charles 86, 173
Boys from Brazil, The viii, 93, 212-213, 289, 293
Brackett, Leigh 173
Bradlee, Ben 68, 70
Brand, Neville 141
Brando, Marlon 9, 15, 23, 49, 83, 220, 222, 260-261, 268, 295
Breakheart Pass 65, 257, 289
Breaking Away ix, 205, 241,

INDEX

254-255, 267, 274, 290, 292-294
Breakout 251
Breezy 296
Brennan, Eileen 24, 57
Brennan, Walter 86
Brewster McCloud 80, 135, 296
Brickman, Marshall 132
Bride of Frankenstein 37
Bridges, Beau 20, 232
Bridges, James 233
Bridges, Jeff xii, xiii, xvi, 112
Bridge Too Far, A 67, 88, 127, 268
Bring Me the Head of Alfredo Garcia 296
Brink's Job, The 147
Brolin, James 63-64, 70, 192-193, 255-256
Bronson, Charles 65, 251, 295
Brooks, Albert 59
Brooks, James L. 262
Brooks, Mel 8-9, 72-74, 88, 123, 169-170, 203, 252, 268, 295
Brooks, Richard 29-30
Brown, Charley 70
Brown, David 19
Browne, Jackson 62
Browne, Leslie 161
Browning, Tod 39
Brown, Jim 251
Brown, Judy 250
Bruce, Lenny 64
Buccaneer, The 122
Buckley, Betty 98
Bucktown 32
Buddy Holly and the Crickets 190
Buddy Holly Story, The viii, 189-191, 195, 210, 259, 290, 293
Buffalo Bill and the Indians, or Sitting Bull's History Lesson vi, 78-80, 290
Buffalo Springfield 180
Buffett, Jimmy 118, 190
Bug 113, 154
Bugsy Malone 214
Bujold, Geneviéve 175
Bull Durham 121
Burnett, Carol 63, 130, 161
Burns, George 1, 78, 115, 158, 200-201
Burns, Marilyn 141
Burnt Offerings vi, 87-88, 227, 244, 290
Burroughs, Edgar Rice 90
Burstyn, Ellen 224
Burton, Richard 81, 117
Burtt, Ben 226
Busey, Gary 114, 173, 189-192, 259
Butch Cassidy and the Sundance Kid 9, 30, 68, 120, 122, 242
Butkus, Dick 84
Butler, Robert 202
Butterflies Are Free 296
Buttons, Red 63, 156
Buzzi, Ruth 111, 252

C

Caan, James 13, 73, 102, 268, 274
Cabaret 39, 115, 196, 265, 276, 279, 296
Cabot, Sebastian 117, 125
Caesar, Sid 268
Caine, Michael 9, 50-51, 67, 115, 185, 222-223, 268
Cain, James M. 118
Calder, Alexander 60
California Dreaming 255
California Split 119, 193, 296
California Suite viii, 222-224, 289, 293
Caligula 182
Callas, Charlie 73
Cambridge, Godfrey 32, 59
Cameron, James 55
Candidate, The 34, 296
Candleshoe vii, 168-169, 289
Candy, John 268
Can I Do It 'Till I Need Glasses? 157
Cannonball! 109
Cannon, Dyan 173, 198-199
Capone, Al 195, 259
Capone 15, 195, 259
Capote, Truman 78
Capricorn One viii, 10, 70, 175, 192-194, 234, 289
Captain & Tennille 2
Carlin, George 94-95
Carlino, Lewis John 269, 286
Carlson, Richard 117
Carnal Knowledge 45, 63, 296
Carradine, David 14-15, 59, 108-109, 184
Carradine, John 103
Carradine, Keith 22-23, 70, 80, 185-186, 238, 240
Carrera, Barbara 77
Carrey, Jim 120
Carrie vi, xvi, 35, 98-100, 182-183, 256-257, 259, 290-291, 294
Carson, John 153
Carson, Johnny 119
Carson, Lance 192
Cars, The 174
Carter, Jimmy 60, 118, 129, 186, 230
Cartwright, Veronica 226
Carver, Steve 15

Car Wash vi, xix, 53, 94-95, 289, 291
Casablanca xix, 78, 243, 245
Casanova's Big Night 22
Casey's Shadow 42
Cash, Rosalind 265
Cassavetes, John 15, 45, 182-183, 243
Cassidy, Shaun 205
Castle, Nick 216
Castle, William 117
Catch-22 217, 233, 245, 296
Cat from Outer Space, The 4, 10, 283
Cazale, John 40, 173, 217, 219
C.C. & Company 296
Chaffey, Don 159
Chamberlain, Richard 268
Champ, The 282
Chandler, Raymond 26, 166, 257
Chaney Jr., Lon 86
Channing, Carol 201
Channing, Stockard 6, 74-75, 78, 194-195, 259
Chaplin, Charlie 86, 105, 117, 242
Chaplin, Geraldine 23, 70, 78-80, 130
Chapter Two 223
Charade 56
Charisse, Cyd 90
Charley and the Angel 84
Charley Varrick 10, 296
Charlotte's Web 296
Charo 124
Chase, Chevy 201-202, 205, 285-286
Chayefsky, Paddy 100-102
Cheap Detective, The 78
Cheap Trick 230
Cheech & Chong 173
Cheyenne Social Club, The 296
Chicago 2, 278
Children of Paradise 122
Children of Theatre Street, The 162
Children's Hour, The 156
Chiles, Lois 252-253
China Syndrome, The viii, 49, 55, 70, 101, 119, 230, 233-235, 289, 293-294
Chinatown 5, 24-25, 44, 48, 77, 296
Chong, Tommy 199, 242
Chorus Line, A 2
Christie, Agatha 208-209
Christie, Julie 4-5, 23, 63, 182, 198-199, 265
Christopher, Dennis 205, 254-255, 274
Chûshingura 242

Cimino, Michael 217, 219, 292
Cisyk, Kacey 159
Citizen Kane 70, 173, 294
City on a Hill 285
City on Fire 55, 267-268
Clapton, Eric 11, 188-189
Clark, Candy v, xi-xiv, 166, 182, 237
Clark, Susan 32, 34, 252
Clash, The 230
Claudine 30, 296
Clavell, James 2
Claws 113
Clayburgh, Jill xvi, 63-64, 107-108, 135, 173, 181-182, 262-263, 295
Clemons, Clarence 145
Cleopatra (1934) 64
Cleopatra (1963) 219
Cleopatra Jones 155
Cleveland, Grover 79-80
Cliff, Jimmy 39
Clifton, Peter 96
Clockwork Orange, A 52, 212, 214, 231, 296
Clooney, George 285
Close Encounters of the Third Kind vii, xviii, 124, 158, 161-166, 235, 247, 266-267, 272-274, 281, 283, 290-291, 293-294
Close Encounters of the Third Kind: The Special Edition 165
Cobb, Lee J. 59, 86
Coburn, James 29, 268
Coca, Imogene 187
Cody, Buffalo Bill 79
Coffy 247, 296
Cohen, Mickey 60
Cohn, Nik 42
Collins, Joan xiv, 153-154, 166
Collins, Roberta 15
Colombo, Joseph 174
Coma vii, 106, 130, 157, 175, 181, 235, 257, 289
Coming Home vii, 109, 119, 121, 135, 173, 178-180, 182, 217, 244, 289, 292-294
Commodores, The 191
Computer Wore Tennis Shoes, The 3
Conan the Barbarian 191
Conaway, Jeff 195
Concorde ... Airport '79, The 55, 124, 184, 236
Condon, Richard 257
Conn, Didi 159, 195, 259
Connery, Sean 9, 50-51, 66-67, 176, 267-268, 295
Conquest of the Planet of the Apes 296
Conrad, Joseph 260-262

Conroy, Pat 257, 286
Conversation, The 223
Convoy 135, 201, 244
Conway, Tim 32-33, 111, 215
Cook, Jr., Elisha 26
Cook, Robin 257
Cooley High v, 30-32, 95, 122, 205, 259, 289
Cool Hand Luke 215
Coolidge, Rita 114
Cooper, Alice 258
Cooper, Gary 64, 151
Cooper, Jackie 188
Coppola, Francis Ford 244, 260-262
Corey, Irwin 94
Corman, Roger 14-15, 140, 197, 258, 260, 267
Corvette Summer 135, 207, 259
Cosby, Bill 223
Coscarelli, Don 227
Costner, Kevin 121
Cotton, Joseph 55, 123, 268
Cousin Cousine 293
Cowboys, The 63, 86, 129, 296
Cox, Ronny 108
Crane, Bob 174
Craven, Wes 140-141
Crawford, Christina 174
Crawford, Joan 86, 117
Cremer, Bruno 146
Crenna, Richard 65
Crichton, Michael 175-176
Cries and Whispers 219
Crimes and Misdemeanors 21, 210
Cronyn, Hume 70
Crosby, Bing 7, 86, 117-118
Crouse, Lindsay 70
Crystal, Billy 173, 187
Cujo 141
Culp, Robert 37, 188
Cummings, Quinn 165-166, 281
Curry, Tim 37-38
Curtis, Dan 87-88
Curtis, Jamie Lee 157, 173, 215
Curtis, Tony 66, 72, 103, 186
Cushing, Peter 88-89

D

Dailey, Dan 173
Daisy Miller 8, 243, 296
Dale, Jim 159-160, 202
Dalton, Timothy 186, 274
Daltrey, Roger 11-12, 259
Daly, Tyne 225
Damien: Omen II 81, 216
Damnation Alley 154, 271-272

D'Angelo, Beverly 117, 236
Dangerfield, Rodney 285-286
Danner, Blythe 269, 286
Dante, Joe 197
D'Antoni, Philip 188
Darby, Kim 276
Dark Star 138
Darling, Joan 45, 238
Darling Lili 10
Davis, Bette 13, 87, 208, 268
Davis, Brad 213-214, 251
Davis, Cynthia 30
Davis, Judy 117
Davy Crockett, King of the Wild Frontier 125
Dawn of the Dead 216
Day of the Animals 113
Day of the Dolphin, The 296
Day of the Jackal, The 75, 296
Day of the Locust, The 122, 257
Day of the Woman 183
Days of Heaven viii, 10, 128, 210-211, 242, 267, 289, 292-294
Days of Wine and Roses 264
Deadline—U.S.A. 70
Dead Men Don't Wear Plaid 151
Dean, Roger 160
Death on the Nile 139, 208, 268
Death Race 2000 v, 14-15, 42, 109, 290-291
Death Wish 62, 65, 296
Deconstructing Harry 91
Deep, The vii, 139-140, 184, 235, 289, 291
Deep Throat 112, 122
Deer Hunter, The viii, 173, 179, 214, 217-219, 245, 267, 290, 292-294
Dee, Sandra xiii, 237
de Havilland, Olivia 55, 123, 268
Delerue, Georges 242
Deliverance 99, 140, 242, 263, 296
DeLuise, Dom 72-74, 152, 186, 274
Demme, Jonathan xi
Demon Seed 182, 257, 296
Deneuve, Catherine 57, 63
De Niro, Robert xvi, 9, 59, 61, 103-104, 144-145, 217-219, 295
Dennehy, Brian 117
Denver, John 158
De Palma, Brian xv-xvi, 98-99, 182-183
Derek, Bo 117, 153, 241, 264-265
Dern, Bruce 34, 108, 128-129, 178, 206
Deschanel, Caleb 266
Devane, William 72, 245
Devil's Rain, The 7, 157
Devo 174

INDEX

Dewhurst, Colleen 49, 63
Diamond, Neil 174, 189
Diamonds Are Forever 38, 67, 135, 253, 296
Diary of a Mad Housewife 183, 296
Dillinger 250-251, 296
Dillon, Matt 229
Dillon, Melinda 108, 117, 162, 164, 182
Dirty Dingus Magee 296
Dirty Harry 225, 249, 296
Dirty Little Billy 296
Dirty Mary Crazy Larry 135
Doby, Kathryn 279
Doctorow, E.L. 2
Dog Day Afternoon v, 40-42, 45, 49, 52, 103, 122, 267, 289, 291-294
Donen, Stanley 56-57
Donnelly, Dennis 188
Donner, Richard 80-81, 220, 244
Donovan 201
Don't Go in the House 296
Don't Look in the Basement 296
Don't Open the Door 296
Don't Play Us Cheap 296
Doobie Brothers, The 230
Dooley, Paul 255
Dostoyevsky, Fyodor 275
Double Indemnity 132
Douglas, Kirk 35, 105, 182-183, 250
Douglas, Melvyn 283
Douglas, Michael 175, 233-234
Dourif, Brad 47-48, 207, 284
Dove, The 139
Dowd, Nancy 121
Down, Lesley-Anne 176-177, 244-245
Dow, Tony 155
Dracula 168, 257
Drescher, Fran 17
Dreyfuss, Richard xvi, xviii, 26-27, 115, 117, 152, 162, 164-166, 237, 274, 292, 295
Drive-In Massacre 141
Driver, The viii, 15, 75, 88, 135, 206-207, 289, 292
Drowning Pool, The 43
Dr. Strangelove 52
Drum 36
Duchess and the Dirtwater Fox, The 24, 83
Duel 273
Duff, Howard 130
Dumbo 126, 242
Dunaway, Faye 43, 59, 63, 70, 100-101, 182, 207-208, 241, 268, 292
Duncan, Sandy 70, 283

Durning, Charles 40
Duvall, Robert 102, 176-177, 229, 260, 268-269, 285
Duvall, Shelley 22-23, 79-80, 130, 133
Dwyer, Wayne 118
Dylan, Bob 2, 180, 188-189, 232, 262

E

Eagle Squadron 245
Eagles, The 60, 230
Earth 242
Earthquake xi, 74, 120, 149, 155, 212, 234, 296
Earth, Wind & Fire 201
Eastman, Charles 188
Eastwood, Clint 19-20, 53, 82-83, 210, 224-225, 249-251, 295
Eastwood, Kyle 53
Easy Rider xv, 23, 48
Eaten Alive 141
Eat My Dust! 135, 140
Ebb, Fred 144
Ebert, Roger 1, 262
Eden, Barbara 201, 205
Edwards, Blake 264
Ehrlichman, John 2
Ehrlich, Max 7
Eichhorn, Lisa 245
Eiger Sanction, The v, 19-20, 123, 289
Einstein, Albert 56
Einstein, Bob 188
Eisenhower, Dwight 194, 230
Eisenhower, Mamie 230
Eisenmann, Ike 12, 281
Electra Glide in Blue 188
Electric Horseman, The 44, 244, 274
Electric Light Orchestra, The 16
Eliot, T.S. 21, 76, 260
Elliott, Denholm 243
Ellison, Harlan 42
El Topo 39
Embryo 77
Emigrants, The 219
Emperor of the North 296
Empire of the Ants vii, 113, 153-154, 290
Enberg, Dick 84
End of the World 88
End, The 263
Enforcer, The 15, 225
Englund, Robert 141
Enter the Dragon 296
Equus 293
Eraserhead vii, 39, 53, 93,

126-127, 267, 290-291
Escape from Alcatraz ix, 249-251, 289
Escape from the Planet of the Apes 296
Escape to Witch Mountain v, xx, 1, 12-13, 85, 122, 281, 290
E Street Band, The 145
E.T. the Extra-Terrestrial 13, 141, 283
Evel Knievel 155-156
Everly, Phil 24
*Everything You Always Wanted to Know About Sex * But Were Afraid to Ask* 296
Every Which Way But Loose viii, 24, 224-225, 290-291
Exorcist, The xii, xv, 27, 80-81, 115, 147, 158, 166, 215, 227, 256, 263, 281, 296
Exorcist II: The Heretic 33, 81, 236
Eyes of Laura Mars viii, 207-208, 235, 289

F

Face to Face 122
Fail-Safe 268
Falk, Peter 45, 77-78, 147
Family Plot 59, 88, 108
Fantastic Voyage 36
Farewell, My Lovely 26, 166, 241
Fargo, James 224-225
Farley, Walter 266
Farris, John 257
Farrow, Mia 130, 265, 267-268
Fast Times at Ridgemont High 238
Fat City xi-xii, 105, 296
Fawcett-Majors, Farrah 76, 265
Feldman, Marty 72-74, 151, 268
Feldon, Barbara 34, 169
Ferrer, José 75, 268
Ferrigno, Lou 129
Fiddler on the Roof 219, 296
Field, Sally xvi, 128, 134, 229, 232-233, 263-264, 292
Field, S.S. 42
Fincher, David xi
Finch, Peter 59, 87, 100-102, 115, 117, 268, 292
Fine, Larry 1
Finney, Albert 74
First Love 45, 132, 238
Fischer, Corey 80
Fishburne, Laurence 1
Fisher, Carrie 1, 4, 135, 137-138, 157, 265
Fitzgerald, F. Scott 103-104
Five Easy Pieces 48, 219, 285, 296
Fixx, James 174

Flagg, Fannie 195
Flanders, Ed 148
Fleetwood Mac 118, 230
Fleischer, Richard 35-36
Fleming, Ian 150, 253
Fletcher, Louise 1, 47, 49, 292
Flint, Shelby 143
Flipper 153
Flynn, Errol 66, 105
Flynn, Joe 3, 143
Fly, The 27, 226
FM 174, 190-191, 259
Follett, Ken 174
Fonda, Henry 55, 120, 149, 153, 185, 267-268
Fonda, Jane 44, 63, 70, 119, 156-157, 173, 178-179, 181-182, 210, 222-223, 233-235, 244, 265, 274, 292, 295
Food of the Gods, The 113, 153
Footloose 204
Forbes, Bryan 6
Forbidden Planet 37, 137
Ford, Anitra 250
Ford, Daniel 257
Ford, Gerald 2, 60
Ford, Glenn 220, 268
Ford, Harrison 117, 135-136, 237, 244-245, 260, 268
Forman, Milos 47, 49, 236, 292
Forrest, Frederic 268, 270
Forrest Gump 201
Fortune, The 6
For Your Eyes Only 253
Fosse, Bob 53, 276-279
Fosse, Nicole 53, 276
Foster, Jodie xvi, 59, 61-63, 110-111, 168-169, 241, 281
Foul Play viii, xix, 199, 201-202, 205, 242, 289
Four Musketeers, The 296
Foxworth, Robert 83
Foxy Brown 135, 296
Frampton, Peter 60, 200
Frankenheimer, John 17-18, 128
Frankenstein 37-38, 248
Franklin, Gary 120
Frawley, James 74, 244, 251
Frazier, Joe 2
Freaks 39, 199
Freaky Friday vi, 4, 110-111, 168, 289
Freed, Alan 16
French Connection, The xv, 17-18, 40, 137, 140, 147, 208, 278, 296
French Connection II v, 17-18, 289
Frenzy 17, 28, 108, 296
Fresson, Bernard 17
Friday Foster 32

Friedkin, William 18, 81, 146-147
Friends of Eddie Coyle, The 296
Frisco Kid, The 245
Fritz the Cat 160
Frogs 113
Fromme, Lynette 2
From Noon Till Three 24, 65-66
From Russia with Love 66
Front Page, The 63, 70, 112, 296
Front, The vi, 90-92, 94, 123, 232, 290, 294, 296
Full Metal Jacket 269
Funicello, Annette 255
Funny Lady 49, 291, 293
Fun with Dick and Jane vii, 119-120, 289
Furie, Sidney J. 63
Furst, Lorraine 205
Furst, Stephen 205
Further Adventures of the Wilderness Family, aka Wilderness Family Part 2, The 47
Fury, The viii, 182-183, 257, 290
Fuzz 57

G

Gable and Lombard vi, 63-64, 104, 290
Gable, Clark 51, 63-64
Gabor, Eva 142-143
Gallico, Paul 60
Gan, Jennifer 250
Gardenia, Vincent 199
Gardner, Ava 55, 267
Gardner, Leonard xii
Garner, Erroll 118
Garrett, Leif 210
Garr, Teri 158, 162, 266
Gary, Lorraine 197, 274
Gates, Bill 2
'Gator Bait 296
Gauntlet, The 182, 225
Gaynor, Gloria 230
Gaynor, Janet 35
Gazzara, Ben 15, 195, 243, 259
Gelbart, Larry 158
George, Chief Dan 82-83
Georges-Picot, Olga 20-21
George, Susan 35-36
Gere, Richard 1, 133, 157, 210-211, 245-246
Gershwin, George 240
Getaway, The 135, 206, 296
Getty, J. Paul 60
Giant Spider Invasion, The 113, 154
Gibb, Andy 174
Gibb, Barry 200

Gibb, Maurice 200
Gibb, Robin 200
Gibson, Henry 23, 80, 155
Gibson, Mel 117
Gifford, Frank 156
Gilbert, Lewis 149, 252
Gillespie, Dana 90
Girlfriends 187, 239, 241, 267
Gish, Lillian 130
Gladiator 156, 246
Gleason, Jackie 134
Glenn, Scott xi
Godfather, The xvii, xv, 1, 15, 27, 57, 61, 102, 117, 133, 136, 140, 219, 262, 269, 285, 296
Godfather: Part II, The 33, 115, 123, 219, 285, 296
Goin' South 213
Goldblum, Jeff 23, 191, 226
GoldenEye 253
Golden Voyage of Sinbad, The 296
Goldfinger 253
Goldman, James 67
Goldman, William 68, 257
Goldsmith, Jerry 51, 81, 148, 213, 272
Gone in 60 Seconds 135
Gone with the Wind xvi, 35, 95, 103, 117, 136
Goodbye Girl, The vii, 35, 78, 115, 165-166, 181, 223, 274, 281, 289, 291-294
Goodbye, Norma Jean 64
Goodfellas 174, 188
Good, the Bad and the Ugly, The 225
Gordon, Bert I. 153-154
Gordon, Ruth 75, 225, 266
Gordon, Steve 276
Gordy, Berry 37, 188
Gorman, Cliff 278
Gorney, Karen Lynn 167
Go Tell the Spartans 194, 217, 257
Gould, Elliott 23, 70, 80, 192-193, 268, 295
Grable, Betty 87
Graduate, The 92
Grady, James 43
Grand Theft Auto 135, 140, 300
Grandy, Fred 15
Grant, Lee 1, 4, 81, 123, 268
Grant, Peter 96
Grateful Dead, The 39
Gray, Charles 38
Gray Lady Down viii, 55, 138, 184, 242, 285, 289
Grease viii, xviii, 159, 173-174, 194-196, 199-200, 236, 242, 259, 265, 290-291
Greased Lightning 95, 195-196, 296

Great Escape, The 250
Great Gatsby, The 56, 103-104, 112, 265, 296
Great Santini, The ix, 242, 257, 269, 285-286, 290
Great Train Robbery, The 176
Great Waldo Pepper, The v, 9-10, 94, 123, 290
Great White Hope, The 105, 296
Greek Tycoon, The 177, 241
Green, Al 16
Greene, David 184
Greenhut, Robert 92
Grey, Joel 78-79
Grier, Pam 32, 36, 250
Gries, Tom 65
Griffeth, Simone 14
Griffin, Merv 75
Griffith, Melanie 25, 34, 182
Grindhouse 14, 300
Grizzly 46, 113
Grodin, Charles 112, 199
Groove Tube, The 155, 296
Group Marriage 239
Guercio, James William 188
Guffey, Cary 281
Guilaroff, Sydney 146
Guillermin, John 112
Guinness, Alec 78, 135
Guns of Navarone, The 65
Gus 33, 84-85, 111
Guthrie, Woody 108, 110
Guttenberg, Steve 117, 120

H

Hackett, Joan 83-84
Hackman, Gene 1, 17-18, 24-25, 29, 49, 56-57, 220-222, 268, 295
Hagen, Jean 117
Hagman, Larry 37, 75, 188
Hair viii, 196, 236-237, 285, 290
Haldeman, H.R. 2
Hale Jr., Alan 154, 252
Haley, Alex 60
Haley, Jack 146, 229
Haley, Jackie Earle 71-72
Hall and Oates 118
Halloween viii, 157, 173, 207, 215-216, 247, 259, 267, 290, 292
Hall, Tom T. 201
Halpin, Luke 153
Hamill, Dorothy 60
Hamill, Mark 135, 137, 207, 210, 259
Hamilton, George 155, 168, 186
Hamilton, Murray 197, 274
Hamlin, Harry 173

Hammett, Dashiell 78
Handel, George Frideric 52
Hannah and Her Sisters 210
Hannah, Daryl 173, 183
Hanover Street viii, 241, 244-246, 290
Harder They Come, The 39
Harlan County U.S.A. 109, 232
Harold and Maude xi, 35, 107, 109, 178, 180, 266, 283-285, 296
Harper 43
Harper Valley P.T.A. 201, 205
Harris, Barbara 23, 108, 110-111, 252
Harris, Ed 157, 173, 176
Harrison, Gregory 205
Harrison, William 42
Harris, Phil 143
Harris, Richard 152
Harris, Thomas 257
Harry and Tonto 296
Harry and Walter Go to New York 53
Harry in Your Pocket 296
Hassett, Marilyn 20
Hawkins, Ira 70
Hawks, Howard 117
Hawn, Goldie 4-5, 24, 83, 201-202, 295
Hayes, Helen 115, 168-169
Hayes, Isaac 115
Hayes, John 88
Hayward, Susan 1, 87
Head Over Heels, aka Chilly Scenes of Winter 238
Heard, John 70, 215, 238, 251
Hearst, Patty 2, 43, 60, 102, 193
Heart 198
Heartbreak Kid, The 45, 187, 238, 264, 296
Heart of Darkness 260-261
Hearts and Minds 297
Heaven Can Wait viii, 173, 198-199, 236, 290-293
Heckart, Eileen 88
Heckerling, Amy 238
Heidegger, Martin 241
Heifetz, Jascha 252
Heim, Alan 279
Hellman, Jerome 188
Hellman, Lillian 156
Hellstrom Chronicle, The 153, 297
Hell Up in Harlem 297
Hemingway, Mariel 59, 229, 239-240
Hendrix, Jimi 180
Henry, Buck 198-199
Henry, Gregg 251
Henry, Justin 115, 279-281

Henson, Jim 251
Hepburn, Audrey 66-67
Hepburn, Katharine 97
Herbie Goes to Monte Carlo 85, 144
Herbie Rides Again 85, 144, 169, 297
Hercules in New York 129
Here Comes Mr. Jordan 198
Herrmann, Bernard 1, 63
Herrmann, Edward 252
Hester Street v, 42, 44-45, 94, 187, 238, 267, 290
Heston, Charlton 55, 123, 149, 184, 268
Hickey & Boggs 188
Hickok, Wild Bill 66
Higgins, Colin 107, 201-202
High Anxiety vii, 8-9, 88, 151, 169-171, 289
High Plains Drifter 82, 297
High Velocity 188
Hiller, Arthur 107
Hill, George Roy 9, 120, 122, 241-242
Hills Have Eyes, The vii, 140-141, 290
Hill, Walter 206, 231
Hilton-Jacobs, Lawrence 30-31
Hindenburg, The vi, 53-55, 74, 94, 138, 184, 234-235, 289, 293
His Girl Friday 70, 247
Hitchcock, Alfred 59, 88, 93, 107-108, 151, 169-170, 201-202, 208
Hitler, Adolf 160, 212
Hockney, David 223
Hoffa, Jimmy 2
Hoffman, Dustin 59, 68-70, 92-93, 209, 229, 266, 278-281, 292, 295
Holbrook, Hal 69, 193
Holden, William 70, 81, 100-101, 105, 241, 268
Holliday, Judy 279
Holloway, Sterling 125
Holly, Buddy 190, 259
Hollywood or Bust 242
Holmes, Hollye 46
Holmes, Rupert 230
Holm, Ian 246, 248-249
Honeymoon Killers, The 188
Hooper 242, 263-264, 284, 291
Hooper, Tobe 141
Hope, Bob 252, 261
Hopkins, Anthony 268
Hopper, Dennis 268
Hopper, Hedda 64
Horror Express 210
Hospital, The 102
Hot Lead and Cold Feet 85, 202-203

Hot Rock, The 40, 119, 297
Hough, John 12
Houseman, John 44
House of Exorcism, The 122
Houston, Robert 140
Howard, Mel 44
Howard, Moe 1
Howard, Ron 85-86, 117
Howards End 162
Howard, Trevor 220, 268
Howe, James Wong 59
Howling, The 141
Howlin' Wolf 60
Hudson, Ernie 59
Hudson, Rock 10, 55, 77, 267
Hughes, Howard 60
Hulce, Tom 117, 203
Hull, Dianne 16
Hull, Henry 117
Humphrey, Hubert 174
Hunt, Helen 117, 120, 157
Hurt, John 173, 213
Hurt, Mary Beth 238
Husbands 297
Hustle 57, 63, 123, 242
Huston, Anjelica 103
Huston, John xi, xii, 50-51, 153, 284
Hutton, Lauren 130, 156
Huyck, Willard 56
Hyams, Peter 192-193, 244
Hynek, J. Allen 164

I

Ice Station Zebra 65
I Drink Your Blood 183
I Eat Your Skin 183
I Escaped from Devil's Island 251
I Love My Wife 183
Images 80, 130
Immigrant, The 242
In Cold Blood 30
Indiana Jones and the Temple of Doom 8
In Search of Noah's Ark 124
Interiors viii, 133, 209-210, 280, 290, 293
In the Heat of the Night 88, 178
Invasion of the Body Snatchers (1956) 226
Invasion of the Body Snatchers (1978) viii, 226, 236, 244, 290
Invitation to the Dance 155
Ireland, Jill 24, 65-66
Ironweed 285
Irving, Amy 59, 99, 182-183
Irving, John 174

Island at the Top of the World, The 138, 297
I Spit on Your Grave 183
It Happened One Night 1, 44, 47, 274
It's a Mad, Mad, Mad, Mad World 273
It! The Terror From Beyond Space 246
Ivory, James 162
I Wanna Hold Your Hand 183, 201, 259

J

Jackson, Michael 196, 230
Jackson, Sherry 207
Jack the Ripper 273
Jaeckel, Richard 153
James, Anthony 88
James, Bradley 205
Jameson, Jerry 123
Jaws v, xvi-xvii, 1, 17, 19, 26-29, 49, 52, 66, 94, 103, 113, 117, 136, 139-140, 147, 152-154, 163, 184, 197-198, 215-216, 242, 247, 257, 266-267, 273-274, 278, 284, 290-294
Jaws 2 viii, 33, 139, 152, 197-198, 236, 290-291
Jaws 4 28
Jaws of Death, The, aka Mako: The Jaws of Death 153, 210
Jefferson, Thomas 60
Jenkins, Dan 257
Jenner, Bruce 60
Jennifer 99
Jennings, Claudia 63
Jeremiah Johnson 44, 46, 297
Jerk, The ix, 128, 229, 274-276, 289, 291
Jewison, Norman 13
Jodorowsky, Alejandro 39
Joe 297
Joe Kidd 297
Joel, Billy 118, 174
Joffe, Charles 92
John, Elton 12, 16, 40, 166, 191, 232
Johnny Got His Gun 188
Johnson, Ben 29, 57, 65, 268
Johnson, Don 13
Johnson, Dorothy M. 42
Johnson, Russell 149
Johnston, Ollie 143
Jones, Carolyn 141
Jones, Dean 71, 111, 144
Jones, James 118
Jones, James Earl 138
Jones, John Paul 97
Jones, Tommy Lee 176-177, 207-208
Joplin, Janis 270

Jordan, Richard 75, 237-238
Joyce, James xix
Juggernaut 27, 139, 297
Julia vii, 115, 117, 119, 156-157, 162, 219, 290, 292-293
Jungle Book, The 143-144
Jungle Princess, The 242
Junior Bonner 297
Jurgens, Curt 149-150

K

Kahl, Milt 143
Kahn, Madeline 8, 63, 74, 78, 104, 170
Kander, John 144
Kane, Carol 1, 42, 44-45, 63, 152
Kansas 258
Kapp, Joe 65
Kasem, Casey 146
Kastle, Leonard 188
Katt, William 191
Katz, Gloria 56
Kaufman, Philip 226, 232, 244
Kaye, Danny 105
Kaye, M.M. 174
Kazan, Elia 103
Keach, Stacy 184
Keaton, Camille 183
Keaton, Diane xviii, 20-21, 24, 92, 117, 131-133, 182, 209, 239-240, 259, 292, 295
Keaton, Michael 157, 173, 187
Keats, Steven 44-45
Keitel, Harvey 79, 95, 241
Keith, Brian 51
Kellerman, Sally 75
Keller, Marthe 93, 128
Kelly, Gene 97, 156
Kelly, Grace 162
Kelly's Heroes 217, 297
Kennedy, George 19, 123-124, 215, 268
Kennedy, Jackie 177
Kennedy, John F. 23, 155, 193, 233-234
Kenney, Doug 204, 287
Kentucky Fried Movie, The vii, 88, 155, 204, 289
Kershner, Irvin 207
Kesey, Ken 49, 257
Kidder, Margot 7, 70, 220-221, 255-256
Kidd, Michael 34-35
Kids Are Alright, The 12
Kiel, Richard 150, 253
Kill Bill 248
Killer of Sheep 267
Kim, Evan 155

INDEX

King Kong (1933) 37, 112
King Kong (1976) vi, 50, 112-114, 139, 157, 290-291
King, Perry 35
Kingsmen, The 205
King Solomon's Mines 137
King, Stephen 98, 174, 230, 257
Kinmont, Jill 20
Kirby, Bruno 259
KISS 159, 231, 240-241
Kitt, Eartha 32
Kleiser, Randal 194
Kluge, P.F. 42
Klute 24, 63, 119, 210, 265, 297
Knack, The 230
Knotts, Don 32-33, 144, 169, 202
Koontz, Dean 257
Kopple, Barbara 110
Korman, Harvey 169-170
Kosinski, Jerzy 257, 284
Kotcheff, Ted 119
Kotch 188, 297
Kotto, Yaphet 95
Kramer, Remi 188
Kramer, Stanley 273
Kramer vs. Kramer ix, 115, 229, 236, 241, 269, 279-281, 290-294
Kristofferson, Kris 114, 135, 201
Kubrick, Stanley 52-53, 87, 185, 210
Kubrick, Vivian 53

L

La Cage aux Folles 293
Ladd, Diane 210
Ladies and Gentlemen: The Rolling Stones 97, 297
Lady Sings the Blues 30, 37, 140, 189, 270, 297
Lake, Veronica 87
La Motta, Jake 145
Lamour, Dorothy 104
Lancaster, Bill 72
Lancaster, Burt 79, 194
Landau, Martin 268
Landis, John 88, 155, 203-204, 273
Land That Time Forgot, The 90
Lane, Diane 157, 229, 241
Lange, Jessica 59, 112, 157, 278
Langella, Frank 168
Lanier, Susan 140
Lansbury, Angela 49, 268
Lansing, Robert 153
Larson, Eric 143
Lassick, Sydney 48
Last American Hero, The 42
Last Detail, The xi, 5, 45, 48, 63, 285, 297
Last House on the Left, The 141, 297
Last Picture Show, The 56, 243, 297
Last Remake of Beau Geste, The vii, 123, 128, 151, 257, 289
Last Tycoon, The vi, 94, 103-104, 290
Last Waltz, The viii, 39, 174, 188-189, 289
Laurie, Piper 98
Lazenby, George 155, 243
Leachman, Cloris 169-170, 252
Leadbelly 189
Led Zeppelin 2, 12, 39, 96-97, 118, 123, 188, 230, 258
Lee, Christopher 13, 123, 210, 268
Lehman, Ernest 188
Leibman, Ron 232
Leigh, Janet 215
Leigh, Vivien 64
Le Mans 121, 206, 297
Le Mat, Paul 16, 237
Lemmon, Jack 37, 70, 78, 123, 188, 229, 233-235, 268, 279, 295
Lenny 64, 140, 278-279, 281, 297
Leno, Jay 17, 120
Leonard, Sugar Ray 60
Leoni, Téa 120
Lester, Richard 66-67
Let the Good Times Roll 195
Levin, Ira 6, 212, 257
Lewis, Geoffrey 224
Lewis, Jerry 3
Lewis, Jerry Lee 17
Life and Times of Judge Roy Bean, The 210, 297
Linn-Baker, Mark 210
Lithgow, John 279
Little Big Man 63, 83, 266, 281, 297
Little Fauss and Big Halsy 297
Little Nell 38
Little Night Music, A 196
Little Romance, A viii, 122, 157, 241-242, 290
Live and Let Die 140, 149, 159, 297
Lloyd, Christopher 1
Lloyd, Harold 87
Locke, Sondra 24, 82, 182, 224-225
Loden, Barbara 45, 188, 238
Loeb, Philip 91
Logan, Robert 46
Logan's Run vi, 53, 75-77, 205, 265, 290
Lolita 132, 185
Lombard, Carole 63-64
Lombardo, Guy 118
Longest Yard, The 57, 121, 134, 250, 263, 297
Long Goodbye, The 24, 193, 297
Long, Max Freedom 99
Lonsdale, Michael 252-253
Looking for Mr. Goodbar 2, 128, 133, 182, 257
Loomis, Nancy 259
Lopez, Gerry 192
Lord of the Rings, The 161, 236
Loren, Sophia 63
Lorre, Peter 111
Lost Horizon 112, 297
Lounsbery, John 125, 142-143
Love and Death v, 20-22, 91, 131, 289, 294
Love at First Bite 168
Love Bug, The 144
Love Me Tender 242
Love Story xv, 52, 66, 206-207, 265, 297
Loving 297
Lucas, George xi-xii, xv-xvi, 1, 135, 138, 260
Lucky Lady vi, 10, 56-57, 139, 289
Ludlum, Robert 230
Lumet, Sidney 40, 42, 100, 102, 196
Lupino, Ida 7
Lutter, Alfred 281
Lynch, David xi, 39, 53, 117, 126-127
Lynch, Jennifer 53
Lynde, Paul 187
Lynyrd Skynyrd 118
Lyon, Sue 185

M

MacArthur, Douglas 148-149
MacArthur vii, 148-149, 217, 290
MacGraw, Ali 201, 265, 295
Mack, Ted 60
MacLaine, Shirley 63, 161, 283-284
MacLean, Alistair 65, 257
MacMurray, Fred 268
Macon County Line 210, 297
Magee, Patrick 52
Magnum Force 210, 225, 297
Mahogany 35-37, 188
Mailer, Norman 230
Main Event, The 271
Malden, Karl 149, 267-268
Malick, Terrence 210-211
Malkovich, John 173
Malle, Louis 185
Maltese Falcon, The 26, 78
Mame 39, 297
Man and a Woman, A 123, 179
Man Called Horse, A 42, 297
Mancini, Henry 64
Mandingo v, 35-36, 290-291
Man, Frankie 279

Manhattan viii, 92, 127, 133, 210, 239-242, 265, 267, 290, 294
Manilow, Barry 202
Man of La Mancha 63, 297
Manson, Charles 2
Man Who Fell to Earth, The xi, xiii
Man Who Would Be King, The v, 9, 50-51, 290, 293-294
Man with the Golden Gun, The 149, 297
Man with the X Ray Eyes, The 242
Many Adventures of Winnie the Pooh, The vii, 125-126, 142, 155, 289
Manz, Linda 211
Marathon Man vi, xvi, 50, 59, 92-93, 103, 127, 175, 212, 257, 289
March, Fredric 1, 87
Marcovicci, Andrea 91
Marin, Cheech 199
Marshall, Penny 274
Marshall, Sean 159, 281
Mars, Kenneth 34
Martin 128, 244
Martin, Steve 151, 252, 274-275
Martin, Strother 120
Marvin, Lee 295
Marx Brothers, The 21, 97
Marx, Groucho 87, 117
Mary Poppins 126, 159, 169
*M*A*S*H* 23, 78, 80, 95, 158, 203, 245, 254, 269-270, 285, 297
Mason, James 35-36, 198-199, 212
Mason, Marsha xvi, 117, 165-166
Massot, Joe 96
Masterson, Peter 6
Matheson, Tim 34, 204, 259, 268, 273
Matilda 224
Matthau, Walter 70-71, 78, 205, 223, 295
Matuszak, John 270
May, Elaine 45, 187, 199, 223, 238
Mayer, Louis B. 64
Mayron, Melanie 187, 241
Mazursky, Paul 114, 181, 244
McCabe & Mrs. Miller 23, 63, 80, 247, 254, 297
McCall, C.W. 60, 201
McCambridge, Mercedes 55, 124
McCarthy, Kevin 197, 226
McClure, Doug 88-90
McCormack, Patty 154
McCullough, Colleen 118
McDowall, Roddy 187
McDowell, Malcolm 205, 273
McEveety, Vincent 3, 83
McGavin, Darren 169
McGee, Vonetta 19
McGoohan, Patrick 249-250

McGuane, Thomas 188, 257
McIntire, Tim 14, 16
McMahon, Ed 119, 151
McPhee, John 42
McQueen, Steve 206, 251, 295
Mead, Margaret 174
Mean Dog Blues 215, 251
Mean Streets 188, 285, 297
Meatloaf 38
Melchior, Ib 42
Melville, Herman 152
Mengele, Josef 212
Mephisto Waltz, The 226
Merchant, Ismail 162
Meredith, Burgess 55, 88, 104
Merman, Ethel 278
Messiah of Evil 122
Meteor ix, 55, 67, 138, 235, 267-268, 272, 289
Meyer, Nicholas 257, 272
Michael Clayton 285
Michener, James 174
Midler, Bette 16, 166, 229, 270-271
Midnight Express viii, 128, 213-215, 251, 289, 292-294
Midway 67, 94, 120, 149, 217, 245, 268
Mifune, Toshirô 268
Mikey and Nicky 45, 238
Miles, Sylvia 26
Milford, Penelope 178
Milius, John 88, 156, 191-192, 244
Milk, Harvey 174
Milland, Ray 13
Miller, Ann 104
Miller, Chris 204
Miller, Seton I. 42
Million Dollar Duck, The 4, 297
Milne, A.A. 125
Mimieux, Yvette 282
Mineo, Sal 59
Minnelli, Liza 56, 73, 144-145, 268
Minnie and Moskowitz 297
Mirren, Helen 182
Misfits, The 122
Missouri Breaks, The 9, 50, 83
Mitchell, John 2
Mitchum, James 205
Mitchum, Robert xi, xiv, 26, 103, 149, 166, 241, 268
Mogambo 123
Molly Maguires, The 232, 297
Moment by Moment 187, 239
Monroe, Marilyn 66, 155
Monsieur Beaucaire 21
Monty Python and the Holy Grail 35

Moon, Keith 12, 174, 186
Moonraker ix, 138, 236, 252-254, 289
Moonrunners 205
Moore, Archie 65
Moore, Dudley 201-202, 241, 264, 274, 276
Moore, Mary Tyler 102, 262
Moore, Robert 77-78
Moore, Roger 149-150, 252-253, 295
Moore, Sara Jane 2
Moore, Thomas 42
Moran, Tony 215
More American Graffiti xi, 192, 237
Moreno, Rita 63
Morgan, Harry 32, 283
Morgan, Nancy 140
Moroder, Giorgio 214
Morris, Garrett 31, 94
Morris, John 73
Moscone, George 174
Mostel, Josh 205
Mostel, Zero 87, 90-91, 117
Mothra vs. Godzilla 122
Mountain Family Robinson, aka Adventures of the Wilderness Family 3 47
Movie Movie 128, 224
Munro, Caroline 88-90, 150
Muppet Movie, The ix, 229, 242, 244, 251-252, 267, 289
Murder by Death vi, 77-78, 289
Murder on the Orient Express 42, 77, 208, 297
Murphy, Michael 80, 90, 92, 181
Murphy's War 10
Murray, Bill 36, 157, 285-286
Mutrux, Floyd 16
My Fair Lady 236

N

Nabokov, Vladimir 118, 185
Namath, Joe 168
Nance, Jack 126-127
Napoleon and Samantha 110, 168, 297
Nashville v, xvi, 22-24, 34, 52, 70, 80, 130, 254, 267, 290-294
National Velvet 266
Neame, Ronald 267-268
Ned Kelly 297
Needham, Hal 134, 264
Neeson, Liam 157
Nelson, Gary 110-111, 244, 282
Nelson, Jerry 251
Nelson, Willie 44
Neptune Factor, The 139, 184

INDEX

Network vi, 44, 50, 59, 70, 94, 100-103, 105, 115, 182, 208, 241, 267-269, 290-294
Newhart, Bob 9, 142-143
New Leaf, A 45, 238
Newman, Laraine 17, 259
Newman, Paul 43, 73, 78-79, 105, 120-121, 254, 268, 295
Newton-John, Olivia 194-195, 259
New York, New York vii, 9, 24, 144-146, 290-291
Next Stop, Greenwich Village 157
Nicholas and Alexandra 219
Nichols, Mike 6
Nicholson, Jack 1, 6, 9, 11-12, 47-48, 83, 103-104, 213, 285, 292, 295
Nickelodeon 104, 123, 243
Nielsen, Leslie 156, 267
Nightmare on Elm Street, A 141
Night Moves v, 24-26, 34, 182, 289
Night of the Lepus 113
Night of the Living Dead 216
Nimoy, Leonard 226, 271-272
1941 ix, 8, 204, 242, 245, 268, 272-275, 290, 293
92 in the Shade 188, 257
Nitti, Frank 15
Niven, David 77, 168-169, 208, 268
Nixon, Richard 5, 68, 70, 194
No Deposit No Return 169, 282
Nolte, Nick 139, 269
Norma Rae viii, 95, 128, 232-233, 267, 269, 290, 292-294
Norris, Christopher 140
North Avenue Irregulars, The 252
North by Northwest 44, 107, 170-171, 202
North Dallas Forty xix, 269-270
Norton, B.W.L. 237
Norwood 217, 297
Nothing by Chance 11
Novak, Kim 66
Now You See Him, Now You Don't 3-4, 297
Nugent, Ted 258
Nureyev, Rudolf 152
Nutty Professor, The 3

O

Oates, Warren 251
Oberon, Merle 87, 229
O'Brien, Richard 38
Obsession 50
O'Connor, Flannery 257, 284
Odd Couple, The 78, 166
Odessa File, The 70
O. Henry's Full House 155

O'Herlihy, Dan 148
Oh, God! vii, 88, 117, 158, 289
O'Keefe, Michael ix, 184, 269, 285-287
Old Boyfriends viii, 45, 135, 237-239, 241-242, 290
Oliver! 88
Oliver's Story 207
Olivier, Laurence 67, 92, 115, 176-177, 212, 241, 268
Omega Man, The 13, 76, 265, 297
Omen, The vi, 27, 50, 59, 80-81, 205, 256, 290-291
On a Clear Day You Can See Forever 297
On Any Sunday 297
Onassis, Aristotle 177
O'Neal, Ryan 52, 104, 206-207, 268, 271, 295
O'Neal, Tatum xv, 71, 115, 166, 281, 295
One and Only, The 128, 274, 276
One Flew Over the Cuckoo's Nest v, xi, 1, 40, 47-49, 52, 235, 257, 267, 290-294
101 Dalmatians 142-143
O'Neill, Jennifer 7
One Little Indian 110, 168
One of Our Dinosaurs Is Missing 32, 169
On the Yard 215, 251
Ontkean, Michael 120
Orca, aka Orca: The Killer Whale vii, 113, 139, 152-153, 290
Orlando, Tony 114
Osmond, Donny 258
Osmond, Marie 258
Ostrum, Peter 281
Oswald, Lee Harvey 221
Other Side of Midnight, The 150, 241, 257
Other Side of the Mountain, The 20
Other Side of the Mountain Part 2, The 20
Outlaw Josey Wales, The vi, 53, 82-83, 267, 290, 294
Owl and the Pussycat, The 63, 297
Oz, Frank 251

P

Pacino, Al xvi, 1, 40-42, 166, 168, 233, 295
Pack, The 113
Page, Geraldine 49, 142-143, 161, 173, 209
Page, Jimmy 96
Paint Your Wagon 224
Pakula, Alan J. 68-69, 262
Palmer, Leland 276, 279

Palm Springs Weekend 242
Panic in Needle Park, The 63, 297
Paper Chase, The 297
Paper Moon xi, 8, 63, 115, 166, 206, 243, 281, 297
Papillon 214, 250-251, 297
Paradise Alley 106, 274
Parallax View, The 43-44, 69-70, 193, 234, 297
Parker, Alan 59, 213-214
Parton, Dolly 174
Pat Garrett & Billy the Kid 297
Patrick, Lee 26
Patton 148-149, 213, 217, 269, 297
Patton, George 148
Peaches and Herb 230
Peck, Gregory 80-81, 148, 205, 212, 294
Peckinpah, Sam 201, 244
Penn, Arthur 24-25, 83
People That Time Forgot, The 11, 90
Perelman, S.J. 230
Perfect Couple, A 254
Performance 297
Perkins, Anthony 36, 98, 282
Perrine, Valerie 64, 222
Persona 22, 91, 133
Pescow, Donna 167
Pete 'n' Tillie 161, 297
Peter Pan 143
Peters, Bernadette 73, 268, 274-275
Pete's Dragon vii, 42, 85, 159-160, 202, 281, 289
Petrie, Daniel 53, 176
Petrie, Mary 53
Petty, Tom 190
Phantasm 135, 226-227, 229
Phantom of the Opera, The 27
Phantom of the Paradise 39, 98, 297
Phase IV 188
Phffft 279
Phillips, Julia 115
Pickens, Slim 32, 274
Pickford, Mary 87, 229
Pidgeon, Walter 75
Piece of the Action, A 53
Pierson, Frank 114
Pilgrim's Progress 157
Pink Flamingos 39
Pink Floyd 230
Pink Panther, The 1, 264, 291
Pinocchio 163, 165
Piranha 113, 197-198, 216
Pisier, Marie-France 150, 241
Place, Mary Kay 24
Plan 9 from Outer Space 39
Planet of the Apes 13, 213

Plant, Robert 96
Platt, Polly 185
Play It Again, Sam 21, 92, 280, 297
Play Misty for Me 19, 297
Plaza Suite 155, 223, 297
Please, Don't Bury Me Alive! 267
Pleasence, Donald 201, 215
Pledge, The 285
Plummer, Christopher 50, 244
Pointer Sisters, The 94
Poitier, Sherri 53
Poitier, Sidney 53
Polanski, Roman 24
Police, The 174
Pollack, Sydney 43-44, 244
Popeye 80
Porter, Cliff 8
Portnoy's Complaint 188
Poseidon Adventure, The xi, 54, 74, 123, 139, 154, 184, 234-235, 267-268, 297
Posse 35
Potts, Annie 207
Prather, Joan 187
Predator 27, 94
Prentiss, Paula 6
Presley, Elvis 105, 118, 187, 196, 234, 242
Pretty Baby viii, 63, 182, 185-186, 240, 282, 290, 292
Prima, Louis 174
Primus, Barry 144
Prince, Harold 279
Prince, Steven 189
Prinze, Freddie 118
Private Life of Sherlock Holmes, The 297
Prize Fighter, The 33
Producers, The 72-74
Prokofiev, Sergei 21
Promises in the Dark 188
Prowse, David 137
Pryor, Richard 94-95, 107-108, 196, 223, 252
Psycho 98, 100, 122, 171, 215
Pulp Fiction 189
Pumping Iron 129
Purcell, Lee 259
Pursuit of Happiness, The 250
Puzo, Mario 220
Pyramid, The 70

Q

Quadrophenia 12
Quaid, Dennis 254
Quaid, Randy 213
Quatro, Suzi 241

Queen 2, 118
Quigley, Martin 295
Quinn, Anthony 177, 241
Quinn, Patricia 38
Quintet 78, 254

R

Rabal, Francisco 146
Rabbit Test viii, 45, 53, 157, 187, 238, 244, 289
Rabid 99
Raffill, Stewart 46
Raging Bull 145
Raiders of the Lost Ark 50, 204, 274, 282
Raines, Cristina 22
Raitt, Bonnie 285
Ramones, The 97, 258-259
Rampling, Charlotte 152, 241
Rash, Steve 189
Ravel, Maurice 264
Ray, Man 60
Ray, Nicholas 229
Reddy, Helen 159-160, 201
Redford, Robert 9, 43-44, 67-70, 268, 274, 295
Redgrave, Lynn 75
Redgrave, Vanessa 117, 156-157, 209, 245
Reed, Jerry 8, 134
Reed, Oliver 11, 87-88
Reefer Madness 39
Reeve, Christopher 70, 173, 184, 220-222
Reincarnation of Peter Proud, The 7
Reiner, Carl 88, 151, 158, 263, 275-276
Reinking, Ann 276, 278-279
Reitherman, Wolfgang 125, 142-143
Reivers, The 267
Remar, James 231
Remick, Lee 80
Remsen, Bert 80
Reno, Kelly 266, 281
Report to the Commissioner 157
Rescuers, The vii, 9, 125, 142-144, 289
Rescuers Down Under, The 142
Return from Witch Mountain 13
Return of the Dragon 123
Return of the Pink Panther, The 1, 291
Return to Macon County 297
Rey, Fernando 17
Reynolds, Burt 8, 49, 56-57, 73, 104, 134, 242, 262-263, 295
Rice, Anne 60

Richards, Kim 12-13, 282
Right Stuff, The 226, 230
Riley, Jeannie C. 201
Ringer, Robert 60
Riperton, Minnie 241
Ritchie, Michael 34, 71-72
Ritt, Martin 90, 232
Ritz, Harry 73
Rivers, Joan 37, 53, 187, 238, 244
Rivers, Melissa 53
Road Warrior, The 14
Robards, Jason 59, 68, 70, 115, 156
Robbins, Harold 150, 257
Roberts, Judith Anna 126
Robertson, Cliff 43-44, 268
Robertson, Robbie 189
Roberts, Tony 70, 131-132
Robeson, Paul 59, 87
Robin and Marian vi, 66-67, 290
Robin Hood 66, 142-144, 297
Robinson, Edward G. 87
Robson, Mark 173
Rocco, Alex 187
Rockefeller, Nelson 230
Rock 'n' Roll High School 24, 258-259, 290
Rocky Horror Picture Show, The v, xvii, 11, 24, 37-39, 59, 126, 194, 258, 267, 290-291
Rocky vi, xvii, 15, 26, 35, 50, 59, 103-106, 121, 137, 224-225, 238, 255, 267, 290-294
Rocky II 106, 236, 291
Roddam, Franc 112
Rodgers, Richard 230
Roeg, Nicolas xi
Rogers, Ginger 8
Rogers, Kenny 174
Rogers, Roy 34
Rogers, Wayne 205
Rollerball 13, 42, 49
Rollercoaster 120, 149, 157
Rolling Stones, The 2, 12, 16, 174, 180, 188, 258
Rollins, Jack 92
Romancing the Stone 223
Rome Adventure 242
Romero, Cesar 3
Romero, George 216, 244
Ronstadt, Linda 190
Room with a View, A 162
Rooney, Mickey 105, 159-160, 205, 266
Roosevelt, Theodore 51
Roseland 162
Rosemary's Baby 6
Rosenberg, Stuart 255

INDEX

Rose, The ix, 140, 270, 290, 293
Ross, Diana 35-37, 196, 270-271
Ross, Herbert 161, 165-166, 222
Ross, Katharine 6-7, 177, 241, 268
Ross, Marion 140
Rossner, Judith 2, 257
Rothman, Stephanie 239
Rourke, Mickey 229
Rowe, Misty 64
Roxanne 276
Rozelle, Pete 129
Ruby 99
Rule, Janice 130
Runaway Train 250
Runyon, Damon 90
Russell, Harold 178
Russell, Ken 11-12, 53, 152
Russell, Kurt 3
Russell, Nipsey 274
Russell, Rosalind 59, 87
Russell, Theresa 59
Russell, Victoria 53
Ryan, Robert 87
Rydell, Christopher 53
Rydell, Mark 53, 270-271

S

Sadat, Anwar 174
Saint, Eva Marie 107
Saint Jack viii, 8, 88, 243, 257, 290
Saint James, Susan 168
Same Time, Next Year 128, 224, 242, 293
Sampson, Will 47-48, 152
Sanders, George 87
Sand Pebbles, The 272
Sarandon, Chris 41
Sarandon, Susan 9, 24, 37-39, 63, 150, 182, 185-186
Sargent, Joseph 148
Sarrazin, Michael 7, 250
Saturday Night Fever vii, xviii, 35, 42, 118, 161-162, 167-168, 187, 191, 195-196, 200, 235, 267, 290-291, 294
Savage, John 217-218, 236
Savalas, Telly 193
Save the Tiger 235, 297
Sayer, Leo 122, 181
Scaggs, Boz 60
Scandalous John 297
Scarecrow 196, 297
Scarface 15, 94, 202
Scenes from a Mall 91
Schaffner, Franklin J. 212-213
Scheider, Roy 17, 26, 92-93, 146-147, 197, 229, 276-278

Schell, Maximilian 70, 156, 268, 282
Schell, Ronnie 283
Schlesinger, John 92-93, 246
Schrader, Paul 95
Schroder, Ricky 282
Schultz, Derek 53
Schultz, Michael 30, 53, 94-95, 200
Schwarzenegger, Arnold 129
Scorsese, Martin xv-xvi, 39, 61-62, 88, 144-145, 168, 188-189
Scott, George C. 53-54, 148, 295
Scott, Ridley 117, 246
Seabo, aka Buckstone County Prison 215, 251
Sea Gypsies, The 47
Seberg, Jean 229
Segal, George 26, 83, 119-120
Selleck, Tom 176
Sellers, Peter 77, 229, 283-284, 295
Semi-Tough 134-135, 257
Serling, Rod 1
Serpico 41-42, 196, 252, 297
Sevareid, Eric 102
Seven Beauties 59, 115, 187, 293
Seven Brides for Seven Brothers 84
Seventh Seal, The 22
Seven-Ups, The 135, 188, 297
Sex Pistols, The 174
Sextette 186, 274
Sgt. Pepper's Lonely Hearts Club Band viii, 200-201, 259, 290
Shadow of a Doubt 107
Shaft 115, 159, 247, 297
Shaft in Africa 297
Shaft's Big Score! 135, 297
Shaggy D.A., The 85, 111
Shaggy Dog, The 111
Shakespeare, William 166, 210
Shampoo v, 4-5, 49, 157, 178, 199, 265, 290-291, 293-294
Shamus 26, 57
Sharman, Jim 37
Shatner, William 7, 271-272
Shaw, Robert 26, 66, 128, 139, 152, 173, 266
Shaw, Susan Damante 46
Sheba, Baby 32
She Done Him Wrong 219
Sheehy, Gail 60
Sheen, Martin 260-261, 268
Sheldon, Sidney 150, 257
Shelley, Mary 37
Shepard, Sam 210-211
Shepherd, Cybill 8, 61-62, 88
Sheppard, Paula 100
Sherman, Richard M. 126
Sherman, Robert B. 126

Shields, Brooke 59, 63, 100, 132, 185-186, 240, 282
Shine a Light 188
Shining, The 87, 269
Shire, Talia 59, 104, 237-238
Shootist, The vi, 50, 85-86, 94, 290
Shore, Dinah 88, 158
Sidney, Sylvia xiii
Siegel, Don 85, 249-250
Silence of the Lambs, The 47
Silent Movie vi, 72-74, 123, 151, 169, 268, 289, 291
Silent Running 13, 138, 297
Silkwood 235
Silver, Joan Micklin 1, 44-45, 187, 238
Silvers, Phil 3
Silver Streak vi, 11, 59, 107-108, 201, 289, 291
Simon, Carly 150
Simon, Neil 77-78, 155, 165-166, 223, 285
Simon, Paul 5, 60
Simpson, O.J. 193
Sinatra, Frank 9, 170
Sinbad and the Eye of the Tiger 297
Singin' in the Rain 145
Sin of Madelon Claudet, The 115
Siskel, Gene 1, 262
Sisters 98, 297
Sistrunk, Otis 94
Sitting Bull 78-79
Skatetown, U.S.A. 157
Skerritt, Tom 246
Skin Game 297
Skyjacked 297
Slade, Bernard 224
Slams, The 251
Slap Shot vii, 120-122, 182, 242, 290-291, 294
Slaughterhouse-Five 122, 297
Sleeper 13, 21, 131, 297
Sleuth 77, 115, 297
Slugger's Wife, The 285
Slumber Party '57 157
Smile v, 34-35, 72, 182, 289
Smith, Charles Martin 189, 237
Smith, Maggie 77, 173, 208, 222-223, 268
Smith, Patti 97
Smokey and the Bandit vii, xix, 8, 117, 134-135, 161, 225, 233, 263-264, 289, 291
Snodgress, Carrie 183
Snowball Express 85, 297
Snow White and the Seven Dwarfs 122
Soderbergh, Steven xi
Soles, P.J. 24, 258-259

Some Like It Hot 66
Sometime Sweet Susan 123
Sommars, Julie 144
Song of the Islands 242
Song Remains the Same, The vi, 39, 94, 96-97, 123, 289
Son of the Sheik, The 123
Sorcerer vii, 146-147, 214, 290, 294
Sorrow and the Pity, The 122
Sounder 30, 232, 297
Sound of Music, The xvi, 136, 195
Soylent Green xi, 13, 36, 76, 193, 234, 297
Space Cowboys 226
Spacek, Sissy xvi, 59, 98-99, 130, 182, 259
Sparks 120
Speer, Martin 140
Spellbound 171
Sperber, Wendy Jo 274
Spielberg, Steven xi, xv, xvi, 8, 26-28, 66, 162-163, 165, 197, 273-275
Spinks, Leon 60
Spiral Staircase, The 242
Split Image 285
Spradlin, G.D. 260
Springsteen, Bruce 2, 145, 190
Spy Who Loved Me, The vii, 139, 149-150, 170, 235, 253, 289, 291, 293
Squirm 113
Stack, Robert 268
Stallone, Sylvester xvi, 14-15, 26, 59, 104-106, 274, 295
Stand Up and Be Counted 188
Stapleton, Maureen 209
Star Is Born, A (1954) 122, 209
Star Is Born, A (1976) vi, 50, 114-115, 122, 270, 290-291, 293
Starland Vocal Band 60
Starr, Ringo 16, 186, 189
Star Spangled Girl 70
Starting Over ix, 24, 262-263, 280, 290
Star Trek: The Motion Picture ix, 138, 229, 236, 251, 271-272, 280, 290-291, 293
Start the Revolution Without Me 297
Star Wars vii, xvi-xviii, 1, 13, 27, 37, 76, 89-90, 103, 106, 117, 128, 132, 135-138, 146-147, 150, 161-163, 169, 181-182, 207, 210, 212, 226-227, 232, 235, 242, 245, 247, 253, 259, 265, 267-268, 272, 282, 290-294
Stay Hungry 129
Steele, Barbara 197
Steely Dan 118, 190
Steenburgen, Mary 173, 213
Steiger, Rod 64, 255-256

Steinbeck, John xii
Stengel, Casey 2
Stepford Wives, The v, 6-7, 123, 176, 212, 257, 290
Stephens, Harvey 80-81
Steppenwolf 180
Stern, Daniel 254
Stevens, Art 125, 142
Stevens, Connie xi
Stevens, George 1
Stevenson, McLean 283
Stevenson, Robert 169
Stevens, Stella 63
Stewart, Charlotte 126
Stewart, James xiv, 55, 85, 123, 166, 268
Stewart, Rod 60, 174
Stigwood, Robert 200
Sting 12
Stingray 135, 207
Sting, The xv, 9, 35, 43, 56, 94, 115, 122, 297
Stoker, Bram 257
Straight, Beatrice 59, 100, 102, 115
Straw Dogs 183, 297
Streep, Meryl 117, 157, 217, 219, 229, 240, 265, 279-281
Streisand, Barbra 8, 23, 63, 114-115, 174, 181, 208, 270-271, 295
Strongest Man in the World, The v, 3-4, 85, 289
Stroud, Don 189
Stucker, Stephen 155
Student Nurses, The 239
Styron, William 230
Sugarland Express, The 274, 297
Summer, Donna 174, 191
Summer of '42 56, 297
Summer Wishes, Winter Dreams xiii
Sun Also Rises, The 123
Sunnyside 231-232
Sunset Boulevard 132
Sunshine Boys, The 78, 115, 166, 223, 293
Superdad 85
Super Fly 297
Super Fly T.N.T. 298
Superman viii, xvii, 70, 173, 184, 220-222, 236, 244, 267, 290-293
Supertramp 230
Support Your Local Gunfighter 298
Susann, Jacqueline 150, 257
Sutherland, Donald 155, 176, 226
Svenson, Bo 9, 270
Swarm, The 55, 113, 184-185, 268
Swayze, Patrick 157, 229
Sweet Charity 279
Sweet Sweetback's Baadasssss Song 298

Swift, Susan 282
Sword in the Stone, The 126
Szwarc, Jeannot 197

T

Take the Money and Run 21, 131
Taking Off 49
Taking of Pelham One Two Three, The 298
Tales of Manhattan 155
Talking Heads 97
Tangerine Dream 147
Tarantino, Quentin 14, 189
Tarantula! 113
Taxi Driver vi, xvi-xvii, 8, 61-63, 88, 95, 103, 105, 110, 123, 144-145, 168, 185, 188-189, 217, 241, 267, 281, 290-294
Taylor, Juliet 92, 210
10 ix, xviii, 241, 264-265, 274
Tentacles 113, 153
Terminal Island 239
Terms of Endearment 262
Testament 235
Tewkesbury, Joan 22, 187, 237, 239
Texas Chain Saw Massacre, The 123, 141, 298
Thackeray, William Makepeace 257
Thalberg, Irving 103
Thank God It's Friday 191
That's Entertainment! 268, 298
That's Entertainment, Part 2 94, 97
Them! 113, 153
Theodore, Sondra 207
There Was a Crooked Man 250
Theroux, Paul 257
They Shoot Horses, Don't They? 44
They Went That-A-Way & That-A-Way 215
Thieves Like Us 22, 80, 298
Thirty Seconds Over Tokyo 94, 149
This Gun for Hire 242
This Is Cinerama 120
Thomas, Ernest 205
Thomas, Frank 143
Thompson, J. Lee 66
Thompson, Linda 187
Thompson, Neal 155
Three Caballeros, The 84
Three Days of the Condor v, 43-44, 175, 193, 234, 289, 291
Three Musketeers, The 67, 298
Three Stooges, The 1, 37
3 Women vii, 80, 130, 290-291
Thurman, Uma 248
THX 1138 13, 298

INDEX

Tilton, Charlene 111
Time After Time 205, 272-273
To Have and Have Not 78
Tokar, Norman 32, 168
To Kill a Mockingbird 269
Tolkien, Christopher 118
Tolkien, J.R.R. 118, 161
Tomlin, Lily 1, 22-24, 187
Tommy v, 9, 11-12, 53, 200, 214, 259, 290-291
Tom Petty and the Heartbreakers 230, 259
Toolbox Murders, The 138, 188
Tora! Tora! Tora! 11, 67, 149, 217, 298
Towering Inferno, The xv, 54, 74, 184, 268, 298
Towne, Robert 5
Tracy, Spencer 97
Travolta, Joey 231
Travolta, John xvi, 1, 7, 98, 117, 157, 167-168, 187, 194-196, 295
Treasure of Matecumbe vi, 83-85, 290
Treasure of the Sierra Madre, The 50
Truck Stop Women 63, 298
True Grit 242
Truffaut, François xviii
Truman, Harry 148
Trumbo, Dalton 37, 59, 188
Tucci, Michael 259
Tuna, Charlie 120
Turman, Glynn 30-31, 205, 259
Turner, Tina 12, 201
Turning Point, The vii, 115, 117, 161-162, 166, 181, 290, 292-293
Twain, Mark 283
20,000 Leagues Under the Sea 36
Twilight Zone: The Movie 155
Two-Lane Blacktop xi, 135, 206, 298
Two-Minute Warning 55, 75
Two Mules for Sister Sara 63, 298
2001: A Space Odyssey 13, 52, 127, 178, 247, 271, 282
Tyrrell, Susan xii, 160
Tyson, Cicely 124

U

Ullmann, Liv 268
Unforgiven 83
Unholy Rollers, The 135, 298
Unidentified Flying Oddball 138, 283
Unmarried Woman, An viii, 181-182, 244, 280, 290, 292-293
Unsworth, Geoffrey 173
Up in Smoke xix, 199, 242
Up the Sandbox 280, 298

Uptown Saturday Night 30, 298
Up with People 129
Urban Cowboy 195
Ustinov, Peter 76, 83, 169, 208, 268

V

Vaccaro, Brenda 1, 192
Valens, Ritchie 210
Valentine, Karen 252
Valentino 152
Valley of the Dolls 37, 206
Valli, Frankie 195
Vallone, Raf 241
Van Halen 174
Vanishing Point 135, 298
van Pallandt, Nina 131
Van Patten, Vincent 258
Van Valkenburgh, Deborah 231
Velvet Vampire, The, aka *Cemetery Girls* 239
Verdon, Gwen 276, 279
Vereen, Ben 279
Vertigo 130, 170-171, 202
Vicious, Sid 230
Village People, The 174
Villiers, James 243
Vincent, Jan-Michael 3, 154, 191, 264
Vinton, Bobby 83
Viva Knievel 155-156
Vivaldi, Antonio 52, 277
Voight, Jon 70, 173, 178-180, 250, 292
Von Richthofen and Brown 11, 298
von Sydow, Max 44
Voyage of the Damned 293

W

Wagner, Jane 187, 239
Wagner, Robert 55, 268
Wahl, Ken 232
Wait Until Dark 67
Walken, Christopher 162, 173, 217-219
Walker, Jimmie 124
Walk Proud 232
Wallace, Dee 141
Wallach, Eli 241
Waller, Fats 252
Walsh, Bill 1
Walsh, Joe 231
Waltons, The 285
Wambaugh, Joseph 257
Wanda 45, 188, 238
Wanderers, The 232, 242
War at Home, The 262
War Between Men and Women, The 298

Warden, Jack 4, 198, 205
WarGames 235
War Is Hell 242
Warlords of Atlantis 90
Warner, David 80-81, 273
Warner, Jack L. 173
Warren, Jennifer 24
Warriors, The viii, 231, 290, 292
Waters, John 39
Waters, Muddy 36
Waterston, Sam 193
Wayne, John 85-86, 94, 229, 295
Wayne, Patrick 90
Way We Were, The 44, 159, 203, 298
W.C. Fields and Me 64
Weathers, Carl 106
Weaver, Sigourney 92, 117, 157, 246-247
Wedding, A 100, 130-131
Weill, Claudia 187, 239
Weissmuller, Johnny 104
Welles, Gwen 23-24
Welles, Orson 89, 257, 273
Wellman, William 1
Wells, H.G. 257, 273
Wertmüller, Lina 59, 115, 187
West, Mae 111, 186, 274
West, Nathanael 257
West Side Story 231
Westworld 13, 175, 212, 298
Wexler, Haskell 109
What's Up, Doc? 206, 243, 271, 298
When Harry Met Sally... 131
Where's Poppa? 158, 298
Which Way Is Up? 95
White Buffalo, The 66
White Christmas 201
White Lightning 210
Who Are the DeBolts? And Where Did They Get 19 Kids? 162
Who Framed Roger Rabbit 142
Who'll Stop the Rain 140
Who, The 11-12, 174, 188, 200, 259
Widmark, Richard 175, 268
Wilder, Gene 74, 107, 151-152, 170, 245
Wilder, Thornton 2
Willard 7, 266, 298
Williams, Billy Dee 36
Williams, John 19, 28, 129, 183, 222, 234, 274
Williamson, Fred 32
Williamson, Nicol 66
Williams, Robin 80, 117, 157
Williams, Treat 236
Willis, Gordon 69, 240

Willy Wonka & the Chocolate Factory 281, 298
Wilson, Michael 173
Wind and the Lion, The 51, 88, 191
Winfield, Paul 57
Winger, Debra 59, 157, 191
Wings 60
Winkler, Henry 274, 276
Winner, Michael 104
Winnie the Pooh and the Blustery Day 125-126
Winnie the Pooh and the Honey Tree 125-126
Winnie the Pooh and Tigger Too 125-126
Winn, Kitty 63
Winters, Shelley 55, 153, 160, 267
Wise Blood 128, 210, 257, 284
Wise, Robert 53-54, 271-272
Wizard of Oz, The 23, 64, 84, 146, 155, 170, 196, 247
Wizards 160, 210
Wiz, The 2, 196, 226, 274, 293
Wolfe, Tom 42, 230
Wolfman Jack 201
Woman Under the Influence, A 298
Women in Cages 250
Wonder, Stevie 60
Won Ton Ton, The Dog Who Saved Hollywood 104
Woodard, Alfre 173
Wood, Ed 39, 173
Wood, Natalie 55, 267-268
Wood, Ron 2
Woodstock 188, 298
Woodward, Bob 68, 70, 194
Woodward, Joanne 263
Wopat, Tom 205
Working Girls, The 239
World's Greatest Athlete, The 3, 85
World's Greatest Lover, The 128, 152
Wouk, Herman 174
Wray, Fay 37
Wren, P.C. 257
W.W. and the Dixie Dancekings 8, 123

Y

Yakuza, The 298
Yank in the R.A.F., A 245
Yanks 242, 245-246
Yates, Peter 139, 254
Yes 160
York, Michael 75-76, 151, 205
York, Susannah 220
You Can't Have Everything 281
You Light Up My Life 88, 159

Young, Burt 104
Young Frankenstein 8, 35, 72-74, 108, 123, 151-152, 169-170, 298
Young, Dey 258
Young, Gig 87, 173
Youngman, Henny 73
Young, Neil 16
You Only Live Twice 150, 253

Z

Zabriskie Point 298
Zanuck, Darryl 229
Zanuck, Richard 19
Zelig 21
Zemeckis, Robert 173, 201
Zevon, Warren 174
Zinnemann, Fred 156
Zsigmond, Vilmos 189, 219
Zucker, David 155
Zucker, Jerry 155

INDEX

List of Photographs

Airport '77 124
Alien 228, 246, 247, 249
All That Jazz 229, 277
All the President's Men, 69
American Graffiti xiii
Amityville Horror, The 230, 256
Animal House 172, 204
Annie Hall xv, 132
Apocalypse Now xvii, 261
Apple Dumpling Gang, The 33
At the Earth's Core 89
Bad News Bears, The 71
Barry Lyndon 52
Being There 284
Big Wednesday 191
Black Stallion, The 266
Black Sunday 129
Bound for Glory 109
Breaking Away 255
Buddy Holly Story, The 190
Buffalo Bill and the Indians, or Sitting Bull's History Lesson 79
Caddyshack 286
California Suite 223
Capricorn One 193
Car Wash 95
Carrie 99
China Syndrome, The 234
Clark, Candy xiv
Close Encounters of the Third Kind xviii, 163, 164
Coma 175
Coming Home 179
Cooley High 31
Corvette Summer 207
Days of Heaven 211
Death Race 2000 14
Deep, The 139
Deer Hunter, The 173, 218
Dog Day Afternoon 41
Driver, The 206
Eiger Sanction, The 19
Empire of the Ants 154
Eraserhead 127

Escape from Alcatraz 250
Escape to Witch Mountain xx
Every Which Way But Loose 224
Eyes of Laura Mars 208
Fat City xii
Foul Play 202
Freaky Friday 110
French Connection II 18
Front, The 91
Fun with Dick and Jane 119
Fury, The 183
Goin' South 213
Grease 195
Great Santini, The 286
Great Waldo Pepper, The 10
Halloween 215, 216
Hanover Street 245
Heaven Can Wait 174
High Anxiety 170
Hindenburg, The 54
Jaws xvi, 2, 28
Jerk, The 275
Julia 157
King Kong 112, 113
Kramer vs. Kramer 280
Little Romance, A 241
Logan's Run 76
Lucky Lady 56
MacArthur 148
Mahogany 36
Man Who Fell to Earth, The xiii
Man Who Would Be King, The 51
Manhattan 240
Many Adventures of Winnie the Pooh, The 125
Marathon Man 93
Midnight Express 214
Moonraker 253
Muppet Movie, The 251
Network 58, 102
New York, New York 145
Night Moves 25
1941 273

Norma Rae 233
Oh, God! 118, 158
O'Keefe, Michael 287
Omen, The 81
One Flew Over the Cuckoo's Nest 1, 48
Outlaw Josey Wales, The 82
Pete's Dragon 159
Phantasm 227
Piranha 197
Pretty Baby 186
Rescuers, The 143
Robin and Marian 67
Rock 'n' Roll High School 258
Rocky 59, 105
Rocky Horror Picture Show, The xvii, 38
Rose, The 270
Saturday Night Fever 167
Sgt. Pepper's Lonely Hearts Club Band 200
Shampoo 5
Shootist, The 86
Silent Movie 73
Silver Streak 60, 107
Slap Shot 121
Smokey and the Bandit 116, 134
Song Remains the Same, The 96
Sorcerer 146
Spy Who Loved Me, The 150
Star Is Born, A 114
Star Trek: The Motion Picture 272
Star Wars 117, 136, 137, 138
Starting Over 263
Stepford Wives, The 7
Strongest Man in the World, The 3
Superman 221
Taxi Driver xvi, 62, 63
10 265
Three Days of the Condor 43
Tommy 11
Up in Smoke 199
Wizards 160

ABOUT THE AUTHOR

After composing ten different "about the author" summaries for his previous books, Chris Strodder has decided to change things up by not writing that paragraph in the third person. He'll use the second person instead:

You might be interested to know that this second volume of *The Daring Decade* is the eleventh book Chris Strodder has had published since 2000. Maybe you'll recall that most of his books have been nonfiction works that respectfully celebrate popular culture, including *Swingin' Chicks of the '60s*, *The Encyclopedia of Sixties Cool*, three editions of *The Disneyland Encyclopedia* (named one of the year's "Best Reference Books" by the national *Library Journal*), and *The Disneyland Book of Lists*. You could also look for Chris's writing in print magazines, which have included *Los Angeles*, *The Hollywood Reporter*, *Parade*, and *Movieline*. Possibly you've seen him on national TV programs, heard him on national radio talk shows, or noticed that he added commentary to several documentaries. You can also catch one of the popular live presentations he continues to make. If you were an avid movie fan back in the 1970s like he was, you'll recognize that scene in his author's photo below, which shows what it was like "a long line ago at a theater far, far away…." And finally, as always Chris extends his boundless gratitude to his publishers and to his readers, especially you.

The memory of waiting in line for Jaws back in 1975. The front of the line is off the page to the left; the line continues off the page to the right; the author's position is marked by an arrow. By the time those people at the end finally got to the front, Star Wars (1977) was playing.

Made in the USA
Middletown, DE
13 January 2021